The Rainbow Covenant

TORAH AND THE SEVEN UNIVERSAL LAWS

The Rainbow Covenant

TORAH AND THE SEVEN UNIVERSAL LAWS

Michael Ellias Dallen

Foreword by Rabbi Michael Katz

LIGHTCATCHER BOOKS
Springdale, Arkansas

And

THE RAINBOW COVENANT FOUNDATION
New York, New York

Design and electronic layout by Carol Long

Author photo by Ed Mroz, Mrozfoto@aol.com

Drawings by Inge-Lise Bay MacFarlane

Graphs, tables, and notes on pp. 12-13, within, reproduced from *Comets, Jews, and Christians* by John Hulley (1996, Root and Branch Association, Ltd., Publisher. P.O. Box 8672, 91086, Jerusalem, Israel. Website: www.rb.org.il), by the kind permission of the author. Copyright © 1996 by John C. L. Hulley.

The Rainbow Covenant

TORAH AND THE SEVEN UNIVERSAL LAWS

ISBN 0-9719388-2-2

Library of Congress Control Number: 2003102494

10 9 8 7 6 5 4 3 2 1

Printed in the United States of America on acid-free paper. For information write to Lightcatcher Books, 842 Kissinger Ave., Springdale AR 72762, or visit our website: www.lightcatcherprod.com

I have set My rainbow in the cloud,
and it shall be a sign of the
covenant between Me and the earth.

— Genesis 9:13

Contents

W HEREAS... these ethical values and principles have been the bedrock of society from the dawn of civilization, when they were known as the Seven Noahide Laws; Whereas without these ethical values and principles the edifice of civilization stands in serious peril of returning to chaos....[1]

— Joint Resolution of the United States Congress, March 20, 1991

1. Public Law 102-14, U.S. Congressional Record (Government Printing Office, Washington, D.C.), Vol. 137, 1991.

T hroughout the ages, scholars have viewed the Noahide[1] Laws as... universal norms of ethical conduct, as a basic concept in international law, or as a guarantee of fundamental human rights for all. [2]

— Encyclopaedia Britannica

1. Also called Noahite, Noachite, Noachide - Nó•ach•ide, pronouncing the middle syllable, "ach," like the Scottish "*loch*" or the German "*Ach!*" (Noah, a Hebrew name, is actually *Nó•ach*, with a guttural ending. Hebrew is rich in such throaty, liquid sounds. For another example, "Messiah," with its similarly silent ending "h," comes from *Mashiach* or *Ma•shé•ach.*) "Ch," "h" and "kh" are each sometimes used to try to transliterate these Hebrew gutturals into English. Just remember that none of these letter-symbols are fully up to this job, unfortunately, and that Hebrew has no sound like the explosive "ch" in "chop" or "Chuck" or "church."

2. *Encyclopaedia Britannica,* Inc., Chicago IL, 1991, "Noahide Laws."

God gave the Torah to the
*Jewish people so that all nations
might benefit from it.*

— *Midrash Tanchuma* (ancient rabbinic commentary), *Devarim 3*

Preface

And God spoke unto Noah, and to Noah's
children with him, saying, And as for Me,
behold, I establish My covenant with you,
and with your seed after you.
— Genesis 9:8-9

Seven was a special number to the ancient Israelites. It symbolized the completion and perfection of God's Creation. The people of Israel believed that God gave the whole human race a set of laws which would lead men and all the children of men to a coming glorious golden age.

According to the Hebrews' ancient tradition, God originally gave humanity six Commandments, and the ordinances that accompany them, by inscribing them on the hearts of Adam and Eve. Ten generations later, He initiated the famous Rainbow Covenant of the Bible's Book of Genesis. See Genesis 9. He gave all Seven Commandments, including a commandment forbidding certain vile crimes against the natural world, to Noah and Noah's family.[1]

Noah's descendants failed to completely transmit the Law to later generations. Slavery, tribalism, violence, and all the terrible pathologies of paganism degraded the human race.

So Heaven, still holding out hope for humanity, tried a slower but surer revolutionary, text-oriented approach. Ten generations after Noah, God taught these seven Commandments to the prophet Abraham, and six generations after Abraham, to Moses. Moses taught them to his people, Israel, and inscribed them in the Bible with loving care.

The Seven Rainbow Covenant Commandments represent, in essence, a larger Code of detailed, logically implicit moral and ethical statutes, ordinances, and rules.[2] These laws are, according to Israel's tradition, Divinely revealed. **God gave them to humanity's legendary common ancestors for the good of all mankind, forever.** In fact, taking all Seven Commandments together, they constitute the universal, fundamental code of upright human behavior.[3]

Moses directed his ministry to Israel. From Moses' time to the present, Israel's rabbis[4] have taught that, through Moses, the Master of the Universe gave the Hebrews Ten Commandments — including a Code of 613 laws, revealed to Israel in the Sinai desert — and obligated the Jews to serve Him in a unique way.[5]

This Law, Israel's Ten Commandments' Code, makes up the revolutionary constitution — the Torah, the "Guidance," "Teaching" or "Law" — of Moses' so-called "people of priests."[6] It rules Israel, and Israel alone.[7] But Moses taught that God calls on everyone, Jew and non-Jew alike, to live up to the equally revolutionary moral standards — His Code of Seven Rainbow Covenant Commandments — that He gave to Noah and his children.

One cannot understand the Bible's total scheme, the nature or purpose of the Ten Commandments, the people of Israel, or, for that matter, of the whole human race, without coming to terms with these Universal commandments.

The study of the Seven Commandments is said to provide great advantages. Scripture promises the student knowledge, understanding, riches and might.[8] Such study exalts and magnifies a person, according to the Hebrews' ancient law: He[9] will be called friend, beloved of God, lover of God, and lover of humanity.[10] Every human being who lives what he learns of that moral life, who fulfills the Universal Law, merits eternal and infinite reward.[11]

As the Christian Scriptures put it, the Jews and their teachers "sit in Moses' seat" as the "authorized custodians" of God's Law.[12] Israel's obligation to transmit His Universal laws to others is much of the reason, Israel's Sages wrote, for the Jews' dispersion among the nations.[13]

Every Jew is expected to try to establish the laws and true morality of the Rainbow Covenant wherever possible.[14] Because, if the people of Israel know anything about it at all, nothing less than the basic nature of the future is riding on the outcome. As the Jewish prophets and more than a hundred generations of Hebrew sages and mystics have believed and yearned for it, the nations' general acceptance of these laws will usher in a new stage in planetary history, a golden era of realized human potential, which Jewish scholars describe as the Messianic Age.[15]

NOTES

1. See Genesis 9:8-18 (note the seven separate references to 'covenant') and commentaries; *Mishnah Tosefta, Avoda Zorah* 9:4; Talmud, *Sanhedrin* 56a, 74b, *Nedarim* 31a; Midrash, *Genesis Rabbah* 16:6, 24:5, 34:8, *Deuteronomy Rabbah* 2:25. For more on these sources see, particularly, Yehuda HaLevi (c. 1075-1141 CE) *HaKuzari* 3:73.

2. Talmud, *Sanhedrin* 57a (near the end), 74b (in the name of Rava), *Avoda Zorah* 14b, *Hullin* 92a; Rashi (Rabbi Shlomo Yitzchaki, c. 1040-1105 CE) on *Sanhedrin* 75a; Rabbi Moshe ben Maimon (Maimonides, Rambam, c. 1135-1204 CE), *Mishneh Torah (Yad), Hilchot Melachim* 9:9; Rabbi Moshe ben Nachman (Nachmanides, Ramban, c. 1194-1270 CE), *Pirush al haTorah* (Commentary on the Torah) on Genesis 26:5; Rabbi Menachem ben Shlomo Me'iri, *Beit haBechira* (c. 1270 CE) on *Sanhedrin* 59a; *Sefer HaHinnuch* (c. 1300 CE), Imperative 424; *Encyclopedia Talmudica* (Talmudic Encyclopedia Institute, Jerusalem, Israel, 1992), Vol. 4, "Ben Noah"; Aaron Lichtenstein, *The Seven Laws of Noah* (The Rabbi Jacob Joseph School Press/Z. Berman Books, New York NY, 1981, 2d ed. 1986); Nahum Rakover, "Jewish Law and the Noahide Obligation to Preserve Social Order" with Suzanne Last Stone, "Sinaitic and Noahide Law: Legal Pluralism in Jewish Law," 12 *Cardozo Law Review*, pp. 1073/1137 (New York NY, 1991). That each commandment makes up a representative general category containing many particulars should be obvious: look within, for instance, at the single commandment against sexual immorality, forbidding such various specific sins as adultery, incest, bestiality, etc.

3. Talmud, *Sanhedrin* 56a-56B, 74b, 75a, *Yad Hilchat Malachim* 9:1.

4. "Rabbi" is Hebrew, literally meaning "my master," "my teacher." *"Rabbenu"* — "our rabbi," a term of endearment or special affection.

5. See, e.g., Leviticus 26:42-45; Deuteronomy 7:7-11, Jeremiah 31:33; Psalm 147:19-20. See also Talmud, *Yoma* 4b, *Sanhedrin* 59a, *Shabbat* 87a. "All of the [Torah's] 613 Commandments are included in the Ten Commandments." — Rashi (classic commentary) on Exodus 24:12. The Hebrew for commandment is *mitzvah,* from a root meaning "connection." The Seven Commandments are the *Sheva (7) Mitzvot;* the 613 laws that directly command Israel are known as the *Taryag (613) Mitzvot.*

6. Exodus 19:5; Deuteronomy 7:6. See Isaiah 2:3, 26:2, 45:22.

7. See, e.g., Deuteronomy 4:8 and 33:4: Psalm 147:19-20; Talmud, *Sanhedrin* 59a.

8. See Proverbs 8.

9. Or she, obviously. **This book follows the traditional gender conventions of English grammar. No offense intended: "mankind" and "man" both refer inclusively to womankind and women.**

10. Psalm 1:1-2; Mishnah, *Pirke Avot* 6:1.

11. See Genesis 12:3; Psalm 25; *Mishnah Tosefta, Sanhedrin* 13:2; Talmud, *Sanhedrin* 105a; *Mishneh Torah* (Maimonides' *Yad Hazakah*), *Hilchot Melachim* 8:11. Also see Job 19:26; Ecclesiastes 12:7.

12. Matthew 23:2: "Then spoke Jesus to the multitude, and to his disciples, saying, 'The scribes and the Pharisees [i.e., Judaism's mainstream rabbis and religious writers] sit in Moses' seat: All therefore whatsoever they bid you observe, *that* observe and do.'" See Matthew 5:18-19.

13. 1 Kings 8:41-43; Isaiah 56:1-8. See Talmud, *Pesachim* 87b.

14. See Isaiah 2:3; Psalm 96:3,10; *Sifra* (Midrash) on Leviticus 22:32; *Mishneh Torah (Yad), Hilchot Melachim* 8:10. [Maimonides wrote the *Mishneh Torah* ("Repetition of the Torah," per Deuteronomy 17:18; Joshua 8:32), the *Yad Hazaka* ("Strong Hand," per Exodus 6:1; Deuteronomy 7:8,19), or simply the *Yad* ("Hand" — this also being the name of the customary pointer, a miniature silver hand, that directs the reader of a Torah scroll). The *Yad,* an immensely authoritative work consisting of fourteen volumes — Hebrew letters have numeric values too; the letters that make up *yad* add up to fourteen — of stupendous Torah erudition, precision, and remarkably reliable authority, shouldn't be confused with the much larger and much more ancient *Mishnah* ("Teaching"). The *Mishnah*, together with the Gemara, or Talmud, is regarded as the Oral Torah.]

15. See Isaiah 11:9; Daniel 7:27; Zechariah 2:15; Psalm 96:9-10; Hosea 2:25; Talmud, *Berachot* 54b; *Yad, Hilchot Melachim* 12:4-5.

Foreword

I am certain that in every generation people thought that they were living in exceptional, even Messianic times. Notwithstanding the disappointment of our continuing exile, it is difficult not to believe that our own time is the one in which the eschatological[1] promises will finally be fulfilled. The people of Israel have traveled a great distance in only a relatively short amount of time. Over the span of one generation we have experienced the indescribable agony of the Holocaust, the ecstasy of renewed sovereignty in the land of Israel, and the spiritual heights of an unprecedented number of *yeshivot*[2] all over the globe where more people than ever before in our history are hearing and learning Torah.

Now we are witnessing a rebirth of the most ancient of true religions, the Noachide Covenant. This covenant, entered into between God and Noah upon his exit from the ark, still unites the Creator with His human creation. Later, at Sinai, God entered into a unique covenant with Israel, but He will forever maintain the terms of the original covenant with *B'nai No'ach* — the vast majority of mankind, the non-Israel descendants of Noah.

To a large extent the Jewish community has been caught napping at this remarkable time. The B'nai No'ach have come calling and they are not finding anyone home. After thousands of years of exile and persecution, Jews find it hard to believe that the nations would turn to them with the request foretold in Zechariah 8:23.[3]

I found myself in this singular situation early in 1989 when a group of B'nai No'ach requested an appointment. I was the rabbi of a small community in Chattanooga, Tennessee. When you are the only Orthodox rabbi in a radius of one hundred miles you get some very strange calls, but none were as strange as the call from J. David Davis[4] of the Emmanuel Congregation in Athens, Tennessee. He wondered whether I would be amenable to teaching his congregation of former Southern Baptists what God expects of gentiles.

I had studied in classic yeshivot and this was not a subject that came up in our talmudic debates and dissertations. Where would I be able to find the sources to research in order to answer their myriad questions?

The more deeply one delves into the Noachide Covenant, the more one learns of God's expectations for the nations. And thus began, for me, a fascinating journey into lesser known areas of Torah, Talmud and Jewish history in an attempt to glean whatever information could be used to help point the way for today's non-Jewish seekers of Truth. It is now some ten years since I embarked upon this voyage and it has changed my life. It has brought me into contact with many wonderful and interesting people whom I might never have met and it has led me to a deeper study of portions of the Talmud and its commentaries that I might, otherwise, have treated superficially.

Had I not accepted the challenge from J. David Davis on that memorable day in Chattanooga I would most likely not have met Michael Dallen and enjoyed his insightful study into practical laws for B'nai No'ach. I wish I had had Mike's book available to me when I first began my search for Noachide material.

Because it is the Noachide Laws that will bring the nations of the world to an understanding of Torah as it relates to the unfolding of the grand design that God has for all of us, we need dedicated Jews like Michael Dallen to apply themselves to help with the development and education of the modern Noachide.

Just as there are Jews, from beginners to advanced students, who study Torah on different levels, there are B'nai No'ach who are only just beginning their journey and there are those who are ready for deeper thought and involvement. Michael Dallen's fine book will be of inestimable assistance in helping the searching *ben* (m.) and *bat* (f.) No'ach find their path to true religion. He presents his material in a succinct manner that will appeal to the novice while still providing food for thought to the more advanced student, who will also enjoy examining the footnotes and doing his own further research.

The bottom line is that we need much more research into these subjects and I heartily welcome Michael Dallen's book. Mr. Dallen has embraced the historical importance of the emerging Noachide movement and, with wit and a keen eye for what is essential, he brings this ancient religion into modern times. The reader will feel himself a part of this exciting journey and will, we hope, be inspired to become an added light to the torch that will eventually illuminate the world.

RABBI MICHAEL KATZ
Miami

NOTES

1. Eschatology: concerning the "end of days" — the end of current history; the beginning of a radically different era.

2. *Yeshivot:* plural of *yeshiva,* a school or seminary for learning Torah.

3. Zechariah 8:23: " . . . they [non-Jews] shall take hold . . . of him that is a Jew, saying, 'We will go with you: for we have heard that God is with you.'"

4. J. David Davis, b. 1945. Founder and longtime leader of the Emmanuel Noahide community. Author of *Finding the God of Noah; the Spiritual Joruney of a Baptist Minister from Christianity to the Laws of Noah* (Ktav Publishing, Hoboken NJ, 1996).

Introduction

*Mankind cannot rise to the essential
principles on which society must rest
unless it meets with Israel.
And Israel cannot fathom the deeps of its
own national and religious tradition unless it
meets with mankind.*
— R. Elijah Benamozegh[1]

I set out through this book to provide you with a simple, readable introduction to the Seven Commandments of the Rainbow Covenant. The effort began years ago and "simple and readable" eventually took second place to finally delivering a finished product. Still, the treatment here is really nothing more than common sense analysis based, I hope, on Torah — that immense body of Divine legislation, so closely related to the Noahide Law that God entrusted to Israel. The Noahide laws establish minimal guidelines — practical guidelines — of acceptable human behavior, while also pointing all of us to the Torah's countless welcoming "paths of righteousness."[2]

According to an ancient Hebrew tradition, God revealed the Torah at Mount Sinai in the seventy languages of the nations of the world.[3] Israel says, similarly, that the one Torah shows man seventy faces or dimensions.[4] And it's certain that, if a student happens upon two seemingly contradictory teachings based on Torah, he can often truly say, "I think they are both right—both are the words of the Living God."[5] So long as one studies with humility and pure intentions, even the hottest dispute that revolves around the holy Book will — as the sages say — end with love.[6]

One starts by trying to contemplate just one of the Torah's faces. "When you are able to do so, you won't need words of explanation, for it is the Eternal face that is talking to you, visually and directly."[7]

Keep My Commandments, and live; and My Law as the apple of
your eye. — *Proverbs 7:2*

My effort here has been to reveal a face of the Torah as I see it, to help give you the foundation necessary to discover further dimensions of Torah for yourself. So I incorporated more than a few footnotes — not just as a way of concentrating information, still less to distress you with the style — and earnestly ask you to use them. Please, go to the sources, not only to uncover my mistakes — I hope there aren't many — but to develop your own understanding.

———————

Most religions are man-made. Except for one, all of humanity's religions either: 1) emerged from tribal prehistoric nature myths, lacking any original literate tradition or ethical pretensions, like the amoral nature religions of ancient Greece, Japan and Rome; or 2) began with a single individual who claimed to have a special message. He would gather a following and his followers would spread his word, winning converts until a new religion was born.

Most of the great world religions followed this second pattern.[8]

The religion of Israel did not. While Abraham prepared the way, the Hebrew Revolution really began only at Mount Sinai. God proclaimed His message to an entire people there. Every man, woman and child heard Him; the whole nation of Israel became His priests.

So the religion of Israel, if we can call it that—rather than a mere faith or just a system of belief, it's an entire way of life, a way of eating, thinking, and knowingly trying to embody righteousness — is unique.

The Catholic church speaks of its organic tradition, tracing its authority to propound Christian dogma from the grant of authority of Jesus (*Yeshua ben Yosef*), a Jew, to Peter (*Shimon ben Yona*), another Jew, to build Jesus's church.[9] The mother of Christianity, the Hebrew Revolution, has a different but no less organic tradition, based upon God's instructions from Sinai.

Israel first received the Torah some thirty-three centuries ago. The Hebrew prophets and Israel's greatest scholars have been studying it intensively ever since. Their knowledge, along with their authority, resides in the rabbis of Israel.[10] These immensely literate — and always multi-lingual — masters of the Torah, so deeply schooled in the living Source of humanity's moral wisdom, stand apart from clergy of the man-made religions. The rabbis have the insight, born of years of near-total immersion in Torah, to unfold the layers and layers of meaning within God's laws and testimonies. They have the ability to reveal, in effect, the very process of revelation. But no man, whether rabbi or prophet or both, knows everything there is to know of Torah, and no man, not even the truest prophet, has any authority to effect any change in any of God's eternal laws.[11]

The very Messiah, it's said, won't change the Torah. Rather, he will confirm and explain the laws, as Israel has received them, to more perfectly reveal them.[12] Israel's revelation at Sinai gave man divinely inspired authority binding for all times. This revelation, and no other, had the power to impose eternal Commandments— no other revelation can.[13] This is the Revelation that Israel has been studying so intensively over all the long centuries.

After all these centuries, Israel has learned something worth knowing about it. Much of what can be said has been said, often brilliantly, as one sees by looking into the vast body of accumulated Torah scholarship.

Even a dwarf can reach high if he stands on the shoulders of giants. I saw my main job in writing this book to be arranging the learning from other books, both ancient and modern, and from rare, obscure, or relatively difficult sources. Very few authors have attempted any extensive treatment of the subject. Fewer yet have written for the audience that should be most concerned about these laws — Noahides themselves — as opposed to writing only for their fellow Jews, and then particularly for Jewish scholars!

I tried to write the most practical and down-to-earth guide to the Rainbow laws available. Without forgetting that the measure of such a book isn't great originality but plain honesty, of faithfulness to the ancient received Tradition — that is, to truth.

This is a book that had to be written—that, given the nature of the Tradition and the dynamics of the Hebrew Revolution, was inevitably going to be written.

It might have been more poetically interesting or charming, I suppose, if a non-Jew, a Noahite, were the writer. Whereas I, *Mayer ben Zusman*, am a Jew born and raised, a son of Israel in America. Unfortunately, the fact is that while the Jews are only a tiny minority in the world, and then only a minority of Jews have the background knowledge — let alone the time, the energy, and command of English — needed to write on the subject coherently, even fewer Gentiles today could do it.

Not to disparage anyone's abilities; most of the world has simply never heard of the Noahide Commandments. Awareness of this all-important Law, fortunately and at last, has begun a rapid spread only recently. It has been my privilege to know some of the *b'nai Noah* who are so largely responsible for this progress, who have taken the Rainbow laws out of the realm of the merely esoteric by finally introducing them to plain lay audiences. I'm indebted, incidentally, to these wise and pious Gentiles — they know who they are — for their generous encouragement and advice, for the access to their libraries as well as all the feedback. But even they were not going to write this book — if for no other reason than that they were already too-fully occupied. So were the rabbis who taught them.

Most books on Torah topics are written by rabbis. This book, on a subject only slightly removed from Torah, wasn't. I'm a writer and attorney, not a Torah sage or decisor. But I think that the book here might be better for it.

A rabbi's formal religious training usually begins early in life and continues with ever-increasing intensity into adulthood. It's an incredible education, yet it can also be narrowing or parochial in this sense: One doesn't necessarily get to see how Torah precepts can be applied — and often are applied — in different or non-traditional settings. Here the advantage tends to go to the more worldly Jew. So if one must write a guide to the Noahide laws, it is probably better, even if one knows much less Torah than the rabbis know, to know at least a little more than most rabbis know about the real strengths and priorities of actual Noahides.

On questions of Israel's Torah obligations the rabbis are permitted to render authoritative decisions for Israel. But one doesn't need to be a rabbi, or know all that a rabbi must know, to elucidate the Noahide Commandments.[14] I would say that the best qualifications for that, beyond the basic analytical and research skills that every writer should have, are just: a) common sense; b) general experience, especially if it's supported by some acquaintance with history and law; c) reasonable familiarity with at least the English-language literature; d) and a good grounding in "the general thrust" of Torah; all these being joined to e) a very genuine respect for the King of Heaven.

One does not advise others on matters of Torah ethics casually. To "put a stumbling-block before the blind"[15] — to mislead any person, who may be "blind" in a certain matter, with false information or advice (or even with the truth, if the truth in the wrong context will mislead the listener) — is a lawless act. If the "blind" person sins because of such misleading advice the one who misled him shares the weight of his sin.[16]

To mislead not just a single person but many people — "to cause a multitude to sin" — is something even more terrible.[17] And to mislead them about the meaning or contents of the holy Torah, of all things, would be an act of blasphemy — a profanation of its Maker's Name. So one approaches the writing of such a book with a good deal of care.

Israel is told, "It is not incumbent upon you to finish the task, but neither are you free to desist from it."[18] I wrote this book because I was able to write it, and because no one else was writing it. That is, I didn't feel myself free to desist from the task. A man should pray as if all depends upon God, but act as if all depends upon himself.[19] God requires each of His children and servants to do what we can.

You should find *The Rainbow Covenant* informative but please don't think of it as dispositive. It's hardly that: it's an early study, a provisional work, introducing a huge body of knowledge and a Divine challenge — to interpret the data that God gave us and use it for nothing but good. By studying His laws we learn about His ways. That's a process that should occupy us all, and it could occupy us all for many lifetimes. In fact, it's central to the vocation of being human. So the very most that I could do here has been to try to push the process along. Obviously, I can't legislate for the nations. No one mortal can. The nations, and coming generations, must do that for themselves.

Remember that Heaven's Revolutionary laws are rarely as simple as any one lesson may seem to make them.

Here you will find a method, which I think is the best method, of approaching the Noahide Commandments. I've pointed out many fairly obvious associations and connections between the Torah and the Universal Law, discussing them in terms of possible practical applications and underlying meanings. This discussion must inevitably reflect some personal biases—but you should also know how hard I worked to put my own prejudices entirely aside. **I didn't make up any of the laws here.**

When I first took up this project, for instance, I believed in "gay rights" as a matter of basic principle. In the abortion debates, I was determinedly "pro-choice." Only the undeniable thrust of God's laws forced, finally, certain modifications in those positions.

Reject my conclusions and my reasoning if you must.

Skepticism is wisdom when applied to everything man-made. There are statements within that may represent no more than the opinion of one or several people — hopefully, a respectable group among Israel. You will concur with their point of view or their underlying logic or you won't. There are also many completely reliable — in fact, holy — truths inside. Be sure that you don't throw any Torah out with any thing that you might regard as bathwater.

Writing this book changed me. Which isn't that surprising: it was never far from my conscious thoughts every day over many years. It was a wonderful thing to have this opportunity. I learned a lot; I became increasingly devout as I learned more.

Believe me when I tell you — incidentally, if it interests you — that I thought very little of religion, or what I knew of it, for many years, through most of my youth and early manhood. Like many people, I regarded it, and particularly biblical religion, as wishful and enervating or divisive. I became a "man of faith" not out of any tugging emotional need or yearning for transcendence but only over time, reluctantly and skeptically, more or less despite myself. Thank God, the truth of the Hebrew Revolution — God's Torah revolution — is amazingly persistent. Attribute my "conversion," if you will, to plain pragmatic logic and a growing acquaintance with the facts: to fairly wide-ranging personal experience informed by quite a lot of reading (especially of secular history and economics and comparative cultural analysis or theory), and, ultimately, the strongest intellectual conviction that 1) God blesses those who bless Israel and 2) all true morality reflects or comes from Torah. After that, as I learned personally, the more one learns of Torah, the more one tries to live it.

As for you, my fondest wish is that you will soon find the same thing happening to you. May you start from where the book here stops to climb to new and ever greater heights! The quotations and source notes provided should, as I've said, help you make your own way to the light.

Take advantage of those sources. Again, most of them, including every one that I used or mentioned frequently, have been translated into English. Never in all of history have they been more easily accessible. I'm discussing long-cherished "hidden" things within that, in some circles, are little more than common knowledge. This book could never have been written otherwise.

Many people helped me with the project. Special thanks are due all the following: Linda Booker, Franc Gianino, Rabbi Michael and Toby (Bulman) Katz, Arthur Kurzweil, Michael Joseph Lane, Rabbi David K. Nerenberg, Noah Potter, C. Rachel, Dana Salzman, Jack E. Saunders (my long-time confidant and ally, a Noahide pastor), Rav (Rabbi) Yoel Schwartz, Rabbi David Sears, and Rabbi Yechiel Sitzman. Of course none of these good people bear any responsibility for anything wrong within.

By far my greatest debt is to my mother, Naomi Shana Dallen, daughter of Reb Mayer Moshe Ellias, son of Reb Yitzchak Noah Ellias of Kovno/Kaunas, Lithuania. Let the memory of these two righteous men of Israel — who became, with their families, such proud Americans — be for blessing. And may my excellent mother, and all her tribe of dedicated librarians and teachers, never lack anything good.

Naturally, I apologize for any errors, whether of commission or omission. Compared to everything that could be said, all that I managed to get in barely amounts to a spoonful from an ocean. To acquire real wisdom, go to the sources and study with a teacher. This is no more than a guidebook, an introductory work, an invitation to further study.

Michael Ellias Dallen

NOTES

1. From *Israel and Humanity* (France, 1914), title page, quoted by Aimé Pallière, *The Unknown Sanctuary; A Pilgrimage from Rome to Israel*, (Bloch, New York NY, 1985, final page).

2. Psalm 23:3.

3. Talmud, *Sotah* 36a.

4. Midrash, *Genesis Rabbah* 13:15.

5. Talmud, *Eruvin* 13b.

6. Talmud, *Kiddushin* 30b with Rashi.

7. Rabbi Israel (Friedman) of Rizhyn, Ukraine (d. 1850). Quoted in Martin Buber, *Tales of the Hasidim* (Schocken, New York NY, 1948) Vol. 2, and Lewis Glinert, *The Joys of Hebrew* (Oxford University Press, London, 1992) p. 70.

8. *Kuzari*, supra, 1:6. See Aryeh Kaplan, *Handbook of Jewish Thought* (Moznaim Publishers, New York NY/Jerusalem, 1979), 4:40.

9. See The Christian Gospels According to St. Matthew, 16:18.

10. See, e.g., Leviticus 10:11; Deuteronomy 17:9-12, 19:17; Talmud, *Moed Katan* 17a, *Hagigah* 15b.

11. See Deuteronomy 4:2,13:1; Talmud, *Zevahim* 80a; *Yad, Mamrim* 2:9; *Sefer HaMitzvot* 2:313-14.

12. *Yad, Hilchot Melachim* 11:1-4, *Yesodey HaTorah* 18:3.

13. See, e.g., Leviticus 27:34; Numbers 36:13; Deuteronomy 4:40; Isaiah 59:21; Talmud, *Shabbat* 104a, *Yoma* 80a; *Yad, Hilchot Melachim* and *Yesodey HaTorah*, ibid.

14. Based on the principle that, while the Torah in all its details is best known to the rabbis of Israel, the details of the Universal Law are, ultimately, for each nation to determine for itself.

15. Leviticus 19:14.

16. See *Sifra* (Midrash) to Leviticus 19:14; *Sefer HaMitzvot* 2:299.

17. *Yad, Hilchot Teshuvah* 3:14,19; See *Yad, Hilchot Sanhedrin* 11:5.

18. Mishnah, *Pirke Avot* 2:21.

19. See Emil Fackenheim, "The Jewish Concept of Salvation," in *Quest for Past and Future: Essays in Jewish Theology* (Beacon Press, Boston MA, 1968), p. 167.

Book One

The Rainbow Covenant

The Permanent Revolution

SINAI

When the Law of Sinai came into the world,
freedom came into the world.
— Mishnah Torah, Pirke Avot 6:2

Call to Me, and I will answer you, and I will
tell you great and mighty things which you
do not know. — Jeremiah 33:3

Some manner of convulsive, out-of-the-ordinary event, dramatically described in the Bible's Book of Exodus, took place among a disorderly assemblage of nomads in the ancient Middle East. As a matter of historical fact, and whatever its exact nature, it changed the Hebrew people radically. It raised a free nation out of slaves. It forged a revolutionary Law. And the people, in accepting the Law, became a nation of revolutionaries, who would radically change the world.

Describing the Hebrew Revolution as merely religious grossly distorts the truth of the matter.

It was a violent revolution. It waged a continuing battle with right-wing ("conservative") reactionaries — like the party of the "Golden Calf"[1] — and left-wing radical revisionists — like the party of Korah.[2] It bloodily fought off challenges from retrogressive foreign opportunists: nations like the Amalekites,[3] the Moabites and Midianites.[4]

Moses, the nominal leader of the Revolution, turned the economic, political and moral basis of Hebrew society upside down. He was "history's first revolutionary." His was the prototype for all successful revolutions, the model for later, lesser revolutionaries — Paul (Saul of Tarsus), Muhammed, Luther, Cromwell, Tom Paine, Jefferson and Franklin and Washington, Robespierre, Frederick Douglass, Lenin, Gandhi, Malcolm X, etc. — to aspire to and emulate.[5]

Directed by the God of freedom, Moses crafted a complete system of police and courts; he organized the Hebrew masses with revolutionary discipline.[6] Creating a special cadre of supervisory officers — while cultivating two hereditary classes, the priests and Levites — to watch over the people and each other, he installed a permanent hardcore revolutionary body to keep the Revolution pure.[7] He purged a whole generation of his own people, and left them to die in a wilderness.[8]

The Hebrew Revolution raised a free new nation from out of the slavish dregs of ancient Egypt. Then, before Moses died, he invested his people with the purpose and ability to carry on his cause.

PERMANENT REVOLUTIONARIES

The essence of this Revolution, the principal object of the Rainbow Covenant as well as the Covenant of Sinai, and the axis around which the whole Law — along with all true morality — turns, is to blot out the pagan impulses in the human heart, to make the existence of idolatry impossible.[9] God and history and Moses forged the Jewish people as an instrument to attain that goal.[10]

> The Hebrews have done more to civilize men than any other nation. If I were an atheist, and believed in blind eternal fate, I should still believe that fate had ordained the Jews to be the most essential instrument for civilizing the nations. — *John Adams*[11]

The cause is humanity's, but the Hebrews received the first call. Their mission is permanent.[12] Moses promised that the new nation, though "the fewest of all peoples," would become an eternal nation.[13] History has obliged.

THE CENTRAL CADRE

Almost 140 generations have come and gone since Israel burst forth from Egypt. Moses' armies fought their first battles with bronze weapons, more than 3200 years ago.[14] Hundreds of nations and great civilizations have risen and vanished into oblivion in the interval. But the people of Israel — the Hebrews, the Jews,[15] the embodiment and vanguard of the Hebrew Revolution — remain.

These Hebrews make up a "peculiar" people, as the Bible says.[16] Today, living among many nations, the Jews constitute a singular nation of practically every nationality and of every race and class and color. They remain one of the "fewest of all peoples"— comparing them to the rest of humanity, America's Mark Twain likened the world's Jewish population to "a nebulous dim puff of star dust lost in the blaze of the Milky Way."[17] According to the most *generous* current estimates, only about .3 percent (.003) of the world's population, or (actually) probably far fewer than three out of every *thousand* people alive, can be counted among Moses' "people of priests."[18]

> Yet these same rude, unpopular and often unintelligent folk, from time almost immemorial, have been the chief dreamers of the Western world, and beyond all comparison its greatest poets. — *H.L. Mencken*[19]

Persecution, ignorance, apathy and assimilation continually drag their numbers down. Uncommonly vicious enemies, in every generation, persistently try to rid the world of them.[20] But this, apparently, cannot be accomplished, because the people of Israel were created to embody Moses' Revolution.[21] Insofar as they choose to live by the Revolution's Law, the Jews make the Law — "the Word" — flesh.[22] God incarnated His Law in a whole people -- an eternal nation, as the Bible says, unlike other nations.[23]

How odd of God to choose the Jews — *Lewis Browne* [24]

It's not so odd. The Jews chose God. — *Leon Roth*[25]

Israel was "chosen"[26] for a vocation. Sinai's Law isn't meant to guarantee the Jews instant peace and tranquility. Rather, so long as Israel obeys it, it guarantees the Jews' service. By living the Law, Moses' people serve God and humanity as "a kingdom of priests and a holy nation"[27] — "a light unto the nations."[28]

> [Moses] took a poor shepherd family and made a nation of it — a great, eternal, holy people: a people of God, destined to outlive the centuries, and to serve as a pattern to all other nations, a prototype to the whole of mankind. — *Heinrich Heine*[29]

Such people aren't supposed to just go along to get along.[30] They were created a nation so that other nations could learn from the laws that Moses put into their custody.[31] The Jews challenge others to be more than they are. God offered Israel the chance to fill the role of the cadre — the hardcore, the "priests" — of a permanent and universal revolution. The people of Israel chose to answer the call.[32]

Consequences of that choice are everywhere.[33] So, for instance, the vast majority of the world's characteristic ideas, concerns and causes — from the teachings of capitalist economics to Marxism to Ayn Rand's[34] so-called Objectivism, from Freudianism to digital computing and atomic physics, from Hollywood and rock 'n roll to feminism and holistic medicine, from America's "pro-choice" abortion movement to the Bible-beating "pro-life" movement, to offer just a very few examples — originated from, were transmitted through, or at least were distinguishably shaped by Moses' "peculiar" people.[35]

> And in your descendants shall all the nations of the Earth be blessed; because you have obeyed My voice. — *Genesis 22:18*

Israel's Revolution sparked the genesis of Christianity and Islam.[36] Jesus, Joseph and Mary, John the Baptist, and Jesus' Twelve Apostles were all Jews; Paul (Saul of Tarsus), the great Christian scriptural author, Catholic saint and "Apostle to the Gentiles," proudly described himself as a former rabbinic student.[37] Later, not one but two of the most beloved wives of Islam's Prophet Muhammed, while he was issuing The Koran (Qur'an) — the "Bible" of Islam, which repeats at least as many precepts from Israel's Oral Tradition as the Christian Scriptures do[38] — were Jewish.[39] Other remarkable Jews profoundly influenced subsequent Christian and Muslim renewal movements.

> Has God cast away His people? God forbid. For I also am an
> Israelite, of the seed of Abraham, of the tribe of Benjamin. God
> has not cast away the people which he foreknew. — *Romans 11:1-2*

Many scholars argue that Sinai underlies the modern Scientific Revolution.[40]

Israel's Revolution taught that nature is a unity, governed and ordered by the God of law. It taught that time isn't just a meaningless and endless cycle, or a path of constant degeneration from some mythical golden past, but a progressive, purposeful movement to a better future.

The fixed conviction of the religious Jew that the universe has only One cause, that God is rational and His creation is rational, that He loves truth, and that He gave humanity the right and the obligation of dominion over the material world, has been one of the greatest constants of human history.

> He will not forsake you, nor destroy you, nor forget the Covenant
> with your fathers which He swore to them. — *Deuteronomy 4:31*

FREEDOM ROAD

"How very much besides religion we owe to the Jew!" President Woodrow Wilson exclaimed.[41] The Bible promises that this people will be "a blessing to all the families of the Earth."[42] As Moses' agents, and the soldiers of his Revolution, no other nation or people has done so much to shape the minds and hearts of humanity.[43] The Jews, for thousands of years, have pressed upon the world *"the most fundamental of all principles and the basis of all learning"*: the knowledge of the existence of the Supreme Being.[44]

Man may have only One true Master. This constitutes the core of the Revolutionary faith. No other idea, philosophy or worldview has done more to uplift the species; nothing has contributed more to the cause of human freedom.

This Revolution aims at nothing less than the utter eradication of every contrary idea — to blot them out of existence.[45] So

Israel has introduced and has continually pressed on humanity the doctrines of radical, historically based monotheism. These include:

- The absolute unity and holiness of God;
- the oneness of His Creation;
- the oneness of humanity;
- the sanctity of human life;
- the sacredness and dignity of the human personality and human free will;
- the uniform application of law, due process, and proportional justice;
- the Sabbath and the seven-day week;
- the efficacy of prayer;
- the immortality of righteous souls;
- and the promise of worldly redemption in the coming Messianic age.

An underlying theory of the Revolution is that good is contagious.[46] Moses deposited the new Law with his own people, Israel, and the "mixed multitude"[47] from other nations who had followed him out from Egypt. Later, different peoples, like the Gibeonites,[48] the Kenites and the Rechabites,[49] as well as countless individuals,[50] joined his followers.

Israel's Law is designed to free the Jews from the sickness, the inertia, and the barbaric wickedness of paganism. It released the Jews' energies. But it has also condemned them to be a people who can't rest, as the old joke goes, and who won't let anyone else rest either. As a nation created to battle blind taboos, oppression and idolatry, their Law won't let them.[51] Moses gave his people a revolution to fulfill. Through their Bible and their lives, the Jews would reintroduce the human race to God's Rainbow Covenant with humanity's legendary common ancestors.[52]

AMERICAN REVOLUTIONARIES

Proclaim liberty throughout the land unto all the inhabitants
thereof — *Leviticus 25:10*[53]

North America's first laws, from the Seventeenth century's
"Pilgrim Code" of Plymouth Colony and the "Body of Liberties"
of Massachusetts, were confessedly based on Moses' Torah. The
American and English Puritans revered the Pentateuch, the Bible's
first Five Books; the Pilgrims tried to pattern American society
upon the Torah's moral teachings.[54]

Our Jewish Bible has implanted itself in the table-talk and
household life of every man and woman in the European and
American nations. — *Ralph Waldo Emerson*[55]

New England's Pilgrims gave themselves Hebrew "Christian
names" — anglicized Hebrew names like Sarah and Samuel,
Ezekiel and Ebenezer and Hannah, or more conventional
Hebrew-rooted names like Ann, John, James, Mary, Judy,
Deborah, Thomas, and Benjamin — for a reason: they believed
that they were building a new Israel in the New World.[56] Israel's
Bible formed a central part of the curriculum in early American
schools. The new nation's revolutionary founding fathers were **all**
schooled in it. It has even been said that Americans like Thomas
Jefferson and Benjamin Franklin, and other intellectuals, had an
education in the Seven Commandments laws specifically.

Hugo Grotius, or Hugo de Groot, the philosopher and legal
theorist of the Dutch Renaissance, might have been their teacher.
He was a great teacher, this brilliant Gentile seeker. Having
explored Israel's Oral Torah he had come upon the Seven
Commandments Code. He built on it.

Grotius's Latin-language treatises on law and nature were
widely translated. His masterwork, *On the Law of War and Peace*, had
a tremendous influence on eighteenth century thought. Indeed, it
remains the basis of international law today.[57] America's leading
revolutionary intellectuals most likely read it.[58]

Grotius's faith in the God of Moses, and his belief in a basic,
God-given universal Law permeates his writings. These works,

especially as they influenced thinkers like Hobbes, Paine, and Locke, shaped the intellectual climate that gave birth to the American Revolution.

Scholars see plain evidence of Grotius's influence in Jefferson's and Franklin's language in the Declaration of Independence. They see it not only in the Declaration's optimistic approach to the moral instincts of the international human family, but in its faith that all people are equal before God, and its ringing appeals to "nature's God" and "natural Law."[59]

RAINBOW UNIVERSALISM AND HEBREW PARTICULARISM

In morals, Jew and non-Jew stand under the same Law.
— *Midrash*[60]

With study, almost anyone may become one with Israel by converting to Judaism.[61] But the Holy One doesn't require anything of the kind. His "house" belongs to all peoples.[62] He cherishes the righteous of every nation.[63]

God designed the Rainbow Covenant Law to govern everybody, *including* the Jews. For everybody *except* the Jews, obedience to the Code of Seven Commandments constitutes the basic test of human righteousness.[64] This was the sole test, in Biblical times, applied to "Noahites," or non-Jews, who sought the status of permanent residents — the equivalent of the United States government's Immigration Service's Green Card — in the Jews' Holy Land.[65]

The Rainbow laws are God's Universal laws. Coming from a time long before the birth of Israel, they set out humanity's *minimal* moral obligations.

God eventually created Israel as a vehicle or catalyst to help establish the Seven Laws in the world. But Israel, through its Torah, can point the nations to an even greater understanding of His way than that.

According to the Bible, the people of Israel are supposed to serve Him as His "priests."[66] The Ten Commandments and the Torah's

613 (naturally, Israel has counted them) Ten Commandments laws constitute a comprehensive priestly body of law — a holiness Code.[67]

Moses presents the Ten Commandments in the Books of Exodus and Deuteronomy.[68] Unequivocally and unmistakably, the Scripture emphasizes, each time, that these Ten Commandments are the special "inheritance of the people of Israel."[69] Introducing the Ten Commandments, Exodus specifies, "Tell the people of Israel . . . ."[70] Deuteronomy proclaims "Hear, O Israel . . . ."[71] The First Commandment identifies God as the One who rescued the Jews from Egypt's slavemasters. These Commandments obviously aren't directed at Egypt's slavemasters.[72] They are clearly **not** universal.

UNIVERSAL REVOLUTION

Sinai's Ten Commandments form the core of Israel's unique Law. *While these Ten Commandments provide guidance to all who seek to follow God,* they don't directly command or apply to anyone except the Jews.

Moses describes the Fourth Commandment, for example, with its injunction to keep the week's last day — the Sabbath, from a Hebrew root meaning "to cease" — holy, as "a sign for all time between Me and the Children of Israel."[73] The other Commandments, and the Torah "statutes and judgments" that follow, include all the Jews' separatist, distinctive tribal rules, like their famous national ban against eating pork.[74]

The Jews constitute a people — an ethnic group, like the Swedes or Armenians — as well as a sacred society. The Torah's laws are meant to permanently maintain Israel as both.[75] God commands the Jews to obey the Ten Commandments, and the Ten Commandments Code of 613 laws.[76] He expects the daughters and sons of Israel to follow this Law, so that they will be worthy to serve Him by bringing humanity — all the daughters and sons of Noah — His most fundamental, Universal laws.[77]

> And I will say to them that were not My people, 'You are My people,' and they shall say, 'You are my God.' — *Hosea 2:25*

Anyone who seeks true understanding of God's universal laws

or of His divine Will as it relates to humanity needs the light provided by Moses' instructions to Israel.[78] But the two sets of Law, the Code of Seven Commandments and Israel's Ten Commandments Code, while having many parallels in each other — the Universal laws against theft and murder, for instance, almost exactly mirror the related prohibitions in Israel's Ten Commandments Code — are ***not*** the same. The former sets out a minimal set of obligations for everyone. The latter, a demanding, highly detailed Code, is for His "priests."[79]

Priests don't minister in a vacuum. Moses pointed his followers to a small land at the crossroads of Europe, Asia and Africa. The "wisdom and understanding" that their revolutionary Law gave the people permitted them to take the land — to rescue it from the defilements of idolatry.[80] The same great Law, at the same time, afforded individual Jews and their families a tremendous advantage elsewhere, out among the nations.

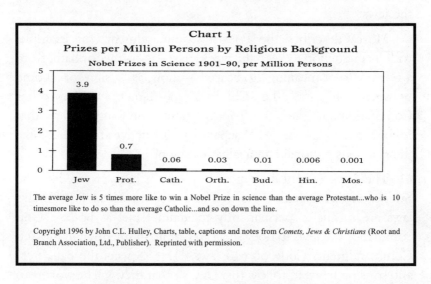

Chart 1

Prizes per Million Persons by Religious Background

Nobel Prizes in Science 1901–90, per Million Persons

The average Jew is 5 times more like to win a Nobel Prize in science than the average Protestant...who is 10 timesmore like to do so than the average Catholic...and so on down the line.

Copyright 1996 by John C.L. Hulley, Charts, table, captions and notes from *Comets, Jews & Christians* (Root and Branch Association, Ltd., Publisher). Reprinted with permission.

Look, for instance,[81] at Charts 1 through 3, and the following tables and statistics. They're certainly worth a look. According to one Harvard study, taking just the United States in the thirty years from 1965 to 1995 (where Jews constituted ***less*** than two percent of the population), they made up 50 percent of what the study called the top two hundred intellectuals, 40 percent of American

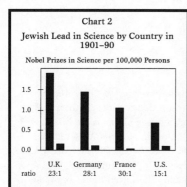

Chart 2

Jewish Lead in Science by Country in 1901–90

Nobel Prizes in Science per 100,000 Persons

	U.K.	Germany	France	U.S.
ratio	23:1	28:1	30:1	15:1

The reliability of Jewish excellence in science is tested here by comparing their record with that of gentiles in the four nations with the most Nobel prizes. The extraordinary lead of the Jews shows up consistently in all four countries.

The combined total for other prize-winning countires is too small to show on this chart; the ratio there is even higher—52:1.

©Copyright 1996 by John C.L. Hulley.

Nobel Prize winners in science and economics, 20 percent of the professors at the country's leading universities, 40 percent of the partners in the leading law firms in New York and Washington, 26 percent of the reporters, editors and executives of the major print and broadcast media, 59 percent of the directors, writers and producers of the fifty top-grossing movies from 1965 to 1982, and 58 percent of the directors, writers and producers of two or more primetime television series.[82]

Chart 3

Nobel Prize-Winners in Science by Religious Background

Religious Background	Prizes 1901–90	% of Total	Population (millions)	Prizes per Million
Jewish	54.4	22.0	14	3.89
Christian				
Protestant	157.9	63.9	213	0.74
Catholic	26.2	10.6	435	0.06
Orthodox	4.1	1.7	120	0.03
Buddhist	2.2	0.9	170	0.01
Hindu	1.9	0.8	301	0.006
Muslim	0.3	0.1	324	0.001
TOTAL	247	100		

Sources: Nobel prize-winners in science: The totals are compiled from B. and J. Schlessinger (eds.) *The Who's Who of Nobel Prize Winners 1901–90*, 2nd ed., Oryx Press, Phoenix, Arizona, 1991. Designations such as "most probably Christian-Protestant" or "most probably Catholic" or "Jewish sympathies" are here classified under the heading for Protestant, Catholic and Jewish respectively. Where the individual has no religion, but that of his parents is given, the latter is shown; if the parents held to different religions, half is assigned to each. Although indications like these may not reveal the beliefs of the individual, they should be fairly reliable in reflecting his or her cultural background. For almost a quarter of the awards (59.3) the religious identity is listed simply as "Christian"; these are here prorated among Protestants, Catholics and Orthodox according to the number of awards already identified for each. For a small number of awards (8.5) the religious identify is given as "unknown" or "none", without any information on the orientation of the parents. There are here prorated among all the religions in a similar way.

Religious population: D. B. Barrett (ed.), *World Christian Encyclopedia*, Oxford, 1982, p. 6. The estimates given here are intrapolated from his data for 1990 and 1970, so as to yield a figure for 1932. This is approximately the midpoint of the research period for the Nobel prizes in science.

©Copyright 1996 by John C. L. Hulley.

NOTES

1. Exodus 32.

2. Numbers 16. Korah, or *Korach*.

3. Exodus 17.

4. Numbers 31.

5. See Wilfried Daim, "The First Revolutionary," *The Center Magazine* (Center for the Study of Democratic Institutions, Santa Barbara CA, September/October 1972) pp. 38-49; Daim, *Christianity, Judaism and Revolution* (Frederick Unger Co., New York NY, 1973); Lincoln Steffens, Moses in Red: *The Revolt of Israel as a Typical Revolution* (Dorrance & Co., Philadelphia, PA, 1926). Mosaic imagery and direct appeals to Mosaic truths and Mosaic history suffuse the works of all these men and, often even more so, of the movements they led. Israel's Bible is 'the Magna Carta of the downtrodden,' the greatest instigator of revolt against despotism.-T.H. Huxley, *Controverted Questions* (1892). "Since the Exodus," said Heinrich Heine, "freedom has always spoken with a Hebrew accent." (*Germany to Luther*, 1834).

6. Paramilitary discipline, extending to every family group, organizing the whole nation into structured, responsive units of tens, fifties, hundreds, etc., under Moses' own handpicked officers. See Exodus 18:20-23.

7. Exodus 32:29, 40:12-15; Numbers 1:48-53. "Who is on the Lord's side?" Moses called, at a critical moment early in the Revolution. By their decisive response, the people of the tribe of Levi earned these badges of obligation and honor for themselves and their descendants forever. See Exodus 32:26 with Rashi.

8. Numbers 14.

9. *Moreh Nevuchim* 3:29. See Exodus 34:13; Deuteronomy 7:5, 12:2. "People make their bellies their gods, their fine clothes their law, and their home maintenance their ethics," R. Bachaya ibn Yosef (Spain, c. 1160), *Hovat HaLevavot* 9:2. "The law against idolatry outweighs all other Commandments," Midrash, *Mechilta* to Exodus 12:6. See *Sifre* to Numbers 15:22: "Whoever rejects idolatry affirms the entire Torah."

10. See Exodus 19:6; Isaiah 43:12, 49:6; Jeremiah 22:29; Zechariah 14:9,16-17.

11. Letter to F.A. Van der Kamp, February 16, 1809. Adams was the second president, a revolutionary founding father, and the second president, of the new United States. He continues, "[...]civilizing the nations. If I were an atheist of the other sect, who believe or pretend to believe that all is ordered by chance, I should believe that chance had ordered the Jews to preserve and propagate to all mankind the doctrine of a supreme, intelligent, wise, almighty sovereign of the universe, which I believe to be the great essential principle of all morality, and consequently of all civilization."

12. Exodus 31:16; Leviticus 26:42-45; Deuteronomy 4:30-31, Jeremiah 16:15-19, 31:35-37; Zechariah 8:23.

13. Genesis 17:7. 49:10; Exodus 32:13; Leviticus 26:44; Deuteronomy 7:6-9. Also see, e.g., Jeremiah 31:35 with Hosea 2:21, 11:8-11. "Forever" means forever.

14. Hebrew tradition indicates that Moses died in the year 1273 BCE. **One uses "BCE" (Before the Common Era) and "CE" (Common Era) instead of the Christian terms "BC" (Before Christ) and "AD" (Anno**

Domini — Latin: "Year of the Lord [i.e., Yeshua ben Yosef, or Jesus])."

15. See Jeremiah 34:9, c. 580 BCE, for the Bible's first use of this word (in Hebrew, *"Yehudi"*) as a synonym for "Hebrew" or "Israelite." That usage began after the Assyrian holocaust but before the Babylonian exile. While Israel didn't make much representational art (See Exodus 20:4), murals, sculptures and mosaics from ancient Egypt, Assyria, Babylon and Rome show that the Jews of those days had relatively long noses and a Western Asian or European ethnic look, as do most Jews today.

16. Exodus 19:5; Deuteronomy 14:2, 26:18.

17. "Concerning the Jews," *The Writings of Mark Twain*, Vol. 12, Author's National Edition (Harper & Brothers, New York, NY, 1899) p. 275 / Jewish Publication Society, Philadelphia, PA, 1985 (reprinted from *Harper's Magazine*, September 1898). This statement issued *before* the Holocaust in mid-20th century Europe.

18. *Encyclopaedia Britannica, 1995 Annual.* Some 47 percent of the world's estimated 13 million Jews live in either the U.S. or Canada, but even in the U.S., according to 2000 and 2002 surveys, Jews make up less than 2 percent (down from almost 4 percent in 1940) of the country's total population. Note that religious affiliation is not a Census topic, and all these statistics are based upon the somewhat self-interested estimates of Jewish organizations themselves. No group attracts support by minimizing the number of its members: if anything, these estimates of Jewish numbers are bound to be inflated.

19. *Treatise on the Gods* (revised edition, Vintage Books, New York NY, 1946) p. 262.

20. See, e.g., Psalm 74:8; Esther 3:8. Yet the Bible also tells of God's unconditional pledge to Israel, to "bless those who bless you and curse those who curse you," Genesis 12:3, 27:29. See Exodus 34:7; Isaiah 42:6; Jeremiah 2:3. In fact, the historical record tends to support the proposition that this Divine promise evidences itself, even if only on a naturalistic level, as a basic historical principle. It seems that anti-Semitism isn't just futile and unseemly, but also ultimately self-defeating.

21. Genesis17:1-21, 22:17-18; Exodus 19:5-6.

22. Deuteronomy 26:16-19; Isaiah 49:3,6. Also see Christianity's Gospel According to St. John 1:14.

23. Numbers 23:9; Leviticus 20:26; Deuteronomy 12:28.

24. Browne, an American writer, 1897-1949. *How Odd of God to Choose the Jews*, 1934. This phrase is also attributed to Lord Alfred ("Bosie") Douglas (best known to history as Oscar Wilde's lover), in his London magazine *Plain English*.

25. Quoted by Leon Roth, editor, *Jewish Thought* (Harper & Bros., New York NY, 1954) p. 39.

26. Isaiah 41:8, Psalm 33:12. Chosen, that is, to serve as the incarnation of the Torah, any failure by the people to do so involving direct and serious penalties. See Deuteronomy 26:16-19; Jeremiah 31:33; Hosea 2:23.

27. Exodus 19:6.

28. Isaiah 49:6.

29. *On the History of Religion and Philosophy in Germany,* Vol. I (Berlin, 1834); quoted in J.H. Hertz, *The Pentateuch and Haftorahs* (2d ed., Soncino Press, London, 1969), p. 209 — Commentary to Exodus 2.

30. See Leviticus 20:23; Deuteronomy 7:6, 26:18.

31. Isaiah 43:10; Talmud, *Pesachim* 87b.

32. Exodus 24:7; Ezra 10:5.

33. See, e.g., *The Gifts of the Jews; How a Tribe of Desert Nomads Changed the Way Everyone Thinks and Feels*, by Thomas Cahill (Nan Talese/Doubleday, New York NY, 1998); *Jews, God and History*, by Max Dimont (Simon and Schuster, New York, NY, 1962).

34. Ayn Rand was Alicia Rosenbaum (before she changed her name).

35. Shelves and shelves of books attest to that proposition. See such titles as *The Jewish Contribution to Civilization, The Jewish Mystique, How the Jews Invented Hollywood,* etc. Yet most standard reference works downplay the Hebrew origin of many important Hebrews. They commonly prefer to describe people like Albert Einstein, for instance, only as a German or American.

36. For Christianity, see, e.g., The Gospel According to St. Matthew 5:17-18, 19:17; Luke 16:17, 18:18; Romans 7:12,22. See also James McKenzie, *The New Testament Without Illusion* (Thomas More Press, Chicago IL, 1980); Hugh J. Schoenfield, *Those Incredible Christians* (Grove Press, New York NY, 1968). For Islam, see, e.g., The Koran, *Surat* 2:39-74, 3:33, 5:3, 6:145, 17:32-35, 24:2-3,33 (Ahmed Ali translation, 1984; Princeton University Press, Princeton NJ, 1988); Will Durant, *The Age of Faith* (Simon & Schuster, New York NY, 1950) pp. 184-186.

37. Galatians 1:14. Saul apparently attended popular lectures given by R. Gamliel ben Shimon ben Hillel (Gamaliel I), in the time of King Agrippa. On Rabban Gamaliel, see, e.g., Talmud, *Sotah* 41a, *Gittin* 61a, *Rosh HaShanah* 23b.

38. See Will Durant, ibid. For example, the rabbinic teaching, "He who destroys a single life is considered as if he had destroyed the whole world, and he who saves a single life is considered as having saved the whole world," Talmud, *Sanhedrin* 4:5, later repeated in the Koran, Sura 5:32, became one of Islam's favorite sayings. Not that this means that Islam is any more sympathetic than Christianity to the Hebrew Revolution generally.

39. Martin Lings, *Muhammed* (George Allen & Unwin, Ltd., London, 1983) p.233; Aisha Abd El Rahman, *The Wives of the Prophet* (Dar El Hilal, Rabat, Morocco, 1971) pp.165-170.

40. Even leading "anti-religious" figures speak movingly of Sinai's contribution to Western thought. See Alfred North Whitehead, *Science and the Modern World* (The Lowell Lectures, 1925. The Free Press, New York NY, 1967)p. 12-13, "Origins of Modern Science"; Thomas H. Huxley, *Science and Christian Tradition* (D. Appleton & Co., New York NY, 1899), pp. 54-58. Also see, e.g., Louis I. Newman, *Jewish Influence on Christian Reform Movements* (Columbia Univ. Press, New York NY, 1925); Herbert Hovenkamp, *Science and Religion in America* (Univ. of Pennsylvania Press, Philadelphia PA, 1978). While most writers give more credit to the ancient Greeks, they often forget how quickly Greece's glory faded, as well as the role played by all the Jewish Hellenist enthusiasts who first translated and popularized the ancient Greek philosophers. See Cecil Roth, *Jewish Contribution to Civilization* (Harper & Bros., New York, NY, 1940) p. 55. Further, such secular philosophical systems as Stoicism and Confucianism (known as "The Way of the *Ju*" [sic] or "the Scholar") probably also derive, at least in part, from the forces

originally set loose at Sinai. But this subject would make another book. See Sidney Shapiro, ed., *Jews in Old China; Studies by Chinese Scholars* (Hippocrene Press, New York NY, 1984); Michael Pollak, *Mandarins, Jews and Missionaries* (Jewish Publication Society, Philadelphia PA, 1980).

41. *The State* (Harper & Bros., New York NY, 1890) p. 143; quoted in Cecil Roth, *Jewish Contribution to Civilization*, supra, p. 40.

42. Genesis 12:3, 28:14.

43. See, e.g., Genesis 12:2-3; Isaiah 2:3; Thomas Cahill, supra, and Cecil Roth, supra.

44. Psalm 83:19. See *Mishneh Torah (Yad)*, *Hilchot Yesodey HaTorah* 1:1.

45. *Yad*, ibid.; *Moreh Nevuchim* 3:29. Every idea and practice contrary to the basic principles of pure monotheism is idolatry — paganism. See Exodus 34:13; Deuteronomy 7:5, 12:2; and commentaries.

46. See Genesis 12:2-3; Exodus 19:5-6; Deuteronomy 4:5-7.

47. Exodus 12:38.

48. Joshua 9.

49. Jeremiah 35; I Chronicles 2:55.

50. See, e.g., Ruth 1:16-17; 1 Kings 18:3; Esther 8:17. Besides Ruth, another great biblical gentile who chose Judaism was the prophet Obadiah, author of one of the Bible's Books. — Talmud, *Sanhedrin* 39b.

51. See Exodus 19:5. "Anyone who repudiates idolatry is a Jew." — R. Yochanan ben Nappah, Talmud, *Megillah* 13a.

52. See Isaiah 49:6. "The Torah is a unified plan for all humanity." — Midrash, *Genesis Rabbah* 1:1.

53. Liberty Bell inscription, c. 1776, Independence Hall, Philadelphia.

54. Roth, supra, p. 15; Newman, supra, ibid.

55. Emerson, writing in *Representative Men: Plato* (1845).

56. See, e.g., Cecil Roth, supra.

57. See "Grotius"/"International Law," *Encyclopaedia Britannica*.

58. See Isaac Husik, "The Law of Nature: Hugo Grotius and the Bible" (*Hebrew Union College Annual*, Cincinnati OH, Vol. 2, 1925) pp. 381-417; Max Wiener, "John Toland and Judaism" (ibid., Vol. 16, 1941) pp. 215-242, 234.

59. Id. Also see Ethel and Stanley Marks, *The Impact of Judaism upon the American People* (Bureau of International Affairs, San Marino CA, 1990); Cecil Roth, supra, pp. 300-303.

60. *Sifra* 85b (Midrash to Leviticus 18:6).

61. *Shulchan Aruch*, *Yoreh Deah* 268:2. See Lawrence J. Epstein, *The Theory and Practice of Welcoming Converts to Judaism* (Edwin Mellen Press, Lewiston NY, 1992).

62. Isaiah 56:7.

63. Talmud, *Sanhedrin* 105a.

64. See Leviticus 18:5; Talmud, *Sanhedrin* 56a-75a; *Yad, Hilchot Melachim* 8:10, 10:12.

65. See Exodus 23:33; Mishnah, *Yevamot* 8:1; Talmud, Tractate *Avoda Zorah* 64b-65a; *Sefer HaMitzvot* 2:51.

66. Exodus 19:6; Deuteronomy 7:6.

67. See Mishnah, *Avoda Zorah* 9:4, *Sanhedrin* 56a-60; *Yad, Hilchot Melachim* 10:9.

68. Exodus 20:2-17; Deuteronomy 5:6-21.

69. Deuteronomy 33:4. See Psalm 147:19-20; Talmud, *Sanhedrin* 59a.

70. Exodus 19:3.

71. Deuteronomy 5:1.

72. Exodus 20:2; Deuteronomy 5:6.

73. Exodus 31:17.

74. See Leviticus 11:7; Deuteronomy 5:1, 14:8.

75. See Friedrich Nietzsche, "The Jews are beyond all doubt the strongest, toughest and purest race [sic] at present living in Europe," in *Beyond Good and Evil*, Sec. 251(1885).

76. Deuteronomy 33:4; Midrash, *Mechilta* to Exodus 20:2; Talmud, *Shabbat* 87a, *Yoma* 4b; Rashi on Exodus 24:12; Maimonides (Rambam), *Sefer HaMitzvot* 1:1.

77. See Exodus 19:5-6; Jeremiah 13:11, 33:7-9; *Yad, Hilchot Melachim* 8:10.

78. See Isaiah 8:16, 51:7; Zechariah 8:23; Psalm 25:14.

79. Exodus 19:5-6; Isaiah 45:22, 56:1-8; Jeremiah 31:33.

80. Genesis 15:16; Leviticus 18:21-30.

81. Not to make too much out of any bit of evidence. But the overwhelming weight of all the evidence categorically supports the central thesis here. The facts and figures are, at the very least, far too spectacular to be so steadily ignored. As for Jewish political power, the greater the power or influence acquired by individual Jews, it seems, the less the people — each doing "what is right in his own eyes" (See Judges 21:25) — tend to have as a nation. Mark Twain, for one, memorably criticized the Jews in this regard, comparing them very unfavorably to the Irish in this matter. (1899, *Literary Essays, Author's National Edition,* Vol. 12, supra, pp. 265-267). The Fast of Gedaliah, following the New Year, *O*, in the Hebrew calendar, exists, in large part, to help Israel mourn its peculiar lack of national political cohesiveness and judgment (See Jeremiah 40-41; Zechariah 7:5; Talmud, *Rosh HaShana* 18b).

82. Seymour Martin Lipset and Earl Raab, *Jews and the New American Scene,* (Harvard University Press, Cambridge MA, 1995), pp. 26-27.

The Torah Revolution

REVOLUTIONARY TEXTS

If they tell you that there is wisdom among the nations" — the "Gentiles," or "clans," from the Latin; the *goyim*, or "nations," in Hebrew — "believe it," the rabbis teach. "But if they tell you that there is Torah among the nations, **don't** believe it."[1]

Torah knowledge makes a difference; it's the most liberating thing on earth.[2] The Jews, carrying their Torah with them, were meant to eventually spread and settle, forming communities across the world. They were meant to expose the people of their new countries and communities to their Revolution.[3]

> That they may know that You alone, whose Name is God,[4] are the Most High over all the earth. — *Psalm 83:18*

Conservative critics of revolution usually deny the possiblity of real revolutionary change. They say that human nature never changes. Slaves will always be slaves, they argue; the slave mentality is passed on from generation to generation. Slaves need the will and the strong hand of a master.

Moses not only created a free people out of just such slaves, he committed them to carry out the terms of a universal revolution. Moses' Egyptian contemporaries probably told him, "it cannot be done."

The Hebrew Revolution stands for the proposition that people **can** change. Today, almost thirty-five centuries after Moses' death, his Revolution continues to spread. Whatever happened at Sinai, it represents one of no more than two or three watershed events in the history of the human race.[5]

Science without religion is lame; religion without science is blind.
— *Albert Einstein*[6]

Scientists say that, in a universe almost 14 billion years old, on
an earth more than 4.5 billion years old, early variants of man
appeared less than 4 million years ago.[7] True men, identical to
those today, classified immodestly but scientifically as *homo sapiens
sapiens* — "wise, wise man" — appeared in the late stone age, only
about 100,000 years ago. Even then, however, the species — a
varied collection of unique animal beings, radically and amazingly
different even from their closest animal cousins — barely
managed to rise above the level of the animals.

Less than 35,000 years ago, human culture exploded.
Anthropologists describe what occurred as a world-wide cultural
revolution. In the age known as the Upper Paleolithic, 35,000 to
11,000 years ago, people all over the planet suddenly began
painting symbols of themselves and animals on cave walls, carving
sophisticated tools with designs in them, wearing clothes and
making jewelry, and keeping track of time.

Students of human pre-history speak wonderingly about this era, the so-called Paleolithic Revolution.[8] To a non-scientist reader of their works, it seems almost as if humanity was touched, during this era, by a wonderful cosmic magic wand. Perhaps people acquired the ability to express complex thoughts through language?[9] At any rate, the human race suddenly took a great leap forward, and no one knows exactly how or why.[10]

Moses described these events — the Upper Paleolithic Revolution, and God's awesome Creation of the universe — poetically and magnificently in the first three chapters of the Bible's Book of Genesis.[11]

There is nothing like it in all of human literature. The supposedly "kindred" Creation myths of Babylon, India, Egypt, Greece and other nations are, by contrast, unrelievedly cruel, wild, amoral and disgusting.[12]

Genesis is utterly monotheistic, optimistic, and — in the sense that it depicts the human race as the crowning glory of Creation — humanistic. Don't think of it as a science textbook, but Moses' account of the Creation anticipates the scientists' famous "Big Bang" theory; his account of life's progress, from the lowest and simplest forms to the most complex and highest, anticipates Darwin.[13]

One may imagine Moses receiving a mental image of the Beginning from the One Who knows. A modern physicist might have tried to put such insight into a set of mathematical formulas. Moses, a man from the Bronze Age who, working at God's command, had to write a Torah for the ages, put his Knowledge into vivid Hebrew poetry and prose.[14]

> The Jews were the only ones whose sacred Scriptures were held in
> ever greater veneration as they became better known.
> — *Jacques Benigne Bossuet*[15]

If the Paleolithic Revolution was humanity's first great revolution, the Hebrew Revolution at Sinai was the second.

The cultural revolution of the stone age lifted the whole human race to a higher plateau. The cultural revolution of Sinai, as it continues to unfold, points in the same direction. The Paleolithic Revolution prepared mankind to accomplish great new deeds and to take on greater challenges. Just so, but on an infinitely higher level, Sinai's Revolution continues, slowly but surely, to pave the way to a new stage in human history.

> The Jewish Messianic faith is the seed of progress which has been planted by Judaism throughout the whole world. — *Jacob Klausner*[16]

IN COMING TIMES

Torah promises that, as part of God's Rainbow Covenant, humanity will live to see the next stage realized. People won't go the way of the dinosaurs: no cosmic catastrophe or new upstart species will bring an end to our dominion over the earth.[17]

The Torah represents the emergence of men and women from primitive prehistory as the start of one new era.[18] Then it uses exactly the same language to promise Israel and all humanity another watershed revolution.[19]

Sinai's Five Books foretell the coming of this era.[20] It will be on earth; "it is not of heaven," Moses taught.[21] The latter prophets, the Psalms and other Scriptural Writings, together with Israel's Oral Law, interpret and elaborate upon these predictions.

The Messianic Age may come to pass within the ordinary laws of nature. But it will still constitute a miracle. "The Messianic era will be a free will act of God, but it is a gift which has been promised. And that raises its beginnings above the level of nature, even if they do occur under natural conditions."[22]

Human potential will explode into genius, and into great and wonderful works.[23] War will come to an end.[24] Though there may still be rich and poor and strong and weak, oppression will end.[25] Likewise, it will be very easy to make a living — a minimum of labor will produce great benefits.[26]

The people of Israel will be reconnected to a free and peaceful land of Israel, to produce great sages — certainly including scientists — and prophets.[27] God may reveal His Presence to humankind again, as He did at Sinai.[28] As people become, like the prophet Abraham, better and more pleasing to God, many may come to know Him at a level of intimacy and directness akin to Abraham's. Individuals, families, races, tribes and nations will join together in unity with Israel, like a magnificent universal symphony.[29] These non-Jews, Children of Noah, will work and worship as one with the Children of Israel.[30] The human life span will be extended.[31] Eventually, even death will be defeated.[32]

REVOLUTIONARY TEXTS

These prophecies are extremely ancient. Moses, as everyone knows, lived in a physically harsh and a technologically primitive age. The people of Isaiah's time, 27 centuries ago, couldn't very well imagine all the complicated possibilities of scientific progress. But the Hebrew Revolution, through the ages, is what made such progress possible. It revolutionized the way that people see the world.

> If you seek it as silver, and search for it as for hidden treasures;
> then you shall understand the fear of the Lord and find the
> Knowledge of God. — *Proverbs 2:4*[33]

> O, how I love Your Torah! It is my meditation all the day.
> — *Psalm 119:97*

The Hebrew Scriptures contain the Hebrew Revolution's manifesto. Israel attributes the Bible's first Five Books — the Pentateuch or Written Law or *Torah*: Genesis, Exodus, Leviticus, Numbers and Deuteronomy — to Moses, Israel's greatest prophet.[34] One regards Moses' revelation not just as prophecy, but as a totally different, higher kind of spiritual experience.[35] In fact, it's said that even the *least* among Israel who *accompanied* Moses to Sinai reached spiritual heights beyond any level ever attained even by such great later prophets as Ezekiel.[36]

Moses wrote the Five Books of the Torah over a period of forty years, inscribing them on scrolls and sections of parchment which he later joined together.[37] The Bible also includes Proverbs and the scrolls of the Prophets, the Psalms, the other Writings and the histories, through the Second Book of Chronicles. But Moses' Five Books are the Bible's heart and core.[38] They reveal every law and ordinance of the Seven Universal Laws.[39]

ISRAEL'S HISTORY BOOK

The Bible begins on a universal basis, with the Creation, and then narrows the focus of the story further in slow progressive stages. It sets out the genealogy of the Hebrews, follows an offshoot of this people to Egypt, and describes their transformation, at Sinai, into the revolutionary nation known as Israel. It ends with its focus on the Jews — the living "remnant of Israel."[40] They have become known by the name of the Judah, Israel's largest tribe.[41] The Bible finishes with some of these Jews returning from foreign exile, to try — not for the last time in history — to reestablish their nation back in the land that God ordained for them.[42]

Jews call their Bible the *Tanach*, based on the initials letters of the Bible's three main sections: *Torah*, T; *Nevi'im* (Prophets), N; and *Chetuvim* (Writings), CH. All of these are Torah, although Moses' Five Books, and the Oral Law which accompanies them, are considered the basic Torah.[43]

Israel is taught that, while Moses was Judaism's foremost prophet, the Bible's later writers, prophets, poets and sages faithfully unfolded Sinai's teachings, increased the knowledge of the truths already revealed through Moses, and made explicit what had been only implicit.[44]

Please understand that this book does not treat the *Tanach* or Bible as if it were some kind of objectively, factually always accurate or "literally inerrant" science text. God didn't, in His wisdom, restrict His spokesmen to textbook-style literalism alone. The Almighty didn't carry Israel out from Egypt upon real "eagles' wings," for instance; while His "strong hand" sustains every atom in the universe, it isn't an actual, material hand.[45]

Israel's Oral Law teaches that this Bible speaks in human terms — not just literally, but in metaphors and poetry, and through prophetic visions. One must never treat every Biblical passage as being necessarily literally true.[46]

This book treats the *Tanach* as Truth, with a capital "T." That is, it approaches the Bible as a complex masterpiece — as a deep and frequently allegorical collection of utterly essential wisdom — which must be read and studied on its own terms.

This Bible is obviously no ordinary book: it's a culture-creator; it's not just a product of human history but a chief agent of human progress. If Moses' God intended the people of Israel to serve Him, in all their generations, by continually trying to introduce God's Law to the world, then Israel gave the Bible to the world to serve the exact same purpose. Like Israel's people, Israel's Bible was designed for interaction.[47] It aims for the heart, as well as the head — and it's designed to elicit a response. It was created to serve all the generations, as a multi-layered argument and a permanent tool of the Hebrew Revolution.[48]

Not just as history, and more than as mere myth, every single expression in this Scripture, Israel is told, abounds in wisdom and wonders to those of proper understanding.[49] The Bible contains many lessons at many levels, but they need to be decoded. Beneath the Scripture's sometimes puzzling surface lies a treasure house of endless wealth.[50]

NOTES

1. Midrash, *Aicha Rabbati* 2:17. *Goy* and *goyim* are biblical words, incidentally, which aren't pejorative at all. See, e.g., Deuteronomy 4:3.

2. See Mishnah, *Pirke Avot* 6:2. Also see David S. Landes, *The Wealth and Poverty of Nations: Why Some Are So Rich and Some So Poor* (W. W. Norton, New York NY, 1998): "If we learn anything from the history of economic development, it is that culture makes all the difference."

3. See Isaiah 42:6, 49:6.

4. Here the original Scripture uses, instead of the title "God," the Holy Name — the Holy Tetragrammaton — of four letters (in English transliteration: Y, H, V, and H). See the discussion further within.

5. The following section borrows from current theories about prehistoric origins. Because such theories often change, one approaches them somewhat skeptically. This section merely reflects today's conventional wisdom, and the classic Jewish tradition that warns against treating Genesis's Creation story completely literally. See Maimonides (1135-1204 CE), *Moreh Nevuchim* 2:30, "Philosophical Interpretations of Genesis 1-4." But also see *Challenge: Torah Views on Science and Its Problems*, Aryeh Carmell and Cyril

Domb, eds. (second ed., Association of Orthodox Jewish Scientists/ Feldheim Publishers, New York NY, 1978) pp. 124-186, for other approaches to ancient prehistory.

6. *Out of My Later Years* (Philosophical Library, New York NY, 1950) p. 26. Another Hebrew genius, Saadya Gaon, elaborated upon this same point earlier in *Emunot VeDeot* (classic work, c. 930 C.E.) 10:14. For the view, based solely on traditional sources, that the Universe is 15 billion years old, see Aryeh Kaplan, *Immortality, Resurrection and the Age of the Universe* (Ktav, Hoboken NJ, 1993) p. 9.

7. Moses wrote that Creation occurred in six uninterrupted stages or "days" — the Hebrew word is "*yomim*" — and most Gentile biblical literalists argue that this refers to six 24-hour days. But *yomim* probably refers only to indeterminate (though uninterrupted) periods of time, like Isaiah's "Day [*yom*] of the Lord." (Isaiah 13:6). Certainly, if Genesis' *yomim* were days, they must have been very unusual, since the Earth's sun wasn't created until the fourth day. (Genesis 1:14).

8. See Charles Brace, *The Stages of Human Evolution* (second ed., Simon & Schuster, New York NY, 1979); Robert Wenke, *Patterns in Prehistory* (Oxford University Press, London/NY, 1980).

9. See Derek Bickerton, *Language and Human Behavior* (University of Washington Press, Seattle WA, 1995).

10. Bickerton, id., and Brace and Wenke, supra, ibid. Later, just about 6,000 years ago (i.e., with the advent of the first man, Adam), humanity took another great leap forward, and began constructing cities.

11. See Hermann Gunkel, *The Legends of Genesis: the Biblical Sagas and History* (Schocken Books, New York NY, 1964); Gerhard von Rad, *Genesis* (Westminster Press, Philadelphia PA, 1961); J. H. Hertz, *The Pentateuch and Haftorahs*, supra, p. 194.

12. Finite gods with huge animal appetites are reputed to have created the world, in these myths, through actions — vomiting, excreting, dripping sperm, or raping, eating, or punishing their fellow gods — which aren't merely arbitrary but also incidental to their real goals: the expression of uncontrolled wrath or jealousy or the satisfaction of a hunger for food or sex. See, e.g., Sir James George Frazer's classic work, *The Golden Bough; a Study in Magic and Religion* (Macmillan, New York and London, 1922).

13. If one understands that phenomena like the animal eye and the human brain are creations of Will — that is, of design, rather than purposeless accident — there is nothing in evolutionary theory that contradicts Genesis. See Hertz, supra, ibid.

14. Israel is taught — and one has good reasons for believing — that every phrase and word and letter of the Bible's first Five Books was put there for one reason: because God wanted it so. See Numbers 16:28; Rambam (Maimonides), the *Siraj,* or *Commentary to the Mishnah* (c. 1168 CE): Introduction to Sanhedrin 10, Israel's Thirteen Principles of Faith, Principle 8. (For the entire Thirteen Principles, see Appendix).

15. (Catholic) Archbishop of Mieux, France — *Discourse on Universal History* (Paris, 1681), Part 2, Ch. 13.

16. *The Messianic Idea in Israel* (Macmillan, New York NY, 1955) p. 531.

17. Genesis 9.

18. Genesis 4:3.

19. Genesis 49:10; Numbers 24:24. See Aryeh Kaplan, *The Living Torah* (Moznaim Publishing Co., NY/ Jerusalem, 1981) p. 10.

20. Numbers 24:17; also see, e.g., Deuteronomy 28:9-30:20.

21. Deuteronomy 30:12.

22. Gershom Scholem, *The Messianic Idea in Judaism* (Schocken, New York NY, 1971) p. 31. See *Yad, Hilchot Melachim* 12:1-2. For the proposition that this era will unfold step by step, in stages, see, e.g., Midrash, *Song of Songs/Shir haShirim Rabbah* 6:16; Jerusalem Talmud, *Berachot* 1:1 and *Yoma* 3:2.

23. Isaiah 11:9; Jeremiah 31:33.

24. Micah 4:3.

25. Psalm 96:10; Talmud, *Berachot* 34b, *Shabbat* 63a, 151b, *Pesachim* 68a, *Sanhedrin* 91b, 99a; *Siraj, Thirteen Principles of Faith*, supra, Principle Twelve.

26. Principle Twelve, supra.

27. See *Yad (Mishneh Torah), Hilchot Melachim* 12:4-5.

28. Deuteronomy 4:30, 30:6; Isaiah 2:2; Talmud, *Avoda Zorah* 3b, *Sanhedrin* 97a-98b.

29. Isaiah 2, 11.

30. Isaiah, ibid.

31. *Yad, Hilchot Melachim* 12:4-5.

32. Isaiah 25:8.

33. "Fear of the Lord." See Deuteronomy 10:12, Proverbs 1:7, 9:10; Mishnah, *Pirke Avot* 1:3. Not just dread or shame but intense feelings of awe and reverence before His infinite majesty, related to one's special love for God. On love, see Deuteronomy 6:5, the most all-embracing injunction in the Bible.

34. Numbers 12:6-8; Thirteen Principles of Faith, supra, Principles 7-9.

35. Exodus 33:11; *Moreh Nevuchim* 2:33.

36. Midrash, *Mechilta* 37a; Exodus 15:2 (Rashi); *Moreh Nevuchim* 3:6.

37. Talmud, *Gittin* 60a.

38. Deuteronomy 4:2; Midrash, *Sifre* to Deuteronomy 18:15.

39. Talmud, *Sanhedrin* 59a.

40. See Isaiah 10:20; Jeremiah 6:9.

41. See, e.g., Jeremiah 34:9; Esther 3:6: Zechariah 8:23. *Yehuda*/Judah comes from Hebrew roots meaning "Praise the Lord." See Genesis 29:35.

42. 2 Chronicles 36. The Bible is complete at this stage, at the beginning of a cycle of blessing and renewal. While Israel's story must necessarily continue until the ends of history are realized, the archetypal patterns of Jewish history have all been revealed. "Whatever happened to the fathers is a portent for the sons." See Ramban (Nachmanides, R. Moshe ben Nachman), *Pirush al haTorah* (Classic commentary, c. 1250 CE), Introduction to Exodus.

43. Mishnah, *Pirke Avot* 1:1; *Sanhedrin* 91b, *Berachot* 5a. See Deuteronomy 17:8-10.

44. Maimonides (Rambam), *Sefer HaMitzvot* 1:172. See *Sifre* (Midrash) to Deuteronomy 18:15.

45. Exodus 19:4, 13:9. See the authorities cited immediately below.

46. See, e.g., Hosea 12:11; Talmud, *Berachot* 31b; *Yad, Hilchot Yesodey HaTorah* 1:9; *Siraj*, Rambam's Introduction to the Mishnah, Sanhedrin 10:1, *Israel's Thirteen Principles of Faith*; *Moreh Nevuchim*, Introduction. And see Aryeh Kaplan, *Handbook of Jewish Thought* (Moznaim, NY/Jerusalem, 1979) 7:75. There are four conditions under which a Torah passage should not be taken according

to its literal meaning: 1) where common human experience contradicts the literal meaning (e.g., can people fly on literal "eagles' wings"?); 2) where obvious logic contradicts it — as when a passage speaks of God having such human attributes as eyes, a hand or mighty arm, etc.; 3) where obvious Scripture contradicts a literal reading and/or 4) where a clear talmudic teaching contradicts the literal sense. See Kaplan, ibid.

47. See Genesis 18:19; Isaiah 8:16; Jeremiah 33:3; Psalm 19:7.

48. See Isaiah 2:3, 43:10, 66:5; Psalm 1:2, 19:7.

49. Psalm 119:18,197; Job 11:9. See the *Siraj*, Maimonides' Commentary on the Mishnah, supra, Principle 8.

50. See, e.g., Psalms 1:2, 19:7, 119:18; Proverbs 2:4; *Yad, Yesodey HaTorah* 1:9.

Written Law
and Oral Law

THE OTHER TORAH

Moses, God and history appointed the people of Israel custodians and interpreters of Israel's Torah, including the so-called Written Law, the Bible's first Five Books.[1] "You are My witnesses, says God, and My servant, whom I have chosen."[2] So the Hebrews themselves, though many nations deny this, have some national special expertise when it comes to interpreting and recognizing the Hebrews' own national Way. Israel's ancient Oral Law, the oral Torah, the Written Torah's "other half," provides a key — the master key — to unlock the Scripture's myriad secrets.[3]

BIBLES AND THE WRITTEN LAW

Practically every edition of the *Tanach* available today includes everything that's usually called "The Bible," up to but not including Christianity's New Testament. This Christian Bible — its title, based on the Latin word "*testamentum*," literally means "new covenant" — was originally an entirely Greek-language work. Written by followers of *Yeshua* ("Jesus" in Greek) *ben Yosef* as a sort of supplement to the Tanach, it begins with The Gospel According to Saint Matthew. Note that, whenever the New Testament refers to Scripture or "the Scriptures," it's referring to the Hebrew Scriptures, the "Old Testament."

> To have bound this New Testament, so completely rococo in taste, with the Old Testament into one book, as the Bible, is perhaps the greatest piece of audacity and "sin against the Holy Spirit" which literary Europe has on its conscience.— *Friedrich Nietzsche*[4]

The different Protestant and Catholic versions of the Old Testament all deliver the Hebrew Scriptures in distinctive ways. Their arrangements of the latter Books and Writings vary slightly; they often add interpretive page and chapter headings which totally contradict Israel's ideas; and bits of the text have been translated differently. Catholic Bibles also usually include several additional "apocryphal" or "hidden" books, like *Tobit* and *Maccabees*, which Israel regards as unworthy or unreliable. Still, a reference to a sentence in the Hebrew Bible — Deuteronomy 8:6, say — can usually be found in the same place, or only a sentence or two away, in a Christian edition. The Table below shows the different arrangements of the Books:

ISRAEL'S BIBLE[5]

Originally written in Hebrew thoughout, except for portions of Daniel, Ezra and Nehemiah, which also include some Aramaic — a closely related language stemming from Chaldean, the everyday tongue of the Babylonian exiles — written in the same script as Hebrew:

Torah: 1) Genesis 2) Exodus 3) Leviticus 4) Numbers
5) Deuteronomy

Prophets: 6) Joshua 7) Judges 8) Samuel 9) Kings 10) Isaiah
11) Jeremiah 12) Ezekiel 13) The Twelve: Hosea, Joel, Amos, Obadiah, Jonah, Micah, Nachum, Habakkuk, Zephania, Haggai, Zechariah, Malachi

Writings: 14) Psalms 15) Proverbs 16) Job 17) Song of Songs ("Song of Solomon") 18) Ruth 19) Lamentations 20) Ecclesiastes (*Koheleth* or "The Preacher") 21) Esther 22) Daniel 23) Ezra and Nechemiah (one scroll, originally) 24) Chronicles

The Roman Catholic (New American) Bible

Pentateuch: 1) Genesis 2) Exodus 3) Leviticus 4) Numbers
5) Deuteronomy

Historical: 6) Joshua 7) Judges 8) Ruth 9) I Samuel 10) II Samuel
11) I Chronicles 12) II Chronicles 13) Ezra 14) Nehemiah
15) Tobit (Apocryphal) 16) Judith (Aprocryphal) 17) Esther
18) I Maccabees (Apocryphal) 19) II Maccabees (Apocryphal)

Wisdom: 20) Job 21) Psalms 22) Proverbs 23) Ecclesiastes 24) Song of
Songs 25) Wisdom (Apocryphal) 26) Sirach, or Ecclesiasticus
(Apocryphal)

The Protestant (King James) Bible

Pentateuch: 1) Genesis 2) Exodus 3) Leviticus 4) Numbers
5) Deuteronomy

Historical: 6) Joshua 7) Judges 8) Ruth 9) I Samuel 10) II Samuel
11) I Kings 12) II Kings 13) I Chronicles 14) II Chronicles
15) Ezra 16) Nehemiah 17) Esther

Wisdom: 18) Job 19) Psalms 20) Proverbs 21) Ecclesiastes 22) Song
of Songs

Prophets: 23) Isaiah 24) Jeremiah 25) Lamentations 26) Ezekiel
27) Daniel 28) Hosea 29) Joel 30) Amos 31) Obadiah 32) Jonah
33) Micah 34) Nahum 35) Habakkuk 36) Zephaniah 37) Haggai
38) Zechariah 39) Malachi

The Christian Scriptures, beginning with Matthew and ending
with The Revelation of John, are all originally Greek-language
works. Both the Roman Catholic and the Protestant versions of
these writings follow the same one arrangement.[6]

Scholars have translated the Hebrew Bible into every human
tongue. But Hebrew is a unique language — the King of the
Universe seems to prefer it to every other earthly language[7] — and
no translation has ever duplicated the concise and amazing clarity
of the Hebrew, let alone each layer of subtle meaning beneath the
merely literal. Obviously, even the best Bible translators must fail
in some respect.[8]

Probably the most spectacular example of a misleading
translation involves the very Name of God.

His Name

Israel knows Him by a Name that represents a compound of
the Hebrew verb "to be." The holy Tetragrammaton — four
Hebrew letters corresponding to the English consonants *Y, H, V*,
and *H* — spells out the fact that God is the One who always will

be, who eternally was, who is.[9] It denotes God's utter transcendence, as well as the Power that faithfully sustains the universe.[10]

The Tetragrammaton appears almost 6,000 times in every Hebrew Bible. Too sacred to pronounce,[11] as its use presumes a more-than-human insight into God's supernal Essence, most Bible translations don't print it.[12] Rather, they use the word "God," or replace it with "Lord," one of God's titles.

Tragically, this has encouraged many Christian readers to confuse Israel's coming Messiah — literally, "the anointed one," who sometimes also gets the title "lord" (a Hebrew honorific, like the English "mister," "master" or "sir") — with the very mortal Messiah's infinite and unchanging Creator.[13] But this is an error that must never be made. It is idolatry and a blasphemy — a terribly soul-coarsening mistake — to confuse God with even the greatest of His creatures.

THE ORAL TORAH

Let my teachings drop as the rain, let my speech distill as the dew.
— *Deuteronomy 32:2*

Every word and letter of Moses' Five Books — the Written Torah — was canonized, or firmly set into the current form, by Ezra's time, in the 4th century BCE.[14] Long before this, Israel had the Oral Torah.

Most Gentiles don't even know of the Oral Torah's existence. But the Bible can't be understood without it, as even the Christian Scriptures suggest.[15] The Oral Torah is the Written Torah's "other half."[16] The two can't be separated: each represents an essential part of the one sacred Torah.[17]

This shouldn't be a secret: Moses didn't write down everything he knew. His Five Books teach that he merely "declared" — that is, orally communicated — many of his Teachings.[18] Moses and the Elders of Israel handed down countless verbal judgments, clarifying the Written Torah, relating the many details and intricacies that explained the Torah's broader points to others, so that Israel's leaders could teach them.[19]

Moses taught, for instance, that the Written Torah's famous "eye for an eye" language[20] must never be taken completely literally. Rather, it embodies the principle of proportional and universal justice. Evil must be punished, without respect to person, nationality or race, or the high or low status of any individual. One who injures another must pay, in an amount and degree proportional to the victim's loss, and compensate the victim for the loss.[21] Only in cases of murder, Moses taught, must the criminal actually pay with his own "life for life."[22]

Moses orally taught the students of his generation. He wrote, for example, that the men of Israel must wear *totafot* — in English translations, "frontlets" — at certain times, but the Written Torah doesn't define the word.[23] What are *totafot*? Moses gave the answer — they are *tefillin* (in Hebrew), or phylacteries; leather-wrapped cubes enclosing parchments inscribed with portions of Holy Script[24] — by show and tell. It is part of the Oral Torah; he never wrote it out, but saved the law's many details for oral exposition instead. As with the law of fringes (in Hebrew, *tzitzit*)[25] or the rules of animal slaughter — "you shall slaughter your cattle . . . as I have [orally] commanded you"[26] — one must go beyond the Written Torah to Israel's Oral Tradition.

Moses spent almost half a century, some 35 centuries ago, explaining God's Law to his followers. This was Moses' Torah, a Teaching consisting of the first Five Books of the Bible, together with their accompanying oral statutes and ordinances, background facts, traditions, stories, and Moses' own, inspired, analytical and problem-solving methods.

He taught his brother Aaron and his own successor, Joshua; Aaron's sons, the priests; the seventy or 140 Elders of the people; the people's lesser judges and leaders; and the whole congregation of Israel together. He made sure that every person should hear these Teachings repeated four times[27] — he and the Elders did *everything* they could to transmit the whole Revolutionary Tradition intact. Later, after Moses had died, Joshua carefully went over the whole of the Torah with the people again.[28]

Israel has been continuously discussing it, and trying to live it, in all its details, ever since. Joshua and his fellow students communicated this Torah to the next generation of students. Each generation that followed did the same[29] — living it, and handing it down word for word, as precisely as possible, exactly as it had been taught to them.[30] The people's elders and judges instructed the priests and the prophets — who put portions of the Oral Law into the Bible's latter Books. Sometime in the middle of the 4th century BCE, these great Sages, including Israel's last prophets, instructed the people and rabbis of Ezra's Great Assembly. And the people of Israel kept Sinai's ancient Teaching alive.

In the twelfth century CE, one of Israel's greatest geniuses explained the Oral Torah thus:

> "Whatever is mentioned there received the full assent of all Israel, and those Sages who instituted the ordinances, issued the decrees, introduced the customs, gave the decisions, and taught the correct rulings, constituted the whole body or the majority of Israel's wisest members. They were the leaders who received the traditions concerning the fundamentals of Judaism, in unbroken succession back to our teacher Moses."[31]

Israel is called to believe that this Oral Torah, including the traditional Hebrew interpretation of the Five Books of Moses, is, like the Written Torah, the product of true and faithful Revelation, or Divine Inspiration.[32] But the Oral Torah, unlike the Books of the Bible, was meant to be transmitted by living example and by word of mouth — personally, from master to student directly.[33] So the rabbis refused, at first, to put any of the Oral Torah into writing.[34]

Roman legions under the Emperor Vespasian had literally begun their siege of Jerusalem, in 68 CE, before the rabbis finally began to encode the Oral Torah. They had to: when a danger exists that the Oral Torah might be forgotten, it must be put into writing.[35]

Israel's Temple priests and rabbis, and most of the leading custodians of the Hebrew Revolution's traditions, would die in the ensuing holocaust. Their vast body of mostly unorganized, never-categorized knowledge might have died with them. But just before the fall of the Second Jewish Commonwealth, in 70 CE, the rabbis began organizing formal academies to systematize and teach the oral tradition. By 200 CE they were reducing the Oral Torah to script.[36]

Converting the Oral Torah into this written *Talmud Torah* — literally, the "Learning" or "Study" of Torah — kept it vital. Most of the 63 volumes of the Talmud read like an exhilarating continuing debate — or like the carefully kept minutes of a huge symposium, though one lasting over 1,200 years (from the fifth century BCE to the eighth CE) — between brilliant scholars. The Written Torah gives a good example of its style when Aaron's very human logic prevails, in an exceptional matter, over his brother Moses' prior general teaching.[37]

This is the Revolutionary Way: logical analysis, argument and controversy all grace an investigation that applies the Knowledge of Sinai to the questions of everyday living.

While God's Torah remains constant, its meaning — that is, the ways in which people interpret it — develops and unfolds according to human needs and experiences. New issues are constantly arising, so students must extend and apply the ancient "Guidance" to correctly answer questions that even Moses never faced.[38]

> The inner meaning of Talmudism is unshakeable trust in God and unreserved obedience to His declared Will.
> — *Robert Travers Herford* [39]

As the Talmud itself maintains, the ultimate wisdom of the Torah has yet to be fully fathomed.[40] More than a hundred generations since the beginning of the Common Era have found in that truth a challenge. Over the millenia new writings, including rabbinic judgments, legal opinions, and other clarifications of the Torah and its Talmud have added to man's understanding of God's Way. Thus Israel fulfills its enduring mission.[41]

One finds the Seven Commandments, the Code of the Rainbow Covenant, set forth within this Oral Torah.

NOTES

1. See Deuteronomy 17:9-11, 33:4. Also see, e.g., the Christian Gospels, Matthew 23:2.

2. Isaiah 43:10.

3. See, e.g., Exodus 24:12; Leviticus 10:11; Deuteronomy 1:5, 17:9-11, 33:4; Isaiah 2:3: Jeremiah 17:22; Ezra 10:8; Talmud, *Shabbat* 88a, *Sanhedrin* 99a; *Siraj,* supra, Principle 8.

4. *Beyond Good and Evil,* Sec. 52 (1885): "In the Old Testament of the Jews, the book of Divine righteousness, there are men, events and words so great that there is nothing in Greek or Indian literature to compare with it." Id. Also see Nietzsche, *Genealogy of Morals,* Sec. 3:22 (1887).

5. The Bible quotations used within are from the translations prepared by the Jewish Publication Society of America (Philadelphia) in 1917 and 1985, or the Hebrew Publishing Co. (New York NY, 1939), or by the late Aryeh Kaplan in *The Living Torah* (supra, 1981). Archaic English pronouns like "thee" and "ye" or "thine" and "thy" have been modernized by converting them to "you" or "your."

6. The quotations within from the Christian Scriptures (New Testament) are from the Authorized King James version or from the New American Bible's Revised Edition of the New Testament.

7. It is, for one thing, a remarkably refined language, where natural euphemism replaces the famously crude four-letter words of Anglo-Saxon. Concise, direct and reasonably assertive otherwise, it's also extremely powerful, almost like shorthand, when it comes to discussing questions of conduct and morality.

8. "If one translates a verse literally he is a liar, and if he adds thereto he is a blasphemer and defamer." R. Yehuda ben Ilai, Talmud, *Kiddushin* 49a.

9. Exodus 3:15. See Talmud, *Sotah* 37b, *Yoma* 66a; *Tur, Orach Chaim* 5; *Shulchan Aruch,* ibid, 5:1; Hertz, supra, pp. 215n-216n; Hebrew Siddur (literally "Order," or Prayerbook), *Adon Olam;* Kaplan, *Handbook of Jewish Thought,* supra, 7:80. For an interesting Christian viewpoint, see "The Divine Name That Will Endure Forever," Watch Tower Bible and Tract Society of Pennsylvania (WTBTS of New York, 1984).

10. *Moreh Nevuchim* 1:61.

11. Leviticus 18:21, 22:32; Talmud, *Sanhedrin* 90a, *Kiddushin* 71a.

12. The Jews who gave the world the ancient Bible translation known as the Septuagint, upon which most Christian translations are based, refused — pursuant to the Oral Law (Talmud, *Shavuot* 35a) — to use the Tetragrammaton in any work that might later be mistreated or erased.

13. See James D. Tabor, *Restoring Abrahamic Faith* (Genesis 2000, Charlotte NC/ Emmanuel, P.O. Box 442, Athens TN, 1991) pp. 8-9.

14. Nechemiah 8-13; Talmud, *Bava Batra* 15a.

15. Matthew 23:2.

16. See Exodus 23:2; Deuteronomy 17:8-11; Mishnah, *Pirke Avot* 1:1; Talmud, *Shabbat* 88a, *Hullin* 11a, *Zevachim* 80a; Rambam, *Sefer HaMitzvot* 1:175, 2:314; *Siraj,* Israel's Thirteen Principles of Faith, supra, Principles 8 and 9.

17. Id. Also see, e.g., Numbers 15:38 and Deuteronomy 6:8 and 12:21, regarding the crucial but unwritten details of the highly detailed laws of

fringes *(tzitzit), tefillin* and animal slaughter *(shechitah)*, respectively.

18. See, e.g., Exodus 18:16-26; Leviticus 23:44. The Written Torah has often been likened to a mere outline of the Oral Torah, the Revelation at Sinai serving, in large part, to confirm the Teachings received from the great mentors of the Jews, the patriarchs and matriarchs of Genesis. Gifted, in many cases, with prophetic understanding of the true spiritual nature of the universe, they passed on a heritage of Torah to their descendants *before* Sinai. See Genesis 26:5; Mishnah, *Kiddushin* 4:14; Talmud, *Kiddushin* 82a, *Berachot* 26b, *Yoma* 28b.

19. See, e.g., Exodus 18:26; Leviticus 19:37.

20. Exodus 21:24; Leviticus 24:20; Deuteronomy 19:21.

21. See Numbers 35:31; Talmud, *Bava Kamma* 83b-84a.

22. Exodus 21:23; Numbers 35:30-33; Rambam, *Sefer HaMitzvot* 1:236-246.

23. Exodus 13:16; Deuteronomy 6:8, 11:18.

24. Four sections of Torah. Specifically: Exodus 13:1-10 and 13:11-16; Deuteronomy 6:4-9 and 11:13-21.

25. Numbers 15:38.

26. Deuteronomy 12:21.

27. Calculation by Aryeh Kaplan, *Handbook of Jewish Thought* (supra) 9:18 (p. 181). See Exodus 18:20, 24:3,12, Leviticus 9:1, Deuteronomy 1:5, 33:4 and commentaries; Mishnah, *Eduyot* 8,7; Talmud, *Eruvin* 54b.

28. Joshua 8:31-35.

29. See Deuteronomy 6:7; Proverbs 22:6.

30. See, e.g., the cogent discussion in Aaron Lichtenstein, *Seven Laws of Noah* (Rabbi Jacob Joseph School Press/Z. Berman Books, New York NY, 1981 (second. ed. 1986)) pp. 27-29, and the sources cited there.

31. Rambam (Rabbi Moshe ben Maimon, "Maimonides"), *Mishneh Torah (Yad)*, Introduction.

32. See, e.g., Exodus 24:12; Leviticus 9:1, 10:11; Deuteronomy 1:5, 4:29, 17:9-11; Joshua 1:8; Psalms 25:14, 94:14-15; Malachi 2:7; Ezra 7:10; Nechemiah 9:13-14; *Israel's Thirteen Principles of Faith*, supra, Principle 8. Please note: the nation of Israel is presumed to have some special expertise when it comes to recognizing the Law of Israel. See, e.g., Genesis 49:10; Exodus 19:6. Just as all Israel collectively affirmed and ratified the holiness of those Books that make up the Hebrew Bible, so did it affirm and ratify the holiness of the Talmud, the Oral Torah. Yet the Talmudic Sages came only after "the spirit of prophecy departed Israel" (Talmud, *Sotah* 48b; See Joel 3:1). On the distinctions between prophecy, Inspiration and Guidance, see Kaplan, *Handbook of Jewish Thought*, supra, Vol. 1, Ch. 6.

33. Talmud, *Gittin* 60b. Maimonides' classic formula, "In the name of my father and teacher, in the name of his teacher, who in turn heard it from his teacher," fails to describe one aspect of this age-old procedure: the extraordinary *care* that Israel's leaders in learning took to ensure the purest and most accurate possible transmission of this precious inheritance. Even the ancient accents have been preserved. See Rambam, *Siraj*, the Commentary on the Mishnah, on Eduyot 1:3 (*Mishnayoth*, translated by Philip Blackman (Judaica Press, New York NY, 1965) Vol. 4, p. 391). Also see, e.g., Lichtenstein, supra, pp. 28-29.

34. See Talmud, *Gittin* 60b.

35. Talmud, ibid.

36. That is, Hebrew script. The Sages wrote the first part of the Talmud, the Mishnah — literally, the "repetition" or "teaching" — in Hebrew. The second part of the Talmud, the Gemara — the "completion" — elaborates or comments on the Mishnah in a combination of Hebrew and Aramaic.

37. Leviticus 10:16-20.

38. See Talmud, *Menachot* 29b; Midrash, *Seder Eliyahu Zuta* 2.

39. *Menorah Journal* (London, 1919), paras. 204 and 206.

40. Talmud, *Sanhedrin* 34a. See Job 11:9; *Israel's Thirteen Principles of Faith*, supra, Principle 8.

41. Deuteronomy 19:17. See Midrash, *Seder Eliyahu Zuta* 2.

The Rainbow Covenant

WISDOM FOR THE WORLD

Our race's — the human race's — Seven Commandments are extremely ancient. While Israel's Oral Torah warns against probing into Genesis' account of Creation too literally or too deeply,[1] as Genesis tells the story, God gave the human race portions of His Universal Law even before man became completely self-aware.[2] Later, according to the Oral Tradition, Enoch was teaching the law in a formal school setting, seven generations after Adam.[3]

Ten generations after Adam, God entered into a compact, the Rainbow Covenant, with Noah and his family.[4] The human race receives the whole of this law, all Seven Commandments. Noah, on behalf of his family and all his descendants, accepts God's terms. From here on, God will hold every human being responsible for living up to these conditions: obedience to the Seven Commandments is now a fundamental obligation of all mankind. Finally, God takes the rainbow, a pre-existing phenomenon, and invokes it to serve as the eternal sign of His covenant with humanity.[5]

Based upon this section of Genesis, later generations have described the Code of Seven Commandments as "Noahite" or "Noahide" laws, Rainbow Covenant laws, or "the Seven laws of Noah and his children."[6]

Israel is told that Shem, Noah's son and an ancestor of the prophet Abraham, became a great scholar and teacher of the Seven Commandments Code.[7] Shem seems to have left behind something of an oral, family legacy. Abraham apparently knew of Shem's teachings; some scholars wonder if Melchizedek, the priest

and — literally — "righteous king" of Genesis 14, might actually
have been Shem himself.[8] Abraham thought so highly of this
good priest that he happily gave him a tithe, or tenth, of his —
Abraham's — own net income.[9]

Abraham, and the Bible's other matriarchs and patriarchs
before Moses, are said to have generally guided themselves by
God's Universal laws.[10] But others forgot or confused this Law so
completely that Moses had to insist that the only version of the
Seven Commandments that can be considered binding is the one
that he received and taught at Sinai.[11]

THE SEVEN COMMANDMENTS IN OTHER TEXTS

The first non-Biblical text to specifically mention the Noahide
laws seems to be the Book of Jubilees. This apocryphal Hebrew-
language work, sometimes also known as "The Little Genesis,"
was published fairly late in history, probably in the third century
BCE — that is, less than 300 years before the Common Era.
Jubilees 7:20 teaches that certain Rules, given to Noah, must be
observed by all humanity, and it lists several Noahide laws.[12]

Later, in the Mediterranean world at the beginning of the
common era, the mysterious third, fourth and fifth volumes of the
Sibylline Oracles, a set of originally Greek-language works, had an
enormous impact and an immense following among the pagan
Romans.[13] Virgil, the great Roman poet, quoted from them.[14]

Written in the name of the ancient pagan prophetesses or fortune-tellers known as Sibyls — the famous Oracles of Delphi were Sibyls — these writings have been called "Jewish propaganda under a pagan mask."[15] They helped smooth the way for Christianity.[16] Each contains a somewhat crude and early summary of the Seven Commandments Code.

Paul (Saint Paul), the former rabbinic student, produced what are probably the world's most quoted lists of Noahide laws. While Jesus apparently advocated total compliance with "even the least" of the Torah's ordinances,[17] Paul did not. Writing that the Torah is "good, holy, and just,"[18] and that he himself "delights in the Torah,"[19] he also realized that many of its laws are meant only for Israel. In the second half of the first century CE he and James (Saint James, or Jacob/*Yakov ben Yosef*), the new movement's leaders, decided against "troubling" or "burdening" Gentile converts to Christianity with the complete Law of Moses.[20] Instead, the Christian Scriptures give converts just a few "necessary rules" — such as those against drinking blood, "sexual immorality," and eating meat from animals that had been either cruelly killed or consecrated to idols — which all stem from the Noahide Law.[21]

Islam's Prophet Muhammed, in the seventh century CE, emphasized the holiness of Israel's Torah. Through the Koran, he offered his followers lessons that first were proclaimed in the Written and the Oral Torah.[22] He particularly emphasized some of the Oral Torah's holdings concerning the Universal Law, and repeatedly tried to teach them to his followers.[23]

Back among Israel, rabbinic *midrashim* — literally, "investigations" or "inquiries" — exploring the Bible's meaning appeared in written form during the early Middle Ages. These books contain some of Israel's most ancient oral lore, legends and traditions. Two of the most important midrashim, *Genesis Rabbah* and *Deuteronomy Rabbah*, present short summaries of Noah's Code.[24]

THE SEVEN COMMANDMENTS

Israel's Talmudic Sages had recorded the basic Seven Commandments by about 200 CE — the doctrine of the Rainbow Covenant was one of the first things they wrote out.[25] But the rabbis didn't have much of a chance to teach or further develop the Rainbow Covenant Code. God and Rome and history scattered the Jews among the nations. And if God had designed the Torah's Rainbow Covenant laws to guide the nations, the nations were still mostly illiterate, and very rarely interested.

For Israel's rabbis, the preservation of the core values of the Hebrew Revolution, and of the people of the Revolution, had to come first.

Mere survival was a struggle. Over millenia of troubles and anti-Jewish persecutions, the study of the Seven Commandments Code became an almost academic exercise. Other subjects seemed more urgent. Most Jews didn't know anything at all about the Torah's universal precepts; the few who did entertained extremely varied and confused notions about the doctrine.

Some authorities claimed that the Code of Universal Law includes thirty commandments.[26] Others seemed to argue that Noah's Code contains a total of only seven laws.[27] Obviously, so long as the nature of this Code remained so vague and uncertain in the minds of Israel's teachers, the common people of Israel couldn't be expected to be its forceful advocates.

Only in recent times, following the establishment of history's Third Jewish Commonwealth, has the confusion begun to clear. The creation of the modern State of Israel took the Rainbow Covenant Code out of the ivory tower. If nothing else, the law has vital current implications for the Jewish State's foreign, internal and immigration policies.[28] The Seven Commandments Code has also come to represent a compelling interest for many non-Jews who, coming from Islam or, seek to understand those faiths' ethical — and originally Hebrew — roots.[29]

Every one of Your righteous ordinances is everlasting.
— *Psalm 119:160*

Mankind has done more reading and thinking about the

Torah's Universal laws in the past thirty years than in the past three hundred. One imagines that Moses would be pleased to see this happening, but probably not surprised. History is unfolding in a way to bring the different strands of his ancient prophecies together.

In ages past, every book had to be handwritten, on costly parchment or papyrus. Students had to struggle to possess even something as basic as a complete copy of the Bible. Further, since Moses' Revolution spreads through the power of ideas, the Revolution's enemies have done their best to suppress the Revolution's texts. Today, not just Bibles, but almost all of Israel's basic texts, are readily and easily accessible — in English, in Hebrew, and in several other modern languages.

With literacy almost universal, for the first time in human history hundreds of millions of people can finally read the Revolutionary texts for themselves. The interpretive works of scores of long-dead geniuses have reached a new, critical mass of students.[30] These students have been able, in their turn, to penetrate and clarify many of the obscurities in Israel's ancient Torah. And as knowledge spreads, so does interest in the Universal Law.

In Europe, Africa, North America and Asia, men and women of the most varied backgrounds are committing themselves to living by the Torah. Japanese students have come to recognize in Torah what they call "a higher Shinto."[31] Rabbis have begun working with Gentile congregations to help explain and interpret the Torah's terms; newspapers, newsletters and Internet groups have sprung up to teach the Seven Commandments Code. The gates are open: precious information is getting out there.[32]

> Open my eyes, that I may see wondrous things out of Your Torah.
> — *Psalm 119:18*

"All the paths of the Lord are lovingkindness and truth, to those who keep His Covenant and His testimonies."[33] The Jews have their Covenant of Sinai; the vast majority of humanity, the rest of the Children of Noah, have the Rainbow Covenant, yet ultimately man's obligations are the same — obey God's laws.[34]

It should go without saying that people must **study** these laws if they wish to know how to keep them.[35] Faith alone can't lead anyone to holiness; God requires more than good intentions from those who claim to love Him.[36] Study and understanding are essential.[37]

"You shall love your neighbor as yourself," the Torah commands.[38] It's a vitally important, major principle of the Hebrew Revolution.[39] But human beings need more in the way of Guidance (Torah) than any such general principle or abstract admonition can provide. The Bible teaches that, when Moses gave his people specific commands, they usually managed to follow them "exactly."[40] When he gave them abstract or general instructions they usually failed.[41]

Critics like to denounce the Torah as "legalistic," harsh and overly restrictive. These charges originate from ignorance. *Why would God impose an unworthy Law on His followers?* Man was created for the Torah.[42] The problem is that people living in an unredeemed world have a genius for doing the wrong thing, as Moses discovered, and a chronic tendency to follow false gods.[43]

Even at Sinai, Moses had to repeatedly spell out the meaning of God's general Commandments — including even the apparently self-explanatory Commandment against having any gods before God.[44] Moses found that he had to give Israel extraordinarily detailed, exacting, specific instructions on the proper forms and manner of truly monotheistic worship.[45] Otherwise the people went astray. People — real people, not angels — will do that.

Today prayer substitutes for Israel's ancient sacrificial rites.[46] Those rites provided the people with an example, among other things, of the purity and loving care that God's service requires.[47] Naturally, the Creator of the universe has no need for sacrifices.[48] He didn't free Israel from Egypt because He needed the Jews to flatter Him with burnt offerings.[49] But the nations of the time, including the Jews, considered sacrifice part of the very essence of worship. God simply channeled the worship that the people would otherwise give to idols to Himself.[50]

Moses taught the Jews to be ever-mindful of the Revolutionary Law, for otherwise they would follow false gods — or worship God through unholy means. It takes clear thinking and disciplined attention as well as ready knowledge to avoid idolatrous habits of thought and immorality.

The Hebrews who built the Golden Calf, for instance, or who joined in their pagan neighbors' rituals, probably didn't intend to slight the awesome One Lord of their ancestors. More likely, they imagined that their idolatrous devotions pleased the Ultimate.

They considered that the One God can be worshipped, conciliated and obeyed according to purely human ideas. Perhaps the Holy One transferred some portions of His Essence or His Power to certain earthly creatures? God did, after all, create calves and cows and clay. These pagan Jews imagined, no doubt, that their neighbors' man-made religions offered acceptable alternative ways to pay allegiance to Him. But God is One and He is Holy.[51]

Holiness includes every characteristic of goodness, kindliness and mercy.[52] So God in His mercy has given man His Torah — a Teaching verified by worldly signs and historical lessons — so that man may know how to truly please and worship Him.

Don't turn up your nose before a gift from God.

The Psalms call the Torah "truth," a "delight," and "perfect."[53] Christianity's Jesus preached the holiness of the whole Oral and Written Torah,[54] and St. Paul, who wrote of his great love for Torah, repeated the same praise.[55] Islam's Muhammed considered The Holy Koran to be a "verification" of the Jews' Torah, and lavished praises upon it similarly.[56]

So people who claim to find true spirituality only in the Muslim or the Christian Scriptures and nothing but harsh and ugly legalisms in Torah obviously are missing something. Yet generations of both Muslim and Christian believers have condemned actual observance of the Torah as "judaizing," a terrible sin, which would ensure the soul's damnation. (Similarly, in frequent demonstrations of their superior Muslim or Christian ethics, they inhumanly persecuted the Jews — the very people who, according to the Christian Gospels, would bring humanity salvation.[57])

> Great is the Torah, for it gives life to those who practice it, both in this world and in the world to come. — Mishnah, *Pirke Avot 6:6*

Torah is demanding — because God requires nothing less than the totally committed, fully focused "service of the heart."[58] He demands it all the time and from everyone, Jew and non-Jew alike.[59] This is how the Torah directs humanity to freedom: man is God's servant, rather than a "servant of servants," or the servant of other men.[60] All its "ways are ways of pleasantness," the Scriptures teach, "and all its paths are peace."[61]

SOONER OR LATER

One day, Moses promised, God shall send Israel a second teacher, who will be comparable to Moses himself.[62] And the next stage of human evolution — the era of the Messiah, and of his pious, learned, yet-to-be born descendants — will begin.[63]

Over more than a hundred generations, people have asked, "When will this day finally come?" The Psalmist answers, "Today, if you will hear God's voice."[64] The human race has the power to hasten the redemptive arrival of the human future.[65]

Moses' own people have a leading role in carrying out the terms of this Revolution: the Jews serve, among other things, as a sort of bellwether, or litmus test, measuring the human race's readiness to accept redemption. The people of Israel represent the world in microcosm.[66] But every person, tribe and nation has a unique genius, and the potential to make, whether for good or evil, a unique contribution. Israel is a leader, in the Revolutionary scheme of things, but also a follower. The moral health and status of the Jews depends upon and is shaped by the prevailing status of humanity.

If only because of the Bible itself, the "people of priests" are internationally notorious for their rebelliously "stiff-necks."[67] Many non-Jews actually regard the name "Jew" as a dirty word and a curse. The Bible repeats, as a constant theme, the Jews' very human tendencies to disobedience, negligence, and paganism. Israel's prophets worked tirelessly to keep their people from becoming ensnared in the savage idolatries of their neighbors.

This teaches that neighbors matter: human beings are creatures of their surroundings and their times.

God judges people individually, yet He also judges men collectively, in their nations and their generations.[68] When the Jews' neighbors lived in fear of nature spirits, devils and demons, so did many Jews.

Moral pollution cannot be confined. When these nations renounced their old crippling ways and adopted portions of the Universal Law, through Christianity and kindred systems of belief, they didn't just improve themselves. As they advanced their own moral, spiritual and intellectual health, they advanced the health of their neighbors.

Humanity is a unity. The health and purity of any one part depends upon the health and purity of the whole. If this was true before, today, in an age of speed-of-light communications, it's truer yet, and it will probably be even truer tomorrow. No nation can exist in isolation. The world's cultures will evolve or degenerate together.

One day these cultures will make themselves holy through the Rainbow Covenant, the Seven Commandments and the Torah.[69] Israel's great Sages speak of the whole human race walking forward, hand-in-hand, to history's next stage.[70] The Jews will finally achieve redemption through the redemption of the nations.[71] Israel is obligated to proclaim the Oneness of God and the holiness of His Universal Law not just to save the nations but to save Israel.[72]

A rising tide lifts every boat. Sooner or later, the permanent Revolution will permanently succeed — it is a biblical guarantee.[73] The nations will pool their genius; they will make awesome beautiful music together.

If the Paleolithic Revolution brought about the first sophisticated human languages, the Messianic Age will probably bring the perfection of language.[74] Science will work miracles; man will reclaim the earth's poisoned wastelands and heal the planet's scars. The world of the future will be like a rich and glorious garden. In those times, "the earth shall be full of the knowledge of the Lord, as the waters cover the seas."[75]

The key to this future — the Way of the just,[76] and the next step in human evolution — lies in the study, understanding and acceptance of the laws of God's Rainbow Covenant with mankind, the Code of Seven Universal Commandments.[77]

NOTES

1. Mishnah, *Hagigah* 2:1; Midrash, *Genesis Rabbah* 1. Getting confused over the mostly unstated details of Genesis 1-3 isn't likely to increase man's fear nor love of Heaven. Mishnah, ibid.

2. See Genesis 2:16,17; Talmud, *Sanhedrin* 568b; Moshe Chaim Luzatto, *Derech HaShem* 2:4,6 (Classic work, c. 1740 CE).

3. *Targum* Jerusalem Talmud, Genesis 5:4. See Genesis 5:23.

4. Genesis 9:1-9:18. A covenant — the Hebrew word is *b'rit, b'ris* or *b'rith* — is no mere contract but a sacred, specifically enforceable agreement, pact or mutual pledge designed to be absolutely inviolable, secure against any trespass of any kind. In this one short passage God invokes the word precisely seven times.

5. Genesis 8-9. See Genesis 8:21, 9:2-4,11,17; Talmud, *Sanhedrin* 56a,

Bava Kamma 38a. The Creator promises — unconditionally, just as mankind's covenantal obligations are unconditional — not to destroy the world again by flood. See S.R. Hirsch on Genesis 9. The rainbow is the eternal symbol of God's vow that, no matter how bleak the future may seem, God will lead us to its ultimate goal.

6. Talmud, id. Also see *Yad, Hilchot Melachim* 8-11; *Sefer HaHinnuch* (classical work, c. 1250 CE, translated by Charles Wengrove, Feldheim Books, New York NY, 1978), Imperative 424; Aimé Pallière, *The Unknown Sanctuary; a Pilgrimage from Rome to Israel* (Louise Waterman Wise, translator, Block Publishing, New York NY, 1985) p. 135; Aaron Lichtenstein, *Seven Laws of Noah,* supra; Chaim Clorfene and Yakov Rogalsky, *The Path of the Righteous Gentile; an Introduction to the Seven Laws of the Children of Noah* (Targum Press, Southfield, MI/Jerusalem, 1987); Yoel Schwartz, *A Light unto the Nations* (Jerusalem Academy of Jewish Studies/Yeshivat D'var Yerushalayim, Jerusalem, 1988); Yirmeyahu Bindman, *The Seven Colors of the Rainbow* (Schueller House/Feldheim Publishers, Nanuet NY, 1995).

7. Rashi on Genesis 14:18-24; Midrash, *Genesis Rabbah* 36:88, 63:7,10.

8. Rashi, id. See Talmud, *Nedarim* 32b.

9. Genesis 14:13-24.

10. *Yad, Hilchot Melachim,* 9:1. But at some point in his life Abraham is said to have logically or prophetically acquired — and lived by — the entire Torah, long before Sinai. See Genesis 26:5; Mishnah, *Kiddushin* 4:14.

11. Talmud, *Sanhedrin* 59a, *Shabbat* 135a-b, *Bava Kamma* 64b.

12. See David Novak, *The Image of the Non-Jew in Judaism: an Historical and Constructive Study of the Noahide Laws* (Edwin Mellen Press, Lewiston NY, 1983) p. 10.

13. See E.H. Hudson, *A History of the Jews in Rome* (Hodder & Stoughton, London, 1882) pp. 45-56.

14. In Virgil's Fourth Ecologue. See Joseph Klausner, *The Messianic Idea in Israel* (Macmillan, London/NY, 1955) p. 379.

15. See Emil Scheurer, cited in Klausner, supra, p. 370.

16. Klausner, supra, pp. 370-381; Hudson, ibid. See "Sibylline Oracles," *Encyclopaedia Britannica.*

17. Matthew 5:17-19.

18. Romans 7:12, Galatians 1:13-14. Perhaps inconsistently, he also called it a curse, Romans 7:7, Galatians 3:13, Philippians 3:5-6. One sometimes wonders about Paul/Saul. See 1 Corinthians 9:19-22.

19. Romans 7:22. For Paul's apparent Scriptural source, see Psalm 119:16, 24.

20. Acts 15:19, 28. Or perhaps James and Paul only meant to set forth minimal requirements facing non-Jews desiring to associate with Jews in divine worship and study.

21. See Acts 15:20, 28-29, 21:25; 1 Corinthians 5-10. Also see. e.g., Alan Segal, *Paul the Convert* (Yale University Press, New Haven CT, 1990) pp. 187-223.

22. Koran. See, e.g., Surat 2:29-74, 3:33. Also see Will Durant, supra.

23. Koran. See, e.g., Surat 2:173, 5:3; 6:145; 17:32-35, 24:2-3,33.

24. See *Genesis Rabbah* 16:6, 24:5, 34:8; *Deuteronomy Rabbah* 2:25.

25. See Mishnah, *Tosefta Avodah Zarah* 8:4; Talmud, *Hullin* 141a-b, *Seder Olam* 5, *Sanhedrin* 56a-59, *Bava Kamma* 38a; Midrash, *Genesis Rabbah* 16:9, 24:5,

34:8, *Deuteronomy Rabbah* 2:17, 2:25, *Song of Songs Rabbah* 1:16; Jerusalem Talmud, *Kiddushin* 1. Also see David Novak, supra, pp. 3-35.

26. See Talmud, *Hullin* 92a-b (Rashi); Talmud, *Sanhedrin* 56a-57a; Azaryah d'Fano (the Rama MiFano), *Asarah Ma'amorot* (c. 1570 CE, Hebrew only); Aaron Lichtenstein, "Noahide Law from the Genizah: the Thirty Laws of Samuel Ben Hophni Gaon," 28 *Hebrew Studies,* p. 113 (New York NY, 1987).

27. See Talmud, *Sanhedrin* 74b; Rambam, *Sefer HaMitzvot* 1:9. Modern encyclopedias reflect this confusion: see "Noahide Laws" in the *Encyclopaedia Britannica* and *The Universal Jewish Encyclopedia*, "Laws, Noachian" in *The Jewish Encyclopedia*, and "Noachide Laws" in *Encyclopaedia Judaica*.

28. See Exodus 23:33; Deuteronomy 7; Talmud, *Avodah Zarah* 64b; *Sefer HaMitzvot* 2:51; Nahum Rakover, "Jewish Law and the Noahide Obligation to Preserve Social Order," supra. However, the modern State of Israel operates as a deliberately secular republic, not as a Torah government.

29. See Aryeh Gallin, ed., *The Root and Branch Noahide Guide,* 1991-5752 (The Root and Branch Association Ltd., Jerusalem/NY, 1991); James D. Tabor, *Restoring Abrahamic Faith*, supra.

30. Despite all of modern Jewry's losses to persecution and assimilation, more Torah scholars in more *yeshivot* — rabbinic study centers — are studying and writing today than ever before in history. See David Landau, *Piety and Power; the World of Jewish Fundamentalism* (Hill & Wang, New York NY, 1993) p. 171.

31. Abraham Kotsuji, *From Tokyo to Jerusalem* (B. Geis Associates/ Random House, New York NY, 1964) p. 66.

32. See *The Root and Branch Noahide Guide*, supra; *The Gap* (a newsletter published by the Emmanuel congregation of Athens TN); *The Researcher* (a newsletter published by Vendyl Jones Research Institutes of Arlington TX). Also see James D. Tabor, *Restoring Abrahamic Faith*, supra, pp. 36-47; Aaron Lichtenstein, "Who Cares about the Seven Laws of Noah? A Status Report," *Jewish Law Association Studies* No. 4, Boston Conference Volume (B. Jackson, ed., Scholars Press, Atlanta GA, 1990) p. 180.

33. Psalm 25:3.

34. Ecclesiastes 12:13.

35. Joshua 1:8; Psalms 1:2, 19:7, 119:142.

36. Jeremiah 16:19.

37. Deuteronomy 6:7; Proverbs 2:3-5; Mishnah, *Pirke Avot* 2:5.

38. Leviticus 19:18. "This is *the* great principle of the Torah," *Sifra* (Midrash) to Leviticus 19:18.

39. See Hillel, Talmud, *Shabbat* 31a; R. Akiva, Jerusalem Talmud, *Nedarim* 9:4; Midrash, *Genesis Rabbah* on Genesis 5:1, *Sifra* on Leviticus 19:18.

40. Exodus 39:43. See Exodus 35-40.

41. See Exodus 32; 1 Kings 22:52-54; 2 Kings 17.

42. See Mishnah, *Pirke Avot* 2:9.

43. Exodus 32. Remembering that every "god" but the eternal, holy One God is false.

44. Exodus 20:3-6; Deuteronomy 5:7-9.

45. See Exodus 32; Leviticus 10:1-2; Numbers 28-29.

46. Hosea 14:3; Talmud, *Megillah* 31b.

47. Moreh Nevuchim, supra, at 4:46,47.

48. See, e.g., Isaiah 1:11; Psalm 40:6-7; 1 Samuel 15:22. However, human beings may have some need — some deeply rooted spiritual craving, or characteristic — to offer sacrifices to Him. Beyond that, a genuinely holy sacrifice might affect, in ways that living men can only guess at, the spiritual or metaphysical structures of Creation.

49. See Jeremiah 7:21-23.

50. See Exodus 22:19; *Moreh Nevuchim* 3:32.

51. See, e.g., Deuteronomy 12:30.

52. Mishnah, *Pirke Avot* 1:18; Midrash, Psalm 89:3; *Mechilta* (Midrash) on Exodus 15:2; *Sifre* (Midrash) on Deuteronomy 11:22. See, e.g., Isaiah 5:16.

53. Psalms 119:42, 12, 19:7.

54. See, e.g., Matthew 23:1-3.

55. Romans 7:12,22.

56. Koran, *Sura* 2:41. Also see, e.g., *Sura* 2:39,53.

57. John 4:22. A vast literature covers these subjects. For the impact of such counterrevolutionary doctrines in America's southern hemisphere, see Eduardo Galeano, *Open Veins of Latin America* (Monthly Review Press, NY/ London, 1973) ch. 1; W.E. Browning, *Roman Christianity in Latin America* (Fleming H. Revell Co., New York NY, 1924); John K. Turner, *Barbarous Mexico* (1910/ University of Texas Press, Austin TX, 1969). Generally, also see, e.g., Deuteronomy 28:37.

58. Deuteronomy 4:29; Ezekiel 20:24-26; Psalm 51:18-19.

59. Isaiah 45:22; Jeremiah 33:3; Psalm 145:18.

60. See Talmud, *Bava Metzia* 10a.

61. Proverbs 3:17. See Mishnah, *Pirke Avot* 6:7.

62. Deuteronomy 18:15,18.

63. See Isaiah 42:4; Daniel 7:27; Midrash, *Mechilta* to Exodus 20:2; *Thirteen Principles of Faith*, supra, Principle Twelve. Israel is also taught, "Do not imagine that the King Messiah will perform signs and wonders, ... revive the dead, or do similar things." *Yad, Hilchot Melachim* 11:3. Presumably, we should expect this era to unfold progressively, bit by bit. "First it will glimmer, then sparkle, then shine forth more and more brightly." Midrash, *Song of Songs/Shir ha Shirim Rabbah* 6:16.

64. Psalm 95:7. See Talmud, *Sanhedrin* 98a.

65. Psalm 81:14-17; Talmud, *Shabbat* 118b; Midrash, *Exodus Rabbah* 25:12.

66. Talmud, *Ta'anit* 5b; Midrash *Tehillim* 99:1.

67. See, e.g., Exodus 32:9, 34:9; Deuteronomy 9:6, 10:16, 31:27; Psalm 75:5; Jeremiah 17:23.

68. *Mishneh Torah (Yad), Hilchot Teshuva* 3:1-2.

69. See Isaiah 2:2-4, 11:10-12; Jeremiah 3:15, 16:19; Jerusalem Talmud, *Avoda Zorah* 2:1; *Mishneh Torah (Yad), Hilchot Melachim* 10:9-10.

70. See, e.g., Isaiah, ibid.; Zechariah 8:23; Ezekiel 38:23; *Shulchan Aruch, Orach Haim* 156:1, *Hoshen Mishpat* 266:1, 425:5.

71. See Isaiah 43:21; *Yad, Hilchot Melachim* 12:4-5.

72. See Talmud, *Pesachim* 87b; Midrash, *Leviticus Rabbah, Veyikra* 6:5; *Yad, Hilchot Melachim* 8:10.

73. See Deuteronomy 4:30, 30:1-8; Isaiah 2:2-3; Zechariah 8:3; Micah 4:3; Zephaniah 3:9; Job 19:25.

74. See Zephaniah 3:9.

75. Isaiah 11:9.

76. Isaiah 26:7.

77. *Yad, Hilchot Melachim* 8:10, 11:4. See, e.g., Isaiah 42:4; Psalms 25:3,10,14; Daniel 11:35; Midrash, *Leviticus Rabbah* 18:5; Talmud, *Sanhedrin* 98a.

Revealed Law

BEGINNING NOAHIDE PRECEPTS

**And God blessed Noah and his sons,
and said unto them . . . — Genesis 9:1**

*My ordinances you shall do, and My statutes you shall keep, to
walk in them: I am the Lord your God. You shall therefore keep
My statutes, and My ordinances, which if a man do, he shall live
by them: I am the Lord.*

— Leviticus 18:4-5

*How do we know that even a non-Jew, if he obeys the Law of
God, will thereby attain the same spiritual communion with God
as Israel's very High Priest? Scripture says, "which if a man do,
he shall live by them" — not priest, Levite, or Israelite, but man.*

— Talmud, Bava Kamma 38a[1]

From a nucleus of knowledge[2] confirmed at Sinai and
handed down from generation to generation, the Talmud
sets out the Rainbow Code's basic elements in tractate
Sanhedrin, folio 56:

"*Our Rabbis taught: Seven precepts were B'nai Noah[3]* (the descendants
of Noah) *commanded: social laws* (i.e., to oppose anarchy and to
pursue justice among men by establishing laws, police and courts[4]);
to refrain from profaning God's Name (literally, to refrain from "blessing
the Name" — a euphemism for blasphemy); *idolatry; sexual
immorality; murder; theft; and eating flesh torn from a living animal* [56a].

Rabbi Hanania ben Gamaliel said: Also not to partake of the blood drawn from a living animal. Rabbi Hidka added emasculation (castration). *Rabbi Simeon added sorcery. Rabbi Yosi said: the sons of Noah were prohibited everything which is mentioned in the* [Scriptural] *section on sorcery* [i.e., Deuteronomy 18:10-12. God punished the Canaanites who indulged in such wickedness by driving them out of their homes before the people of Israel]. *Now,* [the Almighty] *doesn't punish without first prohibiting (i.e., warning). Rabbi Eleazar added the forbidden mixture (i.e., cross-breeding species)* . . . [the descendants of Noah] *are forbidden to hybridize heterogeneous animals and graft trees of different kinds."* [5] [56b]

Just from this excerpt we see that the Talmud is unique; clearly, it has a style all its own.

When the Talmud mentions "Our Rabbis," it's referring to a body or collective of the greatest Sages of Israel, from Moses to Ezra and beyond. It means that Israel's teachers are speaking as with a single voice, without dissent or difference, unanimously.

We can see from this text that the Universal Law contains seven more or less general Commandments, as follows:[6]

1) a broad prohibition against *idolatry*;
2) a broad positive injunction, a command to pursue earthly *justice*;

as well as the following five wide-ranging negative injunctions, prohibitions regarding:

3) the *profanation of God's Name*;
4) *murder*;
5) *theft*;
6) *sexual immorality*; and
7) dietary perversions, or *cruelty to lesser creatures*.

A careful student will also see that the great individual rabbis quoted above — Rabbi Eleazer, Rabbi Yosi, etc. — clearly are not refuting their colleagues' listing of the Seven basic laws.

The Sages' apparent differences and debates actually demonstrate practical unanimity as to the core principles of

Torah. What comes out of the record of their comments is the fact that the Rainbow Commandments aren't just seven stark pronouncements. Rather, this Code of Seven, the *Sheva Mitzvot*, contains other laws, these being revealed statutes and ordinances of greater specificity. Here the Sages speak of several prohibitions — against sorcery, crossbreeding species, and so on — which track, reflect or parallel kindred parts of Torah.[7]

Obviously, the key to the Universal Law lies within the Torah.

Israel has a revealed, revolutionary Torah Code of 613 laws, the *Taryag Mitzvot*,[8] including statutes, commandments, and ordinances.

The question is, which of these 613 laws involve Commands so absolutely fundamental that Heaven has decreed, in effect, that *everyone* must keep them?

> That Your Way may be known upon earth, Your Salvation among all nations. — *Psalm 67:3*

Hebrew Revelation teaches that, as soon as man became a reasoning creature, God tried to instill in us His Universal laws. Genesis also testifies that, in the space of a few generations, men strayed from the right with nasty manmade idolatrous conceptions and habits of thought. That testimony is confirmed, in large part, by the shockingly oppressive ancient legal codes, the Assyrian, the Hittite, and the Babylonian code of Hammurabi — which are also monuments to tribalism and idolatry.[9] The historical record supports the Bible's point: when men stray from the One God they stray from the right.

It should be apparent, even if the Rabbis had never said so, that the Code of basic human virtue is, like the Torah, essentially an anti-idolatry code.[10] All of God's laws begin and end with the principle of man's personal responsibility to his Maker.

Because God's Universal Law and the Torah both come from the same Holy source, we know that they follow the same principles: that is, the principles of justice and righteousness between man and man, between man and the lesser creatures, and between man and the One God.

Similarly, as with Mount Sinai's Ten Commandments, each of the Seven Rainbow Covenant Commandments forms a heading for a specific area of Divine legislation, a separate legal category.

The pattern is plain: where each of Israel's Ten Commandments leads to a broad field of more specific Guidance and law,[11] the Seven Noahide Commandments each point to a field or category of logically related, associated Torah Guidance and law.[12] Clearly, as the Talmud itself maintains, our subject isn't just seven terse commandments but the Seven Universal Commandments — *together with all their offshoots.*[13]

So we see that God's two sets of laws are actually not so very different. Indeed, in countless particulars, they are basically the same. They differ somewhat in their purpose and their scope but they both point to the same One God, Who designed them both to make us better, wiser, and holy.

God gave Israel the Torah at Sinai for the whole world's good. The Torah introduces man to the Universal Law, our species' common inheritance from times long before the birth of Israel.

> The main body of the Torah is contained in the Seven
> Commandments with their details. — *Me'iri*[14]

Israel possesses the details of God's Law. Children may stray from their elders' teachings, and human memory will always fade, but the Torah stays the same. Thus the modern man or woman who seeks God's Way must learn it from the Torah. We can know humanity's Universal laws — that is, know them with certainty, reliably, and well — only because of Torah. Because the Torah isn't just man's best guide to true justice and morality but, as it has been through history, humanity's standard — *the* Guide — for all that man *knows* to be moral, just and upright.

Often, the Rainbow Law and the Scriptural Law are precisely the same — as Rabbi Yosi, who was quoted just above, and other Sages tell us.[15] But every Torah scholar doesn't necessarily agree with Rabbi Yosi or his colleague, Rabbi Gamaliel, that the Code of Rainbow Commandments definitely includes the detailed prohibitions which they pointed out, against sorcery and so on, beyond the basic Seven laws. Unanimity disappears when it comes to the question — obviously, an extremely difficult question — of which Torah laws reflect the *minimal* laws of upright human conduct.

Israel's ancestor Abraham, a wise man who became a prophet, a giant of world history, studied, learned and kept these Noahide laws.[16] Israel is told that God later directly commanded Moses to arrange to bring all mankind to accept the Noahide Code.[17] And it is a Biblical promise that all mankind will one day come to do that.[18]

But gaps exist in the Tradition received from Moses. For the time being at least, God has left it to man to fill in the spaces. Accordingly, pursuant to His ultimate plan for us, the Father of Mercy has given us the tools we need to do so.

Man probably can't know all that there is to know about the Universal Law until and unless God sends us, as He promised, another great teacher and leader "like unto" Moses."[19] Yet it's also true that, in the meantime, God requires us to obey all of His Rainbow Covenant laws. More precisely, the Torah teaches that He commands man to keep **every detail** of the Universal laws.[20] So this aspect of Heaven's plan for us — for the species that calls itself *homo sapiens sapiens*, or wise, wise man — is clear:

> A ruling derived from common sense is also designated by the rabbis as 'Words of Torah.' — *Rabbi Tz'vi Hirsch Chajes*[21]

Our Creator demands that we keep His laws now, immediately, at present. So we cannot wait for revelations based upon some hoped-for future prophet's insight. Obviously, God would have us develop ourselves as we develop our understanding of His Law.

Since we *can* do this, we *must* do it, by the only means available to us — as the rabbis command, "by rational inquiry based upon the general thrust of Torah."[22] That is, through humble human logic, building from the Torah's laws and Testimonies, and from the logical problem-solving methods and procedures contained within the Torah.

Blessed are they who keep His Testimonies, and who seek Him
with the whole heart.— *Psalm 119:2*[23]

Because God demands man's whole heart, and our full
compliance with His Law, it seems like a kind of blasphemy —
as well as a basically impossible task — to try to delimit which
of His Torah laws are minimal. The Torah sets out Israel's Law,
the special "inheritance of the congregation of Jacob."[24] But
if, as the Scripture says, all the Torah's "ways are ways of
righteousness,"[25] then it must also be true that the Torah can
lead us to the basic elements comprising human righteousness
and virtue.

So Israel is warned: Unless Torah sources explicitly call
attention to a dissimilarity between the two systems, the Torah
and the Noahide Law, "one should not presume to exclude the
Noahide from Mosaic principles."[26]

Rabbi Nissim Gaon, a renowned 10th Century sage, taught
that mankind is obligated by every one of the Torah's 613 laws
which are discoverable by rational inquiry.[27] In other words, all
men must conform to all the Scriptural laws which, based upon a
faithful overview of Torah, commend themselves to ordinary
human logic. Rabbi Nissim's Rule is commonly accepted.[28]

One must understand that these Scriptural laws are Revealed
laws. They are not necessarily what people call "natural laws."

The 18th Century secularists' Natural Law theory holds that,
even if man had never heard of Torah nor ever benefitted from
prophetic Revelation, he would still feel obliged to refrain from
such crimes as incest, murder, theft and perjury, due to simple
logic and a basic moral sense inherent to all men.[29]

Unfortunately, a problem with this theory is that men in a
"natural" illiterate state, and primitive tribes and people generally,
tend not to regard such crimes as crimes — especially when the
victim of the murderer, perjurer or thief is a stranger or outsider.
History also shows us, for instance, that scores of millions of

people, including even some of our proudest ancient ancestors, used to shamelessly practice incest.[30]

Most respectable people who come from modern literate cultures — that is to say, cultures already markedly uplifted by Sinai's Revolutionary legacy, with its Teaching that the individual human being is sacred — share an almost instinctive revulsion against such crimes. Simple logic and long-established habit, based upon commonly held Torah principles, have begun to raise these moral laws nearly to the level of universal instinct.

The descendants of those who reviled the Jews for denouncing their pagan crimes no longer treat the killing of babies or old people or the robbing of luckless travellers as customary "natural" practices.[31] Today, most of us "naturally" tend to feel, as well as think, that these are terrible crimes, that even the crudest human societies must abhor.

This constitutes the most fundamental kind of progress —

moral progress, upon which all man's other technological, political, economic, and artistic achievement depends. But the human race still has far to go. While every one of the Noahide laws appeals to simple logic and man's "natural instincts," this is so only if our logical facilities and our instincts have been refined by more than a few of today's "commonly held Torah principles."

If you want Truth, turn to Torah. As the rabbis' statements above, against such mysterious crimes as sorcery, drinking blood, interbreeding species, etc., should indicate, the Universal laws can't be understood without reference to the kindred laws and philosophy of Torah.

One could easily spend a lifetime in such study. Fortunately, this is the sort of inquiry that isn't just accessible to those who lack formal academic or rabbinic training in the Torah, but positively invites the common man's participation. This means you, and all of us. Few pursuits offer greater rewards.

Study holiness. Heaven reveals humanity's fundamental laws to us by means of ordinary human rationality combined with knowledge of "the general thrust of Torah."[32]

NOTES

1. Also see Talmud, *Sanhedrin* 59a. Living refers to real life — the good life — both in this world and in the world to come. "The righteous are called alive even in death; the wicked are called dead even when alive." Talmud, *Berachot* 18b. See Deuteronomy 30:20.

2. Yehudah HaLevi (c. 1105 CE), *Kuzari*, 3:73. See also *Mishnah Tosefta, Avoda Zarah* 8.4 (in some editions, ch. 9); Midrash, *Seder Olam Rabbah*, ch. 5 (both in Hebrew only). Even more ancient than the Talmud, the Midrash (rabbinic commentary) and Tosefta (additions to the Mishnah) both set out the same Seven basic commandments in a form practically identical to the Talmud's. Compare, or see Novak, *Image of the Non-Jew in Judaism*, supra, pp. 3-4.

3. Hebrew, *B'nai* (pronounced B'nay), meaning sons, children, or descendants. Masculine singular, *Ben*; feminine singular: *Bas* or *Bat* (pronounced as Bahs or Baht, with a long flat "a," an "ah" sound).

4. *Mishnah Tosefta*, ibid; Novak, supra, ibid; Rashi on *Sanhedrin* 56b; Nachmanides, *Pirush al HaTorah*, Genesis 34:13; *Yad, Hilchot Melachim* 9:1,14.

5. For example, mating horses and donkeys to make mules; grafting cherry trees with weeping willows to make weeping cherry trees; or,

generally, trying to create an entirely new species, rather than a new variety within a species, by combining one species' genes or reproductive faculties with those of another, separate and distinctive, species. See Leviticus 19:19 and commentaries; Genesis 36:24 with Rashi.

6. No particular sequence or order of importance implied.

7. Lichtenstein, *Seven Laws of Noah*, supra., p. 89.

8. *Mechilta* (Midrash), Exodus 20:2; Talmud, *Shabbat* 87a; Rashi on Exodus 24:12; *Sefer HaMitzvot* 1:1.

9. See Philip Biberfeld, "The Bible and the Ancient Law Codes" in *Universal Jewish History* (Spero Foundation, New York NY, 1948) pp. 129-156; J.M.P. Smith, *The Origin and History of Hebrew Law* (University of Chicago Press, Chicago, 1960) pp. 181-274, 279; Lichtenstein, supra., pp. 1-15; *Encyclopaedia Britannica* (under appropriate headings); Hertz, supra, pp. 403-406. Also see Talmud, *Bava Kamma* 38a. Those nations mandated strict caste divisions between and among their respective privileged classes and all "lesser" men, elevating the former to godlike status and humiliating the latter; denied human status to aliens and slaves, regarding their slaves not as men but as mere "animated tools," totally subject to the will of a master; grotesquely punished even torts of negligence with death, torture, mutilation or slavery — these penalties extending beyond the person who was actually negligent to the innocent members of his or her family; institutionalized ghastly pagan "spiritual" rites, including human sacrifice, incest, "religious whoredom," homosexuality, bestiality, the worship of animal fetishes, etc., etc.

10. *Moreh Nevuchim* 3:29; Y*ad, Hilchot Melachim* 9:2. See Exodus 34:13; Ecclesiastes 12:13.

11. See Midrash, *Numbers Rabbah* 13:15; Exodus 24:12 with Rashi; Yehuda HaLevi, *Kuzari* 1:87.

12. *Sefer HaHinnuch*, supra, Imperative 424; Lichtenstein, supra, p. 15; Elijah Benamozegh, *Israel and Humanity* (1914/1995 by Maxwell Luria, ed., Paulist Press, Mahway NJ) pp. 262-263. So, for instance, men and women may not commit sex crimes, because they are universally prohibited by the Noahide Law, but the details of the pertinent Noahide prohibition, i.e., what does or does not constitute a sex crime — reside in the Torah.

13. In the name of Rava, Talmud, *Sanhedrin* 74-75a. While some authorities disagree, Rava, a towering authority, teaches that Noahides are obligated, much as Jews are, to sanctify God's Name — i.e., even to the point of martyrdom, if necessary — and that this broadly demanding obligation, like other appurtenant Noahide statutes, does not, by any means, lie beyond the scope of the basic Seven Noahide laws. Rather, it is contained in the Noahide Code (like many other, unquestionably appurtenant, Noahide statutes), an inherent part of the Universal Law. Id, 74b. Also see *Tosefot*, and Rashi on *Sanhedrin* 75. Similarly, Ramban (Nachmanides, Rabbi Moshe ben Nachman, c. 1194-1270 CE) explains that Genesis, speaking of "My [i.e., God's] charge, My commandments, My statutes, and My laws," kept by Abraham, refers to Noahide obligations, a very extensive body of law. "The descendants of Noah were commanded all these matters, and Abraham observed and fulfilled the Will of his Creator, observing even the details and strictures of their commandments." *Pirush al ha Torah*, Genesis 26:5. He goes on to describe the enormous depth and complexity of the everlasting human

obligation — not just a Jewish obligation! — to overcome idolatry, citing Talmud, *Avodah Zorah* 14b. One notes, incidentally, that Nachmanides, a classical Torah authority and genius, is greatly respected generally, but especially for his teachings on Noahide matters.

14. See Rabbenu Menachem ben Shlomo Me'iri, *Beit HaBechira* on *Sanhedrin* 59a (c. 1270 CE, Hebrew only), cited in Rav Yoel Schwartz, *A Light Unto the Nations*, supra, p. 34.

15. The Sages frequently repeat the expression, "just as the descendants of Israel are commanded, so are the descendants of Noah commanded." See, e.g., *Mishnah Tosefta, Avoda Zorah* 8:4; Talmud, *Sanhedrin* 74b-75a.

16. Genesis 18:18-19; Talmud, *Nedarim* 32b, *Yoma* 28a; *Yad, Avodat Kochavim* 1:3.

17. See *Yad, Hilchot Melachim* 8:10.

18. Isaiah 11:9, 49:6; Zechariah 8:23; Ezekiel 38:23.

19. Deuteronomy 18:15,18.

20. *Mishnat Rabbi Eliezer, Midrash of Thirty-two Hermeneutic Rules*, Parsha 6, 121, by R. Eliezer ben R. Jose, c. 100 CE (edited and with an English-language introduction by Hyman G. Enelow (F. Levy, pub. New York NY, 1935)). See Rakover, supra, 12 *Cardozo Law Review* , pp. 1073, 1078.

21. *Mebo, HaTalmud* (1845, Jewish Publication Society, Philadelphia 1952) Ch. 4, p. 31.

22. *Yad, Hilchot Melachim* 9:1.

23. See also, e.g., The Christian Scriptures, Romans 7:12,22; Koran, *Sura* 2:53.

24. Deuteronomy 33:4. See Psalm 147:19-20.

25. Proverbs 3:17. See Mishnah, *Pirke Avot* 6:7.

26. R. Moshe Isserles (the Rama, c. 1550 CE), *Sheilot U'Teshuvot Rama*, Responsum 10 (Hebrew only). Cited in Lichtenstein, supra, p. 38. Also see Eleazar ben Yehudah, *HaRokeach* (1237 CE).

27. Introduction *(hakdama)* to the Talmud, beginning of tractate *Berachot*. Cited in Rakover, supra, pp. 1074-1075. Also see *Sefer HaHinnuch*, supra, Imperative 424 (Chavel edition, 1952), cited in Lichtenstein, supra, p. 20; Nachmanides, *Pirush al HaTorah* on Genesis 34 (Vol. 1, p. 191).

28. Id. See *Yad, Hilchot Melachim* 9:1.

29. See the Preamble to the United States' Declaration of Independence (Philadelphia, July 4, 1776).

30. Pagan kings frequently married their sisters, for instance. Some even married their own mothers.

31. Supposedly civilized peoples accepted the most incredibly savage practices — the most fantastic barbarism. "The Roman historian Tacitus deemed it a contemptible prejudice of the Jews that 'it is a crime among them to kill any child!'" Hertz, supra, p. 54.

32. *Yad, Hilchot Melachim* 9:1.

Unfolding the Code

THEORY AND PRACTICE

Even when God entrusted His Holy Torah to His beloved servant Israel, he gave it, in a sense, as raw material: as wheat to make flour and as flax to make cloth, through the Torah's own appointed methods of logical interpretation. — Midrash[1]

Basically, every law mentioned in the Bible's Book of Genesis, if it was also verified by being restated by Moses, during or after Israel's experience at Mt. Sinai, must be considered for inclusion in the Seven Commandments Code.[2]

Only laws designed to govern men for all time — as opposed to such temporary or one-time precepts as those governing Adam, say, or the people of Israel between the Exodus from Egypt and the Revelation at Sinai — are still binding.[3]

If the law involved is serious enough, according to Israel's Ten Commandments Code of 613 laws, to provide for capital punishment — death — as a maximum penalty for violations, then it is also likely to constitute a Universal law.[4] That is, essentially the same law binds Israel, through the Torah, as well as all humanity through the Noahide Code. But if the Hebrew Code sets out some lesser punishment as a maximum penalty, or if the law wasn't specifically mentioned prior to Sinai, it should be examined according to its context in the Torah, and by its logical connection to other laws.[5]

Don't convince yourself, based on the Written Torah, that the King of the Universe loves harsh and bloody penalties. The truth is nothing like that, as the Oral Torah demonstrates. "A court [the Sanhedrin] that effects one execution in seven years is branded a murderous court. Rabbi Eleazar ben Azariah said, 'One in seventy years.' Rabbis Tarfon and Akiba said, 'Were we members of the Sanhedrin, no one would ever be put to death.'"[6]

Scriptural penalties teach us ultimate values. The weight that God assigns to a crime tells us something. But the Torah itself warns against improperly imposing the plain Scriptural penalties literally.[7]

God commands Israel, "Honor your father and your mother."[8] This is the Fifth Commandment of the Ten Commandments, but it is *not* one of the Seven basic Noahide Commandments. Yet it undoubtedly constitutes a basic requisite of human virtue.[9] Why isn't it listed with the Seven Universal laws? Let's examine the issue in light of logic and God's Torah:

First of all, the Noahide laws are meant, in most cases, to be enforceable by courts.[10] The duty to honor parents constitutes a positive obligation in the Torah system[11] — one of Israel's 248 Positive Commandments[12] — and the primary duty of Noahide courts is to enforce only such laws as are logically related to the Torah's Negative Commandments, the prohibitions.[13]

In this case, those who honor their parents are promised reward directly from Heaven.[14] God has undertaken to reward those who do the right thing; He will also deal appropriately with those who don't. Human courts may therefore let the matter rest with Heaven.[15] Noahide judges and legislators may, if they so choose, make it their business[16] — they could impose a duty upon adult children to suitably maintain their needy parents, for instance — but the Universal Law doesn't *require* man's courts to get involved.

And what if one's parents are idolators? Honoring them might involve honoring the things they cherish most — that is, their gods.

Since all of God's laws are designed to obliterate idolatry,[17] the Universal Law allows one to make a complete break with paganism, even should that require breaking away from one's pagan parents. Abraham the righteous did no less.[18] Although ordinarily a righteous person must endeavor to honor even such pagan parents to the greatest possible extent. One accepts one's God-given duties. Thus a Noahide studies the Torah concerning this duty — how to honor parents after their death, for instance; duties to step-parents; to parents who are immoral, abusive or mentally ill; duties to in-laws, etc. — so as to better fulfill it.[19]

Finally, while the Law doesn't require Noahide courts to enforce the positive obligation of honoring parents, such courts still have a duty to prevent anyone from violating the negative prohibitions against *harming* his parents.

God gives no child the right to either strike or (even) curse a parent. The law on this point logically and obviously relates to prohibitory Torah Commandments — two of Israel's 365 Negative Commandments[20] — that forbid such behavior as criminal acts, which (Israel's) courts may punish capitally.[21] So these two bad acts both must be Noahide crimes. We can argue about how these two holy prohibitions are best classified — that is, about which of the Seven Commandments most logically includes them — but God's laws against cursing or assaulting one's parent are clearly universal.[22]

Similarly, the Noahide laws against the crime and the sin of thievery, for instance, are practically identical to Israel's.[23] (See "The Sixth Commandment," within.) And we see that the Noahide Law is surprisingly deep.

Rainbow Covenant law strictly forbids — with a few exceptions — such acts as "borrowing" or taking our employer's supplies without permission, unnecessarily delaying paying a worker's wages, mislabeling or mis-estimating items for sale, or even overcharging for them. It condemns the sneak thief more than the brazen thief; the dealer in stolen goods more than the thief who supplies him. And it warns against the sin of coveting — a complex idea, as we shall see — as it forbids other acts, including crimes of a less clearly larcenous nature than outright robbery, kidnapping or burglary.

There's more. As you go deeper into this study you will encounter the following remarkable principle:

No one is virtuous unless he goes so far as to do the very opposite of whatever the Noahide laws forbid.[24]

A man cannot fully satisfy the Noahide law against larceny, for instance, unless he gives charity; the Noahide law against profaning God's Name unless he acts to sanctify the Name; the Noahide law against murder unless he acts to save the life of the person in danger, etc.

Torah students soon discover that God's Law is not always obvious, nor does it always accord with human intuition. That it comes from a more-than-human, supernatural Source is evident from the incredibile acuity and consistency of its applications and from the awesome wisdom which underlies its details. But God's moral laws, rather like the laws of His physical universe, often defy man's expectations.

As His laws of physics are sometimes counter-intuitive, so is His Torah. And, in much the same way that the laws of physics can't be fully fathomed unless one sees them operating, His moral laws can't be understood unless one puts them into practice. God's Way isn't a mere confession of faith or philosophy but an entire way of life. One learns righteousness only by living rightly.[25]

> You shall be holy; for I the Lord your God am holy.
> — *Leviticus 19:2*

Most of the Universal laws regulate relations between man and man. Although we can't pretend to know all the reasons for God's Commandments — each of His laws has an infinitude of meanings, beyond the reach of mere human intelligence[26] — these Rules all commend themselves to conventional moral logic. The rich and fascinating details of the Torah covering such matters as honesty in business or liability for theft or homicide fall into this category.

Some students call such laws "ordinances."[27] These Torah ordinances have, in effect, a universal application. But other parts of Torah, sometimes known as God's "statutes,"[28] aren't necessarily logical from a popular point of view. These laws regulate relations between man and the lesser creatures, and all things subordinate to man's will, and between man and *his* Master, God.

Torah prohibitions against the sins of drinking blood, interbreeding species, and sorcery, for instance, are assumed to fall into this category of "statutes." The logic behind such laws, given humanity's limited present knowledge, isn't always readily apparent.

BAD BREEDING

We aren't just dealing with human decrees, after all, but with the supernatural laws and reasons of Heaven. One may even feel reluctant, lacking at least a passing acquaintance with the Torah, to classify these forbidden acts or sins as crimes. But crimes they are, according to God's Revelation to Israel, even though the laws that forbid them extend beyond the scope of man's relations with his fellow man — and even though these laws may extend beyond the limits of our current understanding. Our Creator doesn't want any of us to commit any of these acts: these seemingly nonrational, nonlogical Torah statutes are, in that sense, universal.

God Who created human intelligence invites us to use it — to develop ourselves by discovering all we can of the logic and the meaning of His laws.[29]

If we probe we will see that *all* of God's laws are statements of Divine wisdom and, particularly, of His Justice.[30] Scripture informs us reliably that all these laws were given for man's own good.[31] So whenever a logical doubt exists as to whether a Divine precept belongs to the Noahide Code or only to the Torah, Israel's national Code, one is well-advised to resolve all doubts by seeking the stricter, more detailed and virtuous Way of God spelled out by the Torah.[32]

Furthermore, even in cases involving positive Torah precepts having nothing to do with the Seven Universal laws, all men, not merely Israel, can acquire merit by observing almost all of the Torah's commandments with Israel.[33]

> He declares His word unto Jacob, His statutes and His judgements
> unto Israel. He has not dealt so with any other nation: and as for
> His judgments, they have not known them. Praise ye the Lord.
> — *Psalm 147:19-20*

Having given man His laws for man's own good,[34] God would have man heed them. It follows that the Torah is an open book. The King of the Universe invites the whole human race to study His Revelation to Israel, through Israel's Bible and its commentaries and the Oral Law, so that all men may both know and keep His Universal laws.[35] But, keep this in mind, the Hebrew Revolution also has a revolutionary discipline.

Certain Torah observances and laws, mainly involving symbolic matters of worship,[36] concern only Israel — the Jews, who are bound by all of the Torah all of the time.[37]

One who deliberately submits to *all* of Israel's discipline with Israel becomes one with Israel[38] — a Jew, one of God's Revolutionary "priests." This tiny priestly cadre would soon be destroyed if it accepted outsiders without restriction, like many man-made religions, based upon a mere avowal of faith. There is one revolution that must protect its integrity.

> Teaching [Torah to] an unworthy student is [a transgression] like
> worshipping idols. — *Mishnah Tosefta*[39]

Gentiles or non-Jews — let us use the Hebrew term *B'nai Noah*, signifying all the descendants of Noah, as opposed to its subset, the descendants of Israel — may choose to go beyond the Universal Law to accept most of Israel's laws upon themselves. These include the Torah laws that aren't necessarily logical from man's (current) point of view, and which analysis doesn't otherwise link to the Rainbow Commandments.

Many of Israel's national holidays, for instance, like the New Year (*Rosh HaShana*),[40] the Day of Atonement (*Yom Kippur*),[41] the Day of the Revelation of the Torah (*Shavuot*),[42] and of course the end-of-the-week Sabbath (*Shabbat*),[43] have important universal implications.

Just as some B'nai Noah used to come to Jerusalem to worship at Israel's ancient Temple — "a house of prayer," Isaiah teaches, "for all peoples"[44] — all men can take up Israel's laws concerning such matters as family purity, pure diet, and even most of Israel's purely monotheistic prayer and worship services.[45]

Man can refine his soul and receive great reward by doing so. In fact, the Bible teaches that someday all men will do so.[46] *But God forbids any idolatrous baggage at His holy service.* These services must be performed properly, with the right intent.[47]

God forbid that anyone bring anything partaking of superstition, taboo, or a wrong and idolatrous concept of God to God's service.

One cannot import foreign notions stemming from the weird pathologies of idolatry, or obsessions from the collective unconscious of nations that have only known man-made religions, into a service that demands greater purity. The proper mental, spiritual attitude is all-important: man may connect with God through Israel's Torah observances, but only on God's own terms.

B'nai Noah are obligated by, and are bound to enforce (collectively, at the level of local government) the laws of the Rainbow Covenant, not the laws of Sinai. Unfortunately, it is the Universal laws, imposing restrictions upon man's strongest animal appetites and impulses, that are the most difficult of God's laws to keep. But these are exactly the laws upon which B'nai Noah should concentrate, rather than upon the laws by which God distinguishes Israel.[48]

Just as most Jews are *not* bound by the Divine precepts that apply solely to Israel's "priests" — the *cohanim*, the direct (paternal-line) descendants of Moses' brother Aaron[49] — most people, non-Jews, are not legally or directly bound by the Torah precepts that apply solely to the Jews. But anyone can *learn* something from those precepts.

One thing to learn is this: man acquires more merit by performing an obligatory service than by performing one which is only optional.[50] A servant earns greater reward for diligently attending to his appointed task than by performing mere "extra credit" work. One's first concern must be to observe those laws that God definitely requires him to observe.

Praise is due to all who seek to refine themselves through Torah. But it's wrong to try to pick and choose among God's laws. This point can't be over-emphasized. All men should endeavor to keep the Universal laws as best as they can, but dabblers or seekers attracted to some fraction of Israel's unique national Way have *no* business trying to create a new religion from the Torah.[51]

If God doesn't command you, as an individual, to do something, don't say that He does.

That sort of imitation is a sincere form of flattery which does no good. It happens in almost every generation, but it's an insult to God, to His Torah, and to Israel — and it has certainly, historically, caused Israel endless amounts of trouble. Only an arrogant and lawless person would seek to introduce any manmade element to God's Way, or exclude any Divine element from it.

> For this is your wisdom and understanding in the sight of the nations, who shall hear all these statutes, and say, 'Surely this great nation is a wise and understanding people.' — *Deuteronomy 4:8*

Tragically, whenever Israel invites B'nai Noah to share Torah knowledge, some B'nai Noah will always ignore the Hebrew Revolution's discipline to interject pagan elements into God's service.[52]

These conceited Gentiles, having grasped some fraction of the Torah, soon conclude that they are masters of the whole Torah; they consider their understanding to be above Israel's.[53] It's strange but true that B'nai Noah often even claim to *be* Israel, while denying the same status *to* Israel, their teachers. But God maintains a separation between those who are bound by all of the Torah's laws and those who are bound only by His Universal laws.[54]

According to most authorities, the following, especially, constitute special holy "signs"[55] that separate Israel from the nations, which solely concern Israel, and which only Israel may keep.[56] B'nai Noah have no business:

- Keeping the Sabbath, rather than merely remembering and celebrating it, in the same way that the Jews are commanded to keep it — that is, by refraining (except in life-threatening emergencies) from every kind of work and even from all cooking. This observance is a unique sign between God and Israel.[57]
- Keeping the other Jewish holy days, such as *Sukkot* ("Tabernacles") or *Shavuot* ("Pentecost"), in the same manner as the Jews — that is, as with the Sabbath, by refraining from every kind of work.
- Writing a Torah scroll — a parchment scroll, like Israel's, containing a Hebrew handwritten version of the Five Books of Moses.
- Reciting anything, in a prayer derived from the traditional prayers of Israel, that would constitute a lie — as by saying that God has commanded one to do something that He didn't command one to do, or by otherwise claiming, falsely, to have inherited the legacy of Israel.
- Going before a Jewish congregation and, in the course of its regular worship services, reading to it aloud from any portion of a Torah scroll.

- Making, writing, or wearing *tefillin* — the parchment-filled leather-covered cubes known as phylacteries, which, worn at certain times, are another of God's special signs for Israel.[58]
- Writing or posting a *mezuzah* — a rolled-up written parchment containing, as do the *tefillin,* certain pertinent sections of Torah — on the doorposts or gates of any structure.[59]
- Studying those parts of the Torah, through the Oral Law or Talmud, concerning the above special signs — which, since they directly pertain only to Israel, have no bearing on any Gentile's obligations to God, nor much in the way of educational value regarding either his fear of God or his love of God.[60]

NOTES

1. *Seder Eliyahu Zuta* 2. Paraphrase from this ancient homiletic, Midrashic work. See also Deuteronomy 17:11, 19:17; Proverbs 2:3-5.

2. Talmud, *Sanhedrin* 59a, *Shabbat* 135, *Bava Kamma* 64b; *Mishnah Tosefta, Avoda Zorah* 5b.

3. For example, the prohibition in Genesis 2:17 against eating certain Edenic fruits obviously applied only then and there, as do the Torah prohibitions applying to, e.g., the manna in the Sinai wilderness. See *Sefer HaMitzvot, Shoresh* 3 (Principle 3 of the 14 Principles for enumerating the Commandments) — in the Chavel edition, supra, Vol. 2, pp. 377-380.

4. See *Yad, Hilchot Melachim* 9, 9:2 and commentaries. Also see *Mishnah Tosefta, Avoda Zorah* 8:4; Talmud, *Sanhedrin* 57b. Lichtenstein, *Seven Laws of Noah*, supra, pp. 17-18. After the Bible, the most comprehensive and accessible book on Torah-court penalties probably remains the *Sefer HaMitzvot*/Maimonides' Book of the Commandments, Vol. 2.

5. See *Sefer HaHinnuch* on Deuteronomy 5:18 (Imperative 424); Nachmanides, *Pirush al HaTorah* on Genesis 34; Lichtenstein, supra, p. 20.

6. Mishnah, *Makkot* 1:10.

7. See Exodus 23:7; Deuteronomy 19:15, Talmud *Sanhedrin* 86, *Makkot* 16a. Also see Cesare Beccaria, *Of Crimes and Punishments* (Livorno, Italy, 1764/London, 1775/Oxford Univ. Press ed., New York NY 1964) on the great benefits of making all punishment for crime "the least possible in the case given, proportioned to the crime, and determined by the laws." (Last page.)

8. Exodus 20:12; Deuteronomy 5:16.

9. Talmud, *Kiddushin* 31a; Hertz, supra, p. 498.

10. *Yad, Hilchot Melachim* 9:14.

11. Exodus 20:12; See Talmud, *Kiddushin* 31b; *Sefer HaMitzvot* 1:210.

12. Mishnah, *Oholot* 1:8; *Sefer HaMitzvot,* "Concluding Remarks on the Positive Commandments."

13. See *Yad, Hilchot Melachim* 9:1, and commentaries. Also see Talmud, *Sanhedrin* 57b-58a.

14. Exodus, ibid.; Deuteronomy 5:16.

15. Talmud, *Hullin* 110a-b.

16. See A.Y. Karelitz (the Hazon Ish) on (Talmud) *Bava Kamma,* 10:3 (in Hebrew only); Nahum Rakover, "Jewish Law and the Noahide Obligation to Preserve Social Order," 12 *Cardozo Law Review* 1073, pp. 1090-93.

17. *Moreh Nevuchim* 3:29. See Exodus 34:13; Deuteronomy 7:5, 12:2.

18. Genesis 11:32, 12:1; Rashi.

19. See S. HaLevi Edels (the Maharsha) on (Talmud) *Hagigah* 13a (in Hebrew only); *Kitzur Shulchan Aruch* 143:1-22 (popular abridged work, c. 1886 CE); Clorfene & Rogalsky, supra, ch.12.

20. Talmud, *Makkot* 23b-24a.

21. Exodus 21:15,17; *Sefer HaMitzvot* 2:318,319. Speaking of Israel's system of Torah courts, the Sanhedrin, which had the power to impose capital penalties. But the Sanhedrin relinquished all such power approximately 2,000 years ago. Currently, Torah courts exist only in theory, and so you should understand any of the references to "Torah courts" within.

22. See HaMe'iri, *Beit HaBekhira* on *Sanhedrin* 59a, cited in Schwartz, *A Light Unto the Nations*, supra, p. 34, regarding methods of analysis. It's also said that Noahides collectively, historically, voluntarily took up these obligations (to honor and protect their parents). See Genesis 2:24 with Nachmanides; Talmud, *Kiddushim* 31a

23. *Sefer HaHinnuch*, supra, on Deuteronomy 5:18, Imperatives 416,424; Nachmanides, *Pirush al HaTorah* on Genesis 34:13; Lichtenstein, *Seven Laws of Noah,* supra, pp 19-29.

24. See, e.g., Job 29:11-17; Malach: 3:16.

25. Deuteronomy 30:11-14; Proverbs 29:18; *Mishnah Pirke Avot* 3:12,15; Talmud, *Kiddushin* 40a.

26. Mishnah, *Berachot* 5:3, 33b; *Yad, Tefillah* 9:7. See Isaiah 55:8-11.

27. In Hebrew, *Mishpatim*. See Genesis 26:5 with Midrash and Rashi; Leviticus 18:4-5 (Hertz); R. Samson Raphael Hirsch, *Horeb* (1st German ed., 1837/Soncino Press, New York NY, 1962, 5th ed., 1994), Sec. 3.

28. In Hebrew, *Hukkim*. See Genesis and Leviticus, ibid. Also see R. Hirsch, supra, Sec. 4.

29. *Yad, Terumot* 4:13, *Teshuvah* 3:4. See Talmud, *Bava Kamma* 79b, *Bava Metzia* 3a.

30. See Dayan Dr. I. Grunfeld, Introduction to *Horeb* (Soncino ed., supra, 1962/1994) p. lxii.

31. See Deuteronomy 6:24, 10:13; Isaiah 48:17; Psalm 16:11.

32. See *Mishnat Rabbi Eliezer, Midrash of Thirty-two Hermeneutic Rules,* supra; Rakover, supra, 12 *Cardozo Law Review* 1073, 1078.

33. *Yad, Hilchot Melachim* 10:9-10.

34. Deuteronomy 6:24, 10:13; Isaiah 48:17; Psalms 16:11.

35. See *Yad, Hilchot Melachim* 10:9-10 and commentaries. As a general rule with several exceptions, Jews should not teach Torah to Gentiles (See

Talmud, *Sanhedrin* 59a, *Hagigah* 13a; *Yad, Hilchot Melachim* 10:9), since pagans and hostile foreigners always tend to use it improperly. But pious B'nai Noah, who sincerely want to avoid idolatry, need Torah, to learn their obligations under the Noahide Law, to learn how to better serve God, and to increase their knowledge, fear and love of Him. So while *nochri* (heathens/foreign pagans), *akkum* (idolators) and mere dabblers don't deserve and shouldn't have free access to Torah, as the sources above indicate (even though medieval Christian censors may have altered these texts in some respects), other Gentiles — true B'nai Noah — deserve better (See, e.g., Talmud, *Hagigah* 13a with Me'iri, *Sotah* 35b, *Makkot* 9b; Deuteronomy 1:5 with Rashi. Also see Schwartz, *A Light Unto the Nations*, supra, p. 36; J.D. Bleich, *Contemporary Halachic Problems* (Ktav/Yeshiva Univ. Press, New York NY, 1981), Vol. 2, "Teaching Torah to Non-Jews," pp. 311-340, 339-340). Otherwise, how will the world ever come to genuinely appreciate this Torah (See, e.g., Deuteronomy 4:6), and how will it ever learn its ways so as to walk in them (Isaiah 2:2-3)? So, for instance, the great Rav Israel Salanter (1810-1883) worked to get the Oral Torah translated into all the leading languages, to make it, with the Bible, part of the basic school curriculum everywhere in Europe. See Louis Ginsberg, *Students, Scholars and Saints* (Jewish Publication Society, Philadelphia PA, 1928) pp. 160-161.

36. See Deuteronomy 4:45, 6:17, 6:20. These are *Edot*, in Hebrew. See Hirsch, *Horeb*, supra, Sec. 2.

37. Many of these laws, chiefly relating to Israel's Temple rites and priesthood, can't be performed at present. Of the Torah's 248 Positive Commandments, only approximately 126 have any current application; of the 365 Negative Commandments, only about 243 can be presently observed. See Kaplan, supra, 5:5-6.

38. Numbers 9:14, 15:14-15.

39. *Avoda Zorah* 6:18, in the name of R. Shimon ben Eleazar.

40. Literally, "Head of the year." See Leviticus 23:23-24, Numbers 29:1-6. The start of the seventh month according to the old calendar, this month, now known as *Tishrei,* can be said to serve, in a sense, like the year's Sabbath. Every *Rosh HaShana*, like every Sabbath, is a time to stop, rest, recharge -- and then finally restart. Along with the solar new year, around the time of the winter solstice (December 21), it's a time, at the end of the summer (in the northern hemisphere), for new starts.

41. See Leviticus 23:26-32, Numbers 25:26.

42. Literally, "Weeks." See Exodus 19:1-16, Leviticus 23:15; Talmud, *Shabbat* 86b.

43. Genesis 2:1-3, Exodus 20:8, 31:14. See Nehemiah 13:14-22; Talmud, *Yoma* 85b, *Pesachim* 106a.

44. Isaiah 56:7, 2:2-3, 66:20. See Talmud, *Sukkot* 55b.

45. See *Yad, Hilchot Melachim* 10:10.

46. See, e.g., Isaiah 66 and Zechariah 14:16 with Rashi.

47. Right intent means, among other things, without any idolatrous or primitive, superstitious habits of thought, and with the understanding that a Gentile performs these services solely for self-improvement and to acquire Divine merit (by glorifying the Creator), rather than as a matter of Divine obligation. See *Yad, Hilchot Melachim* 10:10; J.D. Bleich, *Contemporary Halachic Problems* (Ktav/Yeshiva University Press, New York NY, 1977), Vol. 1, pp.

316-320, ch. 14, "Black Jews: a Halachic Perspective."

48. Talmud, *Sanhedrin* 59a, *Bava Kamma* 38a.

49. See Exodus 28; Leviticus 21-22.

50. Talmud, *Kiddushin* 31a.

51. *Yad, Hilchot Melachim* 10:10 and commentaries.

52. One must realize that Rabbi Judah (*Yehudah*) HaNasi, the final editor of Israel's great Mishnah (completed 188 CE), omitted all references to the Rainbow Covenant in a work that was bound to be widely known in translation. Introducing the world's pagan masses to the full Torah, even in this way — when they, unready for its discipline, would undoubtedly appropriate it for themselves, misreading and confusing it — might have destroyed Israel.

53. Gentiles often tend to expect too much from the 48 Biblical prophets who came after Moses — like a major theological revelation completely independent of and contrary to Moses' Torah from Sinai! See Talmud, *Megillah* 14a; R. Abraham Isaac Kook, *Orot* (1920; annotated translation by R. Bezalel Naor, Jason Aronson Inc., Northvale NJ/London, 1993), "Israel and Its Renaissance," Sec. 3-5, pp. 105-108n.

54. Deuteronomy 33:4; Psalm 147:19-20. See Talmud, *Sanhedrin* 59a, *Bava Kamma* 38a, *Hagigah* 13a.

55. See, e.g., Exodus 31:13,17. Also see Hirsch, *Horeb*, supra, ch. 2.

56. *Yad, Hilchot Melachim* 10:10 and commentaries; Clorfene & Rogalsky, supra, pp. 41-42. Difficult as it is to describe the exact parameters of this prohibition, some authorities might add to the list here; some might make deletions. But the general rule, whenever one has a doubt about whether to perform any of the Torah's positive, ritual, ordinances, requires that one refrain from its performance.

57. Exodus 31:13, ibid. See Talmud, *Sanhedrin* 58b, *Keritot* 9a and *Yevamot* 48b with Rashi. Also see J.D. Bleich, *Tradition* (Rabbinical Council of America, pub.) Vol. 25:3, Spring 1991, pp. 46-62. B'nai Noah are well-advised to honor this holy day, and their Maker, by refraining from some, but not all, workaday activities. Briefly, generally, Rashi (Rabbi Shlomo Yitzchaki, 1040-1105 CE) indicates that a Gentile — the term that has come down to us is *nochri/heathen* — who has accepted the Noahide Covenant and renounced idolatry should definitely keep Shabbat, because desecrating the Seventh Day is itself idolatrous (Talmud, *Yevamot* 48b). Maimonides speaks only of an *akkum* — a follower of false religion — as someone who must not fulfill nor otherwise dabble with Shabbat or other characteristic Torah observances (*Yad, Hilchot Melachim* 10:9). But medieval church censors have interfered with these texts, and Maimonides was probably referring here to any Gentile — i.e., to any Gentile living in the land of Israel, as a permanent or long-term resident, in Messianic times (Id.). This would be a Ben Noah who just wants to enjoy Shabbat and certain other benefits of Torah that particularly move him, while he stands aloof from the rest of Torah and the balance of God's commandments. This person wants to pick and choose Torah practices and rituals as from a cafeteria counter, to create, in essence, a new religion. He should instead either accept upon himself the whole Torah or just fulfill the Noahide Law — the whole moral Law, minus Sinai's Torah-dependent rituals. As for Shabbat, the day in all its glory does not belong to him; he has no right to observe it as though it does — i.e., observe it exactly in the

manner of observant Israel. To do so would be to intrude on Israel's special national relationship to Shabbat, the liberationist aspect (See Deuteronomy 5:15), beyond the Sabbath's elemental connection to all existence (Exodus 20:11). Of course this does *not* mean that he should desecrate the Sabbath — as by treating it, God forbid, like part of the workaday world. Rashi, above, makes this point very clearly. No one should desecrate Shabbat. (Rav S.R. Hirsch, among others, based partly on the *Yad* cited here, disagrees, asserting that any conscious, specific observance of Shabbat by Gentiles is harmful. See Hirsch on Exodus 20:8. Oddly, these scholars never seem to articulate just *how* it might be harmful, even in the face of the many palpable bad consequences flowing from the nations' general non-recognition of Shabbat.)

58. See Exodus 13:9,16; Deuteronomy 6:8, 11:18. Also, see Talmud, *Shabbat* 49a (R. Yannai). As for the Laws of *tzitzit*, or symbolic fringes (See Numbers 15:38), and the Laws of *mikvah*, or ritual immersion (See Leviticus 15:16), one cannot say that their observance requires nearly as much in the way of either knowledge or personal purity (on the part of the person performing the ritual) as do the laws of *tefillin*. Don't take this remark as a ruling, though. Before a Ben Noah adopts any such observance he should confer with a rabbi personally.

59. See Deuteronomy 6:4-9, 11:13-21. Never treat a *mezuzah* like a (magic) amulet — Yad, *Tefillin* 5:4. The broader prohibition, above, against use of all these objects, might not apply to a Ben Noah who understands the use of the *mezuzah*. That such use can indeed benefit a Ben Noah, see Midrash, *Genesis Rabbah* 35:3; Jerusalem Talmud, *Pe'ah* 1.1.

60. Although a Gentile who has begun formal proceedings to become one with Israel — conversion — by taking up the full "yoke of the Torah" must learn about these observances and study these portions. One may also say that every part of Torah does in fact concern B'nai Noah, as well as B'nai Israel, in some way, since everything in Torah "serves a certain purpose in connection with religious teaching. It either helps to establish a principle of faith, or to regulate our actions, and to prevent wrong and injustice among men." *Moreh Nevuchim* 3:50, and also see 3:28 and 3:29. So, after all, it may be that no aspect of Torah, except the actual performance of some commandments, need remain off-limits for study by a qualified (even though non-converting) Ben Noah.

Who Decides What?

NEW APPROACHES

Declare ye among the nations, and publish, and set up a standard; publish, and conceal not. — Jeremiah 50:2

B eyond the strict Revolutionary imperative to maintain the distinction between Israel and B'nai Noah, Israel has a special reason for reticence in speaking of the Rainbow laws.

God makes man chiefly responsible for himself. So long as B'nai Noah have the God-given obligation to keep these laws themselves, then it's reasonable that B'nai Noah must also, ordinarily, determine the details of these laws for themselves. This responsibility obviously falls outside the scope of the authority of the rabbis.

Israel's rabbis, the devout Orthodox scholars of our own generation,[1] are the guardians and judges of the Torah. They "sit in Moses' seat" as the teachers of the Revolution. As such, their first duty, naturally, is to Israel. They have the right and the obligation to prescribe God's laws to Israel.[2] While they also have an obligation to others,[3] their duty, as they have seen it, is less one of *prescribing* the details of God's Noahide laws than of simply *describing* matters of Torah to B'nai Noah — and usually even then, only upon being asked. Indeed, some rabbis would go further, saying that Israel should point the nations to Truth — to freedom and the blessings of the good life[4] — solely by means of Israel's silent example, rather than by teaching the nations any specific precepts of Torah.[5]

The Jewish people stay safer when they stay quiet about their Torah before the general public. But the same Torah is clear that the God of Abraham and Israel doesn't want Israel to keep silent, and hasn't restricted Israel to passive witnessing alone.[6]

The rabbis' great expertise, of course, is in Torah. Applying such expertise to questions involving the Noahide Law obviously represents something else again.

While the rabbis may have a great deal of wisdom in such things, God has not given them official authority,[7] as He has regarding their Torah judgments for Israel.

Generally, concerning B'nai Noah, the rabbis have only so much authority as their B'nai Noah students grant them. Then too, largely through such Hebrew influences as the Bible, the nations have already taken upon themselves portions of the Law.[8] They can — they shall — build on that foundation. And we must finally assert that the nations have both the continuing obligation and the right to determine their own laws — including the details of the Universal laws — for themselves.

If this rule has any real exception it concerns B'nai Noah in the Holy Land, the Land of Israel.[9] God commands Israel to eliminate every trace of the nations' idolatries in the one country that He bequeathed to Israel.[10] But Israel, practically speaking, can only do so — by giving aliens in Israel a choice between leaving the country or accepting the Noahide Law[11] — when Israel's government is both obedient to Torah and in full control of the land. These two conditions haven't been met for thousands of years. So the rabbis' habitual reluctance to prescribe to B'nai Noah has been reinforced by a historic lack of opportunity.

Furthermore, there *is* another approach to the Noahide Code. It emphasizes man's dependence upon Revelation while de-emphasizing Torah-interpretations based upon mere common sense. Thus many students have tried to reveal the Rainbow laws, to isolate and define them, by an imaginative examination of the Scriptural text alone.

This is called the exegetical method. It puts a magnifying glass to the individual words of Torah, and sometimes even to the letters making up the words, in an effort to discover allegorical or poetic truths lying deep beneath the text's plain meaning. It's based on the belief that the Written Torah, in those portions concerning God's revelations to mankind's common ancestors — to Adam and Eve and to Noah and his family in legendary times — contains hidden clues that spell out the substance of these Revelations. It stresses the idea that the rabbis of ancient times knew of these things and that man's obligation today is to discover the ancients' secret lore.

An allegorical interpretation of Genesis 2:16-17, for instance, is said to reveal all seven of the Seven basic Noahide Commandments.[12]

Conceivably, every detail of the Rainbow laws could become known to us through the same method. Many students have used it in a search for said details. But this technique is too conjectural to serve us as our only reliable guide.[13] Men can hardly base life-or-death decisions of law upon mere allegories.[14] A passive, dependent method, it ignores the utility of plain common sense. And it's a fact that most of the answers that have come down to us from the Sages' ancient exegesis merely confirm or mirror conclusions attained more certainly through simple Torah-based logic.[15]

Given the confusion regarding method — and probably inevitably, in the light of all the circumstances — Israel's approach to Noahide jurisprudence hasn't always been a model of clarity or logic.

Anyone reading the older works will see that some treatments partake more of solemnity than of seriousness, stressing the Law's great majesty and importance over a rigorous consideration of its contents. Israel has also occasionally mistaken its Sages' passing descriptions of various nations' laws — mere empirical observations — to be prescriptions — normative instructions — concerning the Universal Law.[16]

Several writers have said, in effect, that the notoriously harsh and unjust laws of benighted countries like ancient Syria, Rome and Persia provide humanity with examples for enlightened Noahide courts to follow.[17] Solemnly, they argue that Gentiles may properly enforce their own laws with horrible severity, and that the regular, statutory punishment administered by Noahide courts must always be capital punishment, the death penalty.[18]

This sort of ghastly misconception does little credit to the logic of the Law. Analysis reveals the error. The key teaching is Maimonides', in his seminal work, the *Yad HaChazaka* or *Mishneh Torah* ("Repetition of the Torah"), *Hilchot Melachim* ("Laws of Kings"): "A Ben Noah who transgresses one of these Seven Commandment laws shall be executed by the sword."[19]

Let's take a close look at this:

- **Execution by the sword:** this means, as the Torah teaches, that society shall effect the death penalty only by the quickest and least painful method possible, decapitation in one stroke.[20] The grotesque final penalties so often imposed in humanity's bloody history — flaying, drawing and quartering, keelhauling, burning at the stake, and other mutilating tortures to kill men really, *really* dead — are forbidden.
- **Must every convicted criminal be executed?** Must every teenaged shoplifter be punished just as murderers are punished? The context of this passage, setting out the duties of Israel's kings once the line of (King) David has been restored to sovereignty and the Messianic era has begun, explains everything. Plainly, it directly pertains only to B'nai Noah who have elected to live alongside the people of Israel, within the land of Israel, in the future — that is, in Messianic times, when "the earth shall be full of the knowledge of the Lord as the waters cover the sea."[21]

Recently, many scholars have taken us deeper into this supposed harsh rule of Maimonides. Love and mercy make up the bare bones of the Law and here we have another instance where the exemptions, exacting safeguards and loopholes of divine jurisprudence make a harsh penalty — capital punishment — mostly important only as a symbolic legal benchmark. God wants us to know just how seriously He takes our every failure to live up to our humanity, to His minimal moral expectations for us. Every time we fail to act fully human we die at least a little anyway; the symbolism of the harsh general penalty — the technical penalty — ought to bring that moral value home. As for the practical working details of Noahide jurisprudence, actual penalties are for each nation to determine for itself, based on the facts and circumstances of every case and over time. [22]

It is fundamental Revolutionary doctrine, scholars insist, that the Torah holds Israel up to the strictest standards[23] — that "nothing is permitted to a Jew that is forbidden to a Gentile"[24] — yet Jewish defendants in Hebrew Torah courts don't face the death penalty for every crime.[25] With all the safeguards, exceptions and limitations that make up so much of God's Law, defendants almost never face the death penalty for any crime. Of course, the God of forgiveness, love and mercy is the Universal God of second chances: He doesn't desire the sinner's death but our repentance and return to Him.[26]

Similarly, Israel has always recognized that Heaven's specifications of minimal thresholds or minimum quantities that must be at stake before the Torah requires any legal penalty — a Jew, for instance, must steal an object worth at least a nickel or two before he can be held liable for theft[27] — don't apply to B'nai Noah. These are details of God's Revelation to Israel, not to B'nai Noah.[28]

Does this mean that there is no place in the Universal Law even for the concept of minimal amounts? Must every employee who takes a corporate notepad home with him from work be tried as a thief and punished as a felon? Or does it mean that B'nai Noah may establish minimal amounts — a specific legal threshold, where that may be an issue — for themselves?[29]

God doesn't act as a tyrant to His creatures.[30] The fact is, persuasive ancient as well as modern scholarship insists, that *God has established the substance of His Law while He grants B'nai Noah freedom to legislate its details.*

Such details include minimal amounts or threshold quantities and the mechanisms for the Law's enforcement, to be determined in accordance with their — the nations' — own communal needs. So the nations may devise whatever structure or hierarchy of penalties they think appropriate to secure compliance with their laws.[31]

Looking at this system logically, we see that it must be so.[32] Which means that we can say plainly: B'nai Noah legislators have the *right* to enact the death penalty to punish any crimes committed under the Noahide Law. After all, these aren't just crimes committed against other men, offensive to the good order of society. They are crimes of idolatry, committed against God and His sovereignty, which are directly offensive to Him.[33] But a legal right is not an obligation: a right need not be exercised.

God's Universal laws are also laws of sublime justice. They aren't merely ideal or far off, designed for application only in some spiritual or Messianic future: it is another Revolutionary principle that God's laws are practical laws, meant to govern man's practices *now*.[34] We see that He has designed them accordingly, to commend themselves to the enlightened conscience and sense of justice of every nation. The nations can adjust the details to suit themselves.

NOTES

1. Deuteronomy 17:9-12,19:17; Talmud, *Rosh HaShanah* 25b. "Orthodox" means, essentially, scupulously faithful to the letter of the ancient Revolutionary Tradition. Among Israel, unfortunately, it is largely or entirely only Orthodox Jews who are entirely serious about the whole of the Torah.

2. See Leviticus 10:11; Deuteronomy, ibid; Talmud, *Moed Katan* 17a, *Hagigah* 15b; *Yad, Talmud Torah* 4:1. *Yad, Hilchot Melachim* 8:10.

3. See Exodus 19:6; Isaiah 42:6-7, 43:10, 49:6; *Talmud, Pesachim* 87b.

4. "That man alone is free who has God for his leader." Philo (c. 30 CE), *Every Good Man is Free*, p. 1; See Deuteronomy 30:15,19; Proverbs 10. Only he is free who learns and lives the Torah, and he will be exalted. — Mishnah, *Pirke Avot* 6:2.

5. See Talmud, *Sanhedrin* 59a. But then see Talmud, *Shabbat* 88b; Midrash, *Genesis Rabbah* 49:2; *Leviticus Rabbah* 6:5; *Shulchan Aruch, Yoreh De'ah* 268; J.D. Bleich, *Contemporary Halakhic Problems*, supra, Vol. 2 (1983) ch. 16, p. 311-340.

6. J.D. Bleich, id., note 82. Also see *Avot d'Rabbi Nathan* 23a (Midrash); *Kuzari,* (the whole work) supra; *Sefer HaMitzvot* 1:3.

7. Except in the Land of Israel. See *Yad, Hilchot Melachim* 8:9.

8. Not to ignore the influence of Christian Europe and, particularly in modern times, the revolutionary United States.

9. *Yad, Hilchot Melachim* 8:10, and also 6:1-4, 10:11.

10. Exodus 23:33, 34:13, Deuteronomy 7:5, 12:2-3; Talmud, *Sanhedrin* 90a; *Yad, Hilchot Avodat Kochavim* 10:7; *Sefer HaMitzvot* 1:185, 2:51.

11. Deuteronomy 20:10-12, Rashi; *Yad, Hilchot Melachim* 6, 8:9; *Sefer HaMitzvot*, ibid.

12. "And the Lord God commanded Adam, saying: Of every tree in the garden you may freely eat. But of the tree of the knowledge of good and evil you may not eat, for on the day that you eat of it you shall surely die." See

Talmud, *Sanhedrin* 58b.

13. Yehuda (Judah) HaLevi, *Kuzari* 3:73. Professor Lichtenstein, in *The Seven Laws of Noah*, supra, p. 15, notes that "As careful a traditionalist as Judah HaLevi considered this exegetical derivation far-fetched and but a mnemonic device of the Oral Tradition."

14. See *Mishnat Rabbi Eliezer*, supra.

15. For instance, a mere common-sense examination of Genesis 2:24 — "Therefore shall a man leave his father and his mother, and shall cleave unto his wife, and they shall be one flesh" — reveals five of the universally forbidden degrees of incest. See *Yad, Hilchot Melachim* 9:5.

16. See e.g., Talmud, *Sanhedrin* 59a with Rashi, concerning trivial theft offenses which Noahide courts have punished capitally. Rashi observes that the nations' comparative cruelty, or unwillingness to act forgivingly when it comes to small injuries, helps explain the severity of their laws. Also see Novak, *Image of the Non-Jew in Judaism*, supra, pp. 229-331. However, one must also recognize that every Rainbow Covenant violation threatens, in some way, the good order of society; to keep order, society needs to punish violators with all necessary severity.

17. These nations were infamous for their generally casual approach to capital punishment. See above.

18. See *Yad, Hilchot Melachim* 9:14; Clorfene & Rogalsky, supra, 4:15, p. 44. In unsettled or frontier conditions society may need to execute malefactors like horse thieves and rapists, but other penalties become possible once civilization takes hold.

19. Yad, ibid.

20. See Talmud, *Sanhedrin* 52b; *Yad, Hilchot Sanhedrin* 15:12; *Sefer HaMitzvot* 1:226.

21. Isaiah 11:9. Even then — in Messianic times — and there — in the land of Israel, it's possible that capital punishment may never be part of any operative schedule of penalties. (See, again, *Yad, Hilchot Melachim* 9:14, and the variant readings different jurisprudential schools give to it.) Or, conceivably, society will invoke it only as an ultimate penalty, reserving it solely for the most heedless and incorrigible of felons. See the sources quoted in the note below, or the further discussion in "Laws Against Lawlessness," below.

22. See, e.g., J. D. Bleich, "The Death Penalty in the Noahide Laws," *1 Jubilee Volume in Honor of Rabbi Joseph D. Soloveitchik* (Yeshiva University, New York NY, 1984) p. 149 and "Capital Punishment in the Noachide Code" in *Contemporary Halachic Problems*, supra, Vol 2, pp. 341-367 (holding that God's Law imposes various devices that combine to make capital punishment everywhere impractical or impossible to legally invoke); Nahum Rakover, "Jewish Law and the Noahide Obligation to Preserve Social Order," 12 *Cardozo Law Review*, (supra) p. 1073, with Dr. Arnold N. Enker, "Aspects of Interaction between the Torah Law, the King's Law, and the Noahide Law in Jewish Criminal Law," p. 1137, and Prof. Suzanne Last Stone, "Sinaitic and Noahide Law: Legal Pluralism in Jewish Law," p. 1157. Also see Michael J. Broyde, "The Obligation of Jews to Seek Observance of Noahide Laws by Gentiles," in *Tikkun Olam* (Jason Aronson, Northvale NJ, 1997) pp. 116, 138. Generally, see the discussion in Talmud, *Sanhedrin* 56b, between R. Yochanan and R. Yitzhak, R. Yochanan arguing, in effect, that Noahides must legislate

their own laws for themselves and R. Yitzhak arguing, in effect, that the Noahide Code is fundamentally similar to Israel's Torah. R. Yitzhak teaches that the Noahide Law doesn't just constitute a few general precepts but is, like Israel's Law, genuinely comprehensive, extensive and holy. If both rabbis are correct then the Noahide Law is not identical to but only very closely related to Israel's Law — the view of both Maimonides (See *Yad, Hilchot Melachim* 10:12, presupposing a valid set of Noahide laws separate from Hebrew law) and Nachmanides (on Maimonides' *Sefer HaMitzvot, Shoresh* 14), holding that the Noahide laws are "similar [i.e., not identical] to the laws that Israel was commanded." Most scholarly views to the contrary seem to trace back to a probable small error, a false dichotomy, in a legal opinion by R. Moshe Isserles (Ramo), *Responsa Ramo* 10 (Hebrew only). See Nahum Rakover, *Law and the Noahides* (Library of Jewish Law, Israel Ministry of Justice, Jerusalem, 1998) pp. 55-74 (including the views of many later authorities and clearing up the record).

23. See, e.g., Exodus 22:30; Leviticus 11:44; Amos 3:2, and commentaries.

24. Talmud, *Sanhedrin* 59a.

25. For instance, a Hebrew Torah court doesn't impose death but only the duty to make appropriate monetary restitution if it convicts a Jew of thievery. Exodus 21:37; *Sefer HaMitzvot* 1:239, 2:244. It is inconceivable that Heaven should permit a Jew to pay restitution and go free, while requiring B'nai Noah in their own lands to execute a Gentile, but not a Jew, convicted of the same crime.

26. Ezekiel 33:11. See, e.g., Genesis 4:7; Exodus 34:6-7 with Rashi; Isaiah 1:18, 55:6; Joel 2:13; Mishnah, *Pirke Avot* 4:11, *Yoma* 86a-b; *Pesachim* 119a; *Yad, Hilchot Teshuva* 2:2, 3:4. However, again, where Rainbow Covenant violations threaten to destroy society, society certainly has every right to punish violators as severely as necessary.

27. I.e., worth a *p'rutah* or date or fig, or the value of the smallest conceivable commercial transaction, like "two pins" or a grape or a couple of grapes from a market, but not something as trivial as, e.g., a splinter from a fence rail, "stolen" for use as a toothpick. See Mishnah, *Kiddushin* 1:1; Talmud, *Sanhedrin* 59a, *Kiddushin* 3, 11.

28. Talmud, *Eruvin* 4a; *Yad, Hilchot Melachim* 9:10.

29. Obviously, these thresholds must be set low enough to prevent injustice. But if B'nai Noah in their own countries agree to deny their courts jurisdiction over certain trivial wrongs (perhaps to address them unofficially), and are also all comfortable enough not to agonize over inconsequential thefts, or other very minor crimes or injuries, how can one call this wrong? Nothing could be clearer that the Law of Israel and the Noahide Law differ in some respects — See, e.g., Talmud, *Sanhedrin* 57b. It should also be self-evident that every sovereign nation has the right and obligation to legislate for itself, in the matter of determining legal limits as in legislating other details of local law, this representing, for the citizenry of the nation, a key aspect and characteristic of being fully human. See Rakover, supra, ibid, for an enumeration of authorities, from Rambam (Maimonides) and Ramban (Nachmanides) to Rav Naftali Tzvi Yehuda Berlin (Netziv, c. 1817-1893, *HaEmek She'elah* 2:3) and Rav Avraham Yitzhak Kook (c. 1865-1935, *Etz Hadar*, chapter 40 n. 11, chapter 41 n. 13), who teach us that Noahides need

not conform to all the details of Israel's Law but should instead determine
the details of their own laws for themselves, basing their own (Noahide)
legislation not just on Torah sources but on their own national experience
and conventions.

30. Talmud, *Avoda Zorah* 3a.

31. J.D. Bleich, et al, supra. The single exception involves the crime of
murder. However, Prof. Stone suggests that even murder needn't be
punished capitally, but only appropriately, as determined by society. See
Stone, supra, ibid.

32. General rules or principles — in Hebrew, *kllalim* — must have
greater weight in adjudicating matters of Noahide law than of Torah, since
so much more of the Torah has been specifically Revealed.

33. *Sifre* (Midrash) to Numbers, No. 2.

34. Deuteronomy 30:11-14; Proverbs 6:22; Talmud, *Avoda Zorah* 3a.

Book Two

The Seven Universal Laws

The heavenly call is to the righteous of the generation — not to the sinners. The sinners cannot hear the call; they look at the rainbow and see but a colorful spectrum. Their spiritual senses are deadened. But the righteous of the generation can hear and see; and they can interpret the heavenly sign. It is to them that God calls, and it is for them to respond by praying, coming closer to Torah, and trying to bring others along with them.

— Rabbi Mordechai Gifter[1]

1. Commentary on Genesis, *Torah Perspectives* (Artscroll/Mesorah, New York NY 1986) p. 98.

Common Principles

GENERAL RULING PRINCIPLES

As you read the laws and commandments and the statutes and ordinances that follow, you should try to keep these basic general principals in mind:

1) Men and women are equal in their responsibility to God; the Rainbow laws apply with the same force to both genders.[1] This does not mean that humanity's courts must ignore all differences of sex or gender. Only a female can — Heaven forbid — be an adulterous wife, as only a male can homosexually engage another male. Where matters of gender define the very nature of an act, the Law always takes gender into account.

2) Ignorance of the law is no excuse for violating the Law. But a person who lacks criminal intent because he is ignorant of some *fact* which might make his act a crime — in the matter of adultery, for example, he who has sex with a married woman whom he honestly believes to be single is said to lack adulterous intent — may not be punished (for adultery) by the courts.[2]

3) One's thoughts and feelings are one's own. Man's courts can't invade this personal sphere except in cases where the personal becomes public — when thoughts or feelings become manifest through action. So long as former president Jimmy Carter's

famous self-supposed "adultery" — apparently, mere private "lusting" — was committed only in his heart, for instance, the law must let the matter rest between him and Heaven.

Similarly, where a man might feel some idolatrous or homosexual impulses, so long as the idolatrous impulses aren't translated into an overt act of idolatry, nor the homosexual into illicit physical relations with another man, they are no concern of any court.[3]

4) Very young children and mental incompetents who are not responsible for their actions may not be punished by the courts.[4] Obviously, no punishment will deter the person who has no free will, who cannot tell right from wrong. He who lacks the power to control his acts, or the maturity to understand their significance, is not capable of accepting or understanding legal responsibility. But the child or slow person who can tell the difference between good and evil, who has the power to conform to the law, is obligated to do so, just like any adult.[5]

5) A Ben Noah who lacks free will because of another's threats or coercion is not responsible for his own actions: the courts may not punish one who violates these laws when he acts solely under duress.[6] However, this does not apply to murder. Nobody's blood is any redder than the blood of anyone else; one cannot take an innocent person's life just to save one's own skin, nor even to protect the lives of other innocents.[7]

6) A Jew must sacrifice his own life, if need be, rather than allow himself to be coerced into committing any sin of sexual immorality or idol worship or murder. But Israel's obligation to publicly sanctify God's Name, by publicly defending these central Revolutionary values, is **not** a universal obligation,

legally. Man's duty to protect human life —
including one's own life — takes priority over all
other laws.[8]

7) Complete repentance completely atones for sin,
even including deliberate violations of the most
basic laws. The penitent must make good or erase
all the damage caused by his sin — which is
obviously impossible in the case of murder, or of
other crimes where the damage is not repairable,
committed against one's fellow man — and seek
forgiveness from everyone he injured. Further, he
must seek God's forgiveness, and, truly repenting
his wrongful conduct, sincerely resolve never to
repeat the sin.[9]

> Learn to do well; seek judgment, relieve the oppressed, judge the
> fatherless, plead for the widow. Come now, and let us reason
> together, says the Lord: if your sins are as scarlet, they can become
> white as snow; though they are red like crimson, they shall be white
> as wool. — *Isaiah 1:17-18*

Punishment imposed by a human court for crime helps the
criminal atone.[10] So does suffering imposed by Heaven, through
sickness, loneliness, or poverty.[11] But man shouldn't conduct
himself before God like a slave fearful of a whipping — nor, for
that matter, like a slave hopeful of reward.[12] Rather, one should
do good to be good, to please one's Master, out of love for the
Father of love, for His greater glory.[13]

> Teach me, O Lord, the way of Your Statutes; and I will keep it at
> every step. Give me understanding, and I shall keep Your Law, and
> observe it with my whole heart. Make me to tread in the path of
> Your Commandments; for therein do I delight. — *Psalm 119:33-35*

Let's take a look now, working our way up through the list —
from the narrower or more specific commandments to the
broadest and most comprehensive — at each of the Seven
Commandments.

NOTES

1. See *Encyclopedia Talmudica* (Talmudic Encyclopedia Institute, Jerusalem, 1992) Vol. 4, "Ben Noah/A Noahide," p. 361.

2. *Yad, Hilchot Melachim* 10:1.

3. All depends on one's deeds. See, e.g., Mishnah, *Pirke Avot* 3:19, 1:15,17; *Ta'anit* 2:1 (on Jonah 3:10, recalling that God relented as to the B'nai Noah due solely to their works), *Eduyot* 5:7; Midrash, *Mechilta* to Exodus 12:6; Yehuda HaLevi, *Kuzari* 2:46.

4. *Yad, Hilchot Melachim* 10:2, and commentaries. Naturally, dangerously irresponsible people need protection, for their own good and certainly society's. A decent society protects its weakest members, and also its strongest, from oppression and injustice as well as anarchy. See, e.g., *Yad*, ibid, 3:10 and *Hilchot Rotzeach* 2:4 and commentaries.

5. That is, not necessarily at a pre-determined age, but depending on the actual intellectual maturity of the individual. See *Minchat Hinnuch* 190; Broyde, in *Tikkun Olam*, supra, p. 114. Some very well-regarded authorities hold that usually, by the onset of the first signs of puberty, an individual's full moral responsibility can be presumed.

6. *Yad, Hilchot Melachim* 10:2.

7. Talmud, *Pesachim* 25b; Mishnah, *Sanhedrin* 4:5. Obviously, it is better to disable — the best option — or even kill the guilty person doing the coercing. See Talmud, *Sanhedrin* 72a.

8. Leviticus 18:5; Talmud, *Yoma* 85b; *Yad, Hilchot Melachim* 10:2. Another school of thought holds that Noahides are indeed divinely obligated to sanctify God's Name, their practical responsibilities in this respect being more or less the same as Israel's. See Talmud, *Sanhedrin* 74b (in the name of Rava, a most authoritative sage), Rashi on *Sanhedrin* 75a (applying a slightly different standard), Tosefot, and Ramban (Nachmanides), *Milchemet HaShem*, chapter *Ben Sorrer*, for the argument that B'nai Noah as well as Jews are obligated to sanctify the Name of God — even to the point of death, if necessary. More recently the great Rabbi Moshe Tzvi Neriah (c. 1913-1995) has pointed out that, while there is no difference between the *public* obligations of Jews and non-Jews in this respect, should some Hitlerian evil power try to force the non-Jew to commit, at point of death, any of the three cardinal sins — idolatry, a perverse sexual act, or an act of homicide — privately, out of the public eye, the Noahide is freer than the Jew here. Given the private setting (and assuming, always, that all other forms of resistance are futile), the Noahide may commit the sin, and thereby save himself from martyrdom. The Jew, on the other hand, has no choice; whether the setting is public or private, he must uphold God's Law. See "Are B'nai Noah Obligated in the Sanctification of HaShem's Name?" *Torah SheBeAl Peh Journal* (Mosad HaRav Kook, Jerusalem, Israel, 1972) pp. 119-134.

9. See Psalms 25:8, 145:18; Mishnah, *Yoma* 8:9; *Yad, Hilchot Teshuva* 2:1. True regret stems from love of God and wanting to do right by Him, not just from a fear of ultimate punishment.

10. *Yad*, ibid.

11. *Yad*, ibid.

12. One can always take up righteous practices and observances in order to acquire personal merit before one's Master. See *Yad, Hilchot Melachim*

10:10. The idea that every such good deed doesn't in some way glorify Him, or that a Ben Noah has no power to perform such acts completely disinterestedly — i.e., with no thought of receiving Heavenly (or secular) personal reward — seems unlikely. Also, since the deed's the thing, one may prefer to reserve judgment about other people's motivations. But some scholars approach these issues differently. For a look at the logic of a competing school of thought, see Bleich, *Contemporary Halachic Problems*, supra, Vol. 1, p. 317 (discussing Mishnah, *Pirke Avot* 1:3 and *Yad, Hilchot Melachim*, ibid.).

13. Mishnah, *Pirke Avot* 1:3; *Yad, Hilchot Teshuva* 2:1.

THE SEVENTH COMMANDMENT

Dietary Laws

And God said to Adam: 'Behold My works!
See how beautiful and commendable they
are. All that I created, for your sake I created
it. Pay heed that you do not corrupt and
desolate My world, for there is no one to
repair it after you.'
— Midrash, Ecclesiastes Rabbah 7:28

Every living creature eats. This Commandment requires man to treat the animals he eats — and also, ultimately, every creature subject to human control — with some self-control, self-respect, and at least the semblance of a decent regard for other life.

The Revolutionary Law sweeps away the taboos of paganism.[1] God has given men and women complete dominion over His earth.[2] "Every moving thing that lives shall be food for you; even as the green herb, I have given you everything."[3] But this awesome gift is no license for depravity or piggishness: freedom imposes responsibilities. The Eternal King who elevates us above the animals forbids us from acting like animals.

God created human beings in His image and as His elect.[4] Men and women are obviously totally unlike God in having absolutely undeniable animal needs,[5] but He requires us to behave better than mere animals. People must serve God, rather than use His world as though it exists solely for one's own engorgement. Man's divine right of dominion entails special obligations: human beings are God's planetary stewards.

This Seventh Commandment connects vile gastronomy to idolatry, and to the moral pathologies associated with idolatry, including the pollution and defilement of God's good Earth. It applies equally to men and women, and to their children, in all respects.

Mystics associate the laws connected to this commandment with the rainbow's green.[6]

HISTORICAL ORIGINS

Scripturally, the Seventh Commandment doesn't emerge with Adam, but only as part of a later Revelation: God's Rainbow Covenant with Noah and his children.[7] This gave rise to the Hebrew custom of referring to all the Universal laws as Noah's laws or, more precisely, as the "Laws of the Sons [Descendants] of Noah."[8]

Latest and last of the Rainbow Commandments, this Seventh Commandment, often called "the Law of the Torn Limb," is certainly very old. It is so old, as various wits have joked, that God gave it to man in an age when it was still necessary to tell people to kill their food before they ate it! Yet, quaint as the law here may sound to modern ears, this ancient Rule, focusing on nothing less than humanity's relationship to the natural environment, has earth-shaking current — and eternal — implications. While it can be fully understood only in the context of God's more detailed Revelation to Israel, it exemplifies the whole thrust and spirit of the Rainbow Law.

The Law of the Torn Limb: Statutes

O Lord, You lovingly sustain both man and beast. — *Psalm 36:7*

Every study of the Seventh Commandment begins with God's general but purposeful warning to man: You shall eat no animal while it is still alive; you shall eat no flesh torn from a still-living creature; you shall not eat meat that was taken or torn off the limb of any living being.[9] Man must, at a minimum, kill his food (or have it killed by someone else) before he eats it. This is not a taboo, nor merely an issue of custom or taste, but an absolute and universal moral obligation.

At least three basic principles are operative here:

1) Don't be insensitive to the suffering of animals;
2) Don't be insensitive to the nature of the food you eat;
3) It is savage and sick to be insensitive to both of the above principles in combination.[10]

At least four additional rules are associated with this general, "Torn Limb" Commandment. They are, indisputably, implicit within it. Although man derives them from the originally oral teachings of the Sages of Israel, combined with simple Torah-based logic, rather than from explicit Biblical passages, they are Rainbow laws nonetheless — that is, holy Statutes or universal Ordinances of the Seven Commandments Code.

Certainly, every rabbi of Israel will agree that God abominates and universally forbids:

1) any act of human cannibalism;
2) promoting cannibalism by marketing human blood or flesh for food;
3) cooking or butchering any animal[11] while it is still alive; and,
4) torturing, taunting, or otherwise causing any creature needless suffering before eating it.[12]

These prohibitions are not matters to be left up to individual choice or personal free will. Heaven requires man, a social being, to act collectively to rid the world of such perversions. Whenever an act is a crime under God's Universal Law, God makes each human society responsible for enacting and enforcing laws to prohibit it.[13]

Another rule is also universal, certain authorities say: You shall neither eat nor drink blood.[14] Some authorities say that this prohibition pertains only to blood drawn from a creature while it is still alive.[15] Others — the mainstream — maintain that Noahides have no obligation to enforce even this less comprehensive ban on blood.

Israel is commanded to avoid all blood.[16] This means, precisely speaking, the arterial blood, and every bit of visible blood, from any creature but fish.[17] (As for fish, their vital fluid — their cold blood — is regarded as mere tissue, along with the rest of the animal. It is not defined as blood at all, for the law's purposes; it does not come under any prohibition.[18])

It seems that God does not desire people to dine on His creatures' blood.[19] Blood belongs to the natural world, though one may also *use* it — for medical, experimental, or agricultural purposes, for instance. These are reasonable uses, so they are perfectly acceptable.[20] But one should not try to add blood to one's diet.

Otherwise, rather than having man eat or drink any blood, God tells us to return it, respectfully, to the natural world.[21]

The question isn't whether a righteous person should refrain from supping on blood, but whether the Rainbow Law on the subject is any more lenient than Israel's.

The answer must be yes (it *is* more lenient), despite the mandatory language of Genesis,[22] based on the logic of our analysis.[23] When the greatest Torah authorities hold different opinions, Noahide courts need not follow the most stringent opinion.

Different opinions may be a Providential sign that Noahides

have no obligation to compel other Noahides in such matters. Worldly courts can leave the enforcement of morality in these areas up to God's heavenly courts. It is **not** incumbent upon every society and state to enforce the Scripture's ban.[24]

God tells mankind clearly that we should neither eat nor drink any blood at all. He absolutely prohibits Israel from doing so. Yet His Law leaves the nations with a free will choice to make in the matter. So long, it seems, as the blood being consumed comes from a creature killed before any of its blood was drained off or its parts torn away, man may please himself — with bloody steaks, blood sausages, or soups — or he may, in the alternative, please his Maker. This is not an area where the state need interfere, necessarily.[25] It need not legislate a prohibition.

———————

Israel must never eat carrion, or the flesh of any animal "which [1] died of itself, or which was [2] torn by beasts."[26] Carrion of the second type — "roadkill," or torn and partly-devoured animal flesh — is obviously unfit, not just for Jews but for all human consumption. Man should take such meat and "throw it to the dogs." It is suitable only for animals.[27]

Carrion of the first type — the flesh of animals that weren't deliberately or properly slaughtered or that died only because of accidents like fire or flood — may sometimes be fit for human use. The people of Israel may not eat it but must not waste it, by feeding it to animals, while human beings hunger. Meat of this sort should normally be clearly marked as carrion and either donated or sold as such to non-Jews.[28]

The Biblical lesson is clear. Because Israel may never encourage nor deliberately provide Gentiles with the means to violate any of God's laws,[29] this first kind of carrion is obviously not subject to a univeral prohibition. Still, as a matter of pure free will, in the interests of personal sanctity if not of health, B'nai Noah would surely be well-advised to avoid every kind of carrion.[30]

Analysis

You shall not eat any abominable thing. — *Deuteronomy 14:3*

This Seventh Commandment is man's introduction to an area of great Heavenly concern and law. At first glance it may seem out of place with the rest of the Rainbow Code. After all, the other Commandments refer to such monumental problems as murder, idolatry, and so on, while this one, the Law of the Torn Limb, apparently directs itself only to the mundane matter of groceries — of the food that we put into our stomachs. But the Revolutionary Law makes a strong connection between savagery and diet.

The Torah recognizes that food affects people — physically, mentally, spiritually, and socially.

Cannibals regard their fellow men as a potential source of meat. Hunters like to initiate their children in the rites of the hunt, of predation, death, and killing. People who enjoy dining on blood or carrion — or on rodents, reptiles, insects, dogs, or monkeys — tend to approach life differently than people who refuse to eat such things.

Even if we interpret the Commandment here so narrowly as to include only the minimal, criminal, laws enumerated above, while reflecting none of the rest of the Torah's detailed, instructive moral ordinances and statutes, we see that each of this Commandment's prohibitions refers to an essentially subhuman act — an act of selfish cruelty or heedless rapacity.

When people approach the bounty of the earth like greedy lower animals, they rebel against man's God-given role as His caretakers. The Almighty didn't elect humanity to rule His Creation just so we could abuse it, devour it, or otherwise slake our appetites. Rather, He calls on us to make the world holy by observing His laws for us.

For you are a holy people unto the Lord your God.
— *Deuteronomy 7:6*[31]

Israel received a very extensive, demanding code of dietary laws, as the Scripture makes clear. God calls His "priests" to holiness in all things.[32] He elevates Israel by its diet, among other things.[33]

Torah sets out the foods that are fit and proper — in Hebrew, *kosher* — for a holy people.[34] It presents a universal standard: these are Heaven's own distinctions, dating from long before the birth of Israel.[35]

Plainly, anyone aspiring to greater refinement may profit from its guidance. The "wise" and "righteous" Law that God entrusted to Israel exists to point the way for others.[36] God created Israel to show humanity His Way.[37] But God has also set basic minimum, criminal, standards. All people — the whole human race — must abide, at a *minimum*, by the less demanding dietary Guidelines contained within God's Universal law.

The question is: what are they, and how can man follow them? The answer should be obvious: by exploring the law in the light of common sense and Torah.

Man-Made Prohibitions

History shows us that without clear — that is, Divine — guidelines, the human race has a genius for doing the wrong thing. In every generation, someone tries to restrict human freedom as to alcohol, tobacco, marijuana, meat, or other substances, and justifies the attempt to force a total ban with an appeal to Ultimate Righteousness. We need to recognize that, while this is often man's way, it has nothing to do with God's.

God's Revolutionary law shows us that He gave humanity the produce of the earth for human use.[38] It teaches that alcohol, for instance, is a uniquely human creation, and that its use — always in moderation — is laden with blessings.[39] "Wine makes glad the heart of man."[40] God explicitly calls on the Jews to rejoice before Him with wine and strong drink, on certain occasions; Israel is commanded, at times, to drink and enjoy wine as a sacrament, to honor the Holy King who makes men free.[41]

God prohibits man from creating taboos against things that He has not forbidden.[42] He entrusts humanity with dominion over the material world and the free will and responsibility to make full use of it. But use must not degenerate into abuse. The Torah warns us against misusing drugs, including alcohol. It is specific and emphatic.[43] Noah's own story, of a righteous man reduced to humiliated drunkenness, is instructive.[44]

Abuse, addiction and misuse impair free will and degrade man's most godlike senses — which amounts to a double betrayal of His trust in us.

We insult the God who gives us freedom, who took care to make us in His "image," when we employ the riches of His world to demean ourselves. Most importantly, God's Revelation to Israel at Sinai teaches the great Revolutionary truth: that human beings come closest to Him when their minds are clear.[45]

Don't overdo righteousness. — *Ecclesiastes 7:17*

"Eat your bread with joy," the Scripture tells Israel; "drink your wine with a merry heart."[46] Please consider, in this context, the historic fact of Israel's remarkable national sobriety. The Jewish people have always managed to sustain one of the world's lowest levels — perhaps *the* lowest, of any people who ever touch drugs or alcohol at all — of drug and alcohol addiction.[47] These diseases from civilization's dawn, the scourge of most other nations, have never really made huge inroads against the renowned temperance of the Jews.

This should tell us plainly, as a matter of history, Torah, and common logic, that total abstention is not part of the price that Heaven exacts for redemption.[48] Israel's strict law is significant, in this respect, for all the things that it *doesn't* forbid.

Many people would like to turn man into a vegetarian. They

would prohibit us from eating any meat or animal flesh at all, condemning it as cruel and immoral. The rabbis respond to them, saying: these crusaders "deny the truth of God," because they place a human understanding of mercy and morality above that of the Father of Mercy and of all true morality.[49]

Scripture speaks of man as a being who naturally eats meat.[50] It describes meat-eating as a God-given right.[51] But the Torah and this Seventh Commandment also teach us that people must procure their meat humanely, and eat it, not like animals might, but like the elect of God's Creation.

> A righteous man regards the soul of his beast. — *Proverbs 12:10*[52]

Note that Torah does *not* give rights to animals, nor does it recognize any such thing. The notion of animal rights, or the rights of trees or plants, is simply oxymoronic: only man — a creature with free will — can choose to exercise a right or accept an obligation.

So man has no obligation to ask permission from the natural world's creatures or things when he uses them.

This Revolutionary principle, so foreign to the man-made "nature" religions, tells us that we may, among other things, cut down a tree without offering prayer or sacrifices to the spirit of the tree; we may kill a deer without any need to magically propitiate the soul of the deer. While man has real obligations to the natural world and its life-forms, our responsibility doesn't come from below but Above. Animals don't have rights but Heaven has obligated us to treat them rightly, with justice and humanity. Our responsibilities to our lesser fellow-creatures don't come from them but from God Himself.

The Sanctity of Life

Each living being has a soul, the Torah teaches. If any man should need a living plant or animal, and can take it within the bounds that God has established, then he has a perfect right to it. Otherwise, the rabbis say, even to tear a leaf from a tree without purpose is a sin.[53]

Israel has plenty to say to the world about the basic Seventh Commandment perversions — the beastly behavior that Heaven universally forbids. Directly or indirectly, every such practice involves the crime and the sin of idolatry.[54]

Drinking blood, the Sages tell us, commonly relates to the pagan practice of trying to magically possess the soul of the creature which gave the blood.[55] The Christian ritual of Mass, which attempts to miraculously transmute wafer and wine into a god's body and blood, to devour them, seems to reflect the same idea.[56] So, in a frighteningly similar way, does the modern mythology of vampirism.

Eating living flesh, or meat torn from the body of a still-living creature, often features in the magical rites of paganism.[57] But this sort of vile act, even when it has nothing to do with mystic ritual, conforms to the common pagan notion that the Earth is a foul and lawless world. The savagery of the act reinforces the frankly idolatrous idea that only power matters, or that God's reality — that is, this world — is mere illusion. *It tells man that he may ignore the pain of animals because their pain somehow doesn't matter.* But the Torah generally, and this Seventh Commandment particularly, teaches that life and the world are real, and that God in His goodness doesn't look kindly upon those who abuse them.

> The Lord is good to all, and His tender mercy lies over all His works. — *Psalm 145:9*

A callous approach to taking life for food leads to a callous approach to life in general.[58] The Torah stresses, again and again, God's love for His Earth and for all its lesser creatures.[59] Cruelty to animals constitutes defiance of God. Perhaps incidentally, it also tends to predict whether one will behave cruelly to humans.[60] Every mass murderer on America's death rows has a history, it's said, of cruelty to animals.[61]

Waste, which is bad husbandry of God's gifts, is irresponsible.[62] Humanity's right of dominion implies the obligation of stewardship; good stewards try to enhance and preserve, not impair, the value of their holdings. All creatures are God's property.[63] To waste the Creator's gifts or demonstrate cruelty to His creatures mocks God's elevation of mankind.

Many modern-day, commonly accepted human practices defy even the minimal requisites of the Universal Law. Devouring a living oyster, for instance — as connoiseurs of "fresh oysters on the half-shell" often do — means eating a still-living animal. If this is not a direct transgression of the Law of the Torn Limb, it is, to say the least, unseemly.[64]

So is eating stone crabs. These animals are harvested by hacking off one of the poor creature's claws — which is cooked and eaten — and then returning the beast to the water, to grow another limb. "Mountain oysters," or amputated testicles, removed in the process of gelding living farm animals, are problematic on several levels. As for such choice Pacific Ocean delicacies as *live* lobster and *live* whitebait, a sea animal that squirms and "dances" on the diner's plate,[65] what can one say?

Certain African tribal habits, involving drinking blood or flaying meat from living cattle, are more or less obviously pagan, perverse — and prohibited. The once-common European practice of bull-baiting — that is, of tormenting an animal before slaughter (usually with bulldogs, so aptly-named, who were actually bred for this specific task[66]) to tenderize the meat, is abhorrent and forbidden.

Secrets of the Hebrews

Speak to the earth, and it shall teach you. — *Job 12:8*

The whole Earth, the Torah teaches, is the Lord's.[67] Man must respect the very ground and seas of God's "very good" planet.[68]

When we look at the Seventh Commandment in the context of Torah, it's clear that every human being owes a duty to God to see that His world and His lesser creatures are fairly treated.

Israel's laws, and particularly the dietary laws known as *kashrut* (literally, "fitness") serve as a constant reminder of that fact. The Scripture doesn't explain the reasons that underlie these Statutes, but man[69] has the right and even the obligation to attempt to understand their benefits, together with the logic of their details.[70] These truths are fairly obvious:

All of the Torah's laws exist for man's own good.[71] The laws of *kashrut* inject a sense of holiness into life's most commonplace functions.

By constant practice, rather than mere theory, the Torah and its dietary laws force man to rise above the heedlessness of his lower, animal nature. *Kashrut*, the laws of clean and unclean, instill discipline and precision, in fulfilling laws that demand both; they require, on a daily basis, even from children, conscious self-restraint.

"Sin dulls the heart," the Talmud teaches.[72] But to employ the body for the needs of the spirit — to put one's intimate habits into God's service — is a great and positive thing. The Torah's "dietary laws train us to master our appetites, and not to consider eating and drinking the end of man's existence."[73] One who regulates such an intimate area of life in willing obedience to God's Law confers a tremendous benefit on the soul.[74]

More prosaically, and at the very minimum, Israel's Law bars the Jews, God's "priests," from living like a nation of hunters, pigkeepers, or scavengers. It keeps killing and slaughtering out of Jewish family life, by entrusting these soul-hardening tasks to a corps of pious specialists.[75]

Please consider: most people used to live close to the land. In contrast to the children of nearly every other nation, very few Jewish children, over more than 150 generations, have ever seen their mothers — or their fathers either, for that matter — so much as chop the head off a chicken. Even the concept of going into the yard to casually slaughter the main course for a meal is alien to Israel. Likewise, no child from any Torah-observant family has ever helped his parents fatten and butcher pigs.

Pork

Israel's law requires the Jews to avoid eating any part of any pig.[76]

None of the kosher food animals have anything like the intelligence — speaking relatively — or the sensitive reactions of the pig. Pigs squeal from pain and fright as a human being might. They have unclean habits. Their dung is unusually foul, and copiously excreted. They happily eat carrion, dung, and vermin. They do no work; they cannot be ridden; they produce no milk nor eggs for human use.

Pig farming is an inherently messy, smelly, cynical business. The *only* reason farmers raise and treat pigs well is to fatten them, to kill them for their flesh.[77] This flesh, some say, resembles human flesh, in its texture and aroma.[78] The cannibals of the South Pacific, for instance, didn't see much difference between "long pig" — man — and real pig. Burnt human flesh smells like burning bacon.

To eat the flesh of pigs, the Torah teaches, is an abominable thing.[79]

The Clean Animals

Kosher food animals — that is, the "clean" food animals[80] — are, by and large: cattle, deer, bison, goats, sheep, fish, and poultry.[81] The kosher mammals are all completely herbivorous, they all walk on cloven hooves, and all chew the cud — that is, they chew and then re-chew their food.

Every creature that chews the cud and also walks on cloven hooves has four stomachs. It spends most of its time processing rough vegetable matter. These species of animals are all relatively passive, dull and docile. They can normally be tamed to live peacefully alongside men, even though men eat them. The Almighty seems to have made them for just that — to serve as an acceptable food by which to sustain human beings.

Similarly, none of the livelier birds, the birds of prey or carrion-eaters, the singing birds, or the birds that build complex or artistic nests, are kosher. Chickens, turkeys, ducks, and geese are all clean species, for example; crows and ostriches are not.[82] Birds from all the clean species can be normally be tamed to live peacefully alongside men, even though we eat them.

All the clean birds have a tri-partitioned digestive system, or three "stomachs" — a crop, a fore-stomach, and the main stomach. While some of these birds will eat fish, or will supplement a vegetable diet with insects, they thrive as vegetarians. And none of the clean birds, even including those that eat fish or insects, have what might be called cruel habits: they don't use their feet or claws for eating or tearing their food. Rather, they all pick up their food directly with their beaks.[83]

Shellfish

True fish have both fins and scales. They are permitted for every man to use as food. All shellfish are unclean. So, for instance, activities like shrimping, clam-digging, oystering, lobstering and frog-gigging (i.e., frog-spearing) are almost unknown to Israel.

This sort of food-scavenging often seems to have a brutalizing effect on those who engage in it. Treating living animals as mere objects to be collected and preserved (alive) for the pot tends to harden people to other creatures' suffering.[84] So does the time-honored practice of cooking the poor animals alive. As for the creatures themselves, the Torah tells the Jews (and

anyone else who may be listening), "they shall be detestable to you; you shall not eat of their flesh."[85]

Shellfish are regarded as "passion foods," which act somewhat like aphrodisiacs. Eating them increases the heart rate, raises the blood pressure, and dilates the blood vessels in the skin. A peculiar sort of food, people "lust" to eat shellfish, as they lust to have sex.[86] But this is not the way of human righteousness. Man should think beyond his stomach; the appetite should serve the soul, not the other way around.

Shellfish-rich diets are considered to engender a coarse, callous, ravenous approach to life.[87] Meanwhile, the Torah teaches Israel (and all humanity) that the foods we eat shouldn't master us.

God orders the Jews to purify their diets, to separate the clean from the unclean, and He commends anyone else who decides to do likewise.[88]

Killing to Eat

Israel's Law bars the Jews from hunting mammals or birds for food, except where nets can be used, or in cases of dire emergency. Although deer meat — venison — is a clean food, for instance, an animal shot by an arrow or bullet is not kosher. Such meat is considered to be carrion — it is torn, or in Hebrew, *treyf* — because the animal was not slaughtered in the quick way that the law demands.[89]

"The Jewish method of slaughter is one continuous cut with the sharpest of knives, applied by a skilled operator. Such a cut severs all the great blood-vessels of the neck, and produces *instantaneous* insensibility in the animal."[90]

This technique, besides minimizing the animal's pain, also maximizes the amount of blood that pours out — all kosher meat is as blood-free as man can make it.[91] Other meat is not permitted.

Apparently, God prefers that people obtain most of their animal protein from their own flocks and herds,[92] rather than by hunting. A Jew who hunts just for sport, for the thrill of the kill, is a sinner.[93] Fishing is permitted, and so is fowling with nets, but otherwise kosher meat comes only from domesticated animals —

and then, only from clean animals — after slaughter and inspection by pious experts.[94]

Milk and Meat

Milk means growth and life for the young of all the higher species. Milk is a symbol of motherhood. It represents the providential mechanism by which the higher creatures, including man, lovingly sustain their own kind — their weakest ones, their youngest.

A basic rule of Torah-interpretation, an invariable Principle, holds that the Written Torah contains no excess words, nor even a single surplus letter.[95] Yet the Torah warns Israel no fewer than *three* times, "You shall not cook a kid [a suckling, a young goat or sheep or calf] in its mother's milk."[96]

Obviously, this is a matter of some importance to God. So we look to the Oral Torah for greater understanding. This Oral Torah tells man that it is unholy — it is unrighteous, or certainly insensitive — to eat meat cooked together with the milk of any mother at all. In fact, Israel may not mix meat with milk for any purpose.[97]

Slapping cheese, made from a live animal's milk, onto a slab of meat — dead flesh — can't be said to be an act of outstandingly good taste. Instead of honoring life, so it seems, it verges on swatting life in the face!

Man may kill and eat the clean animals and may take their milk from them as well — milk coming from a clean source is itself clean[98] — but no man needs the added triumph of adding insult to their injuries by devouring both their life's milk and their flesh together.

Furthermore, the combination of the foods is fatty and gross.[99] A person may have milk, which is usually easily digested, and follow it with meat, but to put milk into the stomach right after eating meat leads to feeling heavy and overfull.[100]

Many people seem to like that sensation, of feeling like an overstuffed animal. But this is not the way that God would have us go through life. The people of Israel, at least, must wait some time

— a decent interval — after eating meat before eating or drinking any kind of milk product.[101]

Medicinal Herbs, Magic Potions, and Cures

Israel's Law, and the Revolutionary Law generally, opposes every kind of idolatry, witchcraft and superstition.[102] Unfortunately, physicians and other so-called healers can be superstitious. Still, God permits a sick person to use "whatever is used as medicine" — but only so long as the drug or other therapy "is recommended by reason." Other so-called "cures" are forbidden.[103]

If one hopes that some therapy or potion will heal the body by means of magic, as by an attempt to compel supposed external spiritual forces, the Torah generally will condemn its use: that manner of thinking is idolatrous.[104] If, on the other hand, one hopes that a cure will work in the normal way — that is, through normal psychological or bodily processes — it doesn't matter whether or not anyone can rationally explain how that cure works: the Torah generally will approve of its use.[105] Even therapies that have been associated with idolatry, such as Chinese acupuncture, or some of the "native medicines" of sorcerers or witch doctors, may be permitted. So long as one understands that such cures work, when they work, on a natural level, medicine may use "everything which has been verified by experiment."[106]

Cleanliness and Grace

Personal cleanliness is a general requirement of Torah.[107] For example, Jews must wash their hands before every meal.[108] To eat a meal without first cleansing the hands, the Torah says, is reprehensible.[109] Dirty hands are unfit for the recital of Grace.[110] And saying Grace after meals — that is, a prayer of thanks — is a strict Torah obligation.[111]

Rabbis explain that, just as a guest should thank his host after receiving human hospitality, God's human "guests" on this planet owe thanks to the One ultimate Source of all hospitality.[112] The conventions of ordinary politeness, regardless of Torah regulations, demand no less. So this may be another matter in which a God-fearing Gentile should seek to follow observant Israel's example.[113] Again, the "wise" and "righteous" Law that God gave Israel exists to point the way for others.[114]

Kindness to Animals

Israel's Law, and this Seventh Commandment, teach us that God is King, even in the dining room and kitchen. To the great credit of the human race, children usually understand the lesson readily. It is up to us — adult humanity — to infuse these places with some holiness. This matter does not stop at the dining table. God's mercy extends beyond man to all His creatures, obviously: the discipline that He imposes on the family sitting at its own table extends beyond the table into every aspect of human life.

Cultivate gentleness. — *Talmud, Ta'anit 4a*

God is the Creator and owner of *everything*.[115] As we see from His dietary laws, He cares what we do with our dominion. He requires us to treat it, and particularly the lesser beings under our control, with kindness, with mercy and, most of all, with justice.[116]

Thus the Law of the Torn Limb, the Universal

Commandment, leads us to Torah, which teaches man what God means by justice.

> Loving-kindness is a sin offering for nations.
> — *Talmud, Bava Batra 10b*[117]

To treat our fellow creatures gently is a strict Torah obligation, not an option. So the people of Israel are taught, for example, that one must feed the beasts in his care even before he himself eats.[118] A working animal must not be muzzled to prevent it from eating of the food it sees as it labors.[119] Man should not yoke together two creatures of different species and varying strength,[120] nor slaughter an animal with its young on the same day,[121] nor mutilate any of God's creatures.[122] One may never inflict pain upon an animal out of mere vengeance nor frustration;[123] to neglect to relieve an animal of pain or danger is a sin, the Torah teaches.[124]

While these may seem like small matters,[125] they teach an all-important lesson. Through details like these, the Torah spells out the proper role and place of man in God's Creation.

The Sabbath

> God blessed the Seventh day, and He declared it to be holy.
> — *Genesis 2:3*

Consider the miracle of the Sabbath.[126] The Seventh Rainbow Covenant Commandment here, and the Fourth Commandment of Israel's Ten Commandments, both teach certain very similar things.

Moses commanded his followers to rest even their animals, and also their human servants, along with themselves, every seven days.[127] Clearly, if nothing else, this was history's most radical advance in labor legislation.

No slave has the freedom to take a whole-day holiday completely for himself; compared to the Sabbath, the meaning of the more modern fight for the 40-hour week pales almost into insignificance. *Shabbath*, or *Shabbos*, as most English-speaking Jews call it, or *Shabbat*, as most Israelis pronounce it, recalls Israel's transformation from a slave to a free people.[128] But it also exists to celebrate and commemorate the whole of humanity's exalted place in Creation.[129]

In that respect the message of the Sabbath is unconditionally and absolutely universal. In fact, it's close to that of the no-less universal law that we've been examining here, this broad Seventh Noahide Commandment. We can understand more about both of them if we look at them both in association, in a larger context.

After creating people, the Torah says, God stopped — He took a break.[130] That is, He didn't choose to go on making better and better beings. Rather, He finished at humanity. So He nominated us, ordinary men and women, for greatness, to be His vice-regents on Earth, responsible only to Him.[131]

The Lord's Sabbath stands for the proposition that human beings have the right to stand at the forefront of Creation. More than that, it means that we have God's permission to enjoy our dominion, guided by His Law.[132]

> Happy is the man who does this, and the son of man who holds fast by it: who keeps the Sabbath from profaning it, and keeps his hand from doing any evil. — *Isaiah 56:2*

Just as God ceased from creating on the Seventh day, He commands the Hebrews to do likewise: to rest — with their families, guests, employees and animals, and even their land — from all work, to enjoy the fruits of Creation.[134] It's a holy island in time, to stop, reset, recharge, and then finally restart (when it's over). A day for the spirit, for reading, studying Torah and communing with God, for playing with children, eating, drinking, napping, singing songs and making love, the Sabbath brings man a foretaste of Heaven on earth once a week, every week, 52 days of the year.[135] And then, every Saturday night is a fresh new beginning, a new birth of freedom.

Israel made the seven-day week universal. From the very dawn of time until the end of time as we know it, the Seventh day has always been and will always be *Shabbat*.[136] The time will come, the prophets tell us, when not only Israel but all men — indeed, "all flesh," including our animals — will honor the Seventh day as the Lord would have it honored.[137]

Shabbat expresses the truth that the One God is the Creator, Owner and Master of all, and that man, together with all else, has been called to the service of the One God.[138] It belongs, in all its holiness, only to Israel — to the Jews and to everyone, including animals, who immediately abide with Israel.[139] The symbol of God's rule and man's destiny, God gave the Sabbath to the nation He created to demonstrate man's real task and His eternal Sovereignty to every nation.[140]

Not that anyone of any nation should neglect the Seventh day's uniqueness. Israel must keep and guard the Sabbath; through the Bible and observant Israel's example, God calls on *all* men to remember it and honor it.[141] Which means, among other things, that we — the whole human race — must always try to perceive it in its proper light.

Remember that man-made religion is a contradiction in terms, and that misappropriating what isn't yours is vile. Israel has a special relationship to Shabbat — and to the other Hebrew holy days — and people outside of Revolutionary Israel, unconnected to the whole of Torah, must respect it. B'nai Noah may not create artificial Sabbaths nor invent phony holy days for themselves.[142] They stand in a different relation than Israel to Shabbat — it's simply part of God's plan.

B'nai Noah honor God by respecting Him, His holidays, His Torah, and Israel.[143] The righteous person doesn't try to bend His holy days, entirely appropriate — that is, misappropriate — them, nor observe or invent new and unholy holy days.

This person doesn't try to create any new religions beyond the true religion — the Revolutionary path — that God has given.[144] Rather, he worships God in all aspects of his life, honors the Lord's Name wherever life may take him; and tries, through the practice of goodness as he learns goodness through Torah, to come as close to God as he can.

Our Creator has nominated us all for blessings and honors by appointing us — men and women, the whole human race — to our awesome exalted position in His Creation. The great unconditionally universal message of the Sabbath is one with that, and with the lesson of this Seventh Rainbow Covenant Commandment.

By God's will, man's true occupation is nothing less than the management of the world. We work at this six days out of every seven. Yet as the last, Seventh, day exists to eternally remind us, our authority is borrowed; whatever we may claim to own, our rights of ownership are never absolute.[145] Precisely as this Seventh Noahide Commandment should teach us, *everything* belongs to God, the Creator and Lawgiver, who has set man to rule it according to His will — with wisdom, justice, humility, and kindness.

NOTES

1. Taboo, "a prohibition against touching, saying, or doing something for fear of immediate harm from a supernatural force." *Webster's Tenth Collegiate Dictionary* (Merriam-Webster Co., Springfield MA, 1993).

2. Genesis 1:26.

3. Genesis 9:3.

4. Genesis 1:27. Not that God has any simian or animal characteristics. Having taken man, like "clay," out of the natural, animal world, He somehow infused us with godly, definitely non-animal characteristics — with a rational intelligence, language, and free will that make us somewhat like Him.

5. Talmud, *Nedarim* 10a, *Yevamot* 62b.

6. R. Yirmeyahu Bindman, *Seven Colors of the Rainbow*, supra, p. 112.

7. See Genesis 9; *Yad* (Maimonides' *Mishneh Torah*, the *Yad Chazaka*), *Hilchot Melachim* 9:1; Lichtenstein, *Seven Laws of Noah*, supra, p. 53.

8. Lichtenstein, supra, p. 54.

9. Genesis 9:4 (with Rashi); Leviticus 17:12-15; Deuteronomy 12:23. See Talmud, *Hullin* 102b, *Sanhedrin* 59a. This statute does not apply to creatures that are ordinarily invisible, including the lowest animals — microbes — and other neurologically relatively rudimentary invertebrates, such as the smaller insects. Neither does it normally apply to fish (that is, to true fish; see below) once one has taken them out of their natural element — water. See *Shulchan Aruch, Yoreh De'ah* 13, 84.

10. See Lichtenstein, supra, p. 56.

11. Fish — that is, true fish, with fins and scales — fall into a peculiar category of their own. Once they are removed from the water, their natural element, they become insensible: they may be eaten, cut or cooked, although to do so while they are still alive is a misdemeanor (under ancient rabbinic ordinance) if one is a Jew, and at least "unseemly" if one is not. See *Shulchan Aruch, Yoreh De'ah* 66.

12. On these four prohibitions generally, see Mishnah, *Avodah Zorah* 12:11; Talmud, *Hullin* 91a-92b, *Berachot* 33b, 40b, *Gittin* 62a; Deuteronomy 25:4 with Rashi; *Yad, Hilchot Hovel uMazik* 5; *Shulchan Aruch, Hoshan Mishpat* 420:1. On cannibalism particularly, see J.D. Bleich, *Contemporary Halachic Problems*, supra, Vol. 1, pp. 194-196. The Torah doesn't just speak of cannibalism as an abomination, but as something almost unutterably awful, a monstrous reversal of all natural order. See, e.g., Deuteronomy 28:53-57; 2 Kings 6:28-29; Jeremiah 19:9; Lamentations 2:20.

13. *Yad, Hilchot Melachim* 9:14.

14. See Genesis 9:4; Leviticus 3:17, 7:26-27, 17:12-15; Mishnah, *Tosefta Avoda Zorah* 8:6, 8:8; Rashi on *Sanhedrin* 56b, 59a. "The blood is the life" (Genesis, ibid): for man to dine on a creature's blood [fish blood not being regarded as true blood, at least in this respect] is more or less the equivalent of devouring the creature alive. (Rashi's commentary.) But also see *Yad, Hilchot Melachim* 9:10: despite the Torah-prohibition, there is no sweeping Noahide prohibition against consuming animal blood. In fact, this second view represents prevailing opinion, the holding of most authorities.

15. See Talmud, *Sanhedrin* 56a (R. Hanania ben Gamaliel).

16. See Leviticus, ibid.

17. See Horeb, supra, 4:68, Sec. 451. Non-arterial blood can be burned off or carbonized by heat.

18. *Shulchan Aruch, Yoreh De'ah* 66.

19. Genesis, ibid.

20. Talmud, *Bava Metzia* 32b, *Sanhedrin* 59a, *Moreh Nevuchim* 3:17, 3:37.

21. Leviticus 17:13 with Rashi.

22. Genesis, ibid.

23. Pending an authoritative determination of the exact parameters of this Commandment. See Leviticus 17:14, *Sefer HaMitzvot* 2:184. Punishment is not for human courts but for Heaven's to impose.

24. See *Yad, Hilchot Melachim* 9:10 and 9:14.

25. Similarly, in the case of a live bird with a torn-off wing, a Noahide but not a Jew may be legally permitted to eat the wing. See *Yad, Hilchot Melachim* 9:11 with commentaries. This obviously doesn't mean that the

Noahide *should* do so; rather, a righteous person will usually voluntarily abstain from such torn flesh, even though Noahides apparently have no obligation to legally compel others to this effect.

26. Leviticus 17:15-16. But fish may be eaten even though they may have "died of themselves." See commentaries.

27. Exodus 22:31; Rama Mi Fano, *Asarah Ma'amarot* (c. 1570 CE), supra, *Hekur Din* 3:21; S. R. Hirsch, Torah Commentary, Deuteronomy 12:21.

28. Deuteronomy 14:20 with Rashi; *Shulchan Aruch, Yoreh De'ah* 23, 57. In the United States, many states donate the deer killed in auto accidents to feed the poor.

29. Leviticus 19:14; Deuteronomy 27:18; *Shulchan Aruch, Yoreh De'ah* 151.

30. See Leviticus 17:13-16; Deuteronomy 14:2-3.

31. Regarding food, also see, e.g., Exodus 22:31.

32. See Exodus 22:30; Deuteronomy 7:6, 14:2, 24:15.

33. Exodus 22:30.

34. Leviticus 11 and Deuteronomy 14 list the living animals that are "clean" (that is, not detestable or abominable) for the human diet.

35. Genesis 7:2,8, 8:20. See Leviticus 10:10,11; Deuteronomy 14; Rashi.

36. Deuteronomy 4:6-8; See, e.g., Genesis 7; 1 Kings 8:43; Psalm 19:9; Zechariah 8:23; *Yad, Hilchot Melachim* 10:10.

37. Exodus 19:6; Isaiah 42:6, 45:22, 49:3; Jeremiah 16:17-19; *Yad, Hilchot Melachim* 8:10. Also see the Christian Gospels, Matthew 23:2.

38. Genesis 9:3; Rashi.

39. Genesis 9:20; See Judges 9;13; Psalm 104:15; Proverbs 31:6-7; Talmud, *Nazir* 19a.

40. Psalms, ibid.

41. See Deuteronomy 14:26; Numbers 28-29; Mishnah, *Berachot* 6:1.

42. Deuteronomy 4:2, 13:1. Note that Eve sinned when she characterized God's law as more restrictive than it really was. (Genesis 3:3.) However, society can enact its own man-made ordinances as safeguards, "to make a fence" around the Law (Mishnah, *Pirke Avot* 1:1), to prevent people from violating actual Commandments of law. Leviticus 18:30 with Rashi; Talmud, *Yevamot* 21a. See Deuteronomy 17:11; Talmud, *Berachot* 2a. Regarding marijuana, or *kanbos*, see Talmud, *Eruvin* 29b, *Bava Batra* 92b, *Ketuvot* 17b with Rashi.

43. See, e.g., Deuteronomy 21:20; Isaiah 5:11; Proverbs 24:29.

44. Genesis 9:20-34. See commentaries.

45. Leviticus 10:9-10; Talmud, *Eruvin* 64a; *Sefer HaMitzvot* 2:73. Furthermore, "One who recites the prayers while drunk is like one who worships idols." Talmud, *Berachot* 31b.

46. Ecclesiastes 9:7. See Talmud, *Pesachim* 106a.

47. See Charles R. Snyder, *Alcohol and the Jews* (Free Press, Glencoe IL, 1958/Southern Illinois University Press, Carbondale IL, 1978); Leo Landman, *Judaism and Drugs* (Committee of Synagogue Relations, Federation of Jewish Philanthropies, New York NY, 1973). As a group, traditionally observant Jews suffer far less from alcoholism than do Reform Jews, while Reform Jews have far fewer alcoholics per capita than do completely non-observant Jews. See Snyder, supra, pp. 128-40, 162-167.

48. Ordinarily. But some people suffer from extreme or pathological

reactions to alcohol or other drugs, or cannot use them in moderation. If a risk exists that some substance might endanger one's health or dominate one's life, true morality and common sense urge abstention. See Deuteronomy 4:9, 22:8; *Yad, Hilchot Rotzeach* 11:4; *Moreh Nevuchim* 3:33,48.

49. R. Yacov Culi, *Me'am Lo'ez* (c. 1724 CE) on Exodus 8:22. For an alternative, pro-vegetarian look at these issues, see Richard H. Schwartz, Ph.D., *Judaism and Vegetarianism* (Micah Publications, Marblehead MA, 1988).

50. Deuteronomy 12:20.

51. Id. Still, neither is meat-eating an obligation. One should ordinarily eat no more meat than one's "soul [actually] desires" (Deuteronomy 12:20). But vegetarianism isn't necessarily a measure of enlightenment. See *Me'am Lo'ez,* supra. Further, anyone who eats cheese or drinks milk should know that "a cow has to have a calf every year to keep producing milk, and those calves are raised for beef." Temple Grandin, *Thinking in Pictures* (Doubleday, New York NY 1995) p. 202. According to Dr. Grandin, who should know as well as anyone, the clean or kosher animals really are not bothered by proper herding in the slaughterhouse, or even by the smell of blood, and do not know that they are going to their deaths. Slaughtering them according to the rules of kosher slaughter should cause them no pain or fear whatsoever. Grandin, id, pp. 40-42, 140, 155, 205-206. Conventional non-kosher slaughter is very problematic: the animals are not always stunned correctly and are not always killed by the "sticking" or cutting to bleed them out — the bleed-out is *never* as thorough or complete as it is in kosher slaughter — and the consequences of any such failure are horrendous. See Gail Eisnitz, *Slaughterhouse* (Prometheus Books, Amherst NY 1997), pp. 29, 42, explaining that animals in some mainstream U.S. facilities are sometimes actually butchered alive — contrary to American law (Title 7, United States Code, Sec. 1902, The Humane Slaughter Act) and God's law of basic decency. Obviously, one would not want to eat such meat. But surely the best response to any operation where people kill animals with awful cruelty and then sell the meat for people to eat is not mere abstention from that meat, as by eating only vegetarian or kosher, nor a crusade to stop people from killing animals for food, but to work to stop the cruelty.

52. Or "life" of the beast, but "soul" *(nefesh)* is more accurate. While God actively sustains every particle and atom in existence, He instills a most unusual quality — the miracle of life — in living, animated beings. The heavenly animating force or spirit in living animals and even plants gives each of them a "soul" of a more or less rudimentary type, Torah teaches. But even the most "soulful" animal has nothing akin to the immortal and in some ways almost godlike soul of the least human being. See footnote following, and Psalm 8:5-10; Midrash, *Genesis Rabbah* 14:3; Talmud, *Ta'anit* 11b.

53. Talmud, *Bava Metzia* 32b. See *Moreh Nevuchim* 3:17; Clorfene & Rogalsky, supra, p. 100.

54. All of God's laws are laws against idolatry. *Yad, Hilchot Yesodey HaTorah* 1:1; *Moreh Nevuchim* 3:29. See, e.g., Exodus 20:3,20; Deuteronomy 7:5, 12:2; Psalm 83:18; Midrash, *Sifre* on Numbers 15:22.

55. See Genesis 9:4 and Leviticus 17:4 with Rashi. As English-language dictionaries note, even the word "bless" is derived from "blood," and from the use of blood in pagan consecration ceremonies.

56. See the Christian Gospels, Matthew 26:26-28, Mark 14:22, Luke

22:19-20.

57. *Moreh Nevuchim* 3:48.

58. *Moreh Nevuchim* 3:48.

59. See, e.g., Genesis 1:31; Exodus 20:7-10, 23:5; Leviticus 19:25, 22:28, 25:6-7; Numbers 22:32, 35:33; Deuteronomy 5:14, 22:6-10, 25:4 with Rashi; Jeremiah 2:7; Jonah 4:11; Psalms 36:7, 145:9, 147:9; Proverbs 12:10; Talmud, *Berachot* 33b, 40a, *Gittin* 62a, *Hagigah* 14b, *Shabbat* 128b.

60. See S. R. Hirsch, *Horeb*, supra, Part 4, Chapter 60, Sec. 416.

61. On this subject generally, see R. Lockwood and A. Church, "Deadly Serious; an FBI Perspective on Animal Cruelty," *HSUS News* (Humane Society of the United States), Fall 1996, pp. 27-30.

62. Talmud, *Shabbat* 67b, 105b. See Deuteronomy 20:19-20.

63. *Horeb*, supra, Sec. 4, Ch. 56, Sec. 400-401.

64. If the beast twitches when hit with a splash of pepper sauce, one knows that it is alive and "fresh." Shellfish are unlike true fish in that they linger, alive and sensitive, out of water. People either freeze them alive (which kills them, but not very quickly) and then eat them, or cook or eat them alive. See e.g., Ian Doré, *Fish and Shellfish Quality Assessment* (Osprey-Van Nostrand Reinhold, New York NY 1991) pp. 43-49.

65. See "Moveable Feast," *Newsweek* Magazine, May 20, 1991, p. 6.

66. *Encyclopaedia Britannica.* Bull-baiting remained commonplace well into the twentieth century.

67. Psalm 24:1. See Exodus 9:29.

68. Genesis 1:3.

69. That is, all men (meaning, of course, women too). But one must also understand — this point cannot be too-often repeated — that Israel's Bible is the property of Israel, the Jews. Through the Torah, God guides and instructs all men by means of a Law that directly *commands* only Israel.

70. *Yad, Terumah* 4:13, *Teshuvah* 3:4, *Mikvaot* 11:12; *Moreh Nevuchim* 3:26, 3:29, 3:31. See A. Kaplan, Digest of Torah Thought, supra, 5:38.

71. Deuteronomy 6:24, 10:13. On the kosher food laws and their many undoubtedly significant benefits to human hygiene and physical well-being — these health issues not being treated here — see Hertz, supra, p. 459. One should note that, while kosher meat usually costs more than equivalent cuts of non-kosher meat, it keeps better and stays fresher, since it contains the very minimum of blood, which is a growth medium for bacteria. (In kosher slaughter, the animal loses consciousness and dies *before* the heart stops pumping blood.)

72. Talmud, *Yoma* 39a. Also see Moshe Chayim Luzzatto, *Mesillat Yesharim/The Path of the Upright* (popular commentary, c. 1747 CE), ch. 11 (middle): "Any transgression of God's Law tends to stupefy man's heart, making it coarse and beastlike, and steeped in worldly grossness. This is especially true regarding forbidden foods, since food enters the body and becomes part of one's very substance."

73. *Moreh Nevuchim* 3:35.

74. Leviticus 11:42-44 with Rashi.

75. Slaughtering is the job of the *shochet*, who is learned in the law and theory of *shechitah*, or "ritual slaughter," experienced by means of apprenticeship, and ordained with the diploma called *kabbalah* (not to be confused with the mystic doctrines of the same name). If the *shochet* peforms

poorly, or if other conditions are not right, kosher or ritual slaughter can cause the creature being slaughtered much needless pain, which is, of course, utterly disgraceful. But disgraceful isn't necessarily criminal; in contrast with other methods of slaughter, at least the procedures of kosher "ritual" slaughter guarantee, absolutely and at the very least, that no animal is ever butchered alive.

.   76. Deuteronomy 14:8. The pig seems to tell man, "See, I am pure!" because its hooves, or trotters, are split — that is, cloven. Only by close observation or internal examination does one discover that swine are unclean, as a species that does not chew the cud (see below). So to people who abhor hypocrisy, the pig is a veritable symbol of false appearances. Midrash, *Leviticus Rabbah* 13, *Midrash Tehillim* 80. At the same time, the pig is more sensitive — it reacts to the smell of blood and death, for instance — and also usually less cooperative than any of the kosher animals, so killing it without causing it fear and pain is quite difficult. See the horror stories in Eisnitz, *Slaughterhouse*, supra, pp. 61-105. Also See John Mettler, Jr., *Basic Butchering of Livestock and Game* (Storey Communications, Pownal VT 1986), pp. 39-44.

77. Furthermore, any kind of large-scale pig-farming would harm the land of Israel, or any hot, dry region. Waste disposal is problematic. Also, pigs can't sweat, so they need plenty of moisture to regulate their body temperatures. Neither can they metabolize grass, or other fibrous, dry-land products.

78. Perhaps more importantly, "The pig's stomach resembles that of a human." Talmud, *Ta'anit* 21b.

79. Deuteronomy 14:3. See *Moreh Nevuchim* 3:48. Some say that pork and shellfish will be permitted to Israel in times to come, *Midrash Tehillim* 146:4. But since the law that forbids these substances is eternal — Deuteronomy 13:1 — this tradition undoubtedly refers only to a perfected synthesis of such foods sometime in the future, probably along the lines of today's ersatz crabmeat and vegetable-based "bacon bits."

80. See Genesis 7:2,8, 8:20; Leviticus 10:10,11; Deuteronomy 14.

81. See Leviticus 11. Fish must have scales and fins; no bird of prey is kosher. As a general rule with several exceptions, the clean animals are those that the unclean animals — the omnivores and predators — pursue. Note that horses are unclean, as are dogs, cats, rabbits, bats, shellfish, octopi and squid, catfish, jellyfish, sea mammals, sharks, reptiles, hippos, rhinos, camels, llamas, bears, monkeys, amphibians (including frogs), all insects except for certain grasshoppers (which Israel can no longer identify reliably), kangaroos and all marsupials, and rodents. Leviticus 11, and commentaries.

82. Some birds, such as certain species of doves, and pheasant, grouse, etc., are also clean. In case of doubt, Israel looks for telltale signs of cleanliness, but generally refrains from eating any species that isn't traditionally regarded as a clean species. *Shulchan Aruch, Yoreh De'ah,* Sec. 82. Eggs from the clean birds are clean (Id., 86), so long as no blood is found therein, but the products of the unclean are unclean (Id., 81). So the eggs of ostriches and songbirds, for instance, are considered unclean foods.

83. See Hirsch, *Horeb,* supra, Chapter 68, a fascinating study on the matter of food. But even Rav Hirsch ignores one part of the problem: Some wild bird species, such as the ostrich, simply cannot be farmed — grown and

harvested for food — without causing them excessive suffering. See R. Farinato and D. Kuemmerle, "The Ratite Craze," *HSUS News*, supra, Fall 1996, p. 14-17. (Birds of the ostrich family are known as ratites.)

84. Unlike true fish, shellfish do not die or immediately become shocked or insensible once removed from the water. Rather, they linger, alive and still responsive to the touch; man must prolong their pain to keep them from spoiling. See Doré, *Fish and Shellfish Quality Assessment*, supra, ibid.

85. Leviticus 11:11.

86. See Mishnah, *Pirke Avot* 4; *Moreh Nevuchim* 3:33.

87. Talmud, *Yoma* 39a; *Moreh Nevuchim*, ibid. Anyone who finds this idea hard to accept should visit an expensive seafood restaurant to watch people selecting lobsters from a tank and then devouring them.

88. See Genesis 7; Deuteronomy 4:6-8; Isaiah 56:6; Psalm 19:9, 119:1; *Yad, Hilchot Melachim* 10:10; *Moreh Nevuchim* 3:8: all the laws of Torah aim at the well-being of the body and the soul. Also see Proverbs 3:17. As for the non-kosher animals, it's hard to see much difference in principle between eating pig and eating aardvark, say, or mouse, or bear.

89. See Deuteronomy 12:21, referring to the regulations of the Oral Torah. The rules of animal slaughter are fully set out in the *Shulchan Aruch, Yoreh De'ah* 1-28. Also see J.H. Hertz, *Pentateuch and Haftorahs*, supra, on Deuteronomy 12:21.

90. Hertz, supra, commentary on Deuteronomy 12:21 (p. 803).

91. See Hirsch, *Horeb*, supra, Sec. 451 (1). Salting, to drive out any remaining blood, and repeated washing are also part of the koshering process. Id., and *Shulchan Aruch, Yoreh De'ah* 69-71, 74-78.

92. See Genesis 4:2-5, and commentaries.

93. See, e.g., Talmud, *Avoda Zorah* 18b on Psalm 1:1, describing the way of the sinner.

94. *Shulchan Aruch, Yoreh De'ah* 1. Evidence of certain injuries or disease make meat unfit. Id., 29-59.

95. See Psalm 19:8; Talmud, *Sanhedrin* 99b, *Eruvin* 21b; Thirteen Principles of Faith, supra, Principle 8; *Moreh Nevuchim* 3:50.

96. Exodus 23:19, 34:26; Deuteronomy 14:21.

97. Talmud, *Hullin* 115b; *Shulchan Aruch, Yoreh De'ah* 87-89, 91-97. While the Torah merely forbids eating meat and milk that were cooked (i.e., heated) together, the more extensive prohibition is rabbinic, a "fence" around the Divine law.. That Gentiles might take this restriction upon themselves may seem like an eccentric proposition, but the rabbis of Israel sit, as it were, in Moses' seat, so why should people presume to ignore the rabbinic law here? At the same time, the frightful moral symbolism — even disregarding any bad physical or health effects — of combining animal (i.e., mammal) flesh and milk or milk products, to eat them together, tends to put one off such recipes.

98. As eggs from clean birds are clean. *Shulchan Aruch, Yoreh De'ah* 81. Only two clean foods issue from unclean — not kosher — creatures: mother's milk, for the suckling human infant, and honey.

99. See *Moreh Nevuchim* 3:48. This barbaric mixture also often figures in pagan ritual. It's a natural: to attempt, by combining symbols of life and death, to magically win power over life and death. Id.

100. See *Moreh Nevuchim*, ibid. Also see Genesis 18:8, with

commentaries. The Torah tells us that Abraham would serve his dry and dusty guests cooling milk dishes as a refreshing appetizer and only then offer them meat.

101. *Shulchan Aruch, Yoreh De'ah* 87-89. Six hours is generally accepted; some communities, by custom, permit a shorter interval. Incidentally, pious people also wait after eating hard cheese, which the stomach digests only slowly, before having any meat, lest the two substances be digested simultaneously. Id.

102. See, e.g., Exodus 22:17; Leviticus 19:4, 31; Deuteronomy 11:16, 12:30, 18:10; Talmud, *Shabbat* 67a; *Yad, Hilchot Sanhedrin* 14:3, *Hilchot Avodat Kochavim* 11:14; *Sefer HaMitzvot* 2:30-38; *Sefer HaHinnuch,* Imperative 62.

103. Moreh *Nevuchim* 3:37. See Talmud, *Sanhedrin* 59a.

104. *Moreh Nevuchim,* ibid. See Leviticus 18:3 and Midrash, *Sifra* on Leviticus 18:3. Placebos, even if they supposedly work by magic, are generally permitted. See Julius Preuss, M.D., *Biblical and Talmudic Medicine* (1911), translated by Fred Rosner, M.D. (Hebrew Publishing Company, New York NY, 1983), the best book available on all these issues.

105. That is, so long as the practitioner's attempted cure doesn't require the patient to honor or pay homage to any idol, independent power, or other false god. See Talmud, *Avoda Zorah* 12, *Sanhedrin* 64b; *Sefer HaMitzvot* 2:6.

106. *Moreh Nevuchim* 3:37.

107. See Isaiah 52:11; Talmud, *Shabbat* 50b. *Pesachim* 11b; *Yad, Tumat Ochlin* 15:12.

108. *Yad,* id., Talmud, *Hullin* 106a, Sotah 4b; *Shulchan Aruch, Orach Haim* 4:1, 158:1. However, not every snack is a meal.

109. See note above, and Talmud, *Sotah* 4b. Rabbenu Assi says that it "is like prostituting oneself."

110. See the two notes above, and Talmud, *Berachot* 53b.

111. Deuteronomy 8:10-18; *Mishnah Tosefta, Berachot* 7:1; *Sefer HaMitzvot* 1:19. By logical inference, Israel is also required to say a blessing or prayer of thanks *before* eating or enjoying any good thing. To do so is to refine the soul by acknowledging the true Source of all sustenance; to fail to do so is regarded as being not merely crude, but larcenous. Talmud, *Berachot* 35a. See *Horeb,* supra, Sec. 673.

112. Talmud, *Sotah* 10b, *Berachot* 35a-b; Midrash, *Genesis Rabbah* 54:8. See, e.g., Psalms 92:2, 106:1.

113. See Psalm 117:1.

114. Deuteronomy 4:6-8. See 1 Kings 8:43; Psalm 19:9; Zechariah 8:23.

115. Genesis 1:1; Exodus 9:29; Psalm 24:1; Talmud, *Derech Eretz* 1:1, 24.

116. See Exodus 23:5; Leviticus 22:28; Deuteronomy 20:19-20; 22:6-7, 24:4; and commentaries. Generally, see Deuteronomy 16:20; Amos 5:24; *Horeb,* supra, Sec. 4; *Moreh Nevuchim* 3:48.

117. "The Torah begins and ends with kindness," Talmud, *Sotah* 14. Israel has long held that the quality of compassion distinguishes all who follow Torah. See Talmud, *Beitzah* 32b; *Yad, Hilchot Avadim* 9:8. Also see Proverbs 14:34, discussing the quality of *tzedaka* — righteousness or charity.

118. Talmud, *Berachot* 40a.

119. Deuteronomy 25:4. Not just the "ox treading the corn." This concern applies to every animal. (Rashi.)

120. Deuteronomy 22:10.

121. Leviticus 22:28.

122. Talmud, *Berachot* 33b.

123. *Sifre* (Midrash) to Numbers 22:28.

124. Exodus 23:5; Talmud, *Shabbat* 128b. See *Sefer HaMitzvot* 1:202, 2:270. This biblical obligation supersedes even those rabbinic ordinances that safeguard the Sabbath. Talmud, id.

125. The Christian Scriptures simply don't mention kindness to animals nor the prevention of cruelty against them, at least not directly or specifically. Neither does the Koran.

126. In Hebrew, *Shabbos* or *Shabbot* (see Exodus 20:8 or Deuteronomy 5:12), coming from a root meaning "to cease," "desist," or "rest," and closely related to *Sheva* — "seven."

127. Exodus 20:8.

128. Deuteronomy 5:15.

129. See Exodus 20:8-10, 31:13-17; and commentaries.

130. Genesis 2:2. That is, He withdrew from active creation to invisible guidance of the universe.

131. See Talmud, *Sukkot* 5a; Rashi on Genesis 2:2.

132. Genesis 2:16-17; Talmud, *Sanhedrin* 58b; Rashi.

133. Note that the reference is to man and to the son or descendant of man (in Hebrew, *ben Adam*) rather than to Jews or Hebrews alone. See also, e.g., Isaiah 56:6-8, 66:23; and commentaries.

134. See Exodus, 20: 8-10, 31: 13-17; Deuteronomy 5:12-15; Jeremiah 17:21-22; Isaiah 58:13-14; Rashi on Genesis 2:2; *Kuzari* 2:48, 50; *Moreh Nevuchim* 3:41-43.

135. See Isaiah 58:13; *Genesis Rabbah* (Midrash) 17.5; *Mechilta* (Midrash) to Exodus 31:13.

136. Genesis 2:1-3; Exodus 31:13-17.

137. See Isaiah 56:2, 66:23; Zechariah 14.

138. *Horeb*, supra, para. 139.

139. Exodus 31:17 — it is a special "sign" or symbol between God and Israel forever.

140. See *Horeb*, supra, ibid.

141. Obviously. But note the difference in the nature of these obligations. See Exodus 31:13,17; Talmud, *Sanhedrin* 58b-59a, *Keritot* 9a and *Yevamot* 48b with Rashi; *Yad, Hilchot Melachim* 10:9. B'nai Noah are well-advised to honor this holy day, and their Maker, by refraining from some but not all workaday activities. Also see J. D. Bleich, "Observance of *Shabbat* by a Prospective Proselyte and by a *Ger she-Mal ve-Lo Toval* [a partially committed, circumcised, male conversion candidate]" in *Tradition* magazine, vol. 25:3, Spring 1991, pp. 46-62; Exodus 31:17 with Rashi.

142. *Yad, Hilchot Melachim*, ibid.

143. See, e.g., Exodus 4:22, 19:5, Leviticus 20:26; Isaiah 42:6,49:1; Hosea 2:21; Psalm 148:14.

144. Inventing phony rites and holy days is idolatrous, obviously, and perhaps more specifically, rebellious. See id., and commentaries. This certainly doesn't mean that B'nai Noah can't honor or prayerfully commemorate whatever days or events that seem honorable to them, like national memorials or personal anniversaries. But they shouldn't observe Torah-denying rites or holidays. Torah holidays can be shared by everyone,

upon the Torah's terms. B'nai Noah should refrain from appropriating them as their own complete Sabbath days — Divinely commanded days of feasting, joyful worship, and *total* rest from work. For the work-activities prohibited, see Mishnah, *Shabbat* 7:2. Also see *Yad, Shabbat* 30:2-10, on positive observances. Significantly, Rashi indicates that a Gentile — the texts that have come down to us use the term *nochri*, meaning heathen, or foreign pagan — who renounces idolatry should definitely keep *Shabbat*, because desecrating the Sabbath is itself a species of idolatry (Talmud, *Yevamot* 48b). Maimonides speaks only of an *akkum* — an idolator — as someone who must not fulfill nor otherwise dabble with Shabbat or other characteristic Torah observances *(Yad, Hilchot Melachim* 10:9). Most likely, however, Maimonides is speaking here of any Gentile — i.e., any Gentile living in the land of Israel, as a permanent or long-term resident, in Messianic times *(Yad,* ibid.). This would be a Ben Noah who merely wants to enjoy Shabbat and certain other benefits of Torah that especially attract him, while he keeps aloof from the rest of Torah and the balance of God's Commandments. This person wants to pick and choose Torah practices and rituals as from a cafeteria counter, to create, in essence, a new Gentile religion. He should instead either accept the whole Torah upon himself or just fulfill the Noahide Law (Id.) — the whole moral Law, minus Sinai's Torah-dependent rituals. As for Shabbat, the day in all its glory doesn't belong to him; he has no right to observe it as though it does — i.e., observe it exactly in the manner of observant Israel. To do so would be to intrude on Israel's special national relationship to Shabbat, the liberationist aspect (See Deuteronomy 5:15), beyond the Sabbath's elemental connection to all existence (Exodus 20:11). Obviously — according to Rashi, at least — this does *not* mean that a Ben Noah should desecrate Shabbat by treating it, God forbid, like part of the workaday world.

For the true monotheist, or every follower of the God of Israel, the Seventh day marks the goal and finish of each week. Shabbat sanctifies all the purposeful creative activity — i.e., the "work," or deliberate, foresighted, instrumental activity — that characterizes the workweek. By keeping the Sabbath one imitates God. One commemorates, by personally adopting, God's Own cyclic rhythm of Divine creativity; one dedicates one's own creativity to a completion decreed by Him. To fail to honor Shabbat is to fail to honor Him as the Creator; to honor a different day as one's Sabbath is to honor a different God than the Creator. As for the period of Shabbat itself, which particularly celebrates God's creation of rest, fulfillment, peace and rejoicing, it is especially auspicious for spiritual fellowship and communal worship. Generally, see, e.g., *Horeb*, supra, paras 141-145, 186, 659-660; Yosef Y. Lifshitz, "Secret of the Sabbath" *(Azure,* Jerusalem, Israel. Winter 2001).

145. *Horeb*, supra, paras. 141-142.

THE SIXTH COMMANDMENT

Laws Against Larceny

You shall not steal. — Exodus 20:15

The first human crime, some say, was a Sixth Commandment violation, a crime against property: Adam and Eve ate fruit in the Garden of Eden that was not theirs to use.[1]

God's laws against theft, the Torah tells us, are nearly as difficult to obey as His laws against sexual sins [See the Fifth Commandment, following].[2] Most people possess a natural impulse towards larceny, as the Torah defines the term,[3] and opportunities to commit the crime present themselves almost constantly.[4] But few sins do more to disrupt civil society or degrade humanity's capacity to worthily make use of God's good earth. Larceny, the Torah teaches, actually defiles the Earth.[5]

Mystics associate this Commandment with the yellow of the rainbow.[6]

The broad heading or category of Rainbow Covenant law represented in the universal prohibition here goes beyond the protection of property rights and the sanctity of property. It sets out at least two fundamental monotheistic principles:

- Every human being stands on an equal footing before the Lord. Even against a monarch or a saint, the person who has the best claim and greatest right to a thing is the person who already owns it.[7]

- The Lord is the ultimate Owner of all Creation's riches.[8] The mere things that most people lust after are just "dust" — literally, star dust. Only God and His law are eternal.[9]

Anyone who practices unrighteousness in regard to the possessions of another denies the whole of God's Law and everything that the Bible teaches about God, say the rabbis. "Just as God gave a body to the human spirit as a tool for his human activities, and the body must be respected for the spirit within it; so He gave him (that is, all of us) the Earth with all that is on it and belongs to it so that he may freely acquire it and dispose of it according to his destiny." [10]

The sinner's act of larceny implies that he believes that "the Lord has abandoned the Earth" — that those who sin against their fellow men will not ultimately be punished.[11]

The Torah and the Rainbow Code

You shall not steal anything,[12] God commands Israel; you shall not rob anyone.[13] The Torah forbids theft by stealth or fraud or trickery — stealing — as well as theft by brazen force or threatened violence (robbery).[14]

One who thieves by sneaking is worse, in a sense, than the brazen robber. The robber's crime indicates that he fears society's punishment no more than he fears God's; the sneak-thief's crime tells us that he has no fear of God but only of society.[15] The basic crime in either case is that of taking something that doesn't belong to you (larceny).

God abhors it, regardless of the race, creed, condition, class, gender, age, or national origin of the person doing the taking.

A thief is a thief, whether he steals much or little, from Jew or Gentile. — *Shulchan Aruch*[16]

Practically speaking, this is an area where God, through His law, imposes a single standard of conduct upon the whole human race.[17] Anything less than strict honesty in regard to that which belongs to another verges, at least, upon the felonious. Putting dishonesty into action to effect a deliberately lawless taking is felonious. In this the Torah's laws against larceny are almost identical to the corresponding Rainbow law, this Sixth Universal Commandment.

The only area of significant difference lies in the matter of scheduling penalties, or punishment for misconduct.

Israel's Torah penalties apply only to Israel.[18] So penalties, essentially, are left up to each nation's discretion.[19] Otherwise, the Torah's definitions of larcenous dishonesty and its proscriptions against the crime apply to every nation and to all people[20] — to women, children, and men alike — equally.[21]

Receiving

If there were no receivers of stolen goods, there would be no thieves. — *Midrash*[22]

To knowingly receive stolen property is larceny. The receiver "encourages the thief and induces him to sin." In other words, the receiver not only victimizes the person whose property was stolen but also the thief, as well as damaging the larger society. By accepting stolen goods and giving the thief cash or valuables in return, the receiver more or less creates the crime.

This is a case where the underlying crime — the actual physical removal of another's rightful property — is imputed both to the criminal who first steals the goods and to the criminal who receives them.[23]

Rape and Kidnapping

You shall not "steal" — that is, rape or kidnap — another human being.[24] These are theft crimes, the rabbis tell us, although both are so heinous that they are also likened to murder.[25]

Rape is a kind of kidnapping.[26] The rapist cruelly robs his victim of her basic human right to be secure from violence, from her personhood, her self-worth and her dignity. He takes from her her own body, polluting it, heedless of her own will or self-regard, fiercely denying the fact of her free will — including her God-given right to keep free of pollution.

Rape is an aggravated, intense form of thievery in that it implies such an utter rejection of its victim's humanity: a denial which is equivalent to a denial of the Creator.[27] In kidnapping as in rape, the criminal steals the victim's freedom and tries, in essence, to reduce a human being to the level of an object.[28]

Assault and Battery

Even he who only lifts his hand with the intent to strike another is called wicked. — *Shulchan Aruch*[29]

One who strikes another person, deliberately and without privilege nor permission, is a thief. The batterer serves himself by causing a physical and psychological loss to his victim; his blow robs the victim of the basic right — which society exists to defend — to get through the day secure from others' violence.[30]

Under Israel's Code, a thief must, whenever possible, make restitution: the victim of theft must be restored to his original pre-theft condition.[31] The batterer must pay damages to his victim, fully compensating him for pain, suffering, humiliation, loss of time and wages, medical expenses, and any impairment or disfigurement resulting from the battery.[32] But this iron-clad obligation to make restitution is only Israel's law.

No specific Torah penalties nor rules of restitution apply to B'nai Noah — the Gentile nations — unless B'nai Noah themselves adopt them. And if B'nai Noah do adopt any rule of restitution, they must determine its exact mechanics and ingredients. This seems only natural, really, since what's restorative depends so largely on local social expectations.

Note that, in rape cases, the Torah grants the victim certain equitable, restorative rights — here you absolutely must go to the Oral Torah to make sense of the bare Scripture[33] — but these rights can hardly be called universal. They constitute, for the criminal and his judges, part of a package of legal sanctions or penalties for crime. And, here again, none of the Torah's finely tailored schemes of specific legal penalties for crime apply directly to any nation except Israel. They are details of the Torah, designed for one people only; they are meant to govern Israel and Israel alone. B'nai Noah must legislate their own schedules of penalties for themselves.

Commercial Crimes

If one is honest in his business dealings and the spirit of his fellow creatures takes delight in him, it is accounted to him as though he had fulfilled the whole Torah. — Midrash[34]

Business is central to all civilization: not much happens in the world without money changing hands. In this great sphere of human activity, the Lord of the Universe warns all men: do not try to turn your brother — your fellow man — into your victim; you shall not wrong one another in business;[35] you shall not cheat in business.[36]

Given the breadth of the subject, probably the most that can be done here is to point to some few of the many passages of Torah bearing upon this aspect of the Sixth Commandment, and try to describe their importance:

• You shall not cheat in using measurements or weights.[37]

One who uses imprecise measures can harm countless people in his transactions with them. Even the most repentant trader will find it difficult — if not impossible — to restore the true "benefit of the bargain" to each of them.[38] So transgressions of this law are bound to have extensive consequences.

A merchant who uses weights or measures in business acts in the manner of a judge, the rabbis say. One who uses false measures is like a judge who perverts justice.

This is "sin worse than incest" — a Divinely detested act, polluting and corrupting the land where it happens.[39] As the Bible says, "A false balance is an abomination to the Lord, but a just weight is His delight."[40]

All possible precision in matters of business, in buying, selling, renting, lending or borrowing, is the Torah ideal.[41] You shall give fully unto others that share of your property which is due them.[42]

To steal even a penny from a friend is like taking his life. — *Talmud*[43]

- You shall possess no false weights or measures.[44] "God abhors not only the actual practice of dishonesty, but also the instruments that enable one to commit it."[45]

- You shall not fraudulently shift, remove or change a property mark.[46] This law doesn't just pertain to real estate — real property — but to intellectual property, trademarks and copyrights.[47]

- You shall not oppress an employee by delaying the payment of his wages.[48] The employee, too, is entitled to the benefit of his bargain.

• You shall not wrongfully make off with your employer's property.[49] Embezzlement from one's employer is no less larcenous than brazenly robbing a stranger.

This law prohibits even such "trivial" thefts as taking office supplies from the office or food from the restaurant job, if done without the permission of the employer. Note, however, that an employee who works around food — in a grocery, say, or in a harvest setting — normally expects to snack from the bounty while he works. It is regarded, in certain contexts, as a perquisite of the job. So the employer who denies the employee some such benefit may, in effect, be stealing from the employee.[50]

• You shall not deliberately damage the property that you are paid to tend.[51] The employer, no less than the employee, is entitled to the benefit of his bargain — the work for which he's paying, absent any damage from employee sabotage.

• You shall not demand payment from a debtor at a time when you know that he truly cannot pay.[52] Another name for this is "oppression."

While the precepts above all come under the general ban on larceny, the law adds these specific prohibitions — like those against using false weights — to guard against misunderstanding.[53] Such detailed rules may be usefully extended or applied to help decide similar cases. But the general rule could hardly be clearer: "You shall not wrong one another, but you shall fear your God, for I am the Lord your God."[54]

> When one is first brought [after one dies] before the Heavenly court, the first question asked is, 'Have you [while on earth] dealt honestly?' — *Talmud*[55]

Remember that the Father of justice will certainly exact justice against anyone who abuses any temporary — all things earthly being temporary — power or authority. The power of money gives men authority. Don't wrong your fellow man at all in the course of doing business with him.

A deal is a deal. Do not try to cunningly improve on it once you've pledged your word. God abhors all such "breach of promise" acts, such as non-payment of a loyal worker's wages or his benefits, failing to return a borrowed object, or neglecting to repay a loan. The sin here is to take something of value from your victim while failing to perform your own part of the bargain. It's oppressive, and very close — at least — to outright larceny.[56]

You shall not refuse to pay a just debt,[57] God commands, regarding any unnecessary refusal to pay a legal obligation. Be true to your promises. The Lord didn't bless you with the gift of speech so you could swear falsely — "the check is in the mail," "I've had a long string of bad luck," etc. — in repudiating or refusing to pay a debt.[58]

> The wicked borrow, and pay not, but the righteous deal graciously.
> — *Psalm 37:21*

To oppress someone in your commerce with him is to wrong him as well as the One who bothered to cast you both in His very Image.

Your Creator actively detests any and every act of unfair or unscrupulous price-gouging, whether by a seller or a buyer, as when a seller of food, for instance, dramatically increases his prices to rapaciously "make a killing" in the midst of famine. Or when a purchaser exploits a seller's desperate need for cash to take something at a price ridiculously far below fair market value.[59]

> He who gets riches, and not by right, shall leave them in the midst
> of his days, and at his end he shall be a fool. — *Jeremiah 17:11*

You shall not wrong another human being in "sharp," oppressive or dishonest business dealings,[60] the Torah teaches. You do no credit to the God you purport to follow when you take knowing advantage, for instance, of a seller's mistake in making change.

Perhaps your failure to act in an honest way in the circumstances doesn't constitute a true felony; perhaps no human court will ever punish it. The mistake may be small and your avaricious dishonesty, being passive, may be less a crime than a sin with no penal consequences. But you and your Maker, your Judge, both know that you are trying to get away with something to which you are in no way entitled, that isn't honestly yours, and that doesn't rightfully belong to you.

Crimes of Desire

Coveting is the root from which all crimes spring. — *Midrash*[61]

Israel's Tenth Commandment of the Torah forbids the sin of "coveting" the property or blessings of another.[62] Essentially the same precept constitutes a Rainbow Covenant prohibition. Most authorities agree that it makes up part of the general, universal prohibition against stealing.[63] This law has two parts:

- You shall not "covet," or actively, obsessively and wrongfully, attempt to acquire another's property. [64]

- You shall not "desire" — or allow yourself to consciously crave or obsessively brood about — another's property.[65]

He who sets his eye on what is not his, loses also what is his. — *Talmud*[66]

One who regards his fellow creatures as mere obstacles to the fulfillment of his own desires is a sinner.

Rational self-interest, it should go without saying, is no sin. Without the desires that some might call selfish one would never marry, raise children, build a house nor carry on a trade.[67] Neither does Heaven necessarily condemn the passion of the ardent collector, whether he collects art or stamps or real estate or anything. But the greedy materialism that leads the collector to ignore the rights and feelings of other human beings is perversion.

An ignorant man believes that the whole universe exists only for him. — *Maimonides*[68]

God abhors covetousness; so should we all abhor it. Naturally, society has neither the power nor the right to look inside men's minds. (May God prevent any human court from ever punishing mere emotions.) But people *are* blessed with the capacity to recognize covetous expressions when they hear them. The righteous response is strict personal and social censure.

We who listen approvingly to jealous schemes or lend a patient ear to someone's jealous cravings act like accessories to crime. By showing sympathy to sin, we lead the sinner further astray.

Illicit cravings grow the more one focuses on them. If a man sees a beautiful object belonging to another, for instance, and sets his heart on it and craves it, his love for the object becomes more and more obsessive. If his fellows know about this love and tolerate it, they add to its legitimacy. Eventually, the desirous person will probably devise a scheme or plot to obtain the thing.[69]

Millions of people waste their lives in such nonsense; it's one of humanity's greatest vices. Worse, coveting creates envy, perhaps the most toxic, godless, and contagious emotion of all.

One who covets the possessions of another tends to end up believing that the other person doesn't deserve — isn't worthy — of whatever it is one is coveting. These feelings often lead to stealing, or sometimes even murder, when people convince themselves that justice gives them a right to plunder the victims of their envy.

> What is yours is not yours; then how can you regard what is not yours as yours? — *Talmud*[70]

Charity

Another Torah prohibition, mirroring several positive imperatives of Torah,[71] certainly bears on any discussion of this Sixth Commandment: You shall not fail to give charity. "You shall not harden your heart nor shut your hand to your needy brother." [72]

> If I am not for myself, who will be for me? If I am only for myself, what am I? — *Hillel*[73]

Human title to the good things of the world is always subject to God's. What we have we get from God; how we use what we have is subject to His Divine right to have us, his tenants, use it righteously.

> The rich and the poor meet together: the Lord is the Maker of them all. — *Proverbs 22:21*

The poor have a claim on the produce of the land, a lien on Earth's natural wealth. God is its true Owner, while they, as much as any person, represent His very Image.

So the Jews in the Land of Israel are commanded, for example, to leave a portion of the harvest for the poor. In His words, "And when you reap the harvest of your land, you shall not wholly reap the corners of your field, neither shall you gather every grape of your vineyard; you shall leave them for the poor, and for the stranger: I am the Lord your God."[74] Should one forget or fail in this, or in other, similar obligations, he must substitute an equivalent donation to the poor.[75]

These rules, which aren't just positive injunctions but prohibitive, "you shall not" Commandments, have universal implications.

Israel is taught that severe punishment comes upon the world for wrongfully withholding the dues of the poor.[76] Providing for the poor, the oppressed, and the down on their luck — or rather, helping to provide — is simple compliance with an extensive set of strict Torah obligations. These obligations center on justice, as opposed to pity, kindness or mere sentiment.[77]

A person's duty to give charity is a Divinely created encumbrance on the right to possess property or hold or enjoy wealth. Even the poor, who receive charity, must give charity.[78]

The opportunity to help the less fortunate is a privilege laden with blessings.[79] As the rabbis say, the poor man who receives charity does more for the master of the house, who gives it, than the master does for the poor man.[80]

> He who is gracious to the poor lends to the Lord. — *Proverbs 19:17*

Charity is an attribute of God Himself.[81] Failing to give charity is considered tantamount to idolatry. Commitment to God is inconceivable without compassion for man.[82] A Hebrew Torah court, properly empowered and acting in the land of Israel, can physically compel one who refuses to give charitably. The court has the right to make an assessment for charity and appropriate that amount from the recalcitrant giver's property.[83] Still, whether a Noahide society should ever entrust its courts with similar powers involves different considerations.

> The highest charity is to help someone help himself.
> — *Maimonides*[84]

In this matter of charitable giving — which includes such things as donating time or talent, as well as money contributions — what the Torah offers B'nai Noah is Divine guidance and instruction, rather than outright legal Commandment. Scripture tells us plainly, repeatedly, that God expects and requires man to give charity.[85] This is obviously a huge area of Divine concern as well as Divine legislation. And while the Torah's express legislation directly compels only Israel, the expressed concern of the Master of the Universe should guide and caution everybody.[86]

> If a coin falls out of your pocket and a poor man finds it and
> supports himself by it, you will be blessed on that account.
> — *Midrash*[87]

Charitable giving is a principal characteristic of every man of honor.[88] In fact, it's not too much to say that anyone who wrongly withholds charity is both dishonorable and also something of a thief. So here we have another illustration of that critical principle, mentioned above, that shows us how God wants us to use all these Noahide Commandments: *A person cannot be called truly righteous unless he does the very opposite of what the Universal Law forbids.*

One cannot fully obey God's law against larceny unless he gives charity. Similarly, as we have seen, one must not only refrain from taking what isn't his to take, but must also refrain even from coveting, or obsessively desiring, what isn't his.

This doesn't mean that human prosecutors, police and courts must involve themselves everytime someone may depart from the ideal. Actual virtue, beyond the limits of strict and narrow honesty, can't be compelled by fear of legal consequences but only by one's love and fear of Heaven.

As a matter of universal law the better rule, surely, is to treat these sins of omission, in the area of charity, and all failings of a spiritual rather than a physical nature, as belonging more properly to the realm of the spirit. This means that governments have no duty to intervene: they can leave them up to the individual himself, to society, and to God's Heavenly courts — His courts of final jurisdiction.

> For yourself, give precedence to the soul, but for others, never forego the demands of the body. Your neighbor's physical needs are your spiritual affairs. — *Rav Israel Salanter*[89]

Israel understands that the ideal amounts to give as charity are between one-tenth — 10 percent — and one-fifth — 20 percent — of one's yearly income.[90] But Heaven forbid that even a dishonorable man, who refuses to give anything at all, should fall victim to any (other) thief.

Criminal action is no way to seek redress for someone else's lack of honor. The poor man has an undifferentiated claim on some part of the rich man's surplus property, but no right at all to take anything against its owner's will. Only if life depends on the issue may the poor man seize so much as a piece of bread from its owner, and only then with the intention of somehow paying it back.[91] He who steals, even from a thief or murderer, is himself a thief, a sinner and a criminal.[92]

Lost Property and
Responsibility for Property

Missing property that *can* be returned to its owner *should* be returned to its owner.[93] To seize or convert a lost piece of property for the benefit of anyone else is sin — an act of larceny — so long as the true owner still claims the item, still believes that it can be recovered,[94] and it has distinguishing marks or other characteristics allowing the owner to identify it as his own.[95]

The privilege of property ownership also carries responsibilities. The owner is the guardian of his own property, and must take responsibility for any damage it causes.[96] Israel is told, "even without the verdict of a court of law, even if no claim is put forward by another person, [one] must pay compensation for any harm done to another's property or body for which he is responsible."[97]

Defamation

A good name is better than great wealth. — Proverbs 22:1

While not customarily considered in the category of larceny, the parallels between physical assault — battery[98] — and verbal assault — slander — are too plain to be ignored.[99] Here too, a huge body of Divine legislation and Scriptural admonition show us that this — the sins of the "tongue of evil"[100] (defamation, scandalmongering, and just sheer mindless gossip) — is an area of major divine concern. Not that it necessarily or invariably requires the nations' police and courts to get involved.[101] But God gave our species the unique and wonderful gift of speech to exalt us and to benefit the whole world through us. We pervert His gift and abase ourselves when we use it only to wrong our fellows. Also, as we know, "If you slander, you'll commit other sins too."[102]

> You shall not steal, neither shall you deal falsely, nor lie one to another. — *Leviticus 19:11*[103]

God commands Israel, "You shall not curse the deaf," meaning anyone who cannot hear you and who therefore cannot vindicate himself;[104] "You shall not go up and down as a tale-bearer among your people,"[105] since, as the rabbis say, "even if what he says or repeats is true, the talebearer ruins the world."[106]

The Written Torah itself speaks volumes: "You shall not wrong another, but you shall fear your God."[107] This refers mainly to verbal wrongs.[108]

> Verbal wrong is more heinous than [direct] monetary wrong; because of verbal wrong it is written, "you shall fear your God.
> — *Talmud*[109]

Repeatedly, emphatically, the Psalms and Proverbs condemn the "tongue of evil." They teach, for example, that only he who "speaks truth in his heart," who "has no slander upon his tongue, nor does evil to his fellow, nor takes up a reproach against his neighbor," is in any way qualified for communion with God.[110] The sin involved is essentially one of idolatry. The rabbis say that one who indulges in the tongue of evil shows by doing so that he denies the existence of God. For that matter, God Himself declares, "There is no room in the world for the slanderer and Me."[111]

Seduction/Stealing Feelings

Keep thee far from a false matter. — Exodus 23:7

Telling someone lies about himself to improve his opinion of himself is flattery. Telling someone lies about yourself to improve his opinion of you is hypocrisy. "The Holy One detests him who speaks one thing with his mouth and another in his heart."[112] Pretending, insincerely promising, or telling someone lies to deceive him, to blind him to reality just so you may gain some personal advantage over him, is fraud.

Any of these acts, if they accomplish the deceiver's goal of arousing a false feeling — such as loyalty, love, respect, or trust — in the victim, is a kind of theft. So "stealing the hearts of men," as Israel characterizes the sin, is literally stealing.[113]

Gambling

Finally, while it may come as something of a surprise, the Universal Law does not forbid gambling.

God gives us all free will. One who risks money or other property at games of chance may be motivated by the basest of impulses — the dishonest impulse that leads people to expect something for nothing, or the more plainly idolatrous impulse that leads us to test God by insisting that He prove His love for us through miracles. Still, we have every right to risk our property as we wish.

Gambling resembles robbery: one who bets expects and hopes to take something from another without giving anything in return. A serious gambler never wants to lose, of course; he never wants to leave his money behind. This thinking makes such transactions especially problematic. It's never good for money — valuables — to go from one person to another without goodwill.

Mere recreational gambling — a friendly or lightly regarded card game, for instance — is an innocent amusement. It doesn't (at least, it shouldn't) create ill will. But seriously avaricious gambling is seriously dangerous. It can become a compulsion, so it presents a threat on another level — to one's self-control and personal autonomy, which is another way of describing free will.

When a person's gambling losses cause indebtedness, it has already degenerated into a form of stealing from oneself. Worse yet, addicted gamblers tend to steal from their families, as well as others, causing many of the social problems that other addicts cause.

So if one takes gambling beyond a certain point it's not mere "gaming" but a stepping-stone to larceny.

The compulsive gambler is a slave to his own addiction. The professional gambler's business is necessarily hardening or even cruel. Unlike true commerce, gambling produces no wealth but only transfers it.

Still, while the Torah condemns both the compulsive and the professional gambler as being less than fully worthy citizens, the Lord God who has given us all this Noahide law only forbids cheating — the actual practice of dishonesty — in gambling.[114]

NOTES

1. Genesis 2:17. See Elijah Benamozegh, *Israel and Humanity* (1914/ 1995, supra), p. 263.
2. Talmud, *Makkot* 23b.
3. Ibid.
4. Ibid.
5. Genesis 6:13 with Rashi.
6. Bindman, *Seven Colors of the Rainbow*, supra, p. 72.
7. See Leviticus 19:11,13. However: 1) A properly-empowered court may decree a seizure or forfeiture of property as punishment for crime. See Ezra 10:8; Talmud, *Yevamot* 89b, *Gittin* 36b. 2) Governments, which protect property, obviously have some right to collect part of it back in taxes. See Deuteronomy 20:11; 1 Samuel 8:10-17; *Yad, Hilchot Melachim* 4:1-3. 3) In condemnation or eminent domain cases, a court may order the transfer of property. Talmud, *Gittin* 20a with Rashi. 4) Where life and death are on the

line in real emergencies, one takes — or rather, borrows — whatever property as may be on hand to help effect a rescue, whenever necessary to save life. Property has no higher use than saving life, even if doing so may temporarily violate some of the conventionally inviolable possessory rights of the true owner. See *Shulchan Aruch, Hoshen Mishpat* 359.

8. Genesis 1:1; Deuteronomy 10:14; Haggai 2:8.

9. See Genesis 3:19, 9:16; Proverbs 22:2, 27:24.

10. *Horeb*, supra, ch. 46, Sec. 334. Some right to pass along property as a bequest or inheritance also is an implicit, basic feature of ownership. See Numbers 27:8-11; *Sefer HaMitzvot* 1:248, *Horeb*, id.

11. See *Yad, Hilchot Geneyva* 7:12, and commentaries.

12. Exodus 20:15; Deuteronomy 5:7. This is the Torah's Ten Commandments' Eighth Commandment.

13. Leviticus 19:13; *Sefer HaMitzvot* 2:245.

14. See *Sefer HaMitzvot* 2:244-245.

15. *Yad, Hilchot Geneyva* 1:3.

16. *Shulchan Aruch, Hoshen Mishpat* 369.

17. See Deuteronomy 5:18 with commentaries; *Yad, Hilchot Melachim* 9:9; *Sefer HaHinnuch*, No's. 416, 424. There is this exception: theoretically, a very trivial theft of, say, a single grape, or of anything worth less than about a nickel — i.e., worth less than the minimal amount acceptable for any full transaction — may be punished under the Rainbow Law. This is not the case under Israel's Law: the Torah *requires* Israel to forgive a Jew who commits such a minor taking. See Talmud, *Eruvin* 62a and *Sanhedrin* 59a with Rashi, *Kiddushin* 3a-b, 11a-b. Also see Novak, *Image of the Non-Jew in Judaism*, supra, pp. 224-234; Talmud, *Bava Kamma* 119a.

18. Ibid. Also see Talmud, *Sanhedrin* 57a, 59a, *Yevamot* 47, with Rashi.

19. See *Yad, Hilchot Melachim* 9:9, and our own prior discussion within, regarding the logic of the law and methodology. Following that logic, the threshold levels or the minimal quantities or injuries required for criminal prosecution are also left up to the individual nations — so long as they address the problem seriously and, above all, justly. As a matter of social utility, to prevent the criminal from doing further injury to society while also discouraging others from crime, punishments should usually be chosen and imposed in a manner to make "the strongest and most long-lasting impressions on the minds of others, with the least torment possible to the criminal." Cesare Beccaria, *Of Crimes and Punishments,* supra, chapter 12, "Of the Intent of Punishment."

20. Practically speaking.

21. Parents and other authorities must take great pains to instill a thoroughgoing respect for the sanctity of others' property in children and, in serious breaches, should *physically* admonish them. *Shulchan Aruch, Hoshen Mishpat* 349:5.

22. *Leviticus Rabbah* 6:2.

23. See *Yad, Hilchot Teshuva* 4:5. In the case of a legal transaction, "a person's agent is regarded as the person himself" — Talmud, *Nedarim* 72b, *Kiddushin* 41b — and the principal bears full responsibility while the agent bears none. But "one cannot be an agent for a transgression" — Talmud, *Kiddushin* 42b. One who commits a crime is responsible for that crime, even if he was acting for someone else. The thief is liable for his own act of

thievery. The receiver, who takes what isn't his and conceals or converts it, is responsible for his own larcenous conduct and also for its consequences (i.e., for creating an environment that encourages others to steal).

24. See Genesis 34:2 with commentaries; Exodus 20:15, 21:16. Deuteronomy 24:7. Kidnapping in this sense involves not just wrongful imprisonment or wrongful asportation but also using the victim as a degraded and disposable mere chattel. Also see *Sefer HaMitzvot* 2:243; *Minchat Hinnuch*, No. 35; Genesis 34:13 with Ramban (Nachmanides).

25. See Genesis 34:2,13 with commentaries; Exodus 21:16; *Sefer HaMitzvot* 2:243; *Moreh Nevuchim* 3:41; Lichtenstein, supra, p. 42; Clorfene & Rogalsky, supra, pp. 91, 93.

26. See Genesis 34:2 with Rashi; Exodus 20:15, 21:16; Deuteronomy 21:11-14, 22:23-29; *Sefer HaMitzvot* 2:243. Also see below, footnote 33.

27. See Genesis 1:27. Every human being has property rights in his or her own body, naturally, as well as reasonable expectations of bodily security. Every society has an obligation to defend those rights and expectations. But rape can be a very difficult crime to prove conclusively or to prosecute justly. In fact, the evidentiary and other technical safeguards operative in Israel's Torah courts would make most such prosecutions practically impossible; some scholars, reading Maimonides' *Yad, Hilchot Melachim* 9:14 very narrowly and literally, believe that Noahide jurisprudence should be similarly restrictive. Note that what the Written Torah addresses (see Deuteronomy 22:22-27) isn't necessarily rape but illicit seduction, which is a crime that *can* be proved not merely conclusively but beyond any shadow of doubt.

28. See *Minchat Hinnuch* 35; *Moreh Nevuchim* 3:41. Rape includes elements of assault and battery and also false arrest, or even kidnapping.

29. *Hoshen Mishpat* 420, 421.

30. See Genesis 34:13 with Ramban (Nachmanides); Exodus 2:11 with Maharsha (R. Shmuel HaLevi Edels, c. 1615 CE). Also see *Yad, Hilchot Melachim* 10:6; Clorfene & Rogalsky, supra, 9:15 (p. 93).

31. Leviticus 5:23-24; *Sefer HaMitzvot* 1:194. Some believe that this obligation applies to B'nai Noah as well as to Israel. See Lichtenstein, supra., pp. 26-27; but also see Rashi on Talmud, *Eruvin* 62a: a Gentile, who is subject to criminal penalties only, need not make civil restitution additionally.

32. Exodus 21:18-19 with Rashi; Talmud, *Bava Kamma* 83b.

33. Deuteronomy 22:25-29 and commentaries; Talmud, *Ketubot* 39; *Moreh Nevuchim* 3:49. Due mostly to the singular nature of Israel's Torah court proceedings, including evidentiary restrictions (e.g., no circumstantial evidence allowed) and other technical safeguards, as well as the matter of Israel's Torah penalties, some authorities don't categorize rape as larceny. But all authorities regard it as a heinous felony, pursuant to both the Torah and the Universal Law, that must everywhere be punished. See, e.g., Genesis 34 (the rape of Dinah and its consequences). Finally, because Torah penalties are not Noahide penalties, logic suggests that rape is best defined as a *larcenous* Noahide crime.

34. *Mechilta* to Exodus 15:26.

35. See Leviticus 24:14; *Sefer HaMitzvot* 2:250.

36. See Leviticus 19:13; *Sefer HaMitzvot* 2:247 and commentaries.

37. Leviticus 19:35; *Sefer HaMitzvot* 2:271.

38. See Talmud, *Bava Batra* 82b.

39. Talmud, ibid; Midrash, *Sifra* on Leviticus 19:35.

40. Proverbs 11:1. See The Fifth Commandment, below.

41. Leviticus 19:15,36; *Sefer HaMitzvot* 1:208, 2:271-272; *Yad, Hilchot Geneyva* 7:12.

42. See Exodus 22:6-7,9-10,13-14; Leviticus 25:14,17; Hirsch, *Horeb,* supra, Sec. 344, 357-359.

43. R. Yochanan ben Naffaha, *Bava Kamma* 119a. That is, a person's wealth or money is like part of him; losing it to your thievery may damage him immeasurably. See Midrash, *Leviticus Rabbah* 33:3.

44. Deuteronomy 25:13; *Sefer HaMitzvot* 2:272.

45. Rabbenu Ovadiah Sforno (Italy, c. 1542), Commentary to Deuteronomy 25:13-14. See also Talmud, *Bava Batra* 89b; *Sefer HaMitzvot* 2:272.

46. Deuteronomy 19:14; *Sefer HaMitzvot* 2:246.

47. *Shulchan Aruch, Hoshen Mishpat* 156.

48. Leviticus 19:3; Deuteronomy 24:15; *Yad, Hilchot Melachim* 9:9; *Sefer HaMitzvot* 2:238.

49. See Deuteronomy 23:25; *Sefer HaMitzvot* 2:268.

50. See Deuteronomy 23:25-26; Talmud, *Bava Metzia* 87a-b, 91b; *Sefer HaMitzvot* 1:201; Lichtenstein, supra, p. 24. But to smuggle uneaten food *away* from the workplace is theft. *Yad, Hilchot Melachim* 9:9.

51. See Deuteronomy 23:26; Talmud, *Bava Metzia* 87; *Sefer HaMitzvot* 2:267.

52. See Exodus 22:24; *Sefer HaMitzvot* 2:234.

53. See R. Aaron HaLevi, *Sefer HaHinnuch*, Imperative 577.

54. Leviticus 25:17, 25:14.

55. Shabbat 31a. See *Shulchan Aruch, Hoshen Mishpat* 227-228.

56. Leviticus, ibid. Not that a genuine, unexpected inability to pay or perform an obligation is larcenous, of course, but referring to deliberate oppression, like a material but false promise in business, or refusing to pay what one owes despite being able to pay.

57. Leviticus 19:11; *Sefer HaMitzvot* 2:248.

58. See Leviticus 19:11; *Sefer HaMitzvot* 2:249.

59. See Genesis 34:13 with Ramban; *Sefer HaMitzvot* 2:250 and commentaries.

60. Leviticus 25:14 with commentaries; *Sefer HaMitzvot* 2:250.

61. *Mechilta* to Exodus 20:17.

62. Exodus 20:17; Deuteronomy 7:25.

63. *Sefer HaHinnuch*, supra, No's. 416, 424, on Deuteronomy 5:18. See Lichtenstein, supra, pp. 19, 24; Clorfene and Rogalsky, supra, p. 90, 93-94. Just as everyone is commanded to abstain from committing theft, everyone is commanded concerning deterrents to theft. *Sefer HaHinnuch*, No. 424.

64. Exodus 20:17; Deuteronomy 5:18, 7:25, and commentaries; *Sefer HaMitzvot* 2:265.

65. Deuteronomy 5:18; *Sefer HaMitzvot* 2:266.

66. *Sotah* 9a.

67. Midrash, *Genesis Rabbah* 9:7.

68. *Moreh Nevuchim* 3:12.

69. See *Sefer HaMitzvot* 2:266.

70. *Derech Eretz* 1:1.

71. Deuteronomy 15:11; Leviticus 25:35, 36; *Sefer HaMitzvot* 1:195.

72. Deuteronomy 15:7; *Sefer HaMitzvot* 2:232. See Proverbs 3:27; Talmud, *Bava Batra* 9a, *Sanhedrin* 35a.

73. Mishnah, *Pirke Avot* 1:14.

74. Leviticus 19:9-10; See *Sefer HaMitzvot* 2:210-14; and Deuteronomy 24:19-20.

75. *Sefer HaMitzvot* 2:210.

76. Mishnah, *Pirke Avot* 5:11. See, e.g., Ezekiel 16:49, regarding the punishment of the people of Sodom.

77. See Leviticus 19:9-10; Deuteronomy 26:12. No people is better known for its philanthropies and charities than the Jews, among whom the richest often actually lead by example. See, e.g., Deuteronomy 16:17, Israel's rule of voluntary progressive taxation for charity: "Every man shall give as he is able, according to the blessing of the Lord which He has given you."

78. Talmud, *Gittin* 7a; See *Sefer HaMitzvot* 1:195. Naturally, someone who has only enough for his own subsistence is not obligated to give. Charity begins at home; one must always first support oneself.

79. Proverbs 21:3, 28:27: "Who gives to the poor shall not lack." See Talmud, *Bava Batra* 9; *Sukkot* 49b.

80. Midrash, *Leviticus Rabbah* 34:8.

81. Deuteronomy 10:17-18.

82. Talmud, *Ketubot* 68a, *Bava Batra* 10a; Midrash, *Ecclesiastes Rabbah* 7:1. Every human being is, essentially, Humanity.

83. Talmud, *Ketubot* 49a; *Yad, Mattenot Aniyim* 7:10. However, no such courts presently exist. Further, per Jeremiah 30:20, no collector for charity can be allowed to exact too much. Talmud, *Bava Batra* 8b.

84. *Yad, Mattenot Aniyim* 10:7.

85. See, e.g., Exodus 23:11; Deuteronomy 10:18-19, 15:7-10, 16:11,14; Isaiah 58:5-10; Ezekiel 16:49 (specifically pertaining to Gentiles); Psalms 41:2, 112:9, 132:15, 145:15; Proverbs 10:2, 19:17, 31:20; Job 22:5-9, 29:12-13; Esther 9:12; Nechemiah 8:10. Note that the Torah literally begins and ends with acts of charity — God clothes the naked, Eve and Adam, and He lovingly buries Moses.

86. See, e.g., Ezekiel 16:49.

87. *Sifre* on Deuteronomy 24:19. See *Sefer HaMitzvot* 2:214.

88. See Job 31, the so-called "Code of a Man of Honor." While Israel reads the Book of Job at least partly as parable, rather than as pure non-fiction — no man knows what occurs in Heaven's precincts; does God inflict death and pain upon men whimsically? See Talmud, *Bava Batra* 15a; *Moreh Nevuchim* 3:22 — the story is especially instructive for our study, since Job is depicted not as a Jew, necessarily, but simply as a righteous man.

89. *Tenuat HaMusar*, D. Katz, ed. (Betan HaSefer, Tel Aviv, 1951) 1:273. Sayings of Rav Salanter (founder of the modern *Musar* — or "Hebrew ethical studies" — movement, c. 1810-1883. Classic work).

90. See Talmud, *Ketubot* 50a; *Shulchan Aruch, Yoreh De'ah* 249; *Horeb*, supra, Sec. 572. This is a complex subject; many details and exceptions accompany this general rule. They deserve careful study.

91. *Shulchan Aruch, Hoshen Mishpat* 359; See Proverbs 6:30; Hirsch, *Horeb*, supra, Sec. 337.

92. See *Yad, Hilchot Melachim* 9:9.

93. See Exodus 23:4; Deuteronomy 22:1-3; *Sefer HaMitzvot* 2:269. Likewise, it is forbidden to ignore a lost child, or a person who has lost his way. Talmud, *Sanhedrin* 73a. But these Torah obligations, which suppose a *moral* duty to take some restorative action, are not necessarily a court-enforceable obligation.

94. That is, hasn't yet given it up as irrevocably lost, which would constitute abandonment.

95. See Hirsch, *Horeb*, supra, paras. 558-562. A common coin or other untraceable, apparently ownerless cash lost on a city street belongs to the finder.

96. Exodus 21:33-36, 22:4-5; Deuteronomy 22:8; *Horeb*, supra, Chapter 49 (Sec. 360, pp. 243-244).

97. *Horeb*, supra, p. 244.

98. See discussion above, and Genesis 34:13 with Ramban (Nachmanides). Also see *Yad, Hilchot Melachim* 10:6; Talmud, *Sanhedrin* 58b (re: Exodus 2:11) with Maharsha (R. Samual HaLevi Edels); Clorfene & Rogalsky, supra, 9:15 (p.93).

99. Defamation is often compared to murder — Talmud, *Bava Metzia* 58b-59a — since it is so destructive of its victims' personhood. But in most respects it has more in common with larceny and assault. See *Yad, Hilchot Deyot* 6:8. The Torah invariably treats defamation, unless it involves murderous perjury, as a sin far less heinous than literal murder. It isn't addressed capitally but only by a corporal penalty and/or civil restitutition.

100. In Hebrew, *lashon ha-ra*. The best book on the subject may be Rabbi Israel Meir Cohen's *Hafetz Chaim* (classic work, c. 1873).

101. That is, defamation can be addressed as a private or civil wrong, as opposed to being treated as a felony under Noahide criminal statutes. No Torah court has the power to impose a capital penalty in these sorts of cases, suggesting that defamation can't be treated as a true Rainbow Covenant felony.

102. Rabbi Eleazar HaKappar, Talmud, *Derech Eretz* 7.

103. Also see Exodus 23:7; Hirsch, *Horeb*, Chapter 50, para. 373, pp. 251-252.

104. Leviticus 19:14 and commentaries; *Sefer HaMitzvot* 2:317.

105. Levitcus 19:16 and commentaries; *Sefer HaMitzvot* 2:301.

106. *Yad, Hilchot Deyot* 7:1.

107. Leviticus 25:17. Apparently, cursing ultimately, normally, causes the most harm to the one doing the cursing.

108. *Sifra* (Midrash) on Leviticus 25:17; Talmud, *Bava Metzia* 58b; *Sefer HaMitzvot* 2:251.

109. Talmud, *Bava Metzia*, ibid.; *Sefer HaMitzvot*, ibid.

110. Psalm 15:1-3. See, e.g., Psalm 101:5; Proverbs 10:18, 30:10.

111. Talmud, *Erachin* 15b.

112. Talmud, *Pesachim* 113b.

113. See Leviticus 19:11; Midrash, *Mechilta* to Exodus 22:3; *Shulchan Aruch, Hoshen Mishpat* 228; *Horeb*, supra, para. 373. This is not to say that these kinds of theft offenses either must or should be punished as crimes by any human, Noahide, court. Where the commission of sin causes harm of a spiritual nature exclusively, its punishment is usually best left not to man's courts but to God's.

114. See Judges 14; *Midrash Tehillim* to Psalm 26:10; Mishnah, *Sanhedrin* 3:3; *Tosefta* to *Sanhedrin* 5:2; Talmud, *Sanhedrin* 24b, 25b, *Hullin* 91b, *Gittin* 61b, *Bava Batra* 92b-93a; *Yad, Gezelah v'Avedah* 6:10 and 6:11, *Eduyot* 10:4. Whether gambling debts are legally enforceable presents an intriguing question. Because the debtor-loser entered into the transaction expecting to win, one may say that there was no real "meeting of minds" between the parties beforehand, and therefore no valid contract to be enforced between them.

THE FIFTH COMMANDMENT

Sex Laws

A man shall not lie with mankind as with
womankind: it is an abomination. Nor with
any animal, to defile yourself therewith. Nor
shall any woman defile herself thereby:
it is perversion.[1]
Never defile yourselves in any of these
things: for in all these the nations which I
cast out before you are defiled: And the land
is defiled. — Leviticus 18:22-25

O f all God's laws, the prohibitions that most people find most difficult to keep are those pertaining to perverse sex.[2] Sheer ignorance has a good deal to do with this. If more people simply knew what His law requires, they would surely find it easier to keep.

Human beings are sexual beings. Our Maker knows it. Based on His total awareness of our actual nature, He doesn't command us to suppress our animal urges but only to express and channel them appropriately. His law simply sets out the line between the wholesome and the unwholesome. Guiding animals by their instincts, the same Holy God who created human sexuality gives us law and not just instinct to guide thinking beings — human beings — in His Ways.

Rather than condemning the union of a man with a woman, the Revolutionary Tradition celebrates heterosexual love.[3] Sexual intercourse can — and should — be a source of great holiness and purity.[4]

> Man does not fulfill his destiny without woman, nor woman
> without man, nor the two together without the Divine Presence
> among them. — *Midrash*[5]

Sexual love can bring people much closer to God. Our Creator didn't give us our sexual appetites just to ensure reproduction: the love between a man and a woman expands their capacity to love Him; it can magnify both their power and their inclination to follow Him.[6]

Sex may even be a means to become more directly *like* Him. Mystics say that, just as God has, in a spiritual sense, both masculine and feminine characteristics — He created man and woman "in His own Image," "male and female He created them"[7] — and would be imperfect except as these two aspects of His Being are perfectly united, a man must join with a woman, and a woman with a man, to unite the two aspects, to make a fully complete human being.[8]

Many scholars disdain this mystical theology. God is universally called "He" rather than "She" or "It" because He is an active, not a passive, conscious Force in the Universe.[9] Otherwise, the Almighty Creator of sex and gender, Who made and sustains the Universe not by sexual means but by His pure Will alone,[10] exists far beyond *any* consideration of sex or gender.

Putting aside, for the moment, the deeper secrets of God's Essence, He speaks quite clearly to us on this point: a man or woman alone is almost like a fractional person, a mere part of what God intends each of them to be.[11] Marriage is the human ideal: a man should "cleave to his wife, and they shall be one flesh."[12]

Not all love is holy. God commands humanity — all of us; everyone — to refrain from certain acts of perverted love and self-destructive sexuality. We ignore our species' own inherent seasons and limitations at our peril. Just as sex offers us a means to make ourselves more human, it can also reduce us below the level of the animals.

Without a prevailing law or morality, wrote Sigmund Freud, people can become sexually attracted to just about anything.[13] Human sexuality, and particularly the sexuality of human males, is polymorphous: compared even with animal sexuality, which is fettered by instinct, it can be utterly wild.[14] Yet God loves sexual self-discipline and modesty. He has given our species so much freedom so that we, beyond all other animals, can make something of ourselves.

While God has made countless sexual perversions possible, He restricts, by His law, the range of the sexually permissible. He condemns *incest, bestiality* (sexual relations with animals), *acts of male homosexuality*, and *adultery* as brutalizing, godless, soul-destroying crimes, which corrupt human society and defile the very earth.[15]

Mystics associate the laws of this Fifth Commandment with the rainbow's blue.[16]

Incest

Defined as sexual relations — not just genital intercourse, but any physical contact with romantic or erotic intent — between near relations.[17] Generally, any erotic liason between "both the root and the branch,"[18] as between a man and his mother or a daughter with her father, is both outrageous and forbidden.[19]

Where the Torah singles out eighteen prohibited incestous relationships,[20] the rabbis of Israel, pursuant to their authority to erect "fences around the Torah" for Israel,[21] have defined another twenty forbidden cases of incest.[22] Noahide lawmakers possess similar powers, to define the details of the Universal law against incest for their own respective nations.[23] They are not bound by the specifics of Torah in this but can be stricter or more lenient.[24] They might, perhaps, permit a relationship, such as the union of a father with his widowed daughter-in-law, which is forbidden by the Law of Sinai.[25] Or they might forbid a relationship, such as the union of a woman with her first cousin, which the Torah permits.[26] The laws that they decree are to be obeyed as the Law.[27]

Every society must, at a minumum,[28] prohibit these relationships, being any union between a man and: a) his mother; b) his step-mother; c) his maternal sister;[29] d) his daughter;[30] e) his father's sister, his aunt; or f) his mother's sister, his aunt.

Adultery

Defined as sexual intercourse — genital coitus, with vaginal (or anal) penetration — between a man and any other man's wife.[31] But any erotic contact between a man and any other man's wife is unholy if it might prospectively lead to intercourse.[32]

A woman is married within the general definition of this Statute if she and her husband have had intercourse with the understanding that they are married, and so long as she has not publicly separated from him.[33] But this — divorce — is a complicated subject. God hates divorce but does not forbid it.[34]

Naturally, different nations all have somewhat different family customs, laws and needs. A betrothal or engagement to marry, for instance, can mean one thing among one group, depending on their expectations, and entirely another thing to others. Whose meaning prevails, in most matters of that nature, depends more on local etiquette than on universal moral logic. A people or nation must decide for itself the details of its own laws concerning marriage and questions of divorce. God blessed Israel with a body of wise legislation concerning both.[35] The nations may look to it, or not, to suit themselves.[36]

Bestiality

Defined as sexual relations — not necessarily genital intercourse, but any erotic touching — between any human being, whether male or female, and any animal.[37]

Acts of Male Homosexuality

Defined as sexual relations — again, not necessarily genital intercourse, but any erotic touching — between a human male and any other human male.[38] Like a crime of bestiality or incest, this is perversion, a corruption of nature, the violation of a basic Divine *value,* as well as a felony in His law.[39] God follows His plain Command, "A man shall not," with the plain Teaching that this is a thing which is intrinsically vile — "it is an abomination."[40]

All these prohibitions, concerning adultery, homosexuality, adultery and incest, apply equally to the person who initiates the illicit contact as well as the person who receives it.[41] Only if one participates unwillingly in an illicit act — if one is forcibly coerced or free choice is denied — then the victim, of course, is innocent of the sin. Innocent, that is, in both Heaven's sight and in His law.[42]

Beyond the Basest

Other kinds of vulgar sexuality — lesbian acts,[43] masturbation,[44] harlotry and sex with harlots,[45] and sexual frivolity generally[46] — are regarded as "lewdness."[47] Such acts are patently less than holy and may even be destructive. But it's impossible to characterize them logically as criminal violations of the minimal provisions of this Commandment.

The Holy One does not deal despotically with His creatures.
— *Talmud*[48]

God universally prohibits the great sins, the crimes that reverse the natural order. Where He defines incest, for instance, as a capital crime,[49] the Written Torah never even directly mentions masturbation. Yet every sexually impure act is defiling in some way.[50]

Distinguishing between the merely lewd, or morally pointless, on the one hand, and the abhorrent, on the other, can be a real problem for anyone who seeks to keep God's Way.[51] True virtue is obviously more than just a matter of avoiding the basest crimes. Still, at the level of the Universal Law, and the minimal rules that *every* society *must* lay down in the sphere of sexual morality and conduct, things are much clearer.

Analysis

God is patient with all sins except those involving sexual immorality. — *Midrash*[52]

Because God has not revealed them fully, no mortal can pretend to completely understand the reasons underlying *any* of His laws. Heaven's laws concerning sexual morality must be especially mysterious, because sexuality is so closely bound up with the ultimate mysteries of life and death.[53] We should obey these laws because God has enacted them and it's our life's task to carry out His will.[54] But we have the right to speculate and the duty to try to understand His will as it applies to us.[55]

Probably the best way to understand this Fifth Universal Commandment is by recalling that the Rainbow Code generally, and this commandment particularly, represents a revolutionary Law, which makes a radical break with the "extreme moral degeneracy" of idolatry.[56] These laws make up an integral part of His Plan to utterly obliterate the perverse habits, customs and impulses of idolatry, which keep people enslaved by keeping us from Him.[57] Each of these laws, and all of them together, exist for our own benefit, for the whole world's good. Each of them, and all of them together, reflect His perfect wisdom, His justice, and His eternally abiding love.[58]

Remember that the appetite for sex isn't like the need for food or air. Nobody dies from unsatisfied lust. As human beings — as free willed beings — we have the power to contain our sexual appetites and control our own actions. Alone of all earth's creatures, we can consciously use our sexuality to elevate ourselves to higher levels of purity, true humanity, and holiness.[59]

> Man is perfectly capable of sublimating his impulses and living in moderation. — *Talmud*[60]

Every sexual felony — each of the major Fifth Commandment crimes — contradicts the truth that God has not only given human beings our bodies but cares about how we use them.

Each of the sexual felonies, sharing all four of these features in common only with the other sexual felonies, can be said to: 1) raise sex to the level of a "god," or of a supreme good or craving, regardless of one's obligations to the One God; 2) defile a holy gift by blurring Heaven's own clear distinctions between either a) animal and human, b) male and female, c) married and unmarried, or, in incest, between d) "root and branch" relatives;[61] 3) threaten the stability, purity and peace of the heterosexual family; *and* 4) degrade the status and security of women in society.

A Man Shall Not Lie With Mankind as With Womankind

Kings in Egypt used to marry their sisters, and even sometimes their mothers. French and German landlords used to sexually, legally, violate the new brides of their tenants — a vile rite known as the *droit du seigneur*. Priests and priestesses and royalty, not just lonely farmboys, used to commingle, sexually and lasciviously, with animals, in great public displays supposed to do their people good.[62] So one must never say that progress is impossible. Incest, adultery, bestiality — today most people think of these crimes differently, as deplorable acts, as sin, as crime, as evil.

Much of our most highly valued cultural heritage has been acquired
at the cost of [unrestricted] sexuality. — *Sigmund Freud*[63]

Human freedom — true freedom — and savagery are
incompatible. Here, as in so many cases of Torah from Sinai, the
sublime Rules that paganism used to reject as mere interfering
Hebrew prejudices have been all but universally accepted as
universal moral laws. But even today one invites huge storms of
criticism by daring to condemn the Divinely forbidden practices
— actually, the crimes — of male homosexuality.

Surely, one can and should disparage homosexual practices
without disparaging the humanity of practicing homosexuals. This
is a condition, not an apology. One must always defy evil; one
must also, accordingly, always distinguish between the sinner and
the sin. God loves the sinner but hates the sin; so should all of
us.[64]

None of this is "homophobia." It cannot be phobic — that is,
pathological — to clearly, calmly denounce a wrongful *act* as
wrongful. The Creator tells us that acts of male homosexuality are
evil just as incest or bestiality (or larceny, or murder) are evil. If we
consider the Torah true we must agree. This fact hardly prevents
us, of course, from asking further questions.

Man and Woman/Male and Female

Circumcision is a sign of the Covenant between man and his
Creator, not to pollute himself with licentiousness.
— *R. Abraham Ibn Ezra*[65]

Homosexual acts between men are felonies; homosexual acts
between women are not. There must be some difference either in
the nature of the respective acts or in the nature of the respective
actors or, most likely, between the actions and the actors both.
Every male's basic sexual equipment is very unlike woman's, and
this alone could be determinative. But the differences between the
sexes go beyond the merely physical: gender changes everything.

Women are a nation apart. — *Talmud*[66]

Women, compared to men, probably constitute the higher
form of life. In the Biblical worldview Creation proceeded in
ascending order: from the earlier and less advanced forms to the

latter and more advanced. Adam — whose name literally means "Man," from a root meaning "Earth" — came *before* Eve — in Hebrew, *Hava* (literally "Life").[67] Men may have more size and muscle and upper-body strength but the human male seems to belong to the lesser sex, which in some ways must also be the weaker.

> A man's mate is from the Holy One. — *Midrash* [68]

Looking at Eve's status as Adam's "helper,"[69] we see that woman tends to have certain qualities — the emotional capacity to lovingly and permanently attach herself to one particular partner, along with a relatively cooperative, tolerant or deferential nature — which complement the comparatively aggressive, egocentric, domineering (bossy?) nature of man.

> A man should always be careful to honor his wife, for blessing enters the home only because of the wife. — *Talmud* [70]

Women tend to possess greater faith than men, as well as greater powers of discernment.[71] God commands the prophet Abraham, for instance, to obey his wife in everything that she tells him.[72] Not a single verse anywhere in the Bible instructs any wife to similarly heed her husband. Women tend to be more compassionate than men,[73] reach adulthood faster,[74] and often, in adulthood, have greater maturity of judgment.[75] Women relate to time and its passage, perhaps due partly to their monthly cycles, somewhat differently from men, and tend to have more regular habits.[76]

Women are at least equally as likely as men to serve God as His prophets.[77] They can teach the Torah to men[78] and rule over men from civic office.[79] Israel's rabbis believed women to be more diligent, generally, in observing His Commandments.[80] Only because of the righteous Hebrew women, they explain, did God redeem Israel from Egypt.[81]

> It is the way of men to follow the opinions of women.
> — *R. Pinchas ben Yair* [82]

One's God-given biology inevitably does affect one's destiny. Women have their own mission, but seem to be "created closer to God's ideal of satisfaction."[83] They have society's most essential work cut out for them. Our whole species' life depends on prevailing over the risks inherent in human reproduction and in the tremendously sensitive, dangerous and difficult matter of child-rearing. But motherhood and fatherhood are not naturally equivalent, since — obviously — motherhood naturally takes more from a woman than the minimal contribution necessary to turn a man into someone's father. Men are made freer to behave irresponsibly. Biologically, women have fewer choices and fewer chances to go wrong.

> The recurrent problem of society is to define the male role satisfactorily. — *Margaret Mead*[84]

Having more of a natural inclination to do the right thing helps. A boy in most cultures has less of a chance to grow up into a real man — a worthy man, an independently strong and responsible person[85] — than does a girl into a worthy woman.[86] Men, especially, can be extremely promiscuous. Lifetime marriage ties and responsible fatherhood aren't necessarily "natural" to the sex.[87] So one of the more obvious reasons for God giving us His laws is to raise men above the moral levels of tomcats, or of the average fourteen year-old boy, by making marital "family values" paramount.

> Where there are no men, try to be a man. — *Hillel*[88]

Calling these values "traditional" ignores their genuinely radical, revolutionary nature, as well as their fragility.[89] Most, if not all, human societies have some form of marriage, but the Revolutionary ideal of marriage — a largely self-contained, romantic, biological, financial, and legal joint enterprise between husband and wife, to the complete sexual exclusion of all other men, in a permanent but voluntary partnership — seems to be historically and anthropologically unique.[90]

The Hebrew word for marriage, *kiddushin*, literally means "sanctification," or "holiness." That an arrangement like this has become known as the "Western" or "standard" model of domesticity is truly remarkable testimony to the universal human potential for good.

More than man desires to marry, woman desires to be married.
— *Talmud*[91]

Scripture paints the picture of such a marriage, and of the freedom and power of a wife, in a passage recited in Jewish homes at the start of every Sabbath.[92] The Bible's ideal woman governs her own home — she anticipates the needs of her family and provides for them. God-fearing, a fully adult soul, she manages other business too, planning, hiring and directing employees, manufacturing and selling goods, and even buying and developing land. Generously, she personally gives charitably to, and insists on justice for, those in need. A faithful, joyful person, she counsels and instructs others in the ways of wisdom, and especially, of kindness.

> If he is a good man, she will be his helpmate; if he is not a good
> man, she will be his adversary. — *Talmud*[93]

One thing the Biblical model-woman does *not* do is work at a wage-paying job. She is exempt from wage labor, as she is exempt from performing almost all of God's commandments — positive, ritual Commandments — that must be performed at a regularly specified time.[94]

Her time is too important; she must be free to attend to the unscheduled or irregularly scheduled needs of the people in her life (including herself). Among other things, she doesn't merely *guide* her husband in all household concerns,[95] excepting only matters of religion and the education of their children; she *is*, in a real sense, her husband's home.[96]

> 'Praised be Thou . . . Who has not made me a woman.' This is said
> daily, for a woman is exempt from many of the Commandments.
> — *R. Yehuda ben Ilai*[97]

God assigns different missions to different groups of people. The purity and chastity of women is the foundation of all true civilization. Women are "the guardians of tradition, the molders of character, children, and family."[98] There can be no wholesome homelife unless woman keeps herself wholesome or, at the very least, sexually exclusive to her mate. She who unchastely betrays him with another man or men commits a terrible felony — as does her sinning partner in crime — which threatens civilization and defiles everyone it touches. Adultery is homewrecking.[99] On the other hand, acts of lesbianism, or feminine homosexuality, present a different sort of threat to homelife. They aren't necessarily criminal. Even though it's vulgar and unchaste, the woman who "rolls with woman"[100] doesn't necessarily corrupt the family's purity nor disturb her mate's sanity as she would if she were having sexual relations with another man.

> Why children, if one is unable to provide for them? . . . Why rear
> them, unless they grow in knowledge and wisdom?
> — *R. Saadia Gaon* [101]

Masculine homosexuality must threaten virtue in a way quite unlike its feminine counterpart. How could this be? In its actors, for one thing: the first involves men, probably the weaker and certainly the less naturally rooted sex.

Male sexuality, whether hetero or homo, is penile. Penile sex, unlike woman-to-woman sensuality, can be — among other things — almost entirely anonymous, heedless, irresponsible, and dominating. It tends to be more volatile, and also more polymorphous. This may be why male (but never female) homosexuals, even though total strangers to each other, often come together in places like public lavatories or sex clubs to satisfy their sensual — penile — urges. It's telling, in this connection, that homosexual men tend to be so amazingly much more promiscuous — perhaps *fifty* times more so — than homosexual women.[102]

> Wherever you find sexual license you may expect disease.
> — *Midrash* [103]

Compounding the peculiarities of one male ego with another, and the nature of their sexual equipment, male homosexual sensuality doesn't just mirror its feminine counterpart. Men are less naturally balanced, and far more competitive and insatiable. So male homosexuality tends, among other things, to be a remarkable vector for disease. Also, recalling the combination of at least two male drives, male homosexuality must be unlike lesbianism in the way it can turn sex into a predator's unloving instrument of power and aggression.

If God created man to be the sexual pursuer rather than the pursued, as the Torah tells us,[104] the man or boy pursued by another man for sensuality must find it confusing. If youth is perceived as especially attractive, as it so often is by men, then mature men are probably less generally attractive than boys as the objects of homosexual passions.

It must be hard on the boy who, confused as most boys are about his own identity and lacking confidence concerning the female of the species, becomes such an object. Flattery, bribery and cajolery, the common tools of the sexual seducer, aren't wholesome nourishment for any boy or man.

> Flatterers are destined for Gehenna. They will ultimately fall into the hands of those they flatter. — R. Eleazar[105]

God gives a complete monopoly to woman as man's only legitimate sexual partner. If woman doesn't always relish such power or this status, she ought to consider the historical record. Those cultures that have been most tolerant of male homosexual sensuality, from ancient Greece to China to the Muslim world,[106] have been least likely to recognize woman's independent legal or civic rights, or even, often, her basic humanity.

Those cultures, the Jewish and then the Christian, that historically have been the least tolerant of male homosexual sensuality, have offered women — by far — the greatest freedom, opportunity, and status.[107] Is that merely coincidence? It seems that women prosper, as a class, when society defends this part of His Plan, and suffer, as a class, when men pursue other men.[108]

> Every man may do with his wife whatever he wishes to do.
> — Talmud[109]

Women's status in the world ultimately depends on the decency and humanity of men. Men need to study faith and kindness and compassion to rein-in their aggressive ego-driven appetites; women can rise to much the same level without so much bookish study.[110] As the larger, more ego-driven and aggressive gender grows in maturity and responsibility, women naturally rise with men — or even a little ahead. Generally, when men are good, women tend to be better.[111]

> Nothing is more precious to the Holy One than modesty.
> — *Midrash*[112]

One of the great purposes of God's Law is to restrict the sphere of human sensuality, to direct man's lusts and appetites and channel them for good. Civilization is possible only when men can keep their minds off sex long enough to do their share of the work of civilization. Perhaps man is distracted enough by sex without introducing it into male-only environments. Perhaps man is confused enough by women without confusing him further with other men and boys.

Does this commandment — does God — create unreasonable hardship for the man who says that he can't help being homosexual? Everyone has the option to overcome or at least not act upon his criminal impulses. Many supposed homosexuals manage to father children; many have had extensive heterosexual experiences, but simply find a "truer" or "higher" level of sexual satisfaction with males.[113] Perhaps they find male partners less demanding than female partners, more comfortable, or easier to find.[114]

> Idleness leads to lewdness. — R. *Eliezer ben Jacob*[115]

At any rate, the Rule is clear. A man may feel a homosexual impulse or cravings and not violate this commandment. He may even consider himself to be a homosexual, whether by nurture or nature, and remain entirely guiltless. But he must refrain from the always abominable *practice* of homosexuality — of physically "lying with man as with woman."

One can control any contrary impulse. If a policeman is at one's elbow, even supposedly irresistible impulses somehow become resistible. The practice of male homosexuality is a choice, like other choices, conditioned by law and social norms. Under the Creator's law, it is a crime, a felony. Society may devise whatever mechanisms it thinks best, in law and justice, to defend itself against it.[116]

Adultery and Bigamy

Many embark on matrimony: most succeed, some come to grief
— *Midrash*[117]

Every nation has its own marriage customs and family laws. The nations can determine the details of their own marital laws for themselves. However, this is not a detail but a basic Universal value: adultery — a married woman betraying her spouse by

having sexual relations with a different man — can destroy civilizations. Romantic or sexual relations between any man and any woman who is married to — or even merely engaged to marry[118] — any *other* man are evil, abhorrent and criminal.[119]

Beyond this the marriage laws of different nations may differ in their details. But the God of the Universe universally forbids polyandry — the combination of a woman with more than one man.

This prohibition reflects our species' nature. A man needs his mate to be *exclusive* to him; most women, apparently, can at least function if their mates are only *devoted* to them. Local cultural expectations aside,[120] it follows that polygamy — meaning in this case polygyny, the combination of a man with more than one (eligible) woman, in or out of a marriage relationship — is not universally forbidden. We see that in the lives of Israel's great Patriarchs.[121]

> Enjoy life with your wife that you love all the days of your life.
> — *Ecclesiastes 9:9* [122]

As we also see from the lives of the Patriarchs, polygamy means trouble. It strays far from the human ideal. Virtually every polygamous relationship described in the Bible was miserably unhappy,[123] fraught with envy, jealousy and conflict between wives and children alike. The preferred path for our entire species, as the union of Eve and Adam suggests, is one man, one wife, for life.[124] Of course the nations may enforce this preference by means of legislation. Or individuals can write a marriage contract to the same effect.

> Who can find a virtuous woman? Her worth is far above pearls.
> — *Proverbs 31:10*

It may be appropriate to note one further Torah prohibition in this connection: a man may not have sexual relations with his wife's sister so long as she — his wife — is still alive, even if there has been a divorce.[125] This is incest, according to the Torah. This prohibition is also a plain Rule of righteousness which may or may not commend itself to everyone.

Other Crimes and Perversions

Necrophilia A crime not listed above because it probably more properly belongs, like rape, in the category of larceny.

Involving some manner of sexual contact with a corpse, this crime robs the dead of their dignity. A cruel, heedless act of desecration — and, like rape, an aggravated form of thievery — it is, among other things, an attack on the totally defenseless. It defiles and disgraces the dead as it defiles and disgraces its perpetrator.[126]

Cross-Dressing "A woman shall not wear that which pertains to a man; neither shall a man put on a woman's garment."[127] Humanity isn't unisexual: the conventional outward distinguishing marks between women and men shouldn't be blurred.[128]

Human beings are the only earthly beings to make and wear clothes — or need to. So fashion is a uniquely human thing that can be used either in the service of sexual modesty or immodesty. Cross-dressing is modesty's opposite: the look that's adopted is a look that's erotically charged.

"The interchange of dress begets lust and leads to immorality."[129] It blurs modesty's distinction between the masculine and feminine by offering up the cross-dresser — literally, the transvestite — as a new erotic ideal: a woman with the sexual availability and openness of a man, or a man with the feminine allure of a woman.[130] It promotes — at least it partakes — of the extreme gender-confusion of homosexuality.

The licentious age early. — *Talmud*[131]

Naturally, fashions change, and every society has its own styles. Adornments like long hair, earrings, kilts or pants or neckties don't belong intrinsically to any one sex. But when the members of a community associate any such adornment with one particular sex, those who choose to wear the fashions of the other sex cross an important moral line.

God makes cross-dressing a crime, though not a capital crime, for Israel.[132] Other peoples may approach the problem differently. Because it isn't one of the minimal prohibitions of the Univeral Law,[133] they have no obligation to make such a prohibition part of their law. Yet they should be aware that, in the Lord's words, "whoever" commits this act, of cross-dressing, or transvestism, "is revolting to God."[134]

Scripture's ban against cross-dressing includes a prohibition against women arming themselves as though for battle.[135] Israel's law tries to prevent the reversal of gender roles. In a decent society men try to shield their women from violence, rather than expecting women to do battle for their men. Yet the Torah doesn't speak against women learning to use arms. Women may always take up weapons in emergencies, or whenever necessary to safeguard life.[136]

Intercourse During Menstruation This is a crime, under Israel's law, and a serious one, but not a capital felony. Violators incur a terrible spiritual penalty — the Torah warns of the soul's total extinction upon the violator's death — from Heaven.[137] But the severest punishment that any human court can impose, even theoretically, on even the most egregious transgressor, is corporal.[138] And a legal prohibition that isn't even conceivably capitally enforceable can't ordinarily be described as a Noahide legal prohibition. Still, can the perverse act under discussion here be somehow acceptable to God if a Gentile commits it, when He so despises it if a Hebrew does?

Here, too, where the Law of Sinai commands Israel, it offers everyone moral guidance, by pointing to the path of greater righteousness. Generally, the Bible insists that there is "a time to embrace, and a time to refrain from embracing."[139] This is simply a matter of family purity[140] — and purity, the Torah teaches, leads to holiness.[141] God calls on all people to make themselves holy.[142]

> Even those things in the world that seem superfluous have a Divine purpose. — *Midrash*[143]

Israel's law commands the men of Israel to refrain from intercourse with a woman while she is menstruating, and also during the seven days following her last blood flow.[144] Even then, before any intimate relations are permitted, she must wash thoroughly, and then completely immerse herself in a pool, river or other gathering of pure, unstagnant water.[145]

These holy ordinances tend to achieve some interesting practical effects. Not that such effects are the underlying goals of the law, but if familiarity breeds contempt, periodic abstinence makes the heart grow fonder.

A Jewish couple must abstain from sex for almost half their lives together, for at least twelve days — five days of blood flow or "spotting," plus seven "white" or "clean" days — out of every twenty-eight, during the years of her fertility. This monthly break gives her an opportunity to be herself, when she may be feeling weak or ill, to restore herself. It tends to bring back the art of conversation. And it genuinely helps keep them from getting tired of each other. Further, the approximately sixteen "free" days in the lunar month are usually the time of both the woman's greatest desire for sex as well as her greatest fertility.

Perhaps not surprisingly, those who most scrupulously keep these laws of family purity, as they are known, have both the lowest divorce rates and the highest birth rates among all Israel.[146]

> Everything depends on the woman. — *Midrash*[147]

Another practical effect is hygienic. Menstrual blood and mucus tend to make the body susceptible to infection from the germs that intercourse might carry into it.[148] Women who observe the Torah's laws of family purity seem to be much less subject than other women to uterine cancer, blood-borne diseases like hepatitis and AIDS, and ovarian cysts. They also suffer fewer urinary tract infections, and pregnant women have fewer stillborn births.[149]

> Love that is physical vanishes with the object; love that is not physical is imperishable. — *Mishnah*[150]

God has elevated woman above the animals with a special reproductive cycle. Unlike lesser females, she is usually fertile and capable of breeding all through the year. Corresponding more or less to the cycle of Earth's moon, her periodicity is unique, and enormously sophisticated.[151] Even scientifically, it remains highly mysterious. It distinguishes her from all the rest of Creation, including her male mate. And the less contact that her mate has with it, apparently, the better.[152]

Sexual shamelessness God despises harlotry (prostitution), uncleanliness, or anything that exaggerates the animal in man at the expense of the human spirit.[153] The spirit — the godlike element in man — should be our master and the body our faithful servant, not the other way around.[154] This is less a matter of minimal law than of personal discipline, decency and conscience. In every healthy society these wholesome impulses are also reinforced by powerful social norms.

One should never perform any purely animal function in the public purview. God is there, with us and among us.[155]

Similarly, generally, public nakedness is unholy. Man should "remove his glance from everything animal in man, every animal function of the human body, so that man should never view himself as animal and, grown used to the view, regard only the animal in himself and forget the spirit."[156] These considerations should govern all of us, from Finland to Fiji. Going back to Eden: "When the animal gained the first victory over man, the guardian, shame, awoke, and taught man to cover himself, and the gently guiding Father confirmed this teaching by active help."[157]

Philandering, or flirtatious or erotic conduct between people whose actual union would be illegitimate. The Torah forbids it, subjecting those who transgress to judicial, corporal penalties, as well as further Heavenly punishment. Not merely intercourse — "lying" with someone subject to the incest ban, or with a menstruant, or with a woman engaged or married to another — but merely seductively "approaching" such a person romantically is forbidden.[158]

A Torah statute with obviously universal implications, the prohibition here establishes a fence around criminality. It requires us to abstain from frivolous sexuality, or deliberately provocative flirting, kissing, or petting, which might eventually lead to illicit — i.e., criminal — sexual intercourse.

Contraception and Birth Control

> Everyone is born of three partners: a father, a mother, and the Blessed Creator Himself. — *Talmud*[159]

God did not create the world for a wasteland; He created it to be inhabited.[160] The glory of any kingdom — even including God's — is its inhabitants. So God blesses the reproductive process. "Be fruitful and become many," He told the lesser animals — speechless animals, who surely could not understand His words — and so He spoke to man, who could.[161] Ten generations later God said the same thing to Noah's animals — and also, twice, to Noah and his children.[162]

This is, at the very least, an approving description of His creatures' nature. Clearly, God doesn't give humanity fertility or children as a curse, but intends them both — at least when people follow His law — to serve Him for blessing. The question is, are these words the words of Command and a matter of Universal law or are they something less than law?

Some Torah authorities believe that God does command every Noahide to reproduce.[163] But no authority has ever said that Noahide courts are supposed to enforce that obligation. And, as we've seen before, a duty or obligation that Noahide courts have never been called on to enforce can't be listed as a Noahide law.[164]

Most Torah authorities interpret these words of Genesis simply as words of encouragement and blessing.[165] Heaven never repeated them at Sinai, which suggests that they don't constitute a Rainbow Covenant obligation.[166] Then too, the Torah commands only the men of Israel, but not the women, to reproduce.[167] A Jewish woman isn't obligated to breed or marry — perhaps because "God had no need to reinforce her natural impulses by Divine legislation."[168] Any such legislation might "make the female pursue the male," leading her into immodesty.[169] Excusing her from legal obligation also serves to release the woman, and her family, from destructive burdens — from feeling either that she must rush into marriage or that God unconditionally requires her to risk her life or health in childbirth or pregnancy.

So if the duty to "be fruitful and multiply" — in Hebrew, *pru urvu* — is a Universal law, as some say, just about half of the people of Israel are exempt from it. Of course, this doesn't make much sense. Keeping in mind the clear declaration of the Talmud mentioned previously,[170] that the words at issue are words of encouragement and blesing, we must assume that reproduction is **not** a Noahide law — it is not a universally enforceable legal obligation. But that doesn't mean one can ignore it.

As we have seen before and will see again, righteousness requires more from man than just avoiding what is criminal. In this case Heaven has given us a positive precept to direct us. The method isn't one of legal compulsion but of gentle encouragement. We pursue the Way of virtue by heeding Him; beyond merely abstaining from the vile crimes that His Law forbids, we serve Him by affirmatively following Him in all things.

Finally, since this matter is subject to so many misconceptions, it deserves a minimum of study, even at the cost of ignoring other issues. The Torah does **not** forbid contraception — birth control — at least in certain circumstances.[171] It does forbid certain methods of birth control.

Generally, those methods are best which interfere with the physical and psychological nature of sexual intercourse the least.

Surgical intervention, such as tubal ligation, in the case of a woman, or castration or even vasectomy in the case of a man, is never permitted as a contraceptive technique. It constitutes bodily mutilation — the mutilation, in other words, or maiming of God's property — merely to keep the body from fulfilling its God-given purpose.[172]

As the Bible's story of Er and Onan suggests,[173] our Creator condemns the practice of *coitus interruptus* — of the man's withdrawal just before fully consummating the sex act. Neither that nor anything that might amount to casting semen in vain — that is, deliberately wasting it, as though man's reproductive seed were a useless poison — can be countenanced as a legitimate contraceptive method.[174] The sex act is not complete unless the man's seed enters the woman's body. So a (Jewish) man may not wear a condom as a contraceptive device.[175] In fact, he may never personally employ any nullifying or blocking technique against his own seed.[176]

Feminine contraceptive implants or oral contraceptives, such as the birth control pill, are preferred over chemical spermicides, which are preferred over physical barriers, such as an absorbent internal pad or diaphragm or an internal female condom. While the male's seed must enter the female, she may, if she has to, use such methods to neutralize or block it once he has made his way inside her.[177]

These Torah precepts — righteous Statutes[178] — all have a logically direct bearing upon B'nai Noah. *"One should not presume to exclude the Noahide from Mosaic principles."*[179] Where God condemns any particular practice or contraceptive technique if Israel employs it, the identical methods, if employed by B'nai Noah, hardly seem likely to please Him.

The Lord is with you while you are with Him. — *2 Chronicles 15:2*

Let's close this chapter, finally, with a summarizing reminder. The Divine gift of human sexuality is not an accident nor merely a plaything. Rather, like every other holy gift, it is a wonder, a responsibility, and — when we use it wisely, as Providence intends — a means to both please and refine ourselves with our partners, all courtesy of our infinitely loving Maker.

Study leads to precision, precision to zeal, zeal to cleanliness, cleanliness to restraint, restraint to purity, purity to piety, piety to humility, humility to fear of sin, fear of sin to saintliness, saintliness to the Holy Spirit, and the Holy Spirit to life eternal. — *Talmud*[180]

NOTES

1. "Abomination" — *to'eva*. "Perversion" — *tevel*. See Isaiah 1:13, *to'eva* describing a repulsive sacrificial offering. Or Deuteronomy 24:17, using the same root term, applying it to oppressing strangers and orphans.

2. *Yad, Hilchot Issurei Biyah* 21:1.

3. See Genesis 2:24, 29:18; Deuteronomy 34:7; Proverbs 5:17-18, 18:22. Generally, see Song of Songs (the Song of Solomon), a truly remarkable case in point.

4. See Talmud, *Yevamot* 62b, 63b, 82b; Nachmanides (R. Moses ben Nahman, Ramban, c. 1194-1270), *The Holy Letter* (S. Cohen translation. Ktav, New York NY, 1976).

5. *Genesis Rabbah* 8:9.

6. Midrash, *Genesis Rabbah* 17:7; Talmud, *Sotah* 17, *Yevamot* 63b.

7. Genesis 1:27; Talmud, *Yevamot* 62b, *Sotah* 17a; *Shulchan Aruch, Orach Haim* 231.1.

8. See Genesis 1:27 and 2:18, 24; Isaiah 66:13; Talmud, *Berachot* 32a, 62a; *Genesis Rabbah* 13:14; *Zohar* (the ancient mystic work), *Genesis* 55b (on Genesis 5:2). The biological parents of any person born as a result of a cloning process would be the parents of the person from whom the clone issued. Logically, any human born from cloning is or would be entirely human, possessing all the rights and obligations of every other human being and existing in the same Divine "Image" (Genesis 1:27).

9. Aryeh Kaplan, *Handbook of Jewish Thought* (supra, 1979) 2:27. One notes that every Biblical prophetess or matriarch, as well as all the prophets and the patriarchs, referred to God as "He." Recognizing, in this context, that Hebrew has no neuter gender — an "it" alternative — to "she" or "he."

10. Genesis 1, and commentaries.

11. See Mishnah, *Pirke Avot* 5:21; Talmud, *Yoma* 2a, *Yevamot* 62b-63a,

Kiddushin 29b.

12. Genesis 2:24. See Talmud, *Nedarim* 20b. Only a male and a female, of the same species, can truly "cleave" to each other or become "one flesh" together. Talmud, *Sanhedrin* 58a with Rashi, *Hullin* 98a-b.

13. "Infantile Sexuality," *Three Contributions to the Theory of Sex* (1905), in *The Basic Writings of Sigmund Freud,* A.A. Brill, ed. (Random House, New York NY, 1938/1966) p. 584; "'Civilized' Sexual Morality and Modern Nervous Illness," (1908) in *Collected Papers* (Basic Books, New York NY, 1959), Vol. 2, pp. 76-99.

14. Freud, ibid. See Dennis Prager, "Judaism, Homosexuality and Civilization," *Ultimate Issues* (Los Angeles CA, April-June 1990), p. 2.

15. See Exodus 19:15; Leviticus 20:23, 21:7, 9, 13-15; Proverbs 31; Talmud, *Shabbat* 87a; *Moreh Nevuchim* 3:33, 35,49; *Horeb*, Chapters 66-7. Also see *Mishnah Tosefta, Avoda Zorah* 8:4; Talmud, *Sanhedrin* 57b-58b; *Yad, Hilchot Melachim* 9; Lichtenstein, supra, pp. 49-52; Novak, supra, pp. 202.

16. Bindman, *Seven Colors of the Rainbow,* supra, p. 65.

17. Leviticus 18:6. See *Sefer HaMitzvot* 2:353.

18. *Moreh Nevuchim* 3:39 (middle).

19. Adding that the incest ban has nothing to do with healthy displays of natural affection, but only to contacts between near kin that might arouse a sexual urge. See *Yad, Issurei Biyah* 21:6.

20. See Leviticus 18; Deuteronomy 23:3 and commentaries; *Sefer HaMitzvot* 2:330-345, 351-353; Talmud, *Yevamot* 21a; *Yad, Hilchot Ishut* 1:6.

21. See Leviticus 18:30; Mishnah, *Pirke Avot* 1:1; Deuteronomy 17:9,11.

22. Known as incest of the second degree. See Talmud, *Yevamot* 21a; *Yad, Issurei Biyah* 21:6.

23. Mishnah, *Tosefta Avodah Zorah* 8:4; Talmud *Sanhedrin* 57b.

24. See Talmud, *Ketubot* 12a, *Sanhedrin* 57b, versus *Yevamot* 98a with Rashi, *Horayot* 10b.

25. Ibid, and Genesis 38, regarding Judah (Yehuda) and Tamar, with Leviticus 18:15 and *Sefer HaMitzvot* 2:343.

26. See Isaiah 58:7 and commentaries; *Yad, Issurei Biyah* 2:14; *Shulchan Aruch, Even HaEzer* 15:6-20.

27. See Talmud, *Gittin* 10b; *Tosefta Avodah Zorah* 8:4.

28. See Talmud, *Sanhedrin* 58a on Genesis 2:24. *Yad, Hilchot Melachim* 9:5-6, speaks only of a Rainbow Covenant ban on a man's incest with his mother, his step-mother (his father's wife or former wife or widow), or with his mother's daughter (his maternal sister). But this listing seems to contemplate a society that doesn't recognize biological paternity.

29. See Genesis 20:12: "She is my sister, my father's daughter, but not my mother's, [So] she became my wife." Some authorities speculate that the minimal requisites of Noahide law may not forbid incest between siblings, at least in certain extraordinary circumstances (discussing humanity's legendary ancestors, the children of Adam and Eve). See Novak, supra, pp. 200-204.

30. The rabbis discuss incest between children and parents as an example of the most radically awful conduct imaginable. Lot was a disgusting sinner (Genesis 19:31-38), although his two daughters, who thought to repopulate the world after so much destruction, probably at least meant well. See Talmud, *Horayot* 10b, *Nazir* 23b. Conceivably, adult daughter-father incest might, in certain circumstances, be somewhat less morally abhorrent

than, e.g., mother-son incest. Some speculate that the unadorned Noahide Law might not only forgive Lot's daughters but also Lot himself — if only in that one extraordinary situation. See Talmud, *Sanhedrin* 58b, *Yevamot* 62b-63a; *Yad, Issurei Biyah* 14:12; Novak, supra, p. 204. The sources note that, while every society acknowledges motherhood in some way, not all keep track of paternal ties. Maternity tends to be both more difficult to forget and easier to trace and recognize than biological paternity.

31. Exodus 20:13; Leviticus 18:20, 20:10; *Yad, Hilchot Melachim* 9:7; *Sefer HaMitzvot* 2:347.

32. See *Minchat Hinnuch*, supra, Imperative 188; Lichtenstein, supra, p. 51.

33. *Yad, Hilchot Melachim* 9:7. "Publicly separated" — ordinarily, if she and he have stopped sleeping under the same roof.

34. Malachi 2:16.

35. See, e.g., Deuteronomy 24:1-4; *Sefer HaMitzvot* 1:213, 1:222.

36. As "righteous Statutes" which offer Noahides some guidance. See Talmud, *Nedarim* 66b, *Gittin* 90a-b.

37. Leviticus 18:23; *Sefer HaMitzvot* 2:348-349.

38. Leviticus 18:22; *Sefer HaMitzvot* 2:350.

39. Leviticus 18:22.

40. Leviticus 18:22. Scholars teach that Scripture applies the same term to crimes of oppression, injustice and dishonesty.

41. Talmud, *Sanhedrin* 57b.

42. See Deuteronomy 22:26; Talmud, *Nedarim* 27a; *Moreh Nevuchim* 3:41.

43. Talmud, *Yevamot* 76a; *Yad, Hilchot Issurei Biyah* 21:8.

44. See Genesis 38:7-10 with Rashi, regarding Er and Onan and the discharge of semen in vain. But masturbation by either a male or a female is associated with impurity. Masturbation is thought to encourage immodesty, lust, and pointless pleasure-seeking. See Talmud, *Ketubot* 46a, *Nedarim* 20b.

45. See Leviticus 19:29; Deuteronomy 23:18. Pornography — prurient or lascivious eroticism, in fixed images or print — falls into the same general category.

46. Talmud, *Yevamot* 76a.

47. See Leviticus 19:29.

48. R. Simlai bar Abba, *Avoda Zorah* 3a.

49. Leviticus 18:6-29.

50. See Deuteronomy 18:3, with Rashi; Proverbs 23:7.

51. See Mishnah, *Tosefta Avoda Zorah* 9:4; Talmud, Sanhedrin 58a.

52. *Genesis Rabbah* 26.

53. Hirsch, *Horeb*, supra, chapters 66-67.

54. See *Horeb*, supra, chapter 66, para. 441.

55. Talmud, *Bava Kamma* 79b, *Bava Metzia* 3a; *Yad, Hilchot Terumah* 4:13, *Hilchot Teshuva* 3:4.

56. See Leviticus 18:3; R. Yakov Culi, *Me'am Lo'ez*, supra, on Exodus 8:22.

57. See Deuteronomy 6:5; *Moreh Nevuchim* 3:29.

58. Deuteronomy 6:24, 10:13; Isaiah 48:17; Psalm 16:11; *Horeb*, Introduction, p. Lxii.

59. See sources listed in the note above.

60. *Gittin* 70a. Also see Genesis 4:7; Midrash, *Leviticus Rabbah* 14.

61. *Moreh Nevuchim* 3:49.

62. See Frazer, *The Golden Bough,* supra.

63. *An Outline of Psychoanalysis,* James Strachey, editor and translator (W. W. Norton, New York NY, 1949), p. 114.

64. See Leviticus 11:44, 19:2; Talmud, *Sotah* 14a, *Shabbat* 133b.

65. *Yesod Mora* (classic commentary, c. 1158 CE) ch. 7. See Genesis 17:10. Circumcision, an indelible mark on the male organ of generation (cutting away the infant's penile foreskin), dedicates even man's sexual impulses to God's service and to the truth of His total Unity. See *Moreh Nevuchim* 3:48; Genesis 17:7.

66. *Shabbat* 62a.

67. Genesis 3:18-22.

68. R. Abbahu, *Genesis Rabbah* 68:3.

69. Midrash, ibid, 2:18.

70. *Bava Metzia* 59a.

71. Talmud, *Niddah* 45b, *Berachot* 17a, *Pesachim* 113b. For an interesting look from a secular point of view at some of the differences between women and men, see Carol A. Rinzler, *Why Eve Doesn't Have an Adam's Apple* (Facts on File, New York NY, 1996), and Deborah Blum, *Sex on the Brain; the Biological Differences between Men and Women* (Viking, New York NY, 1997).

72. Genesis 21:12.

73. Talmud, *Megillah* 14b.

74. Talmud, *Niddah* 45b.

75. Talmud, *Niddah* 45b, and Midrash, *Genesis Rabbah* 18:1.

76. See Midrash, *Exodus Rabbah* 28:2.

77. See Midrash, *Song of Songs/Shir haShirim Rabbah* 4:22. Half of ancient Israel's prophets were women. The Bible mentions only seven: Sarah, Miriam, Deborah, Hanna, Abigail, Hulda, and Esther. See Kaplan, *Handbook of Jewish Thought,* supra, 6:84, and its source notes.

78. Talmud, *Eruvin* 63a, *Ketubot* 62b-63a.

79. See Judges 4:4, 5:31; Talmud, *Sotah* 22b.

80. Midrash, *Exodus Rabbah* 28:2. That is, the Commandments incumbent upon women. Many Torah Commandments exempt women entirely and only obligate Jewish men. See *Mishnah Tosefta, Berachot* 7:18.

81. Talmud, *Sotah* 11b.

82. *Pirke d'Rabbi Eleazar,* chapter 41.

83. Commentary to the Siddur (Jewish prayerbook) by R. Nosson Scherman — *The Complete ArtScroll Siddur* (Mesorah, New York NY, 1984) p. 19n, regarding an important liturgical distinction between the genders.

84. *Male and Female; a Study of the Sexes in a Changing World* (William Morrow & Co., New York NY, 1949) p. 160.

85. See Rudyard Kipling's definition of manhood in the poem *If* — "If you can keep your head when all about you Are losing theirs and blaming it on you [. . .] Yours is the Earth and everything that's in it, And — which is more — you'll be a Man, my son!" (London, 1910). Abram/Abraham is the Bible's model man. See Genesis 6:9 with Rashi.

86. But see Ecclesiastes 7:28 — holding women up to a most exacting standard.

87. See Freud, supra, ibid.

88. Mishnah, *Pirke Avot* 2:5.

89. See Prager, supra, *Ultimate Issues*, ibid.

90. Prager, ibid. Also see, e.g., Mead, supra, pp. 192-193; Will Durant, *Our Oriental Heritage* (Simon & Schuster, New York NY, 1959) pp. 36-57.

91. *Yevamot* 113a. Posited as a general rule, with recognized exceptions.

92. Proverbs 31:10-31, known in the Prayerbook as *Aishes Chayil* ("A Virtuous/Accomplished Woman"). Most commentators treat this passage as allegory; a mere human can only try to live up to its ideal.

93. *Yevamot* 63a. Another generalization, with many recognized exceptions.

94. Mishnah, *Kiddushin* 1:7; Talmud, *Menachot* 43b, *Kiddushin* 31a. See, e.g., *Sefer HaMitzvot* 1:10. Women as well as men are obligated to observe the time-specific Commandment of rejoicing on holy festivals (*Sefer HaMitzvot*, supra, 1:54; See Deuteronomy 16:14, 27:7; Talmud, *Hagigah* 6b) and also the Commandment to eat matzah, unleavened bread, on the first night of *Pesach*/Passover (*Sefer HaMitzvot* 1:158; See Exodus 12:18; Talmud, *Pesachim* 120a).

95. See Talmud, *Bava Metzia* 59a.

96. Talmud, *Kiddushin* 29a, *Yoma* 3a, *Yevamot* 62b-63a.

97. *Mishnah Tosefta, Berachot* 7:18, *Menachot* 436, referring to the blessing that is part of every Jewish man's mandated daily prayers. Women, on the other hand, say ". . . Who has made me according to Thy will." Israel's men are bound by all of the Torah's time-specific ritual Commandments, which are only optional for women. The extra burden on men is also a privilege, because it gives men an opportunity to win more merit from faithful observance. In a sense, this is like a Heavenly "affirmative action" program for men.

98. Rabbi Nosson Scherman — commentary in *Complete ArtScroll Siddur*, supra, p. 19n.

99. A husband has a right to know the paternity of his own wife's children. The siege of Troy in Homer's *Illiad* points to the extremely untoward effects of disrespecting the rights of husbands.

100. Talmud, *Yevamot* 76a.

101. *Emunot VeDe'ot* (classic work, c. 925 CE) 10:9.

102. The Kinsey sex researchers reported that lesbians average no more than ten homosexual partners in their lifetimes, while the "typical" male homosexual in America had more than 500. See Alan Bell and Martin Weinberg, *Homosexualities* (Alfred Kinsey Institute for Sex Research/Simon & Schuster, New York NY, 1978) p. 85. Of course these statistics don't reflect changes since the onset of the AIDS epidemic.

103. R. Simlai, *Genesis Rabbah* 36:5.

104. Talmud, *Shabbat* 152a, *Kiddushin* 2b.

105. Talmud, *Sotah* 41b. *Gehenna*, a valley in Jerusalem associated, in very ancient times, with gruesome acts of pagan sacrifice, probably offers the closest Hebrew equivalent to the popular concept of Hell.

106. I.e., cultures tolerant or even approving of a man taking the "male" role in homosexual intercourse, if not of the man who takes or is forced to submit to the "female" role.

107. See Prager, *Ultimate Issues*, supra, p. 11.

108. In every culture some women, an elite, will enjoy broad privileges and powers. One speaks here of the freedom of the average woman to fully realize herself as a woman — as a reasonably materially secure homemaker

and mother and pillar of her community — and not just as a paid producer.

109. *Nedarim* 20b, referring to the enjoyment of sex and the permissibility of different techniques and positions, so as to achieve, as a couple, greater emotional unity and holiness (*kiddushin*). A husband may *never* use force to compel his wife to have sex. Talmud, *Eruvin* 100b. The Torah forbids wife-beating for any reason. *Shulchan Aruch, Even HaEzer* 154:3.

110. See Genesis 21:12; Midrash, *Genesis Rabbah* 18:2; *Sifre*, Numbers 133; Talmud, *Megillah* 14b.

111. See Mishnah, *Kiddushin* 1:7; Talmud, *Menachot* 43b; Midrash, *Pirke d'Rabbi Eleazar,* ch. 41.

112. *Pesikta Rabbati* (I. Friedmann, ed.) Ch. 45, 185b, speaking of sexual modesty — in Hebrew, *tzniut.*

113. Prager, *Ultimate Issues,* supra, p. 14.

114. Not to condemn the caring longterm partnerships that sometimes arise between homosexual men. God forbid. Genuinely selfless love is holy. But homosexual lust is not selfless love. Probably, mutual sexual activity barely even figures in many long-lasting, professedly "homosexual" pairing arrangements.

115. Mishnah, *Ketubot* 5:5. Also see, there, R. Shimon ben Gamaliel II, "Idleness leads to idiocy."

116. Homosexual sodomy and fellatio are still civil crimes in many of the fifty American states. Until the late 1960's, the states generally enforced these laws — and similar laws, prohibiting such things as homosexual kissing and dancing in public — with enough vigor to drive most homosexual activity underground, out of the public purview. According to the logic of our analysis, this approach, depending on conditions in any particular society, would generally suffice as an appropriate legal response to this sort of crime.

117. *Numbers Rabbah* 9:4.

118. Engaged formally, pursuant to a recognized engagement contract, a valid legal agreement.

119. Exodus 20:13; Leviticus 18:20, 20:10; *Yad, Hilchot Melachim* 9:7; *Sefer HaMitzvot* 2:347.

120. A groom's vow of exclusive fidelity to his bride is as binding as any legal agreement and as significant as any vow. But *wherever* monogamy is the norm, a wife's reasonable expectations of an exclusive relationship with her husband deserves protection. See Numbers 30:3; Talmud, *Pesachim* 51a.

121. Also see Deuteronomy 21:15.

122. Note: wife, not wives. Your own wife, not another's. Literally, "a woman that you love."

123. Joseph Telushkin, *Jewish Literacy* (William Morrow & Co., New York NY, 1991) p. 178.

124. See Genesis 2:24; Malachi 2:14; Talmud, *Yevamot* 59a. So, of the approximately 2,800 rabbis mentioned in the Talmud, only one is known to have had two wives, let alone more than two. See Menachem Brayer, *The Jewish Woman in Rabbinic Literature: a Psychosocial Persepective* (Ktav, Hoboken NJ, 1986) p. 51.

125. Leviticus 18:18; *Sefer HaMitzvot* 2:345.

126. Concerning the Torah obligation to protect the dead from any manner of indignity, see, e.g., Deuteronomy 21:22-23, 28:26; Talmud, *Sanhedrin* 46a-b; *Gittin* 61a; *Sotah* 14a. Even the body of an executed criminal

must be promptly and properly disposed of. Concerning these issues of death and defilement, see, e.g., Numbers 19:11-16. Generally, see Hirsch, *Horeb*, supra, Ch. 61.

127. Deuteronomy 22:5.

128. See Brayer, *The Jewish Woman in Rabbinic Literature*, supra, pp. 173-174.

129. *Moreh Nevuchim* 3:37.

130. Brayer, supra, ibid. Also see Marjorie Garber, *Vested Interests: Cross-Dressing and Cultural Anxiety* (Routledge, New York NY, 1992).

131. In the name of Rabbah bar Nachmani, *Shabbat* 152a.

132. *Sefer HaMitzvot* 2:39-40.

133. Even among Israel, a woman may, for instance, masquerade as a man while traveling, in the interests of safety. *Shulchan Aruch, Yoreh De'ah* 182:6. For that matter, a man may, in certain circumstances, masquerade as a woman for comic purpose. Ibid, *Orach Haim* 696:8. Such easy-going exceptions clearly suggest that the prohibition in question is neither absolute nor universal.

134. Deuteronomy 22:5.

135. See Talmud, *Nazir* 59a.

136. Leviticus 18:5; Deuteronomy 4:8, 22:8; Talmud, *Hullin* 10a, *Yoma* 85b, *Sanhedrin* 74a-b. Some commentators point to the Bible's Yael (Jael) — a righteous Gentile woman, who killed a foreign general, Sisera, not with a man's sword, though one was right at hand, but with her accustomed tools, a hammer and a tent pin — as an example of true modesty when it comes to women taking up men's weapons. See Judges 4:21 and 5:26. But Yael surely had every right to use *any* device that she could handle confidently.

137. Leviticus 18:19, 20:18.

138. See *Yad, Hilchot Sanhedrin* 19:1: a Jewish man who has relations with his menstruating wife (a '*niddah*') deserves lashes/a court-ordered whipping; and *Sefer HaMitzvot* 2:346. Also see *Shulchan Aruch, Yoreh De'ah* 183-200, and Mishnah, *Pirke Avot* 3:18.

139. Ecclesiastes 3:5. Even though Gentiles have no legal obligation to follow the Torah precepts here.

140. See Talmud, *Niddah* 17b, 41b; Midrash, *Song of Songs/Shir haShirim Rabbah* 1. "Purity" — spiritual innocence.

141. Talmud, *Sotah* 12a.

142. Isaiah 45:22; Psalm 145:18; Midrash, *Exodus Rabbah* 19:4.

143. Genesis Rabbah 10:7.

144. Leviticus 15:16-33, 18:19, 20:18; *Sefer HaMitzvot* 1:109, 2:346.

145. See ibid, and Leviticus 11:36. The Hebrew word is *Mikva*. See Genesis 1:10, Leviticus 11:36. The Christian baptismal font seems to be derived from *mikva*, while John the Baptist/Yochanan ben Zecharia is famously connected to *tevila*/immersion and *mikva*. See the Christian Gospels, Matthew 3:6, Mark 1:5, Luke 3:7, and Acts 1:5, 22:16.

146. See Talmud, *Niddah* 31b with Rashi; Norman Lamm, *A Hedge of Roses* (Feldheim, New York NY, 1966); Marie C. Stopes, (*Married Love* (an American pre-War standby. Harper Bros., New York NY, 1932), p. 51); David Landau, *Piety and Power* (Hill & Wang, New York NY, 1993), pp. 21, 257, 282.

147. *Genesis Rabbah* 17:7.

148. DeWitt W. Brown, *Journal of Reproductive Medicine*, Vol. 34, November, 1989.

149. Brayer, *Jewish Woman in Rabbinic Literature*, supra, pp. 93-94.

150. *Pirke Avot* 5:20.

151. The passage of time, as time is measured by Israel's Revealed calendar — see Exodus 12:2; Leviticus 23; *Yad, Hilchot Kiddush HaChodesh* 9 — corresponds to the same mysterious forces.

152. Generally, see Norman Lamm, supra, and Aryeh Kaplan, *Waters of Eden* (National Council of Synagogue Youth, New York NY, 1976) pp. 40-46.

153. See, e.g., Leviticus 19:29; Deuteronomy 23:10-15,18, 18:13 with Rashi, Isaiah 52:11, Psalm 24:3; Talmud, *Sotah* 4b; *Yad, Tumat Ochlin* 15:12.

154. See Hirsch, *Horeb*, supra, para. 455.

155. *Horeb*, supra, para. 457. See Deuteronomy 23:10-15,18.

156. *Horeb*, supra, para. 456. Also see Talmud, *Yevamot* 63b.

157. *Horeb*, ibid, citing Genesis 3:7,21.

158. Leviticus 18:3,6,29-30; Midrash, *Sifra* to *Leviticus,* ibid.; *Yad, Hilchot Issurei Biyah* 22:21; *Sefer HaMitzvot* 2:353.

159. *Kiddushin* 30b. Also see *Niddah* 31a; Midrash, *Ecclesiastes Rabbah* 8:13. God provides the spirit or soul, which returns — either diminished or improved — to Him when life is done. See Midrash, id., 12:7; *Moreh Nevuchim* 3:17,24.

160. Isaiah 45:18, Psalm 89:3.

161. Genesis 1:22,28.

162. Genesis 9:1,7.

163. See, e.g., Ramban, *Pirush al HaTorah* on Genesis 9:7.

164. *Yad, Hilchot Melachim* 9:14. Note that the other Universal laws are also all prohibitive, or negative Commandments, rather than positive, affirmative obligations. See *Yad*, ibid, 9:1 and commentaries.

165. See Talmud, *Sanhedrin* 59b, explicitly stating that Noahides are *not* legally obligated to reproduce. And see *Mishneh l'Melech* (R. Yakov Culi, editor; classic commentary, c. 1724; Hebrew only) to *Yad, Hilchot Melachim* 10:7; *Moreh Nevuchim* 3:13.

166. The people of Israel, however, must "be fruitful and multiply" in order to survive all persecution, to fulfill the terms of the Hebrew Revolution. See Exodus 12:24; Deuteronomy 7:6-11; Isaiah 43:10,12, 127:3; Esther 3:8; Talmud, *Pesachim* 87b; *Sefer HaMitzvot* 1:3; *Yad, Hilchot Melachim* 8:10.

167. Talmud, *Yevamot* 65b; *Sefer HaMitzvot* 1:212-213. Hebrew community courts were known, very long ago, to compel young men to marry and start families. See *Shulchan Aruch, Even HaEzer* 1:3, referring to a past practice. Even then, however, the severest penalties for disobedience were (only) corporal.

168. Immanuel Jacobovitz, *Journal of a Rabbi* (Living Books, New York NY, 1966) p. 216, cited in Alex J. Goldman, *Judaism Confronts Contemporary Issues* (Shengold Publishers, New York NY, 1978) p. 112n. Also see Talmud, *Yevamot* 65b, 113a.

169. Talmud, *Shabbat* 152a, *Kiddushin* 2b; Midrash, *Genesis Rabbah* 2:21.

170. Talmud, *Sanhedrin* 59b.

171. See *Mishnah Tosefta* to *Yevamot* 8:4; Talmud, *Yevamot* 12b. Generally,

see David Feldman, *Birth Control in Jewish Law* (New York University Press, NY, 1968); A.J. Goldman, supra, pp. 109-137. After a Jewish man has had two children, a girl and a boy, he may, but only if it is necessary, legally abstain from fathering any more. *Shulchan Aruch, Even HaEzer* 1:1. Contraception is generally permitted if required to protect the life and health of the woman or of any ill or infirm child that still needs her full attention.

172. Deuteronomy 14:1; *Sefer HaMitzvot* 2:45. Naturally, sexual relations with an infertile or a post-menopausal woman, if the union is otherwise permitted, are permitted. See *Tosafot* (Hebrew only) to Talmud, *Yevamot* 12b and *Ketubot* 39.

173. Genesis 38:7-10; Midrash, *Genesis Rabbah* 34:10. See Rashi on Genesis 4:19,23.

174. See Talmud, *Niddah* 13a.

175. See Goldman, supra, p. 120. Conceivably, in very rare or extreme circumstances, a man might, in the context of marriage, be permitted to wear a condom as a barrier to disease, given the primacy of protecting human life and health. See Leviticus 18:5; Talmud, *Hullin* 10a, *Yoma* 85a-b, *Sanhedrin* 74a.

176. Rav Moshe Feinstein, *Iggerot Moshe* (NY 1959), *Hoshen Mishpat*, Vol. 2, No. 69 (Hebrew only). Also see David Feldman and A.J. Goldman, supra, ibid.

177. *Mishnah Tosefta, Yevamot* 8:4 (regarding a "potion of sterility"). See Goldman, supra, and his sources.

178. That offer Noahides moral if not formal legal guidance. See Talmud, *Nedarim* 66b, *Gittin* 90a-b.

179. R. Moshe Isserles (Ramo), *Sheilot U'Teshuvot Rama* (c. 1570 CE; 1835 ed., Hebrew only) p. 7, Responsum 10. Cited in Lichtenstein, supra, p. 37.

180. R. Pinchas ben Yair, *Avoda Zorah* 20b. "Holy Spirit" — in Hebrew, *Ruach HaKodesh* — is the highest humanly attainable degree of godliness, short of genuine prophecy or prophetic revelation.

The Fourth Commandment

Laws Against Murder

Beloved is man, for he was created in the image of God. — Mishnah[1]

God commands all men and all women, including every Gentile and every Jew, "You shall not commit murder."[2] The Hebrew phrase is *lo tir'tzach;* it doesn't mean "you shall not kill" but, in precise prohibitory language, "you shall not deliberately kill an innocent human being."[3]

Behold, all souls are Mine. — *Ezekiel 18:4*

Obviously, people may kill plants and animals for food.[4] Man has a perfect right to kill, at times, as he exercises the privileges of worldly dominion. Since dominion involves duties and responsibilities as well as privileges, God sometimes even requires people to kill, in certain circumstances, to preserve justice and maintain order, as His stewards over the Earth. Soldiers must sometimes kill their nations' enemies in wartime.[5] Courts may execute criminals who have been justly convicted of terrible crimes.[6] A person may, or even must, use killing force if necessary to protect oneself or others.[7]

The real nature of man is the issue here. This Commandment centers around these three very basic Torah principles: everyone on Earth is truly "of" God; every living person is an "image" of and a child of God, and all of us belong to Him.[8] As we all have the same Heavenly Parent, Who also happens to be our Owner, we see that God has made each of us ultimately a brother or sister to everyone else — to the whole species of man.[9]

Further, because God deliberately created all of us, alone of all His earthly creatures, in His very "Image," we understand that God especially cherishes humanity, above His other creations, and that all of us partake, in some sense, of the infinite holiness of our Maker.[10] Since any fraction of infinity is itself infinite, *everyone* born of a human mother — regardless of any bodily, emotional or mental defects, infirmities or wounds — has infinite value. Since infinity equals infinity, we see that man by his very nature must never "trade flesh," or sacrifice even the least of his brothers in order to save one or some of the rest.[11] No one's blood is any sweeter than the blood of anyone else.[12]

> Whoever destroys a single human life is considered by the Torah as if he had destroyed an entire world. . . . — *Mishnah*[13]

No other crime so defiles the earth.[14] Murder deforms civilizations; it pollutes them and the very places where it occurs; it overturns the natural order of the world.[15] Murder constitutes a kind of blasphemy.

> Only a murderer altogether renounces the obligations of brotherhood. — *J.H. Hertz*[16]

God has so much love for humanity, the rabbis teach, that He has made all men aware, and not merely Israel, that man exists in His Holy "image."[17] To deliberately and wrongfully take such a life, before God Himself has called for it, is like erasing God's image, like assaulting the world's Creator. It's a completely irrevocable, terrible, arrogation of Divinity's own jealously held prerogatives. God will hold the murderer to account as if he had diminished God's Divinity.[18]

Mystics associate this Fourth Universal Commandment with the red of the rainbow.[19]

Traditionally, study begins with the Lord's warning and Command to all men: "And surely your blood of your lives will I require; at the hand of every beast will I require it; and at the hand of every man, even every man for his brother-man, will I require the life of man. Whosoever sheds man's blood, by man shall his blood be shed, for in the image of God made He man."[20]

We see from the context that "sheds the blood of man" refers to homicide, the actual taking of life, not the mere infliction of wounds.[21] We also see that, in every case of murder, God commands man to act on His behalf, to exercise actual jurisdiction over our fellow men, if only by virtue of man's resemblance to God.[22]

This Universal law points us to the more detailed, logically associated provisions of the Hebrew Code.

God commands Israel, for instance: You shall not commit murder.[23] You shall not stand idly by when you may save your brother-man from mortal danger.[24] You shall not pity the murderous "pursuer" — anyone who is attempting murder, kidnapping, mayhem, sex crime, etc. — but must deprive him of life if necessary.[25] If it is *not* necessary to deprive him of life, you must not kill him, nor any criminal, without a trial;[26] and, whether with or without a trial, neither you, society, nor any court may kill an innocent man.[27]

That's not all. In no case may anyone accept a ransom — i.e., a payoff, instead of the killer's own "life's blood" — for the life of one who has been murdered.[28] Even if the killer is prepared to give all the treasure in the world, and even if the next of kin are willing to absolve him, no ransom can be accepted as a substitute for justice, "for the soul of the murdered man belongs not to the next of kin but to the Holy One, blessed be He."[29]

Besides these negative Torah Commandments, at least two positive commandments have obvious associations with this Rainbow Covenant Commandment: 1) You shall affirmatively act to save your fellow-man if he is being "pursued" by a murderer, destroyer, or violent vicious kidnapper.[30] 2) You shall destroy a murderous animal.[31]

Finally, we see that there can be no asylum, sanctuary, nor respect to be accorded to the murderer.[32]

Even if he is the most exalted of men, even if he is busy presiding in God's holy Temple at God's own holy service, the killer has no immunity. Justice must take him, wherever he is and whatever he may be doing, and deliver him up to be punished like any man.[33]

The Torah and the Rainbow Code

Recognizing that the two Codes of law, the Rainbow Covenant Law of B'nai Noah and the Torah of B'nai Israel, are *not* the same, that they issued from separate revelations, that each is designed to serve a somewhat different purpose, etc., the practical question before us is, how and where do they differ? We can try to answer that by examining some common issues:

Self-Defense and Defense of Others

He who comes to kill you, kill him first. — *Talmud, Sanhedrin 72a*[34]

He who pursues another to commit murder, mayhem, a violent kidnapping or sex crime must be stopped.[35] It is "homicide" — literally, man killing — to kill the pursuer in defense of the pursued, but this is no crime if other means of defense are inadequate or unavailable. One should use the minimal amount of force necessary to defend the person being pursued. So the defender may grapple with the pursuer, bind him, or even wound or maim him — to use fatal force when fatal force isn't called for is itself murderous — but if the pursuer can't be stopped except by depriving him of life, he must be slain before he can accomplish the evil he intends.[36]

For Israel, rising to the defense of others is a Divine commandment — a Jew must try, whenever possible, to rescue anyone who is in danger of his life.[37] This is a legal obligation that can be enforced (by punishing those who fail to perform responsibly) by a Hebrew Torah court.[38]

Whoever saves a single human life is considered by the Torah as if he saved an entire world. — *Mishnah*[39]

This matter is different in other systems. Unless the bystander has a specific legal duty to act — as does a policeman, say, or the next of kin of the one whose life is at risk — to try to save others, the laws impose no general duty. So an Olympic swimmer may watch and do nothing to save a stranger from drowning, for instance, even though the strong swimmer could have rescued that person easily.

Anglo-Saxon law, including the law in America's fifty states, doesn't obligate the athlete to make the slightest effort.[40] The swimmer may act, but the courts don't require it. If the stranger should drown, the courts leave the strong swimmer's responsibility in the matter up to his own conscience and to Heaven.

Plainly, one who chooses to "stand idly by the blood" of a brother-creature — one who could, without personal risk, save a person at risk, but refuses to do so — demonstrates neither fear of God nor love for Him.[41]

As we have seen before, one must do the very opposite of what the Law forbids before he can be called virtuous: one can't fulfill the law against profaning God's Name unless he acts to sanctify the Name, for example, and one certainly cannot righteously fulfill the whole law against murder unless he acts to save the life of a person in danger. Morally if not legally, one child of God is obligated to rescue, if possible, another child of God. Yet human beings have free will, and courts can't compel us to be wholly righteous.

In this case Noahide courts have no absolute duty to impose their will over the will of the individual.[42] While the strong swimmer in our example *ought* to rescue the one who needs rescue, the Rainbow law doesn't give the drowning person any sort of legal *right* to be rescued. One has no right to depend on the kindness of strangers; one must take responsibility for oneself. The strong swimmer can mind his own business without the law compelling him to mind everyone else's.

Suicide

The Spirit of God has made me and the Breath of the Almighty gives me life. — *Job 33:4*

Suicide is murder: human beings don't belong to themselves alone; rather, each of us belongs to our Maker. This is a Universal Rule.[43] He who commits suicide will ultimately be held to account as though he had killed another — a totally innocent person.[44]

Suicide is cold-blooded premeditated self-destruction. A deranged person, or someone acting upon a sudden or aberrant impulse, is guiltless of the crime. He lacks the freedom of will to form the requisite intent for suicide.[45] Generally, if one's mental balance is disturbed by either chronic or temporary insanity, by pain, or by fear, any act of self-destruction may be presumed to be involuntary. The rabbis tell us that most cases of suicide are really just products of derangement or insanity.[46]

Self-destruction may constitute martyrdom, rather than self-murder, in some extreme or unusual circumstances. For instance, a captured soldier may kill himself rather than risk revealing military secrets under torture. He may not, in any event, attempt to prolong his life by sacrificing the lives of his fellow citizens or soldiers.[47]

Pursuant to Revolutionary Israel's special obligation to hallow and "sanctify God's Name," Jews must — not "may" — choose martyrdom when the only alternative is to profane His holy Name.[48] If some tyrant or oppressor orders a Jew, on pain of death, to commit a particularly egregious sin — not just murder, but any act of idolatry or a gross sexual indecency in public[49] — death is to be preferred to sin.[50]

Rather than betray any of the Revolution's flagship principles, the people of Israel must be ready to die at the tyrant's hands. Yet God doesn't, according to most authorities require the same kind of sacrifice from non-Jews. A Noahide may choose martyrdom, rather than commit an idolatrous act or a sexual crime; the Universal law permits this, but does not command it.[51]

Otherwise, suicide by self-sacrifice is forbidden. Should two travelers who are strangers to each other be crossing a desert, for instance, one of them lacking sufficient water while the other has just enough water for one person to survive the crossing, the one with the water should **not** share it. The Lord calls on man to live by His Law, not die as a result of attempting to observe it.[52] In this example, both travelers will die if they attempt to share the water. God doesn't penalize the traveler with the greater foresight or self-discipline: under these circumstances, one should save oneself.[53]

Self-destructive habits, such as smoking cigarettes, overeating, or heavy alcohol or drug abuse, may pose a future, indirect danger to human life — in some cases they may be clearly suicidal in tendency — but they normally don't pose such a direct, immediate or deliberate threat to life as to treat them as tantamount to suicide.[54] Though the Torah commands the Jew to "look after yourself and take care of your life,"[55] a law of obvious Noahide import, this Fourth Noahite Commandment focuses on the elimination of murder, not the reduction of the general death rate. It doesn't forbid nor criminalize a mere bad habit.

Testing God's promises or warnings, as by exposing oneself to mortal danger needlessly, and then "commanding" God to perform some life-saving miracle, implicates His laws against blasphemy and idolatry, as well as His law against suicide.[56]

"Mercy-Killing," Euthanasia, and Physician-Assisted Suicide

All the above are just pretty names for murder. It isn't for human beings to assess the comparative current value of any human life. Even the life of a suffering person has infinite value to God. Human beings are not like the lesser animals, to be "put down" whenever life becomes unhappy or inconvenient.[57]

> [A]nother right that men and women hold: not to be killed, or pressed to kill themselves, or quietly hustled off in any way before their time. — *Michael Walzer*[58]

A dying person is considered, for all intents and purposes, to be alive.[59] Therefore, no positive, material action may be taken to hasten his death. One may pray for his speedy end. One may remove an impediment to death, such as an annoying noise, or other irritant, which might be artificially prolonging his demise. But one may not touch him, directly or indirectly, as by removing or rearranging a pillow or bedclothes, solely in order to hasten death.[60]

Every human life, including the life of one who is terminally ill, is sacred. God created man not just for pursuit of animal pleasure and avoidance of animal discomfort, but to serve Him. We serve Him by living life to the very last moment until He takes it.[61] Our lives are not whole otherwise; no one has a right to diminish a human life by encroaching on His Divine prerogatives.

Human beings may take animal life, in the exercise of human dominion, but our dominion doesn't extend to our fellow men — only God may take a human life. And our deaths, Israel is told, have unfathomable value. To die in His time and at His command brings man blessing — i.e., atonement.[62] Yet one need not be conscious in order to die, and our Maker certainly doesn't prevent us from administering drugs, or other appropriate therapies, to relieve pain and suffering.

We don't serve Him with our pain but with our lives. Nothing may be done to shorten them.

A "hopeless" person is never to be regarded as a dead person. But God doesn't necessarily require us to pursue heroic measures to prolong the last moments.

One must try to supply even a medically hopeless patient with life's ordinary necessities, such as food, water, air, warmth, and (by transfusion) blood, because the obligation to save and preserve human life is always paramount.[63] Of course physicians have a special duty to try to save the sick.[64] But when the time to die has arrived, a patient may refuse and the physician may withhold treatment by means of surgery, drugs, artificial stimulation, or other extraordinary intervening measures.[65]

War

The self-restraint which Scripture imposed on Israel in regard to Ammon, Moab and Seir carries a prohibition against all aggressive war. — *Nachmanides* [66]

War kills people but doesn't necessarily murder them. A nation or people may fight for life, in self-defense, or for other legitimate reasons. God does not forbid it; He will favor the righteous cause.[67] In a just war, or a necessary war, the nation's enemies are not all legal innocents.

Remember, however, even to tear a leaf from a tree without purpose is forbidden.[68] While soldiers often have to fight cruelly, cruelty for its own sake — purposeless cruelty — is criminal. And one who deliberately but needlessly takes a human life, even of an enemy, even in a war that couldn't be avoided — is a murderer.[69]

Murder by Agency

One's agent is like one's self. — *Midrash* [70]

When a principal says to his agent, "go and kill my [innocent] enemy for me," the agent who does so is a murderer, and so is the principal who sent him. Claiming that one was just following orders is *never* a defense to one's own commission of evil.[71] If the commands of a human master and those of our One Master conflict, we must *always* obey God rather than man.

He who deliberately kills someone indirectly, as by pushing his victim into a busy roadway, is a murderer.[72] But one who inadvertently, helplessly, causes another's death — like the stunned and horrified driver who can't turn in time to avoid hitting the victim in the roadway — lacks any murderous intent and is innocent of any resulting death.[73]

Abortion

This is a far more difficult and complicated subject than most commentaries suggest. Abortion, or feticide, is commonly regarded as "shedding the blood of man in man," and tantamount to "shedding the blood of man by man." So it violates the Rainbow Covenant law against murder.[74]

However, up to forty (40) days — not quite six weeks — after conception a human fetus is considered to be "mere water," "mere tissue," or really little more than a hairy egg.[75] It may be destroyed without the imposition of any legal penalty.[76]

Abortion in the legal context refers to the killing of a fetus *after* the first forty days, anywhere *up to* the point that the baby's head, or the greater part of its body, emerges from the birth canal. That's a significant moment. Only at that point, at birth, according to Israel's law as well as Noahide law, is the child entitled to life on a par with its mother.[77]

After its first forty days but before the moment of its birth, a fetus can be clinically aborted only in the case of compelling medical need — i.e., to save the life and health of its mother. The fetus is still not a true human being — it is not yet a living human soul.[78] So the life of the pregnant woman always has priority over the life of her unborn child.

Should she have a troubled pregnancy, if her life can be saved only by destroying the fetus that endangers it, the fetus *must* be aborted and removed, just like a tumorous growth.[79] That is, the rule here is Israel's law, coupled to the strict Torah obligation to act to save a human life in danger. The life-endangering fetus is like a murderous pursuer, and one should never "stand idly by the blood" of someone being pursued.[80] A fetus before its birth is no more (but also surely no less!) than a potential human life. The people responsible for the mother's care must recognize the distinction.[81]

When abortion is necessary to save the mother's life, one who puts a higher value on the life of the fetus, who acts, knowingly and deliberately, to save the fetus at the expense of its mother, is himself a murderer and an accomplice to her murder.[82]

Suppose that her mere survival isn't immediately at risk, but that her pregnancy very gravely endangers — i.e., unusually, excessively, seriously and directly jeopardizes — her good health. An abortion performed in such circumstances, where it serves a genuinely compelling medical need, can hardly be regarded as a wanton act of criminality.[83] But let us also remember this: every abortion snuffs out a life that God Himself has given.

If the abortion is medically unnecessary, it also constitutes an act of human self-mutilation.[84] The fetus is part of its mother. God gives women the right, as well as the obligation, not to suffer self-mutilation by abortion.

> One who raises an abandoned child is regarded as one who gave birth to the child.— *Talmud* [85]

Against the rights and obligations of women, God gives men no right to make females pregnant — to fill them up — only to vacuum them out for the sake of adult convenience. This sort of elective, optional abortion is, unfortunately, a very ancient practice.[86] One might suppose that it occurs *much* less often among people whose women can count on the support of their husbands, and most often among immoral societies, ridden with promiscuity, adultery and incest, where males are irresponsible and women know it. But even in such immoral cultures, every mother has a duty to realize herself by letting the fragile dependent life that's a part of her develop.[87] The fetus is literally the flesh of her flesh. Its mother should and has every right to love it like herself, since, of course, it *is* herself.

It's extremely difficult beyond this to assign or ascribe any definite legal rights to a child in the womb.[88] You should know that no Torah authority anywhere would *ever* countenance the murder of an abortionist to save the life of a fetus. Both its life and its humanity are entirely contingent, everything depending on the mother's life continuing, her continued healthy pregnancy, and then on her delivering successfully. Who can know the future? Some freak accident might, God forbid, take the life of the mother; even if she lives, a live birth does not naturally follow each and every pregnancy. The fetus remains only *potential* human life. No one, and not the law, can guarantee its future viability.[89]

Where the Noahide law and Israel's law in the matter seem to diverge most strongly is in an area, oddly, of clear Scriptural instruction. God declares to Israel, for Israel, in the Written Torah, that the murder of a living human constitutes a capital crime, but that feticide does not.[90]

If a Gentile deliberately injures a pregnant woman, intentionally causing the fetus within her to die, is he guilty of murder? The Torah provides that a Jew guilty of the same act cannot be held liable by any Torah court for murder, but only for assaulting the woman.[91] This is true even though he has killed the mother's unborn child by causing her to miscarry.[92]

Possibly, as most Torah authorities believe, the Jew in this case will later inevitably be punished by "death at the hands of Heaven."[93] But no Torah court could find him guilty of the unborn child's murder.

By God's will, a Torah court has only one — a capital — penalty for murder. Before it can impose that sentence the court must find, among other things, that the killer's victim was a genuine living person.[94] A fetus is only potentially a living person. Noahide courts, on the other hand, have not just the right but the obligation to treat any such deliberate feticide as a criminal act — as an abomination that they have an obligation to forbid.[95]

Everyone who studies the Noahide law must eventually agree on that point.[96] But this doesn't mean that Noahides must treat every wrongful feticide as murder — that is, as the most despicable and destructive of all felonies. Neither does it suggest that Jews possess any right that Gentiles lack, either to perform abortions or to have them performed.

Noahides must determine the details of their own laws for themselves, including enforcement schemes, and schedules of penalties. Without punishing feticide as murder, they have the power to delegitimize it. So do the Jews. Feticide is a form of homicide that cheapens human life; it isn't all that distantly related to plain murder.[97] The absence, in Scripture, of a specific legal penalty for feticide doesn't mean that Israel must tolerate wholesale fetus-slaughter in its midst. It just means that Jews, like Noahides, have the freedom to legislate their own enforcement schemes against it.[98] It also means that Israel's Torah courts, unlike Noahide courts, lack even the hypothetical power to impose any *capital* penalty for feticide.[99]

So this is yet another area where Noahide societies must determine their own paths for themselves. The law allows for choices by affording human governments the opportunity to fix their own priorities.

But suppose that some state or nation decides, for instance, that in order to minimize the level of infanticide — child killing — or protect mothers from dangerous illicit operations, its courts would be wise, as well as right, to legally permit the abortions that society should abhor. After all, even if God Himself detests them, when society is still divided on the issue, government must also keep the peace.

Give the Creator the benefit of the doubt. None of these considerations should ever outweigh this one: the Noahide law — the Universal Law — absolutely forbids wanton feticide.

God does detest it,[100] and His laws against it are a plain requisite of all moral civilization. Recognizing the huge difference that exists between license and freedom, or total legal acceptance versus regulation, some general prohibition against the wholesale killing of children in the womb is incumbent upon every state and nation. However well-meaning, as it surely was, the idea that [all] "abortion [of every type] should be safe, legal and rare," as former President Bill Clinton put it, still doesn't satisfy the higher Law — the law of God, this Universal law.

Capital Punishment

Whosoever sheds man's blood, by man shall his blood be shed, for
in the Image of God made He man.— *Genesis 9:6* [101]

Of all crimes, murder must be punished. The victim's very
blood demands it; it "cries out" to God for justice.[102] So God
requires every nation to establish and maintain a system of laws
and courts and police to guarantee the appropriate result.[103]

For blood,[104] it pollutes the land, and no expiation can be made
for the land for the blood that is shed therein, but by the blood of
him that shed it. — *Numbers 35:33*

Law's object here is not to reform the murderer, which might
be a very fine thing, nor to fix restitution for the victim's survivors
— which, while it might be nice, doesn't address the real object of
punishment.[105] That object is justice, which involves more than
merely restraining the killer from killing again, or deterring
potential murderers from committing future murders.

Every case of murder must be avenged. Society has an
obligation to the victim as well as God to find, try, and exact
retribution upon the murderer.[106]

Capital punishment, or the death penalty, is a matter of
homicide but not murder. God gives man the right to invest his
courts with the power of life or death over his fellow man.

No crime is more serious than murder.[107] The courts must
show the murderer no pity.[108] Because the law's divine goal is
equal and proportionate justice, courts must remember that every
human life has infinite value; that no one's blood is redder than or
sweeter than another's; and that the murderer has no greater claim
to life or happiness than did his victim.[109]

Does this mean that every court, in every case of murder, must
punish the murderer by extinguishing his life? No.[110] While
Scripture tells us, plainly and repeatedly, that a killer should
himself be killed,[111] penalties normally belong within the area of
those things that the nations must determine for themselves.[112]
But it does seem reasonable that every human court should punish
murder at least as severely as it punishes all other crimes.[113]

All this presupposes that a competent court has fairly judged the accused criminal, justly issued its capital sentence, *and* that the accused is actually and truly guilty of the charged crime.[114] Guilt means moral guilt. A court may not execute a mental incompetent, nor hold anyone criminally responsible who lacks the free will underlying personal responsibility and criminal liability.[115]

All crime, not just murder, must be punished.[116] But a court that executes someone who is innocent of the charged crime commits murder. In any such case the court, quite literally, is guilty of the killing of an innocent.[117]

Where Israel's Torah courts must follow certain extremely stringent rules of criminal procedure,[118] Noahide courts have more freedom.[119] In contrast to the Torah courts, a Noahide court may convict a criminal defendant based solely upon circumstantial evidence, or the accused's own self-incriminating statements, or testimony from his near relatives — even though these relatives may not be the most reliable of witnesses. A Noahide court may also convict upon the testimony of only a single witness.[120] So it's possible — indeed, probable, given time — that the court will mistakenly convict and execute an innocent person.

Organized society can commit crimes worse than those committed by any single individual.[121]

A judicial or capital murder would constitute such a crime, being 1) a fully conscious and carefully premeditated homicide; 2) implicating the very pillars of society, its judges and police, in the organized commission of a totally irrevocable wrong;[122] while 3) permitting the innocent victim no reasonable hope of rescue, nor practical opportunity to resist his killers; and 4) publicly violating the very essence of man's divine obligation to pursue justice, as well as the letter of this Fourth Universal Commandment, forbidding murder.

> Do not execute the innocent or the righteous, for I shall not exonerate the wicked.— *Exodus 23:7*

He who innocently participates in a judicially ordered murder — whether as judge, court officer, witness or executioner — of an innocent yet legally convicted person, cannot be held liable for murder, so long as he was unaware of any perversion of justice.[123] No human court has the right to punish those who do wrong when they commit the wrong wholly unintentionally.[124] But capital murder is still murder, the blood of the innocent still must be avenged, and Heaven knows how to exact a proper penalty.[125]

Vigilante "Justice"

> You shall not do . . . every man what is right in his own eyes.
> — *Deuteronomy 12:8*

Vigilante justice is not justice; the very concept is oxymoronic. Pursuant to the Universal Commandment to establish a system of courts, police and laws, every society must not only establish courts of its own but also use them. Among Gentiles as among Jews, only a duly constituted court has the authority — and even then only after a fair and formal trial — to impose the ultimate legal penalty upon a criminal.[126]

> That the manslayer die not, until he stand before the congregation for judgment. — *Numbers 35:12*

Naturally, one may use all necessary force to stop a crime in progress or, better, before it happens. Obviously, one may use all necessary force to apprehend or stop a killer before he can escape to kill again. But even a gathering of professional judges who are eyewitnesses to murder, who know the killer's identity and guilt beyond any shadow of a doubt, can do no more than bring him to trial — to testify against him there as witnesses before a court made up of *other* judges.[127] Anyone who fails to do so, who deliberately kills a criminal who is subject to legal process without due legal process, is himself a killer and a murderer.

NOTES

1. *Pirke Avot* 3:18, in the name of Rabbi Akiba; See Genesis 9:6.

2. Exodus 20:13; Deuteronomy 6:17. See Genesis 9:5-6; Mishnah, *Sanhedrin* 4:5; *Tosefta Avoda Zarah* 9:4; Talmud, *Sanhedrin* 56b-57a; Midrash, *Genesis Rabbah* 16:9; Yad, *Hilchot Melachim* 9:1,4. Of Israel's Ten Commandments, this is the Sixth. The Rainbow Covenant Commandment here and the Torah's Sinaitic Covenant Commandment are practically equivalent.

3. See above, with commentaries; Mishnah, *Sanhedrin* 9, *Makkot* 2; *Sefer HaMitzvot* 2:289 (with Heller translation, quoted in R. Chavel's standard Soncino Press edition (1967)), and see Lichtenstein, *Seven Laws of Noah*, supra, pp. 46-47. The Hebrew for "kill" is a different and much more general verb.

4. Genesis 9:3; Leviticus 20:27; Deuteronomy 12:15.

5. Exodus 17:10, Deuteronomy 20:17; See *Sefer HaMitzvot* 1:187.

6. See Exodus 21:12-20; Numbers 35:12.

7. Exodus 21:1; Leviticus 19:16; Deuteronomy 22:26-27; and see Talmud, *Sanhedrin* 73a; *Sefer HaMitzvot* 2:293, 297.

8. Genesis 1:26-27; Exodus 15:8; Deuteronomy 14:1; Psalm 8:5, 139:14; Talmud, *Ta'anit* 11b.

9. Malachi 2:10.

10. Psalms 8:5-7, 139:14.

11. Yad, *Yesodey HaTorah* 5:5.

12. Talmud, *Pesachim* 25b.

13. Sanhedrin 4:5. See "Self-Defense and Defense of Others," in this chapter. In a real sense, every human being is humanity itself.

14. See Yad, *Hilchot Rotzeach u'Shemirat haNefesh* 4:9.

15. Genesis 4:10-12, 5:29; Talmud, *Shabbat* 33a.

16. *Pentateuch and Haftorahs*, supra, p. 14, on Genesis 4:9.

17. See Mishnah, *Pirke Avot* 3:14, in the name of R. Akiba.

18. Midrash, *Mechilta to Exodus* 20:13; Talmud, *Sanhedrin* 37a.

19. Bindman, *Seven Colors of the Rainbow*, supra, p. 71.

20. Genesis 9:5-6; See Genesis 4:10; Talmud, *Sanhedrin* 56b.

21. See Genesis 9:6 with commentaries; Exodus 21:24 with commentaries; Talmud, *Sanhedrin*, ibid.

22. See Elijah Benamozegh, *Israel and Humanity*, supra, p. 265.

23. Exodus 20:13; Deuteronomy 6:17; *Sefer HaMitzvot* 2:289.

24. Leviticus 19:16; *Sefer HaMitzvot* 2:297.

25. Deuteronomy 22:26-27, 25:11-12, with Sifre; *Sefer HaMitzvot* 2:293; Yad, *Hilchot Rotzeach* 1:6.

26. Numbers 35:12; *Sefer HaMitzvot* 2:292.

27. Exodus 23:7; *Sefer HaMitzvot* 2:290; Talmud, *Sanhedrin* 33b. Better that a guilty person go free than an innocent person suffer punishment, especially capital punishment; ultimately, God Himself will punish the guilty. "I will not consider the wicked one righteous." Exodus, ibid.

28. Numbers 35:31-32; *Sefer HaMitzvot* 2:295-296.

29. Yad, *Hilchot Rotzeach* 1:4. Also see *Sefer HaHinnuch*, Imperative 412: "[Otherwise] the strong and the rich would kill their opponents and then offer their ransom; thus men would be in constant warfare, and society

would be destroyed."

30. Deuteronomy 25:11-12, with the *Sifre* (Midrash); *Sefer HaMitzvot* 1:247.

31. Exodus 21:28; *Sefer HaMitzvot* 1:237. The animal that kills a man — a human being, a woman, a man, or child — upsets the world's natural order.

32. Exodus 21:14. Among the ancient Greeks, the altar did give asylum to murderers. Later, Christian monasteries and churches offered "sanctuary" even to mass-murderers.

33. *Mechilta* (Midrash) and Rashi on Exodus 21:14. Penalties must be the same for all, depending only upon the nature of the wrong committed. See Mishnah, *Ketubot* 3:7.

34. Also see Talmud, *Berachot* 58a.

35. "He who steals a human being is killed [executed], because he is also prepared to kill him whom he steals." *Moreh Nevuchim* 3:41. A similar presumption applies to criminals who break into homes at night, when the residents are most likely to be home. See Talmud, *Sanhedrin* 72b. Use killing force, if necessary, to stop homosexual, incestuous or adulterous rape. (If those flags of criminality are not there, it is much harder to guarantee that the rapist is truly and in every sense a rapist.) Or to stop a kidnapping, where the kidnapper is likely to murder, or permanently harm the victim, or kill people trying to save the victim. See Mishnah, *Sanhedrin* 1-8.

36. Deuteronomy 25:11-12 and commentaries. See Deuteronomy 22:22-27; Talmud, *Sanhedrin* 73a; *Sefer HaMitzvot* 2:293.

37. Leviticus 19:16; *Sefer HaMitzvot* 2:297. See Talmud, *Bava Metzia* 59b along with *Yad, Hilchot Melachim* 10:12, regarding the rabbinically created obligation for Jews to go to the rescue of non-Jews. However, while Jews do have the right to legally compel their fellow Jews to rescue them, the Torah creates no such right in non-Jews. That is, B'nai Noah may and ordinarily should receive rescue in these circumstances from Jews, but cannot legally compel it. See Leviticus 25:35; Deuteronomy 15:7; *Yad*, ibid, and *Hilchot Mattenot Anayim* 4:22, 10:1.

38. Deuteronomy 17:11; *Sefer HaMitzvot* 1:174, 2:312.

39. *Sanhedrin* 4:5.

40. See *Restatement of Torts 2nd* (American Law Institute, Washington D.C., 1965), Section 314.

41. See Leviticus 19:18; Deuteronomy 10:19; *Sefer HaHinnuch*, Imperative 600.

42. See *Yad, Hilchot Melachim* 9:4 with commentaries; *Minchat Hinnuch*, Imperative 296. At the same time society might decide to *create* a legal duty to rescue, or extend the duty to rescue to a larger class of bystanders.

43. Genesis 9:5 with Rashi; Midrash, *Genesis Rabbah* 34:13; Talmud, *Bava Kamma* 91b, *Sanhedrin* 56a; *Yad, Hilchot Melachim* 9:1,4.

44. See Talmud, *Bava Kamma* 91b.

45. *Yad, Hilchot Melachim* 10:2, with commentaries.

46. See Sidney Goldstein, *Suicide in Rabbinic Literature* (Ktav, Hoboken NJ, 1989) pp. 17-36; Goldman, *Judaism Confronts Contemporary Issues*, supra, p. 257. Physicians and rabbis generally agree on this: most people who commit suicide are clinically depressed. See Dr. Herbert Hendin, quoted in Paul Wilkes's "The Next Pro-Lifers," *New York Times Magazine*, July 21, 1996, p. 26.

47. See Rav Shlomo Goren, in Goldman, supra, p. 251; Talmud, *Pesachim* 25b, *Sanhedrin* 74a. Also see *Genesis Rabbah* 34:13, regarding Genesis 9:5 and the sacrifice — the suicide, or martyrdom — of Israel's King Saul, 1 Samuel 31:4, 2 Samuel 1:14-16. Or see Josephus Flavius (c. 80 CE), *The Jewish War,* Chapter 23, concerning the Zealots who, in 73 CE, killed themselves rather than surrender to the vengefully triumphant Romans at Masada.

48. Leviticus 22:32,with *Sifra* (Midrash); Isaiah 29:23.

49. See Talmud, *Sanhedrin* 74a-b; *Yad, Hilchot Yesodey HaTorah* 5:1-4; *Sefer HaMitzvot* 1:9.

50. Ibid. If it's the oppressor's intention to insult Israel's God thereby, a Jew should give up his life, if need be, rather than commit even the most minor sin in public. *Shulchan Aruch, Yoreh De'ah* 158. However, no human court may punish anyone for a sin committed under life-threatening compulsion or duress — see Deuteronomy 22:26; Talmud, *Nedarim* 27a; *Sefer HaMitzvot* 2:294. Nor will God, if He exacts any penalty, exact the ultimate penalty (of the soul's extinction). See *Yad, Hilchot Yesodey HaTorah* 5:4.

51. Talmud, *Sanhedrin* 74b; *Yad, Hilchot Melachim* 10:2; *Sefer HaMitzvot* 1:9. See the discussion in Common Ruling Principles, supra. Noahides need not necessarily follow the strictest or the most demanding rulings in such matters.

52. See Leviticus 18:5; Talmud, *Yoma* 85b, 88b, *Sanhedrin* 74a; *Yad, Hilchot Yesodey HaTorah* 5:1-4.

53. See Talmud, *Bava Metzia* 62a. However, if the travelers have a special relationship or duty towards each other — if they are husband and wife, parent and child, or, e.g., partners in a common mission — then their relationship is one of mutual dependency or of companions in a joint enterprise, and the duty to share can be presupposed. See Mishnah, *Pirke Avot* 2:4; Talmud, *Bava Batra* 8a.

54. See Goldman, supra, p. 163-164.

55. See Deuteronomy 4:9 with Rashi; *Yad, Hilchot Rotzeach* 11:8; *Shulchan Aruch, Orach Haim* 33.

56. See Deuteronomy 6:16; 1 Samuel 16:2 with Radak (Rabbi David Kimchi); *Sefer HaMitzvot* 2:64. "In danger, one must not rely on a miracle." Talmud, *Kiddushin* 39b.

57. *Yad, Hilchot Rotzeach* 2:6, *Hilchot Teshuva* 3:2.

58. *The New Republic,* June 9, 1997, p. 29.

59. See *Shulchan Aruch, Yoreh De'ah* 339:1.

60. Talmud, *Nedarim* 40a, *Ketubot* 104a; *Kitzur Shulchan Aruch* 4:194, Sec. 1. See R. Immanuel Jakobovits, *Jewish Medical Ethics* (Bloch, New York NY, 1959), p. 306.

61. See Isaiah 56:1-5, with commentaries, regarding Heaven, death and righteousness. Mystics say that man can relate to God in a human way only while he is alive in his own body. Bindman, supra, p. 69.

62. Genesis 3:19 with commentaries; See, e.g., Isaiah 22:14; Hirsch, *Horeb,* supra, Chapter 61. Burial in the planet's earth, bringing with it the total reunion of the mortal self with nature, is also a sacrament, and a last act of atonement. See Talmud, *Sanhedrin* 46b; Deuteronomy 21:22-23 with Rashi.

63. See Talmud, *Ketubot* 19a; *Yad, Hilchot Melachim* 10:2 (regarding Noahide law especially).

64. Exodus 21:19. See Jeremiah 8:22; Job 3:4; Midrash, *Exodus Rabbah*

21:7; *Moreh Nevuchim* 3:27.

65. See Goldman, supra, pp. 177-178. Extraordinary intervening measures — unusual or physically intrusive procedures. Besides fighting death by every means, one can also legitimately accept it when it comes.

66. Ramban's (R. Moshe ben Nachman's) commentary on *Sefer HaMitzvot*, at the end. "Aggressive war" — this pertains to war begun primarily to slake a nation's lust or greed for wealth. It is prohibited to attack a nation that observes the Noahide Law. It is forbidden to attack a nation — any nation — without first trying in good faith to reach a peaceful settlement. The Scriptural reference here is to Deuteronomy 2:5,19. But also see Deuteronomy 23:10 with Ramban: "We [Israel] are not to cause unnecessary bloodshed or do other evil things while fighting our enemies."

67. See Exodus 15:3; Numbers 32:6; Deuteronomy 2:24. Israel's history proves that war can be just, rather than mere national armed robbery. War also tests nations. All else being equal, the morally superior nation, which more generally and closely conforms to the Universal laws, tends to get His blessing, as evidenced in history by many otherwise mysterious and apparently unearned military "breaks" and victories.

68. Talmud, *Bava Metzia* 32b.

69. See Numbers 31:7 with Sifre (Midrash); Deuteronomy 20:10; 2 Kings 3:19; Talmud, *Sotah* 35b; *Yad, Hilchot Melachim* 6:1,7. This Rule applies only when one knows in advance that certain killing is needless. The confusion and secrecy of war often make that impossible.

70. *Mechilta* to Exodus 12:3. See Mishnah, *Berachot* 5:5: "a messenger is the same as he who sent him."

71. Mishnah, ibid; Talmud, *Kiddushin* 42b; Midrash, *Genesis Rabbah* 34; *Yad, Hilchot Rotzeach U'Shemirat HaNefesh* 5:3,4. While a national leader, president or king may have legal immunity from prosecution — i.e., "sovereign immunity" — in his nation's courts (See 2 Samuel 12:9; Mishnah, *Sanhedrin* 2:2; *Yad, Hilchot Melachim* 3:10), the leader's agents must still face justice for any crimes they commit upon their leader's orders. See Talmud, *Kiddushin* 42b, 43a.

72. Even though a Torah court, which must punish a Jewish murderer with death, has no power to do so in these circumstances, when the killing depends on the action of a (murderous) agent. The actual killer, the agent alone, is executed. When a killing is only conditional (i.e., if it depends on the action of another human agent or contingent forces) or potential — or, as we see with abortion, if the life that's taken is only potential human life — a Torah court has no power to impose a capital, maximum, penalty upon the (Jewish) killer. In such cases, the court must turn the murderer over to a secular court, or pass the matter to God (to punish the murderer in the most fitting way). It may also assess a monetary penalty as damages. See *Yad, Hilchot Melachim* 9:4, *Hilchot Hoveil U'Mazik* 4:1, *Hilchot Rotzeach* 1:13, 3:10. But none of these limitations on the power of a Torah court applies to Israel's secular courts — "King's courts" — nor to any non-Hebrew, Gentile or Noahide court. Noahide courts must punish every murder of every kind as appropriately as possible. See *Yad, Hilchot Melachim* 9:4; Rakover, et al, 12 *Cardozo Law Review*, supra. Also see, e.g., Beccaria, supra, Sec. 15, "Mildness of Punishment."

73. See Talmud, *Nedarim* 27a; *Yad, Hilchot Yesodey HaTorah* 5:4, *Hilchot*

Melachim 10:1; *Sefer HaMitzvot* 2:294. However, for B'nai Noah living in savage conditions, where effective courts don't exist and the facts surrounding the death may be unclear, some of the dead victim's family's blame — but not moral or legal guilt — may attach to the inadvertent killer. As for moral responsibility — less than full-fledged guilt — for an inadvertent killing, the killer, just by virtue of having helped cause another's death, should examine all his actions beforehand, and does require some measure of atonement. See the discussion in *Yad, Hilchot Melachim* 10:1.

74. Genesis 9:6. See Midrash, *Genesis Rabbah* 34:10,12; Talmud, *Sanhedrin* 57b, 91b; *Yad, Hilchot Melachim* 9:4. Naturally, in the exercise of responsible dominion, men may abort animal fetuses.

75. Talmud, *Yevamot* 69b, *Keritot* 10a, *Sotah* 2a, *Pesachim* 92 with Rashi, *Niddah* 30a (a fertilized human egg takes at least forty days to develop into a higher form); *Shulchan Aruch, Yoreh De'ah* 305:23; *Kitzur Shulchan Aruch* 61:6 (gender not determined until forty days after conception) and 158:4. But find some opinions to the contrary recorded in J.D. Bleich, *Contemporary Halachic Problems*, supra, Vol. 1, pp. 325-371, "Abortion in Halachic Literature," at pp. 339-347. Go to this article for an all but exhaustive review of the subject of abortion generally, and for a sense of the currently prevailing confusion.

76. Although God may impose a penalty, because the deliberate destruction of a fertilized egg at this stage can be regarded as callous of life. The sin involved in the act, if it is a sin, is said to be equivalent to the destruction of a man's semen through masturbation. See Clorfene & Rogalsky, supra, pp. 82-8. Bleich, supra, explores a wide range of authorities.

77. Talmud, *Sanhedrin* 59a, 72b with Rashi. See Goldman, supra, pp. 49-52.

78. Rashi on *Sanhedrin* 72b, "for so long as it [the fetus] has not emerged into the world [i.e., head from the mother's womb] it is not a human being [*nefesh*, or soul]." See Mishnah, *Ohalot* 7:6. Birth alters being. Departing the womb and entering the world isn't just transformative physiologically but also spiritually.

79. See Talmud, *Gittin* 23b, *Hullin* 58a. Note, however, that the Noahide law doesn't necessarily compel but only urges B'nai Noah to act to save the life in danger. Suggesting that, while no mother should ever sacrifice her own life in order to save her unborn child's, where the law of the land doesn't specifically forbid it, a Gentile mother may legally (if not morally, or practically; see note No. 81 below) have that option.

80. Mishnah, *Ohalot* 7:6; Talmud, *Sanhedrin* 72b; *Yad, Hilchot Rotzeach* 1:6.

81. Whether these caregivers are Jews or Gentiles, so long as they have a legal duty towards the mother. So even if the mother wants to sacrifice her own life for the sake of her unborn child's, any caregiver who actively assisted her in that would be murderously assisting her in a scheme of suicidal self-destruction.

82. Talmud, *Sanhedrin* 80b; *Yad, Hilchot Yesodey HaTorah* 5:7; See Mishnah, *Ohalot* 7:6, and its *Tosefta* (Hebrew only); Clorfene & Rogalsky, supra, 81-7. Also see Novak, supra, pp 185-187; Bleich, *Contemporary Halachic Problems*, supra, Vol. 2, p. 163.

83. The authorities are divided on the issue. See R. Jacob Emden, *She'ilat Yavetz* (c. 1770 CE) No. 43 (abortion permitted in cases of "grave

[medical] necessity") versus Talmud, *Sanhedrin* 72b with Rashi (abortion permitted only where the mother's survival is directly in question). See the discussion in Bleich, *Contemporary Halachic Problems*, supra, Vol. 1, pp. 354-356. Most Torah authorities follow the less permissive opinion but, given the conflict, Noahide legislators have every right to rely upon the more lenient opinion. Even so, compelling medical necessity means exactly that: it's a serious matter, not a loophole permitting casual feticide.

84. See Leviticus 19:28, Deuteronomy 25:3 with commentaries; Talmud, *Bava Kamma* 91a, *Makkot* 22a. Even in cases of rape or incest. See Talmud, *Arachin* 7a; Bleich, supra, pp. 364-366. However, where a pregnancy so seriously threatens the mother's mental health that it endangers her life (as by making her fatally self-destructive), many Torah authorities would recommend aborting it. See Rav Moses Feinstein, *Iggorot Moshe*, supra, *Even Ha-Ezer* 1, Sec. 65; Bleich, supra, pp. 362-363. Still, abortion in the case of this and every medical emergency must be genuinely necessary.

85. Talmud, *Megillah* 13a. Also see Talmud, *Sanhedrin* 19a.

86. See Deuteronomy 29:16 and commentaries (re: abominations of Egypt); *Encyclopaedia Britannica*.

87. See *Yad, Hilchot Melachim* 9:4, and commentaries.

88. See Bleich, supra, pp. 325-371. While all Torah authorities deplore abortion generally, they tend to approach specific cases very cautiously. Note: if the child, out of the womb, needs such extraordinary intervening therapy as intrusive surgery to stay alive, the law imposes no obligation to provide it. In this the child or newborn is like any dying person.

89. Bleich, supra, at p. 359. Also see, e.g., Talmud, *Yevamot* 12a, *Sanhedrin* 72b.

90. Exodus 21:22-23.

91. Exodus, ibid, with commentaries. The offense renders him liable for payment of all her legal damages. If she should die as an unintended result of the blow, he would be liable (to pay all damages) for involuntary manslaugher — only for the death of the mother, not for the death of her unborn child.

92. Note, again, the general rule that stricter standards of moral conduct apply to Israel than to B'nai Noah. Talmud, *Sanhedrin* 59a. So the apparent imposition of a stricter standard upon B'nai Noah in this one area would seem to be anomalous.

93. See *Tosafot* to Talmud, *Sanhedrin* 59a, *Hullin* 33a; Talmud, *Ketubot* 30a; Bleich, supra, pp. 328-331.

94. Proving that the killer fully intended to kill a living human being and that his sin was not committed through ignorance or error. See Talmud, *Sanhedrin* 8b, *Makkot* 16a.

95. Talmud, *Sanhedrin* 57b; *Yad, Hilchot Melachim* 9:4. See, e.g., Bleich, supra, p. 335.

96. Despite many other differences among the authorities, there is no divergence at all among them here. See, e.g., Bleich, supra, p. 335; Novak, supra, pp. 185-187.

97. *Yad, Hilchot Melachim* 9:4 and commentaries.

98. In the state of Israel, history's Third Jewish Commonwealth, the rabbis have consistently pressed for precisely this: an effective, secular, enforcement scheme applying in the matter of abortion. See, e.g., the

popular debates attendant to passage of Israel's Abortion Law of 1977; Leo Trepp, *Complete Book of Jewish Observance* (Behrman House/Summit Books, New York NY, 1980), p. 293.

99. See, e.g., Bleich, supra, p. 326.

100. See, e.g., Talmud, *Sanhedrin* 57b; *Tosafot* to *Sanhedrin* 59a, *Hullin* 33a; *Yad, Hilchot Melachim* 9:4.

101. See Genesis 1:27; Leviticus 24:17, and commentaries.

102. Genesis 4:10.

103. See next chapter, "The Sixth Commandment."

104. That is, bloodshed: homicide. See, e.g., Genesis 9:5-6; Leviticus 19:16; Habakuk 2:12.

105. Numbers 35:31 with commentaries.

106. See Genesis 9:5-6; Exodus 18:22, 20:13, 21:14,23-25; Numbers 35:12; Deuteronomy 5:17, 19:21; *Sefer HaHinnuch,* Imperatives 409, 600.

107. Exodus 20:13; Talmud, *Sanhedrin* 37a; *Yad, Hilchot Rotzeach* 1:4.

108. Deuteronomy 19:12,21; Mishnah, *Sanhedrin* 4 (end); Talmud, *Sanhedrin* 45b. Even though the killer may be poor, abused, or an orphan, the court must disregard that person's background and focus on the crime. See generally, Exodus 23:3 with commentaries; *Sefer HaMitzvot* 2:277, 279.

109. Leviticus 19:15; Deuteronomy 19:13,21.

110. See Bleich, supra, Vol. 2, pp. 341-367, "Capital Punishment in the Noachide Code," at pp. 366-367. Also see Beccaria, supra, Sec. 16 ("Of Capital Punishment"): "It is not the terrible but transient spectacle of a criminal's execution, but the long sustained example of a man's loss of liberty, of a man paying for his offense to society by labors resembling those of a beast of burden, which is the most powerful brake upon crime."

111. Genesis 9:5-6; Leviticus 24:17; Numbers 35:33. "Choose an easy death for him who must be executed." Talmud, *Sanhedrin* 52a, in the name of Rabbah bar Avuha.

112. See "Common Ruling Principles," above.

113. Note that ancient Israel's Torah courts were famously reluctant to impose a death sentence. See Mishnah, *Makkot* 1:10 : "A court [the great Sanhedrin, consisting of at least 23 member-judges] that effects one execution in seven years is branded a murderous court. R. Eleazar ben Azariah said: even once in seventy years. Rabbis Tarfon and Akiba said: Were we members of the court, no one would ever be put to death. R. Shimon ben Gamaliel retorted: They would prefer to multiply murderers in Israel!"

114. See Genesis 9:6; Exodus 23:7; Numbers 35:12; Deuteronomy 17:7; Talmud, *Sanhedrin* 57a; *Yad, Hilchot Sanhedrin* 15:10-13, *Hilchot Melachim* 9:14, 10:5; *Sefer HaMitzvot* 2:290,92; *Moreh Nevuchim* 3:41.

115. *Yad, Hilchot Melachim* 10:2. Society has both the right and the obligation to protect itself by other, nonpunitive means — such as high-security care, custodial therapy, etc.

116. Exodus 21:24; Leviticus 24:20; Deuteronomy 19:19, and commentaries.

117. See Exodus 23:7; Mishnah, *Makkot* 1:10; Talmud, *Sanhedrin* 35a.

118. See, e.g., Mishnah, *Makkot* 1:9-10; *Sefer HaMitzvot* 2:281-291. Israel's secular courts — "King's courts," in rabbinic parlance — have more freedom. Unlike Torah courts, for instance, they may draw conclusions based on circumstantial evidence. See *Moreh Nevuchim* 3:40. Circumstantial

evidence is evidence derived from circumstances. The footprint of a stranger on a desert island, for instance, is circumstantial evidence that there's another person on the island.

119. *Yad, Hilchot Melachim* 9:14; Talmud, *Sanhedrin* 57b. See Novak, supra, pp. 53-83,179. By reading *Hilchot Melachim*, ibid., very narrowly and literally, some authorities argue that this freedom is actually illusory, and that circumstantial evidence is not admissible in Noahide courts.

120. See note above. However, Noahide societies have every right to determine the details of their own jurisprudence for themselves. They may choose to establish more stringent legal procedures of their own, especially in capital cases. See Talmud, *Sanhedrin* 56b; *Yad, Hilchot Melachim* 10:12; Ramban (Nachmanides) on Maimonides' *Sefer HaMitzvot, Shoresh* 14; R. Yosef Albo, *Sefer ha-Ikkarim* 1:25; Rav Avraham Isaiah Karelitz, *Hazon Ish, Bava Kama* 10:3; Nahum Rakover, *Law and the Noahides* (Library of Jewish Law, Jerusalem, 1998), pp. 55-74; S. Stone, pp. 1209, 1214, and N. Rakover, p. 1155, in 12 *Cardozo Law Review,* supra.

121. See, e.g., Novak, supra, p. 171.

122. See Talmud, *Sanhedrin* 37a.

123. Leviticus 19:15; *Yad, Hilchot Melachim* 3:10; *Sefer HaMitzvot* 2:273. Because the responsibilities of a judge require him to render decisions, he can't be held liable for whatever innocent mistakes he may make in the process. Talmud, *Sanhedrin* 33a with commentaries.

124. *Yad,* supra, 10:2. See Deuteronomy 22:26; Talmud, *Nedarim* 27a; *Sefer HaMitzvot* 2:294. While ignorance of the circumstances — the facts — may provide a legal defense, mere legal ignorance, or ignorance of the limits of the law, never excuses crime. See Mishna *Bava Kamma* 2:6; Talmud, *Makkot* 9a-b, with Rashi; *Yad, Hilchot Melachim* 10:1-2.

125. See Exodus 23:7 and commentaries. Also see, e.g, Isaiah 1:13.

126. See *Sefer HaMitzvot* 2:292; *Sefer HaHinnuch,* Imperative 409; *Yad, Hilchot Makkot* 8:10. Also see Lichtenstein, supra, p. 34 (citing N. Berlin, *Haamek Shaela,* pro, and Yosef Babad, *Minchat Hinnuch,* contra).

127. *Sefer HaMitzvot* 2:292. Also see Midrash, *Sifre Zuta* on Numbers 35:12.

THE THIRD COMMANDMENT

Laws Against Lawlessness

Learn to do well; seek justice,
relieve the oppressed, judge the fatherless,
plead for the widow.[1] — Isaiah 1:17

"Where is the God of justice?" asked the prophet Malachi.[2] Not that the prophet didn't know. Oppression and injustice deny God. He Whose very holy Name[3] is Justice is most evident when we live it among ourselves. Accordingly, God commands us — the human race — to stand up for Him on the Earth where He's put us to establish laws and fight for Him against injustice.

This is a negative Commandment, a prohibition.[4] God hates injustice; so should all of us. Man is Divinely obligated to act against it, as a matter of Universal law.[5]

How do we oppose injustice? By setting up a system of laws, police and courts against it, and by refusing to passively accept it as a fixture of social life. Anarchy is not the path of justice; people must live by civic laws.[6]

Note that Moses established Israel's system of courts, police and judges before the people ever even got to Sinai.[7]

Let justice rise up as the waters, and righteousness like a mighty stream. — *Amos 5:24*[8]

Man has no right to leave all judgment up to Heaven. "The Judge of all the world"[9] judges each man and woman individually, but "no man is an island, entire of itself."[10] God created Israel as a unique instrument to promote "charity and judgment" in the world,[11] but the Torah doesn't just speak about Jews to Jews. Rather, "all men are responsible for one another."[12]

Human beings are social beings. Everyone belongs to someone, to some society, nation-state or culture. So God also judges people collectively, in our respective nations and our generations.[13]

> If there is no justice, there is no peace. — *R. Bachya ben Asher*[14]

Injustice is a negation of religion.[15] Because the problem is a social one, this Third Universal Commandment addresses people both as individuals and on the collective level. God requires each of us to pursue justice in his everyday relations with other creatures, to act in a just and upright manner personally.[16]

The Hebrew Revolution's most basic, general Rule of conduct is the Golden Rule: "what is hateful to you, do not do unto another."[17] To fail to act when the time comes to act, to take a decent public stand against injustice, is both hateful and a crime in the Noahide law. In fact, it carries a possible capital penalty.[18] Because the God of justice also commands men to pursue justice collectively, as social beings — as responsible members of society.[19]

Mystics associate this Commandment with the dark brown or deepest red of the rainbow — that is, with the initial band of color, the foundation. In other words, it's seen as the point of departure or the underpinning for the other colors and Commandments. In a sense, this is the reality underlying the whole structure.[20]

Oppression and injustice deny God. Law and order is fundamental to the stability that makes civilization possible.

Laws must be just. Order must not be oppressive. At a minimum, every nation is Divinely obligated to establish effective systems and institutions to justly enforce the terms of the Universal Commandments.[21] They must render decisions founded upon the

Universal Law, and teach and admonish the people concerning the Law's observance.[22]

Beyond this minimal obligation, some commentators argue that the Commandment here — to live by civic laws — obligates the nations to extend the principle of justice. That is, man must bring law and order into every area of life where the absence of law might work an injustice.[23] So besides merely enforcing the Universal laws against larceny, murder, and so on, Noahide authorities are divinely obligated to create and administer suitable, substantive laws of governance, dealing with things like street traffic, the conduct of corporations, world trade, administrative agencies, etc.[24]

This is a wise and logical opinion. Wherever a situation of lawlessness might give rise to anarchy, or the oppression of the weak by the strong, mankind is obligated to impose a just order in its place.

Justice, justice, you shall pursue. — *Deuteronomy 16:20*[25]

God condemns those who default from their responsibility under this Commandment. The challenge is terrific and never-ending. We are the Lord's agents — His stewards — in the world. He created us with almost Godlike capacities and qualities,[26] including the ability to make judgments. He commands our species to use that ability, to judge honestly and precisely, to discover the truth, to decide the issues that rise among us justly.[27] God judges in Heaven. Human beings serve Him, the Father of justice, as His witnesses and judges and police on Earth.[28]

The Book of Genesis illustrates the principle. Long before Sinai, the people of Shechem (Sh´chem, with a guttural "ch" — a town known today as Nablus) failed to prosecute the rape and kidnapping of Dinah, Israel's (Jacob's) daughter. Israel's sons, quite rightly, put a permanent end — a capital end — to the lawlessness of savage Shechem.[29] They killed every man alive.[30]

Were they too cruel? Bloody as it was, the incident teaches us this about the Noahide law: each of us, as individual members of society, has public responsibilities. Every man shares in his own society's obligations under this Commandment. So one sees that the values associated with the United States Constitution — the rule of law, and equal protection under the law — aren't just an American national ideal but an absolute fundamental of divine Universal law.[31]

> One law shall there be for the native and the stranger who dwells among you.— *Exodus 12:49* [32]

Due process is fundamental, despite its apparent absence in Shechem. Procedures must be fair and careful. Courts "shall judge the people with just judgment."[33] They shall "justify the righteous" — that is, the innocent — and condemn the wicked — that is, the guilty.[34]

A court must render justice with complete impartiality to all who come before it, whether they are rich or poor, male or female, strangers or natives,[35] sinners or saints.[36] Every case matters: "A judge shall judge a dispute involving a penny as meticulously as the one involving a fortune."[37]

> Eye for eye, tooth for tooth, hand for hand, foot for foot.
> — *Exodus 21:24* [38]

Heaven's guiding principle for human courts is one of strict proportionality, "eye for eye, tooth for tooth," with neither respect nor favor for the person — the power, or status — of any who come before it. Not mutilation, not personal retaliation, but justice, which must be impartial and finely measured.

"Eye for eye" — not two "eyes" for one; "tooth for tooth" — not just one "tooth" for a mouthful. Whenever a court addresses a wrong, the damages or penalty it imposes must correspond to the wrong — and to any injury so resulting — as precisely as possible.[39] The punishment must fit the crime.[40] In civil, non-criminal law, he who injures another must restore him to his condition before the injury; he who damages another's property must compensate him according to that person's loss.[41]

> The law of the state is the Law.— *Talmud* [42]

The Law of the State: Man and Woman

While women must ultimately share the blame, as well as the credit, for the way that civil society functions, we see from the incident at Shechem that the obligations of men and women under this Commandment are not identical. The men of Shechem were killed for failing to live up to their responsibilities. The women, having different responsibilities, and of course the children as well, were not. Women are not Divinely obligated to involve themselves directly in either society's law-making or its law enforcement.[43]

Perhaps as part of the "affirmative action" plan described earlier,[44] Divine law reserves most civic and religious leadership functions in Israel to the men of Israel.[45] A Jewish man should, if he is able, occupy the greater part of his time in study, teaching, legal deliberation and government, along with spiritual devotion.[46] So the Lord gives Israel's men affirmative, gender-specific commandments in these spheres — for the ultimate benefit of both genders.[47]

Torah defends a different role for women. While men may "sit with the elders," embroiled in questions of law and politics, women aren't required to do so themselves. It goes without saying that the wise man will avail himself of woman's counsel and her insight.[48] But God never commands women — who should lead men both in modesty and gentleness[49] — to participate in a public life that may bring them to hardness or immodesty.[50] Heaven leaves them free to "wash [their] hands in innocence."[51]

This is not to say that God bars women from actively involving themselves in matters of civic justice.[52] Nothing in the Noahide law prevents women from taking any office or serving any function in any Noahide court or government.[53] Still, in a world where leaders lead by charisma and example, where women will accept a fatherly leader but men often can't or won't devotedly accept women as their models, strong civic leadership and woman's leadership can be problematic.[54]

In all events, whether as police, witnesses in court, judges, or the very highest ministers of government, women must, of course, act as righteousness requires. If a woman can give evidence in a court case, for instance, she must do so if asked; if she witnesses a crime she must report it, the same as any man.[55] Wherever society organizes itself to impose the same basic public duties on women as on men, the woman who defaults from her responsibilities is like the man who does the same.[56]

When men dominate institutions of government or justice, fairness — that is, justice — requires them to accommodate woman's special vulnerabilities, if any, and her family-centered needs. A court, for instance, should try to protect the shy and modest woman, to make the ordeal of public involvement less of an ordeal. This is so even at the risk of appearing partial to women.[57] After all, only gentlemen honor women; only dishonorable men treat women dishonorably.[58]

The Law of the State: In the Realm of Religious Ritual

Whatever its intentions, the state has no right to compel a person to sacrifice his moral integrity. God gives no court the power to force His creatures to do wrong. This applies both in the realm of moral, secular obligation — the state may not compel its citizens or subjects to commit murder, for instance, nor violate any of the other Commandments — and in matters of religious rite and symbolism.

Neither the state nor the individual has any right to create any new religion.[59] Still less may the state compel its citizens or subjects to follow a new (or false) religion. Laws enacting man-made religious observances, and other laws conflicting with God's Law, directly discouraging its observance, are illegitimate.

The state may not misuse its power to establish a false religion. Neither may it compel people to follow true religion.[60] God gave man free will and man's law can't reverse the gift. A sin that doesn't directly threaten the good order of society or the rule of moral law shouldn't, just for utilitarian reasons, be the business of the police.[61]

Human transgressions against other humans or even lesser beings are the proper subject of court action. Human transgressions against God alone are best handled by God. Noahide courts need not address them. Certain types of cases, if they can't be informally resolved, must simply be "passed on for Divine judgment."[62] When it comes to any matter of mere religious ritual, or doctrine, as opposed to worldly injuries inflicted on God's creatures, the proper role of the court, and the Noahide state, is to leave such matters to Heaven's courts.[63]

Compromise

What does the Lord require of you: only to do justly, and to love mercy, and to walk humbly with your God. — *Micah 6:8*

If every person feared God and loved Him — if the impulses of conscience were clear, uniform, and irresistibly obeyed — *and* if human memories were perfect, and every promise made became a promise kept, then society would have no need for courts.[64]

An unredeemed humanity does need courts, but that doesn't mean that courts must decide every controversy. Ideally, people should be able to settle their differences out of court, peaceably among themselves.

Pray for the well-being of the state, for if it weren't for men's fear of it, they would devour each other alive. — *R. Hanina* [65]

In civil, non-criminal cases, compromise is often to be preferred to legal judgment. The first — compromise —

promotes peace. The second — judgment — promotes truth. The world depends on a balance of both these values.[66] Should a person suffer a wrong, he need not always seek to avenge it through the strict application of law.[67] Rather, one should "do that which is right and good in the sight of the Lord,"[68] practicing forgiveness, lenience and compassion.[69]

People have a right to rely upon the strict letter of the law — society cannot refuse to grant its members the full benefit and protection of its laws — but one may always forsake a personal privilege. God loves those who walk in "the way of the good, keeping the path of the righteous."[70] The Father of Righteousness cherishes the forbearing person who, rather than pressing for every legal right and entitlement, chooses to follow "the law of the saints" instead.[71]

Sometimes law must take its course — "justice must cut through the mountain" — to condemn wrongs and vindicate rights.[72] But courts can help litigants effect a compromise, and the court that does so deserves praise.[73]

Litigants may also select an impartial arbitrator to settle the controversy between them through compromise. Any such settlement must be honest and fair.[74] Further, because compromise has the same effect as a legal judgment, it deserves to be as carefully deliberated as any legal matter.[75]

Procedures

Bloodshed comes to the world when justice is delayed, and when justice is perverted. — *Mishnah* [76]

For a court to render "just judgment,"[77] it must conform to procedures that are fair and just. These Principles of Torah, most scholars agree, are implicit in this Universal law.[78] That is, the bare rudiments of justice and due process logically require every human society to:

- Appoint judges to serve in every major community, and policemen wherever needed.[79]

- Avoid appointing any judge who lacks knowledge of the law.[80]

- Treat litigants equally before its courts. Each plaintiff, prosecutor and defendant must be allowed a fair opportunity to speak, and an equal opportunity to present a case.[81]

God says to the judges: Think not that you are alone; I am sitting with you. — *Midrash* [82]

- Prevent its court officers from accepting a bribe or gift from — or on behalf of — any litigant appearing before the court.[83] "A judge who accepts bribes brings terror into the world."[84]

- Prevent its courts from showing special favor, respect or honor to any individual litigant. "A judge is disqualified from hearing a case involving either one he loves or one he hates."[85]

- Prevent its court officers from perverting justice out of fear for their own safety, or because of threats made by — or on behalf of — any litigant.[86]

- Prevent its courts from perverting justice out of compassion for the poor or pity for the weak. A court must treat both rich and poor alike — with complete impartiality.[87] Sentiment shouldn't determine legal decisions.[88] It's the business of courts, as of umpires and referees, to render strict and impartial decisions according to uniform established rules. A judge, very like the umpire or referee, must not let pity turn to partiality.[89] God loves charity,[90] but not at the expense of judgment.[91]

One who shows mercy to the cruel will end by showing cruelty to the merciful. — *Midrash*[92]

- Prevent its courts from discriminating or perverting justice against people of bad reputation. Even if one party is a sinner and the other a saint, the court must treat both litigants fairly.[93]

- Prevent its courts from punishing one person for a crime committed by another. Each person bears legal responsibility only for his own acts, or failures to act. A child must not be punished for the crimes of a parent, nor a parent, absent a showing of personal fault, for the crimes of his child.[94]

- Prevent its courts from discriminating or perverting justice against the defenseless, the weak, the stranger or the orphan.[95] "Open your mouth," the Bible commands, "judge righteously, and plead the cause of the poor and needy."[96]

- Prevent its courts from hearing one litigant in the absence of the other. God's justice and due process require the court to grant both litigants an equal opportunity to confront the arguments against them.[97] A court cannot condemn a defendant who isn't present.[98]

- Provide sufficient scope and opportunity for the cross-examination of witnesses. To ensure "just judgment" and to avoid harming the innocent, a court must allow full inquiry into the testimony of each witness.[99]

You must appear justified before men as well as before God.
— Mishnah[100]

- Provide its courts with the power to compel the production of evidence and the testimony of witnesses.[101] Not only that, to help our courts do justice, God requires us, as individuals, to come forward with any evidence we have.[102] "He who suppresses evidence is like one who stands idly by the blood of his neighbor."[103]

- Provide its courts with the power to punish perjury.[104] Further, every individual who gives evidence before a court must testify truly, to the extent that he or she is able. Anyone who bears false witness against another commits an extremely grave crime, a very heinous sin.[105]

By three things is the world sustained: by truth, by law, and by peace. — Mishnah[106]

- Provide a high court among other, lower courts, to decide unusually difficult questions, and to act as a court of final authority.[107] Not every student regards this as a Noahide obligation, but logic indicates that every society needs a court of final authority, if only to review and revise any unjust decisions in its lower courts.

It is joy to the just to do justice.[108] *— Proverbs 21:15*

- Prevent any gross miscarriage of justice by its courts.[109] God gives judges and juries awesome responsibilities. They must judge righteously, carefully, with complete impartiality, and fearlessly.[110]

He who judges arbitrarily, without due deliberation or taking the time to fully consider a case, is both wicked and stupid.[111] But a judge must also judge promptly, without causing others unnecessary suffering by letting a case drag on oppressively.

A judge who needlessly delays judgment or who, either negligently or deliberately, allows a litigant to artificially drag out the proceedings, is an unrighteous judge.[112] Unrighteous judges — and court officials, and police — must be removed.[113]

> [He] said to the judges, 'Take heed what you do, for you judge not for man, but for the Lord, who is with you in the judgment. Therefore now let the fear of the Lord be upon you; take heed and do it. For there is no iniquity with the Lord our God, nor respect of persons, nor taking of gifts.' — *2 Chronicles 19:6-7*[114]

NOTES

1. That is, 1) well-doing should and must be learned, by putting it into practice; 2) justice secures each person's individual rights; 3) relieve the oppressed, or "set right the oppressor" [by opposing his wrong actions]; 4) judge (win justice); 5) plead (take the part of — literally, "strive for") the weak and friendless. See Isaiah 1:17 with Rashi; Hertz, *Pentateuch and Haftoras*, supra, p. 753.

2. Malachi 2:17.

3. The Divine name *Elo[k]im*, usually translated "Lord," connotes His inherent attribute of pure justice (roughly translating) — in contrast to His attribute, expressed by His four-letter "proper" Name, of mercy (roughly translating) and loving-kindness. See Rashi on Genesis 1:1 and Hosea 14:2.

4. Talmud, *Sanhedrin* 57a, 58b.

5. Id., 56a; *Mishnah Tosefta, Avoda Zorah* 8:4; *Yad, Hilchot Melachim* 9:1,14. See, e.g., Isaiah 5:16.

6. See sources listed in the two notes above, referring to *dinim*, in Hebrew, or enforceable, statuatory civic or social laws.

7. Exodus 18.

8. Justice — in Hebrew, *mishpat*, or law/judgment. Righteousness — in Hebrew, *tzedaka*, charity/justice.

9. Genesis 18:25.

10. John Donne, *Devotions Upon Emergent Occasions*, Number 17 (London, 1624).

11. Genesis 18:19 with commentaries.

12. Talmud, *Sanhedrin* 27b. Not to suggest that each group and nation isn't, first of all, responsible for itself. As for Hebrew brotherhood: "all Jews are responsible [i.e., bound to care, like closely related family members] for one another." Midrash, *Sifra* 112a; Talmud, *Shavuot* 39a.

13. See Genesis 4:9 with Rashi; Talmud, *Sanhedrin* 108a, *Kiddushin* 40b; *Yad, Hilchot Teshuva* 3:1-2. People bear some collective responsibility only for crimes that they know about or could have discovered. For completely private hidden sins, committed in utter secrecy, only the individual sinner bears responsibility. See Midrash, *Mechilta* 66b.

14. *Kad haKemach* (thirteenth century CE, Hebrew only).

15. Hertz, supra, p. 821.

16. See, e.g., Leviticus 19:35, Proverbs 11:1, Midrash, *Sifra* 91a; Talmud, *Sanhedrin* 7a; *Yad, Hilchot Geneyva* 7:12; *Sefer HaMitzvot* 2:246, 271.

17. Talmud, *Shabbat* 31a. See Leviticus 19:18, "You shall love your neighbor as yourself." And Deuteronomy 10:19, "You shall love the stranger." See generally, *Sefer HaMitzvot* 1:206, 207.

18. *Yad, Hilchot Melachim* 9:14.

19. See Genesis 34:13 with Ramban; Talmud, *Sanhedrin* 56a; *Yad, Hilchot Melachim*, ibid. Also see, e.g., Ezekiel 16:49.

20. Bindman, supra, p. 124.

21. See *Yad, Hilchot Melachim* 9:14 with commentaries.

22. *Yad*, ibid. See *Mishnah Tosefta, Avoda Zorah* 8:4; Talmud, *Gittin* 9b with Rashi.

23. Ramban, *Pirush al haTorah* on Genesis 34:13 and on *Yad, Hilchot Melachim* 9:14.

24. Ibid. In other words, a Noahide court — as opposed to a Torah court, which is a Hebrew rabbinic tribunal with (theoretically) full secular authority — is, or should be, a regular secular court. Ideally, a Noahide court would be fully self-aware, promoting Noahide precepts that are consciously based on Revealed values.

25. In Hebrew, these first two words are *tzedek, tzedek*. The phrase is often translated, "That which is altogether just you shall pursue." Some commentators interpret it, "Do not use unjust means to secure the victory of justice." See Hertz, *Pentateuch and Haftoras*, supra, p. 820.

26. See, e.g., Psalm 8:5-6.

27. See Deuteronomy 16:20; Talmud, *Sanhedrin* 56b.

28. See Deuteronomy 10:17, 16:18-20; Psalm 58:1; Proverbs 31:9; Mishnah, *Pirke Avot* 1:18.

29. Genesis 34. See *Hilchot Melachim* 9:14 and commentaries. Shechem is called Nablus today. It's said that Israel (Jacob) didn't object to the severe punishment but to the guile, or fraud, by which his sons accomplished it. However, other commentators argue that Israel's sons punished too severely, and also that the looting that followed was itself lawless. See Nachmanides (Ramban) on Genesis 34:13; Novak, supra, p. 55. Also see Genesis 34:30, 49:5-7.

30. But not the women or children. Illustrating the important principle that men — male adults — are primarily responsible for making and administering public law. See the discussion further below.

31. Constitution of the United States (Philadelphia, 1776), Preamble and Article Three; the Bill of Rights (1791) and the 14th Amendment (1868).

32. That is, no distinction in civil (as opposed to religious, or social, rights or obligations) rights between native and alien. See commentaries.

33. Deuteronomy 16:18.

34. Deuteronomy 25:1 and commentaries.

35. Bigotry based on any supposed racial or biological national superiority is nonsense. See, e.g., 1 Kings 8:41-43, Amos 9:7, and Jonah. All of us were made in God's Image. All of us come from the same first family: Adam's. See Mishnah, *Sanhedrin* 4:5; *Mishnah Tosefta, Sanhedrin* 8:4-5.

36. See Exodus 22:21, 23:6; Leviticus 19:15; Deuteronomy 24:17; *Sefer HaMitzvot* 2:275, 277-278, 280.

37. Talmud, *Sanhedrin* 8a.

38. Also, Deuteronomy 19:21. And, with very slightly different phrasing, Leviticus 24:20.

39. Ibid with commentaries; Talmud, *Bava Kamma* 83b-84a. Also see *Moreh Nevuchim* 3:41. This is no man-made "liberal" invention but basic original Torah, as we see from Numbers 35:31, where exact measure-for-measure means exact money damages, or "a ransom," to address most non-fatal injuries.

40. Deuteronomy 25:2. See Deuteronomy 24:16; Jeremiah 17:10; *Yad, Hilchot Melachim* 10:1-2. Also see, e.g., Beccaria, *Of Crimes and Punishments*, supra: too-severe punishments are tyrannical. Further, laws and penalties, even though derived from timeless Revelation, must often be adjusted over time, for the sake of justice, as the needs of the population and other circumstances change. See R. Yosef Albo, *Sefer ha-Ikkarim*, supra, 3:14-15.

41. Exodus 21:18-19, 25, 33-36, 22:4-5; Deuteronomy 25:11. Including compensation for medical bills, pain and suffering, humiliation, lost time, lost wages, and any lasting physical injuries. See *Horeb*, supra, ch. 49.

42. *Dina de-malchuta dina* — that is, the law is the Law. (Or, the law is *our* law.) In the name of Rav Samuel, *Gittin* 10b. Also see Talmud, *Bava Kamma* 113a; *Menuchot* 38b and *Berachot* 49b with Rashi; Novak, supra, pp. 68-69.

43. See Talmud, *Sanhedrin* 57b; *Yad, Hilchot Melachim* 1:5. The women of Israel are excused from such responsibilities. Would God put more of a burden on the women of other nations?

44. See "The Fifth Commandment," Man and Woman.

45. In a Hebrew Torah court, for example, only a man may serve in the office of judge. See Exodus 18:21; Deuteronomy 1:3; *Yad, Hilchot Sanhedrin* 2:1-6, *Hilchot Melachim* 1:5. Likewise, only a man may serve Israel as a rabbi — a rabbi is also a judge — or as a king or monarch. *Yad, Hilchot Melachim*, ibid.

46. See Exodus 18:21; Joshua 1:8; Proverbs 31:23; *Yad, Hilchot Melachim* 12:4-5.

47. Mishnah, *Kiddushin* 1:7; Talmud, *Menuchot* 43b.

48. See Genesis 21:12; Proverbs 31:26; Talmud, *Bava Metzia* 59a, *Niddah* 45b, *Berachot* 17a.

49. Talmud, *Megillah* 14b. See Midrash, *Genesis Rabbah* 18:2.

50. See Mishnah, *Sotah* 3:4.

51. See Psalm 26:6.

52. Note that, even in Israel, the Bible's Deborah/Devorah ruled the Hebrews. See Judges 4:4, 5:31; Talmud, *Sotah* 22b. She may have judged Israel's court cases too — although some say that she didn't actually judge, but restricted herself to instructing her people's judges. *Tosafot* on Talmud, *Niddah* 50a.

53. In the land of Israel in Messianic times, a woman may not, according to Maimonides (*Yad, Hilchot Melachim* 9:14), serve as either a "judge" — in the context, a superjudge, a combination of "elder," social

leader, prosecutor and defense counsel, legal decisor and fact-finder — nor even as a (non-party, fully credible) witness in a criminal, capital prosecution. The reasons for this are various, relate to the special nature of Millenial court procedings, and are too long to go into here. See *Yad, Hilchot Eydot* 9:2. However, following the principle that B'nai Noah are obligated to determine the details of their own Law for themselves, we must presume that no such prohibition exists for them in other times and places.

54. See *Yad, Hilchot Melachim*, 1:5, 9:14. One can only guess at the reasons for these precepts (reserving all official positions of civic authority — i.e., over both men and women — in Israel to Israel's men), subject to the example of Deborah, above. Not to mention the examples provided by history's other great women leaders.

55. Talmud, *Gittin* 10b, supra: "The law of the state is the law."

56. See, e.g., Genesis 1:27, Judges 4, Esther 4:14, and commentaries.

57. *Yad, Hilchot Sanhedrin* 21:6. Assuming that this Torah principle applies universally, as it seems.

58. See Exodus 22:21; Ezekiel 22:7; Talmud, *Yevamot* 100a, *Bava Metzia* 59a.

59. See *Yad, Hilchot Melachim* 10:9. Religion: in this context, not just morality and prayerful worship, but supernaturally meaningful symbolic observances, holy days and rituals. Man cannot invent Divine Commandments. Neither may he modify existing Commandments.

60. Even the Messiah's future government in Israel may not do so. See *Yad, Hilchot Melachim 8:10-11.* Conviction can't be coerced. One accepts and fulfills the purely theological principles of Sinai — as opposed to Sinai's operational Universal moral principles, the laws of common human decency — voluntarily, out of personal conviction and belief, or not at all.

61. A Hebrew's transgression against God, even in the realm of ritual, presents a different sort of threat to the world. A Hebrew Torah court *can* be empowered to punish such transgressions. See Exodus 22:19; Deuteronomy 17:11; *Yad, Hilchot Mamrim* 1:2. Naturally, only overt acts, not beliefs, are punishable. Id.

62. Mishnah, *Bava Kamma* 6:4; Mishnah Tosefta, *Bava Kamma* 6:16-17.

63. So it seems. See *Yad, Hilchot Melachim* 9:2, 10:9 and commentaries. Even in the land of Israel in the Millenium, a Noahide is/will be liable to the death penalty for creating a new religion or misappropriating Israel's observances, but no human court may execute him. Rather, his punishment will come from God.

64. See Thomas Paine, *Common Sense* (Philadelphia, 1776).

65. Mishnah, *Pirke Avot* 3:2.

66. See Mishnah, *Pirke Avot* 1:18; Midrash, *Genesis Rabbah* 39:6.

67. Talmud, *Bava Metzia* 13b.

68. Deuteronomy 6:18, with commentaries.

69. Ramban, *Pirush al HaTorah* on Deuteronomy 6:18 and 12:28; Midrash, *Sifre* 9a, 94a.

70. Proverbs 2:20.

71. See Talmud, *Bava Metzia* 83a; *Mishnah Tosefta, Sanhedrin* 1:3: "It is meritorious to compromise."

72. Rabbenu Eliezer ben Yossi, Talmud, *Sanhedrin* 6b.

73. *Mishnah Tosefta, Sanhedrin* 1:3; *Yad, Hilchot Sanhedrin* 22:4.

74. See *Shulchan Aruch, Hoshen Mishpat* 12:2.

75. Talmud, *Sanhedrin* 32b with Rashi.

76. "And when teachers distort the *halacha* [Israel's observant "Walk," or Torah path]." Mishnah, *Pirke Avot* 5:12.

77. Deuteronomy 16:18, above.

78. See Talmud, *Sanhedrin* 57a (near the end), 74b (in the name of Rava), *Avoda Zarah* 14b, *Hullin* 92a; *Sanhedrin* 75a with Rashi; *Yad, Hilchot Melachim* 9:9, 10:9, 10:12; Ramban on Genesis 26:5, 34:14; HaMe'iri on *Sanhedrin* 59a; *Sefer HaHinnuch*, Imperative 424; Albo, *Sefer ha-Ikkarim* 1:25, 3:14-15; Lichtenstein, *Seven Laws of Noah*, supra, pp. 31-35, Stone, Rakover et al, 12 *Cardozo Law Review*, supra. While Rabbi Yosef Babad argues that Noahides "may judge singly and at once" to rid themselves of any criminality in their midst — *Minchat Hinnuch*, Imperative 409 — virtually all other commentators argue that vigilante "justice" is itself criminal. Babad's dictum would probably only hold true in conditions of pure anarchy; in the case of lawless Shechem, for instance, or a similarly savage environment.

79. See Deuteronomy 16:18; *Mishnah Tosefta, Avoda Zarah* 8:4; *Yad, Hilchot Melachim* 9:14; *Sefer HaMitzvot* 1:176. Hebrews in the land of Israel must set up courts "in every city and town," but outside the land of Israel only in every major city. *Yad, Hilchot Sanhedrin* 1:1-2. So we assume that B'nai Noah must, similarly, conduct themselves more righteously in the Holy Land than outside it.

80. Deuteronomy 1:17; *Sefer HaMitzvot* 2:284; *Minchat Hinnuch*, Imperative 414.

81. Leviticus 19:15; Talmud, *Sanhedrin* 7b; *Sefer HaMitzvot* 1:177.

82. Midrash to Psalm 82:1.

83. Exodus 23:8; Deuteronomy 16:19; *Yad, Hilchot Teshuvah* 4:5; *Sefer HaMitzvot* 2:274.

84. Talmud, *Bava Batra* 9b.

85. Leviticus 19:15; Mishnah, *Pirke Avot* 1:8; *Sefer HaMitzvot* 2:275; and Talmud, *Ketubot* 105b.

86. Deuteronomy 1:17; Talmud, *Sanhedrin* 56b; *Yad, Hilchot Sanhedrin* 22:1; *Sefer HaMitzvot* 2:276.

87. Exodus 23:3; Leviticus 19:15; *Sefer HaMitzvot* 2:277. Although this can require the court to provide an indigent litigant with the means to make a proper presentation. If a litigant is obviously poor (or impressively dressed), clothing might affect the judge. So the judge should try to level the playing field. See Hirsch, *Horeb*, supra, para. 394.

88. Mishnah, *Ketubot* 9:1.

89. If a litigant is poor the judge may, after issuing judgment but not before, give that person charity from the judge's own pocket. Mishnah, *Sanhedrin* 1:4, *Ketubot*, ibid.

90. See Deuteronomy 15:7; Proverbs 10:2; Job 34:28.

91. See Deuteronomy 25:1. The Lord's judgments couple strict justice and infinite compassion. Midrash, *Pesikta Rabbati* 5:11; *Moreh Nevuchim* 3:53. But human judges don't have God's wisdom. They serve Him best when they issue judgment without any sentimentality at all. Mishnah, *Ketubot* 9:2, *Ta'anit* 6:2.

92. R. Shimon ben Lakish, *Ecclesiastes Rabbah* 7:16. See Deuteronomy 19:13,21 and commentaries.

93. Exodus 23:6; Midrash, *Mechilta* to 23:6; *Sefer HaMitzvot* 2:278.

94. Deuteronomy 24:2; 2 Kings 14:6; Ezekiel 18:20; Midrash, *Numbers Rabbah* 19:33. Here lies the Scriptural basis of the U.S. Constitution's provision, Article Three, Sec. 3, prohibiting "Corruption of Blood."

95. Leviticus 19:15; Deuteronomy 24:17; *Sefer HaMitzvot* 2:280.

96. Proverbs 31:9.

97. Exodus 23:1; Talmud, *Sanhedrin* 7b, *Shavuot* 30-31a; *Sefer HaMitzvot* 2:281.

98. Talmud, *Sanhedrin* 79b. But a court can act, despite one party's absence, to preserve others' rights.

99. Deuteronomy 13:15; Talmud, *Sanhedrin* 40a with Rashi; *Sefer HaMitzvot* 1:179. In Israel's Torah courts, a panel of judges examines the witnesses; in Anglo-Saxon jurisprudence, opposing lawyers. But if a lawyer fails to elicit important evidence, the deciding judge or jurors may never get the material they need to judge correctly. The Torah's system probably comes closer to God's ideal.

100. *Shekalim* 3:2. Meaning, among other things, that a judge must avoid even the appearance of impropriety.

101. See Leviticus 5:1; Talmud, *Sanhedrin* 57b; *Sefer HaMitzvot* 1:178.

102. Ibid.

103. *Sefer HaHinnuch*, Imperative 237.

104. See Deuteronomy 19:18-20; Talmud, *Makkot* 5b; *Sefer HaMitzvot* 1:180, 2:285.

105. Ibid. Note that this is the ninth of Israel's Ten Commandments. See Exodus 20:13; Deuteronomy 5:17.

106. R. Shimon ben Gamaliel, *Pirke Avot* 1:18 (citing Zechariah 8:16). See Talmud, *Shabbat* 55a: "The seal of God is Truth."

107. Exodus 18:22,26; Deuteronomy 1:17, 17:11; Talmud, *Sanhedrin* 86b; *Sefer HaMitzvot* 1:174; *Moreh Nevuchim* 3:41.

108. "[T]o the just" — in Hebrew, "to the *tzaddik*," the kindly, wise, righteous person. "[T]o do justice" — to do *mishpat*, true lawful justice/judgment.

109. Leviticus 19:15; Talmud, *Sanhedrin* 7a; *Sefer HaMitzvot* 2:273.

110. Deuteronomy 1:16, 16:18-20, 17:9-10, 25:1; *Yad, Hilchot Sanhedrin* 20:6-7. Rather than execute a person who may be innocent, however, the court must remember that, in difficult cases, God Himself (and not a fallible human court) will punish the guilty. See Exodus 23:7; Talmud, *Sanhedrin* 33b.

111. *Yad*, ibid.

112. *Yad*, ibid. Also see Mishnah, *Pirke Avot* 1:18, 5:12.

113. Talmud, *Shabbat* 139a. This means that society must institute effective mechanisms to justly judge its judges, which, in turn, points to the need for efficient police, reviewing agencies, and higher courts.

114. Also see Deuteronomy 1:17, 16:19. "[R]espect of persons" — i.e., personal favoritism, as opposed to "blind" and impartial justice.

THE SECOND COMMANDMENT

Laws Against Sacrilege

So honest and frank when addressing most other enormities, Israel's Sages refer to this Second Universal law only in guarded terms. They describe the core crime here as "blessing the Name" — the holy Name of God.[1]

The true crime, of course, doesn't involve blessing but cursing, profaning His holy Name.[2]

Name means identity. "As is his name, so is he."[3] Among human beings, the world's only creatures who use language to think, a name represents the essence of its bearer.

You shall not profane My holy Name. — *Leviticus 22:32*

Profaning the Lord's Name — bringing anything directly associated with God into contempt or disrepute, by word or deed — is blasphemy.

But this gets into English semantics, muddling Hebrew Revolutionary concepts. *Profane* comes from two Latin words, *pro* and *fanum*, meaning "outside the temple." That is, secular, desanctified, unholy. *Blasphemy* comes from Greek and means "evil-speaking," or impious, godless, god-defying speaking.

We could wish for tools more precise than all that Greek and Latin offer to handle the deep and important laws within.

Here would be the place to deal with the most abhorrent of
crimes, blasphemy, but the author recoils in horror from doing so.
— *R. Samson Raphael Hirsch*[4]

Blasphemy and idolatry both belong to the same family of crimes. The two Commandments against them are closely linked, each referring to the other. So it's difficult to speak of either Commandment alone, without connection to the other.

Only man — humanity — treasures sacred symbols, ideas, or language; only human beings feel any inclination to protect them. One can define man as a creature who defends the symbols that are sacred to him.

We are also a species, the only species, that both wants and needs to put a fence around the sacred, to protect it from injury — to save it from defilement.

Clearly, no finite being could ever harm the Master of the Universe. He is infinite and eternal; He is the never-changing all-powerful Creator, the Foundation of the entire cosmos, of this and every universe.[5] That any man or men could harm Him, God!, in any way . . . the very suggestion is ridiculous.[6] The truth, which is widely recognized, is that "human nature cannot bear blasphemy."[7] This is a crime that poisons civilizations; a sin — an error and a failing — that attacks man's mind, sickens his soul, and often even goads him into war.[8]

Basically, any human action leading others to denigrate or undervalue the things and beings they should esteem is blasphemous, or sacrilegious.[9]

Blasphemy defames what is holy. It attacks man's important treasure, his individual relationship to the Ultimate — to God. It attacks the proper idea of God.[10]

This, "the most abhorrent of crimes," also presents us with a special challenge.

One turns to the great authorities only to find them reluctant to speak on the subject, or willing to discuss it only in very ginger, general terms. Most treatments focus only on narrow aspects of the crime. Of course "blessing the Name" relates especially to speech — to utterance — and the human aptitude for language. At the same time every sin, to some extent, is blasphemous.[11]

> Whosoever curses his God shall bear his sin. And he who
> blasphemes the Name of the Lord shall surely be put to death.
> — *Leviticus 24:15-16*[12]

By these words the Lord of the Universe sets before the entire world one of the Torah's most explicitly Universal laws.

Mystics associate this Rainbow Covenant Commandment with the color orange.[13] Orange "reflects different aspects of the colors which are similar to it" — such as the rainbow's red (See "Laws against Murder"), the yellow of the laws against larceny, and the deeper red of the laws against anarchy or lawlessness — but which each lack orange's "all-embracing nature."[14]

In fact, these laws touch upon every law. The crime at the core of the Commandment — the outlandish act of "blessing," or really damning, God's holy Name — is the subject of a most stringent Divine prohibition, a universal legal prohibition, which is also incredibly narrow. But it opens our eyes to the most wide-ranging wisdom. It shows us that God grants man not only the power to honor but also to dishonor Him here on Earth, before one's fellow men; that He grants us free will to choose our way; and that He forbids us to dishonor Him.

Proceeding from these simple principles, our subject becomes truly "all-embracing." Man must not profane God at all, in any respect; one exists only to do His will and honor Him. We are dealing, then, not with blaspheming but with glorifying holiness — that is, with the true and literal blessing of His Name.

In narrowest terms, this Universal law forbids the act of cursing the Creator. This is the crime at the core of the Commandment, which gives its name to this whole huge body of laws and — especially — morality.

Anyone who publicly curses or reviles God, wishing Him harm, by His true Name — His utterly unique four-letter proper Name, the Tetragrammaton,[15] known in English by the letters Y-H-V and H — deserves to die.[16] If a second person witnesses and understands the curse the blasphemy is public.[17]

One sinner destroys much good. — *Ecclesiastes 9:17*

Note that the crime here isn't cursing *in* God's Name, but cursing God *by* His Name. And see how precisely Israel defines the offense. This is the only kind of curse, or malicious wish, for which a Torah court may impose the death penalty upon a Jew. At the same time, Israel has protected the four-letter Name so assiduously, to protect it from every blasphemous, presumptuous misuse, that no one today even knows precisely how to pronounce it.[18] So this is an offense that exists almost entirely in theory; as a capital felony, it can no longer be committed.[19]

Base people revile your Name.— *Psalm 74:18*

Still within the realm of courts and crime, one who curses the Creator by any name or title other than the Name, clearly pointing to Him in both the speaker's and a witness's understanding, also deserves punishment. The Torah prescribes corporal, not capital, punishment, for a Jew who curses God, wishing Him harm, damning holy names other than the Name.[20] But a Gentile who blasphemes God in this manner, using the only name or names for Him he knows, comes under a different rule. Under the Noahide Law, he may be punished capitally.[21]

A Ben Noah who curses God's Name, whether he uses God's unique Name or one of His other names, in any language, is liable. — *Maimonides*[22]

People associate the Bible's Job with the crime. His suffering wife spoke to the good man, her stricken husband, so: "Do you still retain your integrity? Curse God [in Hebrew, *Barach Elo[k]im*, or "Bless the Lord," the conventional euphemistic antonym], and die."[23] Righteous Job's righteous response: "What? shall we receive [only] good at the hand of God [*Elo[k]im*], and shall we not [also] receive evil?"[24]

Assuming Job to be a Gentile — a Ben Noah — rather than a Hebrew,[25] this Scriptural dialogue is especially revealing. Neither Job nor his wife use God's proper Name, but only a less hallowed, commonly accepted substitute.

So we see that this is a Rainbow Covenant principle: one must not curse God in any language, using any of His names.[26]

Job never did. Even in his pain he kept his head. Job's story exemplifies the truth that Creation exists not for any one of us nor even for many of us but for Torah, for righteousness and godliness — for God's purposes, far beyond the scope of our imaginings.[27] To "bless the Name" in the criminal sense denies that truth. It is verbal rebellion; it is treason.

> Both the blasphemer and the worshipper of idols deny the fundamental principles of our religion. — *Maimonides*[28]

Revolutionary Israel, still camping at the foot of Sinai, learned how to deal with such treason early on.[29] A full-grown man with a grudge, apparently, the son of a Hebrew mother and a pagan father,[30] decided to curse or cast contempt upon the Name. He did it publicly and he did it as an antagonist, an enemy, of the Revolution's God.

Treason weakens a people. Anyone who suffers exposure to treason has an obligation to bring the traitor to justice.[31] Among Israel, justice must be the same for the Gentile as the Hebrew blasphemer: a Gentile living among Jews isn't bound to worship or believe in the One God but must never actively, publicly, attack Him.[32] If he does attack Him, he deserves to suffer punishment no less horrendous than his crime: a bad death, public disgrace, and — usually — the disgrace even of his family.[33]

Blasphemy as Offensive Speech

If gossip is debased speech, surely the basest qualities that go into gossip are: 1) malice, 2) false superiority, and 3) a sense of disaffection — a lack of solidarity — with the object of the gossip.[34] "Blessing the name" combines *all* of these less than fully human impulses to revile pure Perfection — the King of the Universe, our Father. The voice is man's but the feelings that drive the voice are animalistic.

So this is a crime of relative sophistication — only man can blaspheme his Maker — flowing from ugly and rebellious impulses of crude resentment. It is pathological, a matter of abnormal psychology, as well, of course, as absolutely futile. It defiles the divine gift of speech by cursing its holy Giver. Worse, perhaps, it breaks down the elaborately constructed fences by which men protect their most precious treasure — a true idea of God and holiness.[35]

> Where were *you* when I [God] laid the foundations of the Earth?
> — *Job 38:4*

Obviously, even under God's full-time total sovereignty, human life, at least on a planet yet to be redeemed, involves pain. To suffer and, suffering, declare that the world that hurts *me* is perverse and so is its Maker perverse, is to substitute one's own agenda for the Holy One's. One may think of this crime as an essentially trivial — but thinking, speaking — being's absurd presumption.[36] It's not just illogical or infantile: it's also fundamentally idolatrous.

Only man can ignore God's Will and try to substitute for it his own — the pathology at the root of both idolatry and blasphemy. Only man has the gifts, together with the self-inflated pride, or hubris. Unrestrained by law, the animal in man easily degenerates into perverse childish willfulness and ego-driven presumptuousness.

We all exist as a unique combination of animal elements and godlike attributes. But we sacrilegiously defy the God who made us when we put mere human — really, animal — goals and man-made values ahead of His.

Idolatry is always blasphemous. Blasphemy is always idolatrous. The opposite of both idolatry and blasphemy is the sanctification of the One God's holy Name. Just as the two crimes, idolatry and blasphemy, are connected, so are the Commandments against them. In fact, mystics say that the two operate together, in tandem — the only two of the Seven Commandments that do so — like the legs supporting a man walking.[37]

These two Commandments are unique in other ways. The other Noahide Commandments focus on man's relations with his fellow creatures. Since material harm comes to God's creatures when people violate them, men need no special Revelation concerning God to recognize that those crimes have negative effects. But the Noahide laws against blasphemy and idolatry govern man's relationship with God Himself — with the God "Who hides" Himself,[38] the God of Israel. So anyone seeking to understand these two Commandments should probably be looking at them both together, and then only in their proper context: within God's special Revelation to Israel.

Don't Curse the One God, the Creator

The nations are responsible for criminalizing this if no other kind or degree of "blessing the Name."[39] The offense here, as we have seen, isn't cursing *in* the name of God but cursing God wrathfully or contemptuously *by* name, wishing evil or a sudden loss of status to befall Him.[40] An outlandish act, a crime of treason, it invites the very harshest punishment — whether in Hebrew courts, Heaven's courts, or the nations' civil law.[41]

> Of all those condemned to death by a Court of Law, the blasphemer is the only one in whose case all the witnesses and the judges are required to place their hands, one after the other, upon the head of the culprit and say to him, "Thy blood be upon thy head, for thou hast brought it on thyself. — *Maimonides*[42]

Following the majority viewpoint,[43] the Torah prohibition that governs Israel is *narrower* than the Rainbow Law is here. Hebrews are legally culpable only if they damn the Name — the Tetragrammaton — or (while it isn't said to merit capital punishment)[44] one of the seven holy descriptive Hebrew titles by which God revealed Himself to Israel. A Ben Noah is guilty if he curses God by *any* of the names or titles or descriptive designations by which he knows the God of Israel, the One God, the Almighty.[45]

If that seems like strange jurisprudence, the nations' laws offer many precedents, at least roughly reflecting the same essential proposition.

True, not every nation treats blasphemy as a criminal matter. The law against blasphemy, like the law against idolatry, is still too widely misunderstood; the world's nations as yet haven't learned enough about this law, nor about God. They can hardly be expected to criminalize what they still haven't learned to recognize as crime.

Know that it *is* crime. Note, for instance, that the laws of even the liberty-loving individual American states proscribed blasphemy — generally definable as "scandalous, impious, obscene or profane libel of or concerning God, offensive to religious-minded persons and likely to disturb the public peace" — through most of the history of the United States.[46]

People must be protected from what should be grossly offensive to all men: witnessing one's Father (who is also no less than one's Heavenly Mother), the Creator, being cursed! The Commandment requires no more. Levels of penalties, as mentioned previously, and other details of enforcement, are for each nation to determine for itself.

Beyond this, the stringent law that gives its name to this broad category of Law, our subject — against "blessing the Name" — becomes one mostly of morality, less than the minimal requisites of a Universal Commandment. The precepts below, which logic associates with the Commandment, need not be judicially enforced, though they can be; at the same time, those who try to legislate morality must accept the risk of trampling upon legitimate human freedoms. God's Law proscribes the clearly pathological and criminal so that man can exercise his God-given right to live in freedom. Freedom includes, above all, the freedom to think, and certainly its twin, the freedom to speak.

> You shall not revile God, nor curse a leader of your people.
> — *Exodus 22:27* [47]

Every apparent ambiguity Moses left us in the Written Torah was deliberate.[48] Some authorities interpret the Hebrew word *Elo[k]im,* above, as God; others translate it as Gods, or judges.[49]

Whenever there's a chance that a Heavenly prohibition may be broader than it looks at first, it is best to be careful, to avoid a frightful transgression.[50]

We've discussed the extremely narrow prohibition at the heart of the Commandment already. But logic suggests that this Biblical passage, "You shall not," with its obvious universal implications, must be treated as inclusive, not exclusive, encompassing the following precepts:

- **Don't curse or revile God by *any* of His
  names, even if one of His names has been
  joined to that of a false god.**

Kill me, but do not mock my faith.— *Arabic proverb* [51]

Pagans adore and venerate their idols. Ignorant folk associate
their false gods with the One God. They invest their Athenas with
His wisdom, their earth mothers with His mercy or His infinite
love, their father gods with His omnipotence; etc.[52] So the fierce
public curse or angry taunting insult by which the blasphemer
brings contempt against a mere idol can easily reach beyond its
target — that is, against Him, as pagans think they know Him.[53]

> My name is great among the nations;
> And in every place offerings are presented unto My name,
> Even pure oblations;
> For My name is great among the nations,
> Saith the Lord of hosts.— *Malachi 1:11*

Moses' Revolution spreads beyond Israel by exalting God's
holy Name. It follows that, in this area particularly, God imposes
on His followers a certain duty of care.

The Biblical prophets didn't roam the world insulting other

peoples' idols. Jonah went to distant Assyria not to deflate the infantile theology of the Assyrians but to admonish them because of the violently immoral way they led their lives.[54]

Israel by the fact of its existence stands for the non-existence of every god but God. Still, never has it been the way of Israel — except, of course, among the people or in the land of Israel — to try to keep, taunt, or badger any person away from any god.

> Always respect the public. — *Talmud*[55]

A Jew who follows a pagan god necessarily rejects the One God and His Law.[56] Likewise, in the Holy Land, the land of Israel, there can be no good in any god but God. The Creator commands the Jews to obliterate every shrine to every foreign deity and spirit in their Holy Land — that is, within geographic Israel.[57] In other lands, among other peoples, the issues are somewhat different.

Both idolatry and blasphemy are crimes of treason against God. But an ignorant idolator — one who genuinely knows no better than to worship his people's customary gods — may lack the requisite treasonous intent.[58] He *should* know better than to follow idols but, in fact, he may not be that wise.[59]

Those who stand outside Israel's unique Covenant haven't necessarily benefitted from Israel's history or direct experience with Revelation. In such cases, outside the Hebrews' Holy Land and away from anyone, Jew or non-Jew, who either knows or should know only God, there might even be some real, if temporary,[60] good in the manmade gods of paganism.[61]

> Thou art the Lord, and all beings are thy servants, Thy domain;
> And through those who serve idols vain
> Thine honor is not detracted from,
> For they all aim to Thee to come.— *Jewish hymn* [62]

It is blasphemous to attack what is good. So the Lord of the Universe, who calls on all humanity to worship Him alone, also calls on us to heed Him in this respect. Even if their worship, infamously, goes to a Satan or a Stalin,[63] one should try to lead others to Him — that is, to truth — by emulating and praising Him, rather than by heaping blasphemy, intolerant abuse or ridicule upon their most-cherished beliefs.[64] "Don't provoke one of another belief," Israel is told.[65] The logic here is universal. People who try to push others to the truth by heedlessly dragging down their gods and insulting everything involved with them do Him no service. In fact, the God of truth has provided us with this caution to the contrary.

> All the Torah's ways are ways of sweetness, and all its paths are peace. — *Talmud*[66]

Surely the best thing, as Moses taught, is to "make no mention of the names of other gods": don't pronounce the name of any idol — "don't let it be heard out of your mouth."[67]

Not that righteousness requires a censoring (if self-imposed) ban on honest dialogue. Nothing could be further from the truth.[68] The vice addressed here involves a dismissive, defamatory attack on goodness — even if the good involved is slight, obscure, or fleeting — in a manner perceived by others as insulting if not obscene. So one's manner, and other people's perceptions, matter. If one's audience believes that there is no godliness nor good in Satan nor Stalin, for instance, attacking Satan or Stalin cannot be blasphemous.

What are blasphemies to one man or clan may be no more than platitudes to others. The single rule applicable in all times and places protects the One God as the people present think they know Him. A great deal depends on circumstances. A truly human being should always be sensitive to circumstances.

> Whoso guards his mouth and his tongue keeps his soul from troubles. — *Proverbs 21:23*[69]

- **Still proceeding from the core of Commandment, still dealing with deliberate verbal defamation, cursing one's fellows is problematic. Don't damn the goodness in Creation, even when it's mixed with badness. Don't slight the godly in one's fellow men.**

I don't like low opinions, and when you speak them out it commits

you and you become a slave of them. Talk will lead people on until
they convince their minds of things they can't feel true. — *Saul
Bellow*[70]

"Be rather of the cursed than the cursing," the Torah tells
Israel.[71] Everyone — every person — exists, in a sense, in God's
image; every human being possesses aspects of infinite rarity and
godliness. Then too, some of us occupy an office, or perform
worldly functions, of unusual or special holiness.

> What is there that envy has not defamed, or malice left undefiled?
> Truly, no good thing. — *William Baldewyn*[72]

- **Don't curse a leader. The word** *elo[k]im*
  denotes judges and legal decision-makers, in
  the Torah's text, as well as God *(Elo[k]im),*
  and other elevated beings.[73]

The office of judge deserves honor, even if the occupant is
unworthy.[74] One's secular leader, ruler,[75] teachers, and parents[76]
all fulfill a role that, in some respects, is holy. Demonstrating
respect for them and for the good they may do is to acknowledge
and honor the great potential for goodness in all men. To curse
such figures — to vehemently denounce them, calling on a higher
Power to visit evil upon them[77] — is to commit a kind of *lese
majesty*, an affront to the holy nature and importance of their
offices.

Describing this sort of conduct as "backbiting" suggests the
cowardice involved in attacking someone only when he is absent,
unprepared, or otherwise unable to defend against it. It "recalls
the dog who will tear a dead boar's skin although he dare not look
upon the living animal."[78]

> To allow oneself to be carried away by wrath is as bad as
> worshipping idols.— *Maimonides* [79]

Generally, we should not curse anyone in any respect, even the
most wretched of human beings. "You shall not curse the deaf."[80]
That is, even a person who cannot hear your words[81] — and not
just because he might not be able to defend himself against
them.[82] "Torah has regard not only to the one who is cursed, but

also to the curser, who is told not to be vindictive and hot-tempered."[83] So you shouldn't curse your fellow human being even if your curse doesn't bother him at all. Neither, for that matter, should you ever curse yourself.[84]

"You shall love your neighbor as yourself," the Torah emphasizes.[85] If you can give yourself the benefit of the doubt, you must do so for your fellow. God requires us to judge each other — our living contemporaries — as favorably as we are prone to judge ourselves.[86] Just as one doesn't habitually and cynically ascribe purely self-interested or discreditable motives to one's own actions, one must not do so to others'.

Note that this Rule, the Golden Rule, applies at least as strongly when men speak of their leaders as it does when speaking of everybody else.

In Israel's law, cursing is permitted only when prompted by pure motives, which are selfless motives, and justified by the guilt — the reprehensible conduct — of the person being cursed.[87] Sometimes some people, due to their crimes, deserve others' curses.[88] But ordinarily, when a curse against a person is forbidden, a Torah court can impose no more than corporal, rather than capital, punishment.[89] That level of penalty is revealing.

> You shall not wrong one another, but you shall fear your God.
> — *Leviticus 25:17* [90]

Wrongfully cursing or denouncing a person — invoking a higher Power to cause him harm — is surely a blasphemous and very sinful thing. Call it a kind of sacrilege of the second or the third degree. See the Biblical history of Shimei, a fanatic enemy of King David, who lawlessly cursed the king. Good King David punished him with death, not merely for cursing, but for the utterly ungovernable recklessness that lay behind it.[91]

Israel sometimes hyperbolically equates such lawless speech, and slanderous speech generally, to murder.[92] But unlike actual murder, it isn't, in itself, necessarily directly inimical to all true civilization.[93] Accordingly, unlike actual murder, neither can it be said to constitute a true Rainbow Covenant felony.

You shall not take the Name of the Lord your God in vain; for the
Lord will not hold him guiltless who takes His Name in vain.
— *Exodus 20:7* [94]

•   *Ha Shem* means "the name," in Hebrew;
    HaShem means "the [holy] Name." Even if
    one learns no other Hebrew from this book,
    this is the Hebrew to learn. "HaShem" is
    how Israel, in casual and common usage,
    refers to the Master of the Universe, the Holy
    One, blessed be He. It's respectful
    terminology. It's protective.

As well the stranger as the home-born, when he blasphemes the
Name, [he] shall be put to death. — *Leviticus 24:16*

God's Name, as people may think they know it, is not to be
uttered unnecessarily in common conversation. He is holy and His
public identity is holy, and it is vile and sacrilegious to treat
anything so closely associated with Him profanely.

Death and life are in the power of the tongue. — *Proverbs 18:21* [95]

One should never erase His Name, nor otherwise mistreat it. [96]
One must never invoke it in support of a vain oath — to swear,
for instance, that an existing object is not what it is in fact (as
where one swears that an object of clay is gold, or vice versa), or
that something exists which doesn't. Every such oath makes God a
party, as it were, as a witness and seemingly as a guarantor, to
nonsense. Further, one must never, ever, swear by His Name
falsely. [97]

Because God witnesses every oath, one who violates an oath
testifies, in effect, that God doesn't concern Himself with the
affairs of humanity; that He can be disregarded with impunity.
This, of course, is blasphemy. Likewise, swearing by His name to
violate any of His laws, as by invoking Him to affirm that one will
commit adultery, is perfidious. It denies the validity of His Law; it
constitutes a blasphemous "testing" of the Lord. [98] Similarly, one
must never invoke HaShem to add weight to any banal or trite
assertion — as by swearing, for instance, that the sun rises in the

east, that grass is green, or that a similarly self-evident fact is true.[99]

> Wild beasts [i.e., bloodshed] come into the world because of false swearing and on account of the profanation of God's Name.
> — *Mishnah*[100]

God is to be hallowed, not profaned, by His followers.[101] The sins being described here are classed among the "graver transgressions" of His Law — that is, of Israel's Law, the Torah.[102] Yet the Jew who transgresses unintentionally, or negligently, receives no punishment from a court at all. In fact, even the most willful and guilty violator incurs (from a Torah court) no more than a corporal penalty.[103] So if, as it seems, these Torah ordinances point to universal moral rules, we must remember not to confuse the precepts of a rigorous morality with the Universal legal precepts that all courts must *always* enforce.

The Eternal Lord Who gives man free will allows him to use it. While the path of the righteous should be clear to all men, all men are not held to the standards of Israel. This is an area where conscience, not legal coercion, should be guidance enough for most men.

Censorship is not the essence of civilization. God created us, speaking creatures, for freedom. We can assume that God will justly punish the sinner, even if human courts do not: the Master of the Universe may occasionally overlook other awful crimes, but never the profanation of His Name.[104]

> He who asserts that idolatry is true, even if he does not worship an idol, reviles and blasphemes the Honored and Revered Name of the Lord. — *Maimonides*[105]

- **One of the most consistently radical ideas coming out of Sinai is that there is truth in the world and that people can find it. Naturally, logically, if truth exists, so must its opposite. But "the seal of God is truth."[106]**

You can't adhere to untruths without being immoral in some

way.

Truth is the first of the three foundations (i.e., along with justice and peace) on which the world rests.[107] God calls on His followers to keep far from every false matter,[108] to pursue what is true, if for no other reason than that "God is true."[109]

Blasphemy is supremely evil in that it gives His creatures — one's fellows — a false idea of Who and What their Lord is.

Nothing is more important than a correct idea of God. Everything man strives for stems from his perception of the underlying reality of all existence. A person's concept of the Ultimate is the single central idea around which his universe — his intellectual, moral, and spiritual existence — revolves.

It follows that, while any falsehood betokens a certain level of ungodliness, falsehoods concerning the Master of all things are especially noxious. Indeed, to communicate anything untrue about the nature of Divinity is to blaspheme Him.

Finite man finds it difficult to speak of an infinite God. The words simply don't exist that can describe Him or tell of His perfection.[110] "Can you find out the deep things of God?"[111] "My thoughts are not your thoughts, neither are My ways your ways."[112] It will have to suffice here, at least for the time being, to underline the fact that to represent God as in any way distant or uncaring, finite or unjust is blasphemous.

This means that every idolatrous statement, every idea of multiple gods, or no God, or that "God has abandoned the earth," is blasphemous, as well as idolatrous.[113] So is the idea that man has no power to choose between good and evil — i.e., that God denies man free will.[114]

If man lacks free will, if he is just the plaything of circumstances and not actually responsible for his actions, he cannot truly exist in God's Image. Nor can there be a just punishment for those who do evil, nor any just reward for those who do good.[115]

Falsehoods like those are not merely contrary to what God has told us in His Torah.[116] Any statement, dogma or religion that denies human free will must end by denying that the God of love, the God of Israel, is a true and just and holy Being.

He who oppresses the poor blasphemes his Maker. — *Psalm 14:31*

> • **Blasphemy — "blessing the Name" — is sometimes a matter of utterance but sometimes a matter of non-verbal conduct. One who profanes God's Name — in other words, His infinitely holy Essence — does the opposite of sanctifying the Name. "What is the sanctification of the Name?" Obviously: "Conduct which leads people to love the name of Heaven [His Name; i.e., Him]."[117]**

If you must sin, sin privately, but do not publicly profane God's Name. — *Talmud*[118]

God Who is holy deserves followers who are holy themselves. To follow God is to be associated with Him, to some extent, in one's fellows' eyes. *So as much as any of the Seven Commandments, this Commandment, against defaming His Name, leads promptly to its opposite — the sanctification of everything pertaining to God.* When His followers conduct themselves so as to lead non-believers to love and follow Him, His holy Name is sanctified.[119] Their reputation for goodness exalts His Name; anything less than that profanes it.

This means that God demands more from some people than from others. Look at His instructions to the "priests" — the *cohanim* — of Israel, and all that they must do to avoid anything that might defile His special servants.[120] Similarly, a great leader or Torah scholar who — Heaven forbid! — appears before the public drunk or unkempt incurs a much greater degree of guilt than the lawless savage who behaves similarly.[121]

A man of Torah should be nothing less than an agent of godliness, a vehicle of God. But even the lawless savage bears some guilt under this Commandment. Both the scholar and the savage exist in God's own holy Image. And both, at least compared to animals, are only "a little less than Divine."[122]

One who publicly pretends to serve and honor God but who behaves as if "God has abandoned the Earth" in his secret, personal affairs will eventually, publicly, desecrate His Name. "Expose hypocrites," the Talmud recommends, "to prevent the profanation of the Name."[123] Still, the God of Truth is first of all the God of loving-kindness.[124] So Israel is told, "Speak the truth by all means; but be quite sure that you speak the truth *in love*."[125]

Some men being more closely associated than others with the God of Abraham and Moses, they deserve some deference from all men. Because few people are more closely associated with the God of Israel than the people Israel, to demean a Jew must (all else being equal) be unusually problematic. "The portion of the Lord is His people."[126]

God speaks to mankind through the Bible, to clearly tell us all that the people of Israel are uniquely His own.[127] Scripture is most specific: "Cursed be they who curse you [Israel], and blessed be those who bless you."[128]

The Jewish people are eternally "betrothed" to Him to glorify His Name — sometimes in strange ways — among their fellow creatures.[129] The world has an obligation to respect that. It is especially sinful, because it is especially blasphemous (all else being equal), to wrongly strike a Jew, for instance.[130]

In positive terms, because God created man to "cleave to Him,"[131] it behooves men to cleave to, or respectfully associate with,[132] those who are uniquely called by His Name.[133]

By far the best thing one can do is to love God "with an exceedingly great and mighty love, so that one's very soul shall be bound by his love of God" — like the love of the lovesick lover, who ceaselessly longs after his beloved — and then to act accordingly.[134]

"To avoid a transgression or to perform a holy precept, not from fear or ambition but purely out of love of God, is to sanctify His Name before the public."[135]

One can learn something about this from the Book of Job, focusing as it does on both blasphemy and its opposite.[136] Job's so-called "Code of a Man of Honor" offers amazingly concise guidance — for B'nai Noah as well as B'nai Israel — on truly sanctifying the holy Name.[137]

> You shall be holy; for I the Lord your God am holy.
> — *Leviticus 19:2*

God requires His followers to imitate Him — not, of course, His infinity or majesty, which are beyond human comprehension anyway, nor in anything requiring His omniscient vision, but in His ways of mercy, goodness, gentleness and truth.[138]

His Law — His Torah — is the greatest truth of all.[139] Those who claim to love God but who ignore His Law profane His Name.[140] Further, in positive terms: while it isn't possible to discuss every Torah precept associated with these broad Noahide Commandments, whoever seeks to glorify Him, by avoiding the profanation of His Name, needs to have some knowledge of the following:

- **Correct conduct. Known in Hebrew as the "Way of the World" — *derech eretz*, the "Way of the Land" — or "Worldly Occupation," this immensely important concept teaches, among other things, courtesy, humility, gentleness, and dignified and appropriate behavior.[141]**

Correct conduct isn't merely good manners or a code of etiquette — although the doctrine teaches both etiquette and manners — so much as a way of participating in the world, or at least in one's part of it, as an effective, upstanding servant of the Creator.

> In whom mankind finds pleasure, God finds pleasure. —
> *Mishnah*[142]

One should conduct oneself in such a gracious, sensible,

decent and attractive manner that others, looking on, will want to follow one's example. "You must appear justified before man as well as before God."[143] This imperative is so compelling that it can actually, in extreme cases, excuse certain violations of law. It's based on the theory that "Correct conduct/*derech eretz* precedes Torah,"[144] and that "without correct conduct there is no Torah."[145] Basically, however, correct conduct exists as a means to glorify the Law — and through the Law, its Maker.[146]

> • **Kindliness is the heart of *derech eretz*. Man cannot honor God if he doesn't also treat God's creatures kindly. The story of Abram, or later Abraham, who practiced the most rigorous kindness as a supreme religious obligation, offers us instruction.[147] The Lord God *cherishes* human kindliness. And He requires us to live and practice charity.**

As the Talmud teaches, charity — in Hebrew, *tzedaka,* meaning "righteousness," "justice," or "acts of loving-kindness" — equals all of the other Divine commandments combined.[148] Or see Isaiah: "God Who is holy is sanctified by justice [*tzedaka*]" — in other words, "by charity."[149] Perhaps more than any other human activity, "charity brings near the Redemption."[150]

Not to slight the other values implicit within *derech eretz*. Consider the value of study.

> Learning is more important than action, when it leads to action.
> — *Talmud*[151]

> • **Animals are ruled by their instincts. Man, whose intellect surpasses his instincts, who has the free will to make choices for himself, makes moral choices based on learning.**

"An empty-headed man cannot be a sin-fearing man and an ignoramus cannot be saintly."[152] Without education, even if only of an informal kind, people soon sink below the moral level of the animals.

In fact, study itself is service to God,[153] "for without wisdom there cannot be any good act or true knowledge."[154]

- **Neither can we ignore the importance of work. Human beings are born to labor.[155] The first thing the Lord did for Adam, even before He created Eve, was to put him to work.[156] In the Revolutionary worldview labor isn't a curse but a blessing. Scripture promises, "When you eat the fruits of your labor, happy shall you be."[157] "Great is labor," the Talmud teaches; "it confers honor on the laborer."[158] "Be strong," the prophet says, "and work."[159]**

All work, in a sense, comes from the Lord. He gave men and women dominion over the earth[160] — humanity's ultimate responsibility is "to perfect the world under the rule of God."[161] Obviously, such an enormous task can never be fulfilled without tremendous effort: every little bit helps; every human being has a duty to help. So one should "love work."[162]

As Scripture teaches, "cursed be he who does the Lord's work with a slack hand."[163] As for the great rabbis of Israel, they practiced what they preached: they were "porters, smiths, hewers of wood and drawers of water."[164] They preferred to tire themselves with honest labor rather than accept charitable support from their brethren.[165] People so unfortunate as to have no regular work should still find themselves something to do — "perhaps in a neglected yard or field."[166]

- **As for the negative aspects of *derech eretz*, everything immoral, oppressive, or even needlessly unseemly are offenses, even if they are not otherwise forbidden by His law. Scripture tells us that sexual immorality, particularly, is defiling.[167]**

The God who Created us expects us to direct and channel our animal drives not in ways that abase us — that exaggerate our animal qualities — but in ways that make us better. Neither does He want us to misdirect the animal within us, to bring unnecessary or ugly reminders of those qualities to any aspect of His service.

Worship

You are the children of the Lord your God. — *Deuteronomy 14:1*[170]

Dirt, impurity, nakedness — in fact, everything unseemly — have no place in any place of worship. So one does not pray in a lavatory, for instance; amidst a foul odor; nor in places dedicated to sexual immorality or idolatry.

Man cannot properly direct himself to God's total Purity when distracted by gross impurities. Similarly, the God who loves modesty never asks us to pray to Him with our genitals exposed.[168] Not to say that He desires that we despise our animal parts or feel shame about their functions, only that He bids us to behave in a seemly way, as nobly as we can, when we address ourselves to Him.[169] Approach the King of kings decently.

The general Commandment in this chapter

being truly all-encompassing, we can try to emphasize some main points. Perhaps the most important thing is just to recognize what we discussed before: that we — all of us, every human being, each of us owing everything to our Creator — live with both the power to honor Him and the power to dishonor Him, right here on earth, in our workaday lives, before our fellow men.

Plainly, we should always try to honor Him, which involves more than merely avoiding the sacrilegious and the sinful and disgraceful. We should also — we all have a moral obligation to — pray to Him and,[171] in fact, to acknowledge Him in every aspect of our lives.[172] Some scholars argue that Noahides, like Jews, are even obligated to *die* for Him, if necessary, in the face of persecution, for the sanctification of His holy Name.[173] While other scholars disagree,[174] the issue being most complex,[175] the very nature of the debate tells us that the human — not just the Jewish — duty to affirmatively, positively honor God is almost limitless.[176]

At the very least, our obligations to Him require us all to try with all our might to avoid violating any of His laws (which, anyway, He gives us for our own benefit). *Anyone* who does *anything* "presumptuously" — that is, knowing that an act is Divinely forbidden and doing it anyway, willfully — is a blasphemer; he "reproaches the Lord" by demonstrating that he despises His law.[177]

> Rebellion is as the sin of witchcraft, and stubborness is as idolatry and *teraphim* [idols].[178] — *1 Samuel 15:23*

God has previously clearly revealed, through His Torah, how men may worship Him in purity. He *hates* the presence of *anything* partaking of idolatry, even if men totally devote it to Him.[179] One must never try to bring idolatrous trappings into His holy service. People live down to their haughty, heedless and primitive worst when they try, with impure foreign rites or lawless innovations, to honor Him as they — not He — think He should be honored.[180] So it is a most serious transgression to try to establish any kind of new religion.

B'nai Noah may not try "to originate a new religion or create

Commandments for themselves based [solely] upon their own decisions."[181] The path of Torah and of the Universal Commandments lies open before all men. Men are not to create, as an alternative, a new kind of holiness for themselves, whether "holy" days or "holy" rites, that God has not created.

One cannot mix man-made "religion" with God-made religion in any way to please Him. Instead of a superior synthesis the result necessarily involves putting the real thing into the service of the fake.

Isaiah presents the prophecy that many Gentiles will try to create their own rites and religion in honor of the God of Israel, the Master of the Universe, in violation of these precepts. The prophet immediately goes on to promise that they will suffer for it, but that God in His time will teach them better.[182]

Holiness is optional. God presents all humanity with a choice: His Ways or other ways that are not His. Presuming to import other ways — odd symbolic rites, superstitious customs, founded in impure beliefs; or anything at all unsuitable to God, counter-Revolutionary, irrational or tainted — into His service insults both the Torah and its holy Author. It shows an idolatrous self-will, a lack of discipline, and haughtiness, rather than humility. It's more than just impure: it's defiling.[183]

This phenonemon has certainly been painful for Israel historically. Most of history's many, many movements to effect different syncretizing combinations or partial "compromises" between the Torah and the man-made have devolved into counter-revolutionary movements, neglectful of the real Torah and hostile to the Jews.[184]

A lordly manner is no help before the Lord. No man should ever approach God in any way but humbly. So one should always approach His Torah — the Living God's living Word, Divinely entrusted to holy Israel — properly, with due regard.

Propriety, in this case, requires a certain self-restraint and discipline. B'nai Noah are forbidden to approach the Torah in any way haughtily — meaning arrogantly, presumptuously or pridefully.[185] As the Jews are told, "Approach the Torah with joy, and also with trembling."[186]

Sacrilege Offending the
Good Order of Creation

Finally, we must discuss two laws, or Divine statutes, that are somewhat difficult to categorize. Their purpose is mysterious, given the present state of human science, and they are quite unlike most of the rest of the Noahide ordinances in terms of penalties.[187] But when all is said and done they may be the two most important ordinances to be examined in this book.

Not every scholar agrees that they even are Universal laws. But the Talmud, as it sets out the rest of the Noahide Law, puts us all on notice: 1) to emasculate — castrate — any male of any of the higher species,[188] or 2) to bring together two disparate species to hybridize them, or try to turn different species into a new species, created by man and not by God . . . is playing with holy fire.[189]

These same two restrictions, and related ones, govern Israel.[190] They are explicit Scriptural commandments. Of these, some apply only in the Holy Land,[191] the land of Israel — which God tells us is uniquely precious to Him[192] — but the Torah's narrower prohibitions against castrating individuals and hybridizing species govern the people of Israel everywhere they go.

We can only presume that this is so for the rest of humanity to see and learn. *All* of the Torah's Rules exist for man's own good.[193] Each of them truly expresses the Lord's wisdom, and particularly, His justice.[194]

> Guard yourself against allowing the free use and transformation of this world, which He has granted to you, to degenerate into a God-forgotten, world-destructive presumption.
> — R. *Samson Raphael Hirsch*[195]

God calls on mankind to respect the Divine order in His Creation. We may use a castrated creature or enjoy an emasculated pet as we may use and enjoy the products of hybridization — a mule,[196] say, or a tangelo,[197] or a weeping cherry tree,[198] or the like. As producers, we may selectively breed for favored traits, graft and combine the traits available within a species, and even manipulate the submicroscopic germ plasm — the DNA — of the life on our planet. A principal characteristic of man's dominion is its incredible breadth and scope.

But even this extensive dominion of ours has certain Divinely imposed limits.

One of the conditions of human dominion is that we have no right to tamper with the inherent goodness of Creation.[199] God calls on us to respect the Divine order of the species and the basic nature of each being.

We can't improve on individuals by removing their masculinity, which changes their basic nature. It violates His Will, already clearly expressed, and His pre-existing plan for them.

We can't improve the individuals of any species by trying to breed them with another species. It violates His clear Will, His pre-existing plan, for the members of those species.

Pretending that we can do better than God in either of these two respects is hubris, or exaggerated human pride. It's not just presumptuous or disrespectful: it's blasphemous; it's sacrilegious.[200]

> [This technology] takes mankind into realms that belong to God and to God alone. — *Charles, Prince of Wales*[201]

We — the people of Israel, at least — have no right to castrate anything. That is, to hijack a being that was divinely designed to serve Him as a male and neuter it for man's pleasure, to convert it solely for human uses, to create a being neither wholly male nor female.[202] Who can know all the consequences of such an act? Only God, whose Torah specifically forbids it.

Similarly, while the discussion here and these attempts at classification are only tentative — one can never presume to know all the reasons behind any of God's laws — this last prohibition, especially, invites very close attention. It also treats of a type of sacrilege:

We — at least, the people of Israel — have no right to take or misappropriate any being that God designed to serve Him "after its [own] kind," in the manner of that species,[203] to join it to some other species . . . in any effort to create, for man's sole use and pleasure, a newborn being of a new and artificial species.[204]

"Biological pollution will be the environmental nightmare of the twenty-first century."[205] Even as one writes, people are splicing spider genes — this is not a joke — into live goats and into the cells of live hamsters and cows. Whole countries are refusing to accept imports of "genetically engineered" produce from the United States. Agribusiness has recently introduced such produce — corn, potatoes, soybeans, all combining genes from different species, or "transgenes" — into the economy and ecosystem of North America. Virtually all of us, mostly quite unknowingly, have already eaten of it.

Our species is crossing a threshold. Breeders can now bring qualities from *anywhere* in nature into the genome of a plant, for instance, not just from other plants but from mammals, fish, bacteria, and even from viruses.[206]

No one knows where this will go. It's something new under the sun, a new technology-driven power. It will certainly have unintended consequences, even concerning what has already been done.[207] It won't, given this technology, end with man merely re-engineering plants and animals.[208]

Science can only tell us what we can do, not what we should do. Society already tries, through law, to regulate dangerous science — like nuclear or radioactive research, say, or in the field of poisons, or explosives. Similar controls will eventually, undoubtedly, be extended over the dangerous science of genetic manipulation. Society has every right to exercise control over those who seek to control nature, or who threaten the wider environment. It is a practical issue, and also, especially in this case, a deeply moral one.

Creating living species is not man's prerogative but God's. A Jew who does these things or arranges to have them done merits punishment at the hands of a Torah court. That is, these are not

matters that Israel may leave entirely up to Divine disposition —
the courts of man must act.[209]

Noahide courts either may or must act similarly. But everyone
needs to respect the reality of the Scriptural restrictions here.
These prohibitions were given to Israel for the benefit of all
men.[210]

> The end of the matter, all having been heard: fear God, and keep
> His Commandments, for this is the whole duty of man. —
> *Ecclesiastes 12:13*

Undoubtedly, as humanity develops, our Maker's specific
purposes and larger plan in giving man this law will become clearer.
Day by day, science gives us more power over the natural world; day
by day, we learn more about the consequences of using it.

Science alone should tell us that man can't just tinker with
elemental life-forces like a boy playing with a chemistry set.[211]

> We have caught the first glimpses of our instruction book, previously
> known only to God. — *Dr. Francis S. Collins (June,2000)* [212]

As we marvel over our growing power to manipulate living
genes, to combine them and even reshape the nature of lower or
higher life-forms, we need to respect the wisdom of His law lest
we overstep our limits. God has given us dominion so that we can
make our world a holy garden — *not* a weird and sterile monument
to tragic pride and greed and sacrilege.[213]

NOTES

1. Find the same respectful euphemism in Leviticus 24:16, 1 Kings 21:10,13, and Job 2:9.

2. Talmud, *Sanhedrin* 56a; *Yad, Hilchot Melachim* 9:3. See Mishnah, *Sanhedrin* 7:5; *Sefer HaMitzvot* 2:60.

3. 1 Samuel 25:25. See Exodus 34:5-6; *Moreh Nevuchim* 1:63-64.

4. *Horeb*, supra, ch 94, para. 596.

5. See Psalm 145:13; Daniel 3:33, 4:31; Kaplan, *Handbook of Jewish Thought*, supra, 2:10.

6. Recognizing that blasphemy might, in some unknowable sense, disappoint, disgust or anger Him.

7. Fyodor Dostoyevsky, *The Brothers Karamazov* (St. Petersburg, 1879-1880), Part II, Book V, Sec. 5.

8. See Mishnah, *Pirke Avot* 5:12.

9. See Numbers 15:30-31, with commentaries; Ezekiel 36:20-23; *Sefer HaMitzvot* 2:66; *Yad, Hilchot Avodat Kochavim* 2:6; *Moreh Nevuchim* 3:41. Also see the derivation of "sacrilege" — i.e, profaning, or violating, the sacred.

10. See Hosea 6:3,6; Mishnah, *Pirke Avot* 2:19; Talmud, *Sanhedrin* 92a, *Berachot* 33a, *Nedarim* 41a.

11. See Numbers 5:6 and commentaries.

12. See Talmud, *Sanhedrin* 66a, with Rashi: "Whosoever" — in Hebrew, *ish, ish,* or "man, man." In other words, every human being. So this is a direct Noahide Commandment. "Curses his god" — *kalayl elo[k]av,* a contemptuous slur motivated by defiance, a curse that *elo[k]av,* one's "god," or God, should lose status. "Bear his sin" — receive his just desserts. "Blasphemes" — *nokav,* curses, abuses, disrespects. "The Name of the Lord" — the one Revealed proper Name of God, the Tetragrammaton. Note that Israel customarily accords such honor to God's different names and titles that one deliberately distorts the most evocative of them (such as the Hebrew word for God, above, where '[k]' in the text here substitutes for the actual 'h' sound) in a book — like this book — for readers who may or may not treat such Divine names respectfully.

13. Bindman, *Seven Colors of the Rainbow,* supra, p. 103.

14. Bindman, ibid.

15. See the section "Bibles and the Written Law," above.

16. Exodus 22:27; Leviticus 24:16; Talmud, *Sanhedrin* 56a. This is blasphemy of the first degree. Heaven prescribes not just death but a hard death in the case of a guilty Jew. Deuteronomy 22:24; Mishnah, *Sanhedrin* 7:5,8, *Shevuot* 4:13; *Yad, Hilchot Sanhedrin* 15:10; *Sefer HaMitzvot* 1:229, 2:60. As for the written Name (as it appears in Scripture, or even in translation), one should never treat it frivolously. A believing Jew will rarely even write it out, to prevent its desecration by erasure. See *Yad, Yesodey HaTorah* 6:1-6, treating such desecration of the written Name as (potentially) corporally punishable blasphemy. Also see Leviticus 22:32 and commentaries.

17. *Yad, Hilchot Avodat Kochavim* 2:9.

18. See Deuteronomy 12:2-4; Mishnah, *Sanhedrin* 10:1; Talmud, *Sanhedrin* 101b, *Sotah* 38a; *Yad, Yesodey HaTorah* 6. Only the Tetragrammaton's consonants, not the vowel sounds, are known. Scripture explains, however, that all humanity will eventually come to understand and "pronounce" or use

His Name correctly. Zechariah 14:9; Talmud, *Pesachim* 50a with Rashi; Exodus 6:3 with Rashi.

19. Talmud, *Sanhedrin* 56a and commentaries; See "Blasphemy," *Encyclopaedia Judaica*, supra.

20. Mishnah, *Sanhedrin* 7:5,8, *Shevuot* 4:13; *Yad, Hilchot Avodat Kochavim* 2:7, 3:6. Hebrews who curse God using any of the seven uniquely holy, descriptive Hebrew titles by which He revealed Himself to Israel merit corporal punishment — lashes. *Yad*, ibid. These Scripturally recorded names all describe some attribute of Divinity. See Talmud, *Shevuot* 35a with Rashi; and Exodus 6:2-3 with commentaries.

21. Talmud, *Sanhedrin* 56a and *Yad, Hilchot Melachim* 9:3, a common sense exception to the general rule that God imposes His strictest standards upon Israel. Noahide societies may treat the most vile blasphemy of which a Noahide is capable as equivalent to the most vile blasphemy of which a Jew is (theoretically) capable, and punish it equivalently. See Leviticus 24:15 and commentaries.

22. *Yad, Hilchot Melachim* 9:3. "Liable," that is, fully culpable, and subject to the maximum — capital — penalty. "This law does not apply to Israel [that is, to the children of Israel, the Jews]." Ibid.

23. Job 2:9. That is, subject yourself to the full legal penalty for blasphemy. See Rashi. Yet Israel has a clear exculpatory Rule on this very point: "A man is not blamed for what he utters in agony." Talmud, *Bava Batra* 16b.

24. Job 2:10. These Scriptural references to the crime are also revealing: Leviticus 24:10-23 (the "son of the Hebrew woman," cursing by the Tetragrammaton); 1 Kings 21:1-16 (Naboth, falsely accused by Ahab and Jezebel); Daniel 3:29 (Babylonian laws).

25. Some believe Job to have been a contemporary of Abraham. See Talmud, *Bava Batra* 14b. Still, most of Israel regards his story not as fact but, at least partially, as parable. Talmud, *Bava Batra* 15a; Midrash, *Genesis Rabbah* 57; *Moreh Nevuchim* 3:22. After all, what man ever eavesdropped on Heavenly deliberations?

26. *Yad, Hilchot Melachim* 9:3. See Leviticus 24:10-23; Mishnah, *Shevuot* 4:13.

27. See Proverbs 16:4; Mishnah, *Pirke Avot* 6:11; Talmud, *Sanhedrin* 98b; Midrash, *Genesis Rabbah* 1:4.

28. *Yad, Hilchot Avodat Kochavim* 2:6. "Our religion" — i.e., the religion of Israel.

29. Leviticus 24:10-16. Associated with another rebel's treason, publicly violating the Sabbath's holiness (Numbers 15:32) — both incidents happening at about the same time. Midrash, *Sifra* to Leviticus 24:10.

30. Believed to be the illegitimate son of the Egyptian overseer who Moses killed. See Exodus 2:11 with Rashi.

31. Leviticus 24:11,14,16 and commentaries.

32. Leviticus 24:14,16.

33. Ibid., and 24:11, Scripture identifying the blasphemer with particularity. Criminality has far-reaching consequences — a man's life is not his own to do with completely as he pleases: his disgrace disgraces his parents, his tribe, his city, etc. See Rashi on 24:11 and Hertz, *Pentateuch and Haftorahs*, supra, p. 526.

34. Patricia Meyer Spacks, *Gossip* (Knopf, New York NY, 1985) p. 9.

35. See Hosea 6:3,6; Mishnah, *Pirke Avot* 2:19; Talmud, *Sanhedrin* 92a, *Berachot* 33a, *Nedarim* 41a.

36. But, again, there is no crime (i.e., no blame attaches) if the statement issues from overwhelming personal agony, rather than from a genuine free will choice. Talmud, *Bava Batra* 16b.

37. Bindman, supra, p. 82-83.

38. Isaiah 45:15.

39. See *Yad, Hilchot Melachim* 9:3.

40. See Herbert C. Brichto, "The Problem of Curse in the Hebrew Bible," *Journal of Biblical Literature*, Monograph Series, Vol. 13 (Society of Biblical Literature, Philadelphia PA, 1963, reprinted 1968).

41. Many countries already have laws on their books that proscribe this same offense. See Richard Webster, *A Brief History of Blasphemy: Liberalism, Censorship and "The Satanic Verses"* (Orwell Press, Southwold, Suffolk, England) 1990; Evarts B. Greene, *Religion and the State: the Making and Testing of an American Tradition* (NYU 1941/Cornell University (Ithaca NY) 1959, pp. 97-98; generally, see Leonard W. Levy, *Blasphemy: Verbal Offense against the Sacred, from Moses to Salman Rushdie* (Knopf, New York NY, 1993).

42. *Yad, Hilchot Avodat Kochavim* 2:10. See Leviticus 24:14.

43. *Yad, Hilchot Melachim* 9:3, as to that common-sense exception to the general principle that nothing forbidden to Gentiles is permitted to Jews. See Talmud, *Sanhedrin* 56a; *Yad, Hilchot Avoda Zorah* 2:7.

44. Mishnah, *Sanhedrin* 7:5, 8, *Shevuot* 4:13; *Shavuot* 35a with Rashi; *Yad, Hilchot Avodat Kochavim* 2:7, 3:6.

45. Talmud, *Sanhedrin* 56a; *Yad, Hilchot Melachim* 9:3, *Avoda Zorah* 2:7. This includes such descriptive Gentile-language titles as Lord, Almighty, Eternal, King of the Universe, or Holy One. A nation may expect to hold its Hebrew citizens to the same Noahide standard: "the law of the state ["kingdom"] is the Law." Talmud, *Gittin* 10b. See Jeremiah 29:1-7, on patriotism and obedience to local law.

46. See Evarts B. Greene, *Religion and the State* and Leonard W. Levy, *Blasphemy*, supra; "Validity of Blasphemy Statutes and Ordinances," by Robert A. Brazener, 41 *American Law Reports* (ALR) 3d, p. 519 (1972); 12 *American Jurisprudence* (Am Jur) 2d, p. 375 (1964); 70 *Columbia Law Journal,* p. 694 (1970). Many American anti-blasphemy statutes are Constitutionally invalid due to overbreadth, but blasphemy, like obscenity, "fighting words," and slander, is *not* Constitutionally protected. So the types of curses that are so narrowly proscribed by this Commandment, being malicious, utterly lacking in redeeming social importance, and so offensive to reasonably sensitive "religious-minded persons" as to arouse almost physical feelings of disgust, *can* undoubtedly be properly and Constitutionally prohibited. See 70 *Columbia Law Journal* at 697, 702, 711 (attacking the extant statutes). Please note, in this context, that the U.S. Congress opens its sessions with a prayer, the Supreme Court opens its sessions with "God save this honorable court," the Pledge of Allegiance explicitly puts God above the nation, and even America's coinage declares "In God We Trust."

47. "God" — *Elo[k]im,* the substitute name used by Job. Plural in form, like the sovereign's royal "we," and often translated as "Lord," it literally refers to "High Ones," or gods, chiefs, judges, or God. "Curse" — *saor,* a

curse of fierce anger or envy, that one should shrivel up and have no blessing. "A leader of your people" — one's *nasi* or prince or ruler.

48. Maimonides' *Siraj*, the *Commentary on the Mishnah Torah, Sanhedrin* 10:1, Principle Eight.

49. See Talmud, *Sanhedrin* 66a; *Moreh Nevuchim* 1:2; Kaplan, *The Living Torah*, supra, p 206n; Hertz, *Pentateuch and Haftorahs*, supra, p. 315n. Also see Exodus 21:6, 22:7 with Rashi and Nachmanides. This revealed name particularly evokes the Divine attributes of strict and impartial justice — as opposed to the Name more reflective of His infinite kindness, His mercy and His love: the Tetragrammaton.

50. Mishnah, *Pirke Avot* 1:1; *Moreh Nevuchim* 3:41.

51. Quoted in Webster, *A Brief History of Blasphemy*, supra, p. 31.

52. Jews generally *avoid* advising Gentiles against this (otherwise deplorable) associationism — this habit of associating their own deities, false gods, with the One God in His worship. "The whole Torah exists only for the sake of peace. For the sake of peace, truth may be sacrificed [i.e., in this context, left unuttered]." Talmud, *Gittin* 59b, *Yevamot* 65b. See Talmud, *Hullin* 13a; *Moreh Nevuchim* 1:36; *Shulchan Aruch, Orach Haim* 156 (Commentary of Ramo, Rabbenu Moshe Isserles).

53. See R. Elijah Benamozegh, *Israel and Humanity* (Paulist Press edition, supra) p. 268: "[T]he Noachide law on Blasphemy . . . forbids the Gentile to blaspheme not only the names of the [God] of Israel but also those of the various divinities of paganism, in which Judaism teaches their adherents to discover the scattered fragments of divine Truth." But also see Jonah, etc., below, and Jeremiah 10:11.

54. See Jonah 1:2, 3:8, with commentaries; Amos 1:3-2; Novak, *Image of the Non-Jew in Judaism,* supra, pp. 109-111.

55. *Sotah* 40a.

56. Talmud, *Kiddushin* 40a; *Moreh Nevuchim* 3:29.

57. Exodus 34:13; Deuteronomy 7:5, 12:2-3; *Sefer HaMitzvot* 1:185. Every active pagan shrine defiles the land, but a shrine may be preserved for several reasons, for the sake of peace, or knowledge, etc., at the command of Israel's leaders.

58. See Mishnah, *Avoda Zorah* 4:7; Talmud, *Avoda Zorah* 54b: Gentiles usually commit idolatry because they don't know any better; their worship of no-Gods may be savage, but it isn't necessarily treasonous. See Jeremiah 16:19; Talmud, *Hullin* 13a, "they [merely] continue in the customs of their ancestors."

59. Humanity as a whole should know better. See the discussion in the next chapter.

60. See, e.g., Isaiah 2:12,18; Jeremiah 10:1.

61. Nihilism is lawless, and utterly pagan. Old established belief-systems, even if founded in paganism, always offer *something* in the nature of a civilizing morality. See *Moreh Nevuchim* 1:36.

62. By R. Solomon ibn Gabirol, c. 1050 CE. Translated by Morris Jastrow.

63. Some people actually invest their idea of Satan (in Hebrew, *Sotan*, an "adversary" or prosecutor or spiritual accuser) with good. See Anton S. LaVey, *The Satanic Bible* (Avon Books, New York NY, 1969). As for human "god-kings," millions and millions of simple souls, just in the last century,

have attributed divine powers to their leaders, considering them capable (according to some reports) of omnisciently hearing prayerful petitions, and even of influencing the weather. But then, there are also people who pray to space aliens.

64. See Talmud, *Gittin* 59b, *Yevamot* 65b, *Hullin* 13a. 2 Kings 5:18 (regarding the prophet Elisha and Na'aman, a Noahide) is interesting in this context too. Also see, e.g., Flavius Josephus (c. 38-100 CE), *Against Apion* 2:14, 2:34: "Our legislator [Moses] expressly forbade us [Exodus 22:27] to ridicule or revile the gods recognized by other people, on account of the name of God ascribed to them." Even if only as a matter of custom or good conduct, nothing in the literature explicitly challenges this convention. But also see Midrash, *Genesis Rabbah* 38:13: Abraham, quite properly, smashes up his idol-selling father's inventory, then coolly tells him that the idols destroyed each other in a quarrel. Even here, however, the father's — Terach's — attachment to idolatry may have been more a matter of narrow opportunism than of deep-seated religious belief. No one could know that better than Abraham.

65. Rabbenu Asher ben Yechiel (Rosh, c. 1250-1327 CE), *Hanhaga* ("Conduct," or *Rule for the Health of the Soul*, Sec. 43, 69, 74, 104, 107, 108, 120, 129-131. See *Hebrew Ethical Wills*, Israel Abrahams, ed., (Jewish Pub. Society of America, Philadelphia PA 1926/1976) p. 123. This being said, a Jew who curses a pagan deity commits no blasphemy against God, the Holy One of Israel; neither may any Hebrew Torah court punish him for blasphemy. See Talmud, *Sanhedrin* (*Baraitha*) 56a. Plainly, for a court to punish the curser for blasphemy it must have some belief in the god who is being cursed.

66. *Sukkot* 32a. Also see Proverbs 3:17; Talmud, *Yevamot* 87b.

67. Exodus 23:13.

68. See Jeremiah 10:11-16 with commentaries.

69. Also see Proverbs 10:19, 13:3, 18:21; Ecclesiastes 10:20; Mishnah, *Pirke Avot* 1:17. "Always use refined speech." — Talmud, *Pesachim* 3a.

70. *The Adventures of Augie March* (Viking, New York NY, 1953) p. 219.

71. *Sanhedrin* 49a. See Psalm 34:14, prayerfully recited after the *Amidah* (Israel's standard prayer, the core of the thrice-daily service): "My God, guard my tongue from evil and my lips from speaking deceitfully. To those who curse me, let my soul be silent. . . ."

72. *A Treatise of Moral Philosophie* (London, Edward Whitechurch, 1556) 3.13 (p. 105), quoted by Spacks, *Gossip*, supra, p. 27. See Leviticus 25:17; Talmud, *Bava Metzia* 58b.

73. See Exodus 21:6, 22:7,27 with Rashi; 1 Samuel 2:25; Judges 5:8; Psalms 82:1,6, 138:1.

74. *Sefer HaMitzvot* 2:60, 2:315. See Midrash, *Mechilta* to Exodus 18:13; Talmud, *Sanhedrin* 66a; *Moreh Nevuchim* 1:2; Kaplan, *The Living Torah,* supra, and Hertz, supra, on Exodus 22:27. "A judge [of Israel] must have these seven qualifications: wisdom, humility, fear of God, disdain of gain, love of truth, love of his fellow men, and a good reputation." *Yad, Sanhedrin* 2:7.

75. *Sefer HaMitzvot* 2:316. See Isaiah 8:21; 1 Kings 2:8, 21:10.

76. Exodus 21:17; Leviticus 20:9; *Sefer HaMitzvot* 2:318.

77. See Brichto, "The Problem of Curse in the Hebrew Bible," *Journal of Biblical Literature*, supra.

78. Spacks, supra, p. 27 (quoting various 17th century English writers).

79. *Yad, Hilchot De'ot* 2:3.

80. Leviticus 19:14. See Midrash, *Mechilta* to Exodus 21:17; *Sefer HaMitzvot* 2:317.

81. So long as that person is alive. The prohibition here pertains to cursing the deaf, not the dead.

82. "The penalty of whipping is also incurred for cursing a minor whose sensibilities are wounded." *Yad, Sanhedrin* 26:1.

83. *Sefer HaMitzvot* 2:317.

84. Leviticus 19:4 and commentaries; Midrash, *Mechilta* to Exodus 22:27; *Sefer HaMitzvot,* ibid.

85. Leviticus 19:18. Also see Leviticus 19:33; Talmud, *Shabbat* 31a; Midrash, *Sifra* to Leviticus 19:18.

86. Leviticus 19:18 with Rashi.

87. See Talmud, *Menachot* 64b, *Sanhedrin* 97b.

88. See, e.g., Psalm 69:29. But also see Proverbs 26:2 — wrongful curses "come home" to the curser.

89. *Sefer HaMitzvot* 2:317. Unless the curser invokes the Name of God, a (Torah) court shall not even impose corporal punishment. See *Moreh Nevuchim* 3:41.

90. "This refers to verbal wrongs." Talmud, *Bava Metzia* 58b. Defamation tends to travel beyond its source like confetti in a wind; as only the retrieval of every last scrap of litter can fully remedy an act of littering, only the retrieval, by effective retractions or corrections given to everyone who heard both the original and the recounted statement, can fully cure a defamation.

91. 2 Samuel 16:5-14; 1 Kings 2:8-9, 1 Kings 2:36-46 (death for violating a subsequent royal order).

92. See Leviticus 19:6 with commentaries; Psalm 15:1-3; Talmud, *Arachin* 15b; *Yad, Hilchot De'ot* 7:2-5.

93. In fact, it might occasionally serve for good by providing, among other things, a sort of social safety valve, a method of release. See Spacks, supra, p. 30: "Anyone can invoke the dangerous magic of language: a weapon for the otherwise powerless."

94. "The Name of the Lord" — the Tetragrammaton, HaShem. "In vain" — for any false, unnecessary, or trivial purpose. See Talmud, *Berachot* 33a. Also see Deuteronomy 5:11; Psalm 24:3-4; Micah 3:20.

95. See Ecclesiastes 5:5.

96. See Deuteronomy 12:2-4; Talmud, *Makkot* 22a; *Sefer HaMitzvot* 2:65. A writing, even if it includes the Name, is holy only if written by one conscious of its sacred character and also under a religious duty — see, e.g., Deuteronomy 17:18, 31:19 — to write it. But one who writes God's name, regarding it like any other writing, creates nothing holy. In fact, that writing should optimally be destroyed, "so as to leave no record of infidels or their works." *Yad, Hilchot Yesodey HaTorah* 6:8.

97. Leviticus 19:12; *Sefer HaMitzvot* 2:61. Only when *life* is at stake, as when murderers threaten it, may one take a false oath or vow. Mishnah, *Nedarim* 3:4. To repeat a fundamental Principle: God would have man live by, rather than die because of, His law. Leviticus 18:5; Talmud, *Sanhedrin* 74a.

98 See Deuteronomy 6:16; *Sefer HaMitzvot* 2:64. "You shall not try the

Lord." That is, you shall not treat Him like a loyal dog who performs miraculous tricks upon the commands of His creatures. This prohibits trial by ordeal — a method of judging a person's guilt or innocence by waiting upon a Heavenly sign — while also broadly proscribing the absurd formula, "May God strike me dead if. . . ."

99. *Sefer HaMitzvot* 2:62. See Leviticus19:12; Talmud, *Shevuot* 21a; *Sefer HaMitzvot* 2:61.

100. *Pirke Avot* 5:12.

101. Leviticus 22:32; See Isaiah 29:22-23; Ezekiel 36:20-23; *Sefer HaMitzvot* 1:1-9.

102. *Yad, Hilchot Teshuva* 1:7.

103. *Sefer HaMitzvot* 2:62, 2:65. Again, the corporal penalty is "lashes" — i.e, a whipping, a beating.

104. Midrash, *Leviticus Rabbah* 22:6. Overlook, of course, in the sense of forgive/not count.

105. *Yad, Hilchot Avodat Kochavim* 2:6.

106. Talmud, *Shabbat* 55a.

107. Mishnah, *Pirke Avot* 1:18.

108. Exodus 23:7.

109. Jeremiah 10:10. See the last words of the *Shema*, Israel's basic statement of faith, in the *Siddur*/Prayerbook.

110. Any picture or image that one might hold in his mind of God applies to something other than God. See *Moreh Nevuchim* 1:54; Rabbenu Bachya, *Hovot HaLevavot* (classic work, c. 1161 CE) 1:10.

111. Job 11:7.

112. Isaiah 55:8; See *Yad, Hilchot Teshuva* 5:5.

113. *Yad, Hilchot Teshuva* 3:7.

114. *Yad, Hilchot Teshuva* 5:4.

115. *Yad, Hilchot Teshuva*, ibid., and see Rashi on Exodus 6:2.

116. See, e.g., Genesis 1:26-31, 2:16; Exodus 24:7; Deuteronomy 28-30, 30:15-20; Isaiah 48:17.

117. Talmud, *Yoma* 86a.

118. *Kiddushin* 40a.

119. See Talmud, *Yoma* 86a; *Yad, Hilchot Yesodey HaTorah* 5:10; Novak, supra, pp. 89-92.

120. Leviticus 21:1-24:23, this same section of Torah prescribing judicial punishment for blasphemy.

121. Talmud, *Shabbat* 114a, *Yoma* 86a; *Sefer HaMitzvot* 1:9, 2:63.

122. Psalm 8:5-6; Genesis 1:27.

123. Talmud, *Yoma* 86b.

124. See Exodus 34:6 and commentaries.

125. Emphasis in the original — Hertz, *Pentateuch and Haftorahs*, supra, p. 365 (on Exodus 34:6).

126. Deuteronomy 32:9. See, e.g., Exodus 4:22, 6:7; Deuteronomy 4:7, 7:6; Jeremiah 31:3.

127. See, e.g., Genesis 17:7; Exodus 4:15, 19:5-6; Leviticus 20:26; Isaiah 43:10, Jeremiah 31:37, 33:7-9; Hosea 2:21; Zechariah 8:23; Amos 3:2; Ezekiel 39:25-29; Psalm 148:14.

128. Genesis 27:29; Numbers 24:9. See Jeremiah 2:3.

129. Hosea 2:21, 11:14. See Exodus 19:5; Isaiah 42:6, 43:10, 49:3-9,

54:4; Jeremiah 31:3, 51:5.

130. See Exodus 2:11-12 and Talmud, *Sanhedrin* 58b; *Yad, Hilchot Melachim* 10:6.

131. Deuteronomy 10:20, 21:22. See, e.g., Zechariah 8:23.

132. "To 'cleave unto Him' means to cleave unto the wise men [of Torah] and their disciples." Midrash, *Sifre* to Deuteronomy 21:22. See Talmud, *Berachot* 10b, *Pesachim* 22b; *Sefer HaMitzvot* 1:6.

133. Deuteronomy 28:10.

134. *Yad, Hilchot Teshuva* 10:3. See Deuteronomy 6:5.

135. *Yad, Hilchot Yesodey HaTorah* 6:8.

136. Recognizing that, if Job has a central message, it is that God is always near, immanent and not just transcendant — that He is immediately, intimately somehow "with" each of us and concerned with man in ways that confound even the proudest philosophies.

137. Job 31. Psalm 15 ("God's Gentleman") and Ezekiel 18:5-9 are also great this way. And see Talmud, *Makkot* 24a, *Sanhedrin* 81a; *Midrash Tehillim* on Psalm 16:7.

138. See Exodus 34:6-7; Leviticus 19:2; and commentaries.

139. See Deuteronomy 4:8; Psalm 119; Proverbs 29:18; Mishnah, *Pirke Avot* 5:22.

140. See Numbers 15:30-31.

141. See Talmud, *Derech Eretz Zuta*; Midrash, *Derech Eretz Rabbah*. Patriotism, or loyalty to one's nation and place of residence, is an associated value. See Jeremiah 29:1-7; Hirsch, *Horeb*, supra, paras. 237 and 607, 609.

142. *Pirke Avot* 3:10.

143. Mishnah, *Shekalim* 3:2.

144. Midrash, *Leviticus Rabbah* 9:3.

145. Mishnah, *Pirke Avot* 3:17.

146. See Exodus 24:7; Psalm 111:10.

147. Genesis 18:1-8 and commentaries. Also see Talmud, *Yoma* 28b; *Moreh Nevuchim* 3:43.

148. *Bava Batra* 9b, *Sukkot* 49b.

149. Isaiah 5:16, and see 58:6-8; Mishnah, *Pirke Avot* 1:18; Talmud, *Sanhedrin* 6b.

150. Talmud, *Bava Batra* 10a.

151. *Megillah* 26b.

152. Mishnah, *Pirke Avot* 2:6, in the name of Hillel.

153. See Sefer HaMitzvot 1:5. For Israel, to study and teach the Torah is a positive, explicit, Divine commandment. Deuteronomy 6:7, 11:19, 31:12; *Sefer HaMitzvot* 1:11. See Talmud, *Kiddushin* 40b.

154. *Moreh Nevuchim* 3:36.

155. Job 5:7. See Genesis 3:19.

156. Genesis 2:15. "Man is born to labor," Job 5:7.

157. Psalm 128:2.

158. *Nedarim* 49b.

159. Haggai 2:4.

160. Genesis 1:28, 9:2.

161. Israel's *Siddur*/prayerbook, "*Aleinu*," recited daily.

162. Mishnah, *Pirke Avot* 1:10.

163. Jeremiah 48:10. "Idleness is a curse," Mishnah, *Ketubot* 5:5.

164. *Yad, Hilchot Mattenot Aniyim* 10:18.

165. Yad, ibid.

166. Rabbenu Yehuda ben Batyra, *Avot d'Rabbi Nathan*, ch. 11; See Talmud, *Avoda Zorah* 3a. Naturally, one should first fix up one's own neglected property.

167. Numbers 5:13; Malachi 2:11. See Genesis 34:5,27.

168. Even when a person stands naked in the privacy of a *mikvah*, or ritual bath, and says the blessing, everything below the shoulders must be completely immersed in water. See Leviticus 12:2, 15:5-16; Numbers 19:19; *Kitzur Shulchan Aruch* 162.

169. See Deuteronomy 23:10-15; *Shulchan Aruch, Orach Haim* 2-4; *Horeb,* supra, ch. 69, Secs. 455-463.

170. Directing this statement at Israel, of course, God also tells us in His Torah that all human beings are equally His creatures — i.e., His children. See Genesis 9:6; Mishnah, *Pirke Avot* 3:18.

171. See Exodus 23:25; Deuteronomy 6:13, 11:13, 13:5; *Sefer HaMitzvot* 1:5; Talmud, *Sanhedrin* 74b; Genesis 26:5 with Rambam. "Prayer is the service of the heart," Talmud, *Ta'anit* 2a. "God longs for the prayer of the righteous," Talmud, *Yevamot* 64a. "When you pray, know before Whom you stand!" Talmud, *Berachot* 28b.

172. See Exodus 20:2; Talmud, *Sanhedrin* 74b; *Sefer HaMitzvot* 1:1. To fully acknowledge Him means to submit one's total personality to His, by fully obeying His Law. See, e.g., Deuteronomy 10:12-13.

173. Leviticus 22:32, "You shall not profane My holy Name, but I will be hallowed among the children of Israel." See Talmud, *Sanhedrin* 74; *Sefer HaMitzvot* 1:9, 2:63; Lichtenstein, *Seven Laws of Noah*, supra pp. 79-82. Even if a persecutor puts a gun to his head, for a Jew to publicly repudiate God disgraces the Holy Name. Myriads of Jews have suffered death for just such reasons, historically, for the sanctification of His Name.

174. Arguing against a moral obligation to accept martyrdom (absent any other alternative), it's believed that a Noahide *may* repudiate God if compelled to. See 2 Kings 5:18 (the prophet Elisha to Na'aman, a Ben Noah); Talmud, *Sanhedrin* 74b-75a; *Yad, Hilchot Melachim* 10:2.

175. See Daniel 3; *Yad, Hilchot Yesodey HaTorah* 5:1-4; Lichtenstein, supra, ibid; Novak, supra, pp 89-92.

176. "For such is the duty of all creatures." *Uvmakehlos* prayer, in the Jewish prayerbook.

177. Numbers 15:30-31.

178. *Teraphim*: idolatrous images; small carved or molded household idols. See Genesis 31:19,30.

179. See Leviticus 26:1 with Deuteronomy 16:22.

180. See *Yad, Hilchot Melachim* 9:2.

181. *Yad, Hilchot Melachim* 10:9.

182. Isaiah 19:19-21. Of course this is only one way of reading this passage. Also, please note: the negative promises here, the predictions of coming bad things, aren't absolute. God in His wisdom may avert a predicted coming evil. This is so of all prophecy — see, e.g., Haggai 2:23 on Jeremiah 22:24-30 (repentance annulling a bad decree); Zechariah 1:3; Lamentations 5:21; Mishnah, *Pirke Avot* 4:13; Midrash, *Song of Songs Rabbah* 8:6 — and one of the reasons that fortune-tellers fail. God can turn the future around

if even a single person repents from doing evil. While His promises of coming good are firm, when it comes to punishments He is also, thank God, infinitely merciful. See Exodus 34:6-7.

183. See Leviticus 10:1-7, concerning the two priests, Nadav and Avihu, and their "strange fire" offering. God takes these sorts of transgressions most seriously. Also see, e.g., Exodus 32 (regarding the Golden Calf).

184. See, e.g., Bernard Lewis, *Semites and Anti-Semites* (W.W. Norton, New York/London, 1986).

185. See Talmud, *Sanhedrin* 59a; *Yad, Hilchot Melachim* 10:9.

186. Talmud, *Yoma* 4b. See Mishnah, *Pirke Avot* 2:12, "Fit yourself to learn Torah; it does not come by inheritance." On qualifying as a good student, see, especially, *Pirke Avot* 6:6.

187. The Torah prescribes corporal, not capital, punishment for Jews who commit these sins. See below.

188. As a matter of Rabbinic law (a "fence" around Sinai's Revealed Law), the people of Israel are forbidden to remove or otherwise impair the reproductive organs in human beings, beasts or birds of *either* sex. *Shulchan Aruch, Even HaEzer* 5:11.

189. *Mishnah Tosefta, Avoda Zorah* 9; Talmud, *Sanhedrin* 56b. In the name of Rav Hidka (emasculation), and Rav Eleazar (hybridization). The prohibition against hybridization applies to all life forms of every species.

190. Emasculation: Leviticus 22:24 and Deuteronomy 23:2; Talmud, *Shabbat* 110b; *Sefer HaMitzvot* 2:261. Hybridizing species: Leviticus 19:19; Deuteronomy 22:9; Mishnah, *Kilayim* 8; *Sefer HaMitzvot* 2:215-216. Also see Deuteronomy 22:9,11; *Sefer HaMitzvot* 2:42,193.

191. Leviticus 19:19 (regarding intermixing seeds of different food plants) and Deuteronomy 22:9 (against eating the resulting produce), are Torah prohibitions that apply only in the Holy Land. But the prohibition against wearing wool (an animal product) and linen (vegetable matter) together in the same fabric applies to the people of Israel everywhere. See *Sefer HaMitzvot* 2:42,193, 215-216; Leviticus 19:28.

192. See, e.g., Leviticus 18:25, 25:23; Numbers 35:33-34; Isaiah 2:3; Zechariah 2:16; Mishnah, *Kilayim* 1:2.

193. See Leviticus 18:4-5; Deuteronomy 4: 8, 6:24, 10:13: Isaiah 48:17; Psalms 16:11, 67:3.

194. See I. Grunfeld, Introduction to *Horeb* (Soncino ed., 1992), p. Lxii; Psalm 119:160; Mishnah, *Pirke Avot* 6:6; Talmud, *Bava Kamma* 38a. The work of Creation, introducing the last new species (but not sub-species, nor races), apparently finished, on Earth, some fifty-eight centuries ago. See Genesis 1:31-2:1 and commentaries.

195. *Horeb*, Sec. 57, para 402.

196. The (usually sterile) offspring of a donkey and a horse.

197. The fruit, which is sterile, of conjoined tangerine and orange trees.

198. The (sterile) issue of conjoined cherry and willow trees.

199. See Genesis 1:31; *Yad, Hilchot Melachim* 10:6.

200. Compare it to self-mutilation, or deliberately disfiguring — with tattoos, embedded jewelry, gouges in the flesh, or the like — the human form entrusted to man by God. (No observant Jew has ever willingly taken upon himself a tattoo, let alone scarification.) Or to mourners grieving so excessively as if to indicate, blasphemously, that human life has meaning not

in relation to God but only in relation to the person being mourned. See Leviticus 19:28; Deuteronomy 14:1-2; *Horeb*, supra, para. 430.

201. Michael Pollan, "Playing God in the Garden," *New York Times Magazine*, October 25, 1998, quoting Prince Charles' June, 1998 column in *The Daily Telegraph of London* — including Charles' vow never to eat, nor serve to his guests, bio-technology's new (genetically engineered) hybrids.

202. This restriction applies to the higher species. Obviously, if a matter of life-saving medical necessity, castration is permitted like any therapy. But consider the side-effects: removing a female's ovaries doesn't make her masculine, but the closest equivalent operation on a male — castration — makes him effeminate, or at least neuter; deprives him of normal sexual outlets, pleasures and feelings; and changes his essential nature. Bound to be fairly ineffective as a population-control method — females tend to find other, functional, males — it transforms the male into a different, far more tractable and docile (and sexually confused) creature than the one that God designed.

203. Genesis 1:24-25. See Genesis 1:11-22; Leviticus 19:19; Deuteronomy 22:9-11, and commentaries.

204. The Talmud's R. Yose tells a story indicating that the same honorable, wonderful qualities that inspired the first man to harness fire lie behind this particular impulse — an evil impulse — to play with the forbidden. Talmud, *Pesachim* 54a. Also see *Hullin* 7b, in connection with Genesis 36:24 (Anah in the desert breeding donkeys with horses), offering a good example of a Noahide or a non-Jew performing acts that, though the Noahide laws might not explicitly forbid them, the Scriptural tradition still condemns as evil.

205. Andrew Kimbrell, director of the Center for Technology Assessment in Washington, D.C., in Michael Pollan, "Playing God in the Garden," supra, pp. 44, 50.

206. Pollan, supra; "In Experiment, Mammal Cells Produce Silk Like a Spider's," *New York Times*, January 18, 2002, p. A15.

207. Given our "miserably poor understanding of how [an] organism develops from its DNA," says Harvard geneticist Richard Lewontin, expect "one rude shock after another." Pollan, supra, p. 49.

208. The first birth of a transgenic primate — a male Rhesus monkey named ANDi, bearing DNA from a jellyfish in his basic genetic makeup — was reported in *Science* magazine, Vol. 291, "Genetic Engineering of a Non-Human Primate," January 12, 2001. "The next step," says *Time* magazine (January 22, 2001), p. 42, "is to give monkeys human genes and human diseases."

209. Leviticus 19:15; Deuteronomy 16:18, 17:11. The Torah prescribes corporal punishment, for Jews, for castraters and for wrongful hybridizing, or violating the law against joining different species of living beings. As for wrongfully hybridizing animals, the Torah prescribes court-administered punishment only if one personally, actively assisted in physically joining the different animals. See Mishnah, *Kilayim* 8:1; Talmud, *Bava Metzia* 91a; *Sefer HaMitzvot* 2:215-217; *Moreh Nevuchim* 3:37. The Maharal, Rabbi Yehuda Loew of Prague (c. 1525-1609), in *Be'er HaGolah* (Jerusalem, 1971), pp. 38-39, says that the law here might only apply to Jews — that putting a donkey together with a horse to make a mule, for instance, might only be immoral in the sight

of God if it were done by Jews. One wonders what the Maharal would say of modern industrial attempts (probably mostly by non-Jews) to hybridize a spider with a goat, say, or a monkey with a jellyfish.

210. See Jeremiah 50:2; *Yad, Hilchot Melachim* 8:11, 10:6, 10:10.

211. "[W]hile [this hybridizing] biotechnology depends for its power on the ability to move genes freely among species and even phyla, its environmental safety depends on the very opposite phenomenon: on the integrity of species in nature and their rejection of foreign genetic material." Pollan, supra, p. 49, discussing the dangers posed by "Frankenplants," or any of the molecularly hybridized traits in bio-technology's new varieties of plant-life escaping into the wild.

212. Director of the National Human Genome Research Institute, speaking at a White House ceremony celebrating the completion of the first survey of the human genome. *New York Times,* June 27, 2000, pp. 1, 21.

213. Generally, on respecting the natural order of the species, see *Horeb*, supra, Sec. 57, paras. 402-410, and Additional Note E., *"Chukim,"* (in the Soncino edition, supra, p. 577).

THE FIRST COMMANDMENT

Laws Against Idolatry

Know this day, and consider it in your heart,
that the Lord alone is God in heaven above
and upon the earth beneath;
there is none else.
— Deuteronomy 4:39[1]

T he King of the Universe warns and beseeches not only Israel but every creature with the ears to hear and the brain to heed this eternal, Universal Commandment:

"You shall have no other gods before Me."[2]

For it is the principal object of the Law, and the axis around which it turns, to blot out these [idolatrous] opinions from man's heart and make the existence of idolatry impossible. — *Maimonides*[3]

All Divine law comes back to the same all-important point: You shall have no other god nor gods but God, your Maker; whatever other allegiances you may have, you owe your first and last allegiance to the One holy Lord Who sustains you. He Who Created you to honor, follow and worship Him alone reveals this to you (through Israel, His special agent): you shall follow no spirit, force or deity besides God; you shall worship no one and *nothing* created but only Him, the Creator, your Judge.

People make their bellies their gods, their fine clothes their law, and their household maintenance their ethics. — *Ibn Yosef*[4]

An idol is a false god, a non-god — an imagined or created "god" other than God. Man, the only creature that directly confronts the Universe as he knows it as a thinking individual,[5] must always follow either gods or God. Because man needs to devote himself to a leader, a cause, or at least some concept of ultimate good, to guide him. God Created us so, for our own good, for His greater Glory.[6]

> [T]here is no god but He in Whom the people of Israel believe.
> — *Muhammed* [7]

We — human beings — are creatures who always seek to know who and what and where we are. We constantly need to center ourselves, to fix our position, as it were, in real existence. From the time we can speak we spend almost every waking moment orienting ourselves to personally ruling concepts of ultimate goodness and final purpose. Man takes all those concepts, all his values, from his highest allegiances. In other words, we all pursue either gods or God.

Idolatry describes the act of worshipping a non-god: of following, with attachment and devotion, any thing or being or appetite or power instead of or in preference to the One Eternal God.

Of course some kinds of idolatry are grosser and more overt than others. One thinks of wild pagan blood-cults. But conforming to peer pressure instead of conscience — what one knows or should know to be right, joined to one's fear of the All-Knowing Judge — also exemplifies idolatry.

> And Jesus answered him, The first of all the Commandments is
> Hear, O Israel: the Lord our God is One Lord.— *Mark 12:29* [8]

Introducing as it does the foremost Teaching of the Hebrew Revolution,[9] the law against idolatry outweighs all other Commandments.[10] Maimonides puts it first among the Noahide laws.[11]

Whether one is a Jew or a Gentile, a *Ben Israel* or a *Ben Noah*, whoever professes idolatry rejects the entirety — the basis, the essence — of God's Law.[12] At the same time, as the rabbis say, whoever genuinely rejects idolatry affirms Israel's entire Torah.[13]

Mystics associate this Commandment with the violet, or purple, of the Rainbow. Purple is seen as the royal color, indicating honor and distinction, related to God's Sovereignty.[14] The purple makes up one of the rainbow's borders, lying opposite the band of dark brown or deepest red that forms the other — the two colors together encapsulating all the other colors between them. Further, if this deep red band that constitutes the rainbow's base can be said to symbolize the rule of God's Law,[15] the purple, or violet, that forms the rainbow's other border can only stand for Him: that is, for the perfect Unity of the sole Lawgiver Himself.

So this Commandment, associated with the highest level of the rainbow, represents the source, as well as the highest value, of the entire system — which only stands to reason. One must accept the authority of the Sovereign to faithfully carry out His Decrees.[16]

Biblical exegesis ties the Universal law against idolatry to Genesis 2:16: "And the Lord God commanded it upon the man (Adam), saying . . ."[17] Meaning, in other words, that God put humanity's common ancestors on notice: that He, as the Source of all Commandments, is God; that He and only He should be served.[18]

In still other words, the Scriptural text itself shows us that the Noahide law — the general heading for this broad category of Rainbow Covenant laws and ordinances — and the Torah Commandment of Israel's Ten Commandments' Code are connected. They both command the same one thing: "You shall have no other gods before Me."[19]

We saw before, in the last chapter, that this law, against idolatry, and the Universal law against blasphemy are also tightly bound together. Idolatry is always blasphemous, blasphemy is idolatrous; the opposite of both idolatry and blasphemy is the sanctification of the One God's holy Name.[20] Note that the other Noahide Commandments all focus primarily on man's relationship with God's Creation — on sins between man and man, or between man and lesser, or subordinate, creatures. In contrast, only these two Commandments directly regulate the human relationship with the Ultimate, with God. Which means that they both depend for their enforcement, in mankind's courts, on the knowledge that men have of God.

> Know What is above you — a seeing Eye and a hearing Ear and all your deeds are written in a Book. — R. *Yehuda HaNasi* [21]

For all the quaintness of its name — the apparent old-fashionedness of the concept — idolatry remains vigorously alive today. It permeates this unredeemed world of ours, defiling it. Man must struggle consciously, almost constantly, to resist it. [22] This means avoiding false worship — following the One God in false ways — while also avoiding false allegiances.

> If one wished to write the names of all the idols, all the donkeys in the world would not suffice to carry them. — *Midrash* [23]

Idolatry hoodwinks people, seducing them; it's stubborn; it frequently changes faces. Most of the idolatrous cults of ancient days are merely names in history. Who today follows Zeus, or Athena? The idols of our current era have different names: men serve them in new ways; they supposedly serve men in myriad new and better ways. But every incarnation of idolatry resembles and shares features with the older versions. [24] And the various idolatrous pathologies — the myriad evils inherent in the different species of idolatry — are actually unchanging. They all whirl around man's obsession with death. They all feed off the human ego. They all denigrate or lead men to denigrate God's Law and His eternal Torah's values.

> Ultimately all idolatry is worship of the self projected and objectified: all idolization is self-idolization. — *Will Herberg* [25]

If one doesn't accept man's One True Master — God — one will acquire untrue masters — gods. "The righteous fear only God." [26] Only by directing oneself to Him can one successfully free oneself from false gods, and from the brutalizing, defiling, soul-enslaving distractions of idolatry. [27] So God's first and most important Rainbow Covenant law necessarily involves more than just a negative, a general prohibition.

At least as much as any of the other Seven laws, this Commandment takes us into the positive. Virtue requires one to deliberately work at practicing the *opposite* of everything that this Commandment prohibits. Man must always strive to keep coming closer to God if he hopes to keep from straying, idolatrously, even further from Him.

Pure Monotheism

Jews grow up hearing: "Though all the nations walk each one in the name of its god, we will walk in the Name of the Lord our God forever."[28] Israel stands for sanity. "For all the gods of the nations are idols."[29]

Gentiles — the nations other than Israel — have been historically notorious for worshipping mere created things, or spirits or forces other than the One Creator, God.[30] The error is crippling and also blameworthy,[31] morally if not always legally, because men who betray their Father by following nonsense will be held accountable by Him for ignoring the evidence before them.[32] Their earthly fathers, as the Scripture says, inherited lies.[33] The nations will learn better.[34]

As for Israel, a Jew who even permits the *thought* to enter his mind that there is *any* deity in existence besides God, the One Lord, violates the first Commandment of Revolutionary Israel's negative, or prohibitory, laws.[35]

The Hebrew Code reads sharply here. The Jew who transgresses this Torah Commandment thinks like an outright apostate, an enemy of truth, who has neither merit nor a portion in Israel.[36] As Scripture says, "God is jealous, and the Lord exacts revenge."[37]

Five classes of heretics are proscribed:[38]

1. "One who says that there is no God, and that the universe has no Sovereign Ruler;

2. "One who says that there is a Sovereign Power, but that power is vested in two or more beings;

3. "One who says that there is one Sovereign Ruler,
    but that He has a body and material form;

4. "One who denies that He alone is the First Cause
    and Rock[39] of the Universe; and

5. "One who worships any power beside Him, to
    serve as a mediator between himself and the
    Sovereign of the Universe."

Professing any of these falsehoods constitutes idolatry, a crime against God's Law — as His Law applies to Israel. The rest of the world stands on notice: the Lord's own Truth is in these laws, in His Torah for all to see, for the benefit of all humanity.

But God's Noahide laws, which are minimal laws, don't necessarily require all humanity to live up to this standard, the radical, genuine monotheism of the Infinite Eternal God's eternal Covenant with the Jews.

> He who denies the existence of any deity whatever commits a
> graver violation than he who worships idols. — *Abraham ibn Ezra*[40]

Correct knowledge of God is *not* one of the minimal requisites of decent human conduct. Also note, though it should go without saying, that the Lord God grants no earthly court — not even a Torah court — authority to punish heretics for heresy alone.

One must behave — that is, act — in an idolatrous way to be punished for idolatry. No human court can punish anyone for mere false and harmful thinking, as opposed to wrongful doing.[41]

> [T]he trajectory of divinely guided human history is one which
> maximizes individual human freedom as essential to the reality of
> free choice, which in turn is essential to doing the good and holy.
> — *Rabbi Gerald Blidstein*[42]

Wrongful doing, in the Universal law, means committing affirmative acts of criminal idolatry: of turning against the Eternal One not just by thought but by one's deeds.[43] Idolatry is a crime against God, but at the level of the law that the nations' courts must all eventually enforce idolatry it is a crime against men,[44] an abomination committed in the world of men — where most or all of the damage happens.[45]

> [E]xamining the Torah and the Books of the Prophets, you will not
> find the expressions "burning anger," "provocation," or "jealousy"
> applied to God except in reference to idolatry; and none but the
> idolater called "enemy," "adversary," or "hater of the Lord.
> — *Maimonides* [46]

Men — the whole Gentile world — will accept the Truth about God when He wills it, in His time.

The next great stage or new plateau in human history, the Messianic Age, is coming. "The Earth shall be full of the knowledge of the Lord as the waters cover the sea." [47] God's Truth — in this case, the truth about Him — will surface. All humanity will worship Him directly, and correctly. [48]

In the meantime, the Noahide Law imputes no legal culpability to non-Jews for not *fully* rising to the Revolutionary theology — the pure Monotheism — of Sinai. [49]

Sinai's radical doctrine of God's supernal total Oneness tends to bewilder people — even people who purport to follow only Him.

> God was portrayed now as the Father, now as the wielder of the
> thunder. He might be softened by the intercession of his kindlier
> Son, who again was delineated as an implacable judge unless
> mollified by his mother, who, being a woman, was not above
> cheating alike God and the Devil on behalf of her suppliants; and
> if she were remote, one could enlist her mother, St. Anne. — *Here
> I Stand; a Life of Martin Luther* [50]

Idolatry aims at God, or at some aspect of His godliness, or Truth, but the idolater — the Torah-denier — lives in a complex universe.

Reality consisting only of Creation and its One Creator, idolatry posits a complicated mess of original or intermediate co-creative powers, impulses and spirits. It imagines all existence to be dominated by the clash of fundamentally independent forces — of different vying sources of supernal help and worth and value. The idolator seeks to align himself with forces or impulses of ultimate reality, or genuinely independent creativity, in preference to the Lord — even though the One God is the only such force, source or Creator.

All men pursue the Ultimate in some fashion. But even the most sincere effort to reach Him indirectly, through intermediates or any of His supposed associates, is blasphemous, as well as idolatrous. The Universe is a simpler place than that, a more sensible place, because God Himself is good. He, the Infinite One has both the Divine capacity and the Will to deal full time with every living human being in person, as it were, directly. And the only way He wants men to contact Him, as He tells us,[51] is directly.

Abram, or later Abraham,[52] the father of the Jewish people, discovered all these truths. He taught them in his school and carefully conveyed them to his heirs.[53] God confirmed them again at Sinai, and subsequently in Hebrew history. Israel exists as a nation to carry the message.[54]

So for the Jews, God's special witnesses, to betray the Father who so deliberately revealed His character to them isn't just stupid or ungrateful[55] — it's also always criminal, a violation of the Torah. But for His other children to fail to recognize Him or stray from the clear truth about Him (as He revealed it to Israel) is a different thing. It may not be an actual turning against God at all.

Experience makes the best teacher.[56] The people of Israel know about God through and due to Israel's own experience — the living history of their own people.

Pending the universal redemption promised by the Bible,[57] no other ethnic group or people has ever had such a direct, unmediated national connection to God.[58] Accordingly, the prophet warns, "You only have I known[59] among all the families of the earth. Therefore I will visit upon you all your iniquities."[60] Israel, like the first-born of a family,[61] has special responsibilities in the family of the nations.[62]

This doesn't mean that the Creator's other children have no responsibilities, or that the God of justice doesn't hold us all personally accountable to Him. When it comes to God's transcendent Unity, Israel may be His primary witness, but that doesn't excuse the rest of us from learning from the testimony.[63]

Every straying from God diminishes His creatures. Idolatry denies or distorts the truth that all men are holy; that we each represent, in a sense, the image of Divinity. It enslaves man to false gods, false allegiances, false ideals and a false perspective.[64]

Different writers give us different estimates of which sorts of straying — which kinds and degrees of idolatry — are worst.

Legal Definitions

This First Noahide Commandment criminalizes only those idolatrous activities, described in Scripture, for which the Torah prescribes capital punishment for Jews.[65]

A) God gives no man the right to physically bow down to any idol, nor before any object of worship other than God Himself;

B) nor the right to serve an idol, a no-god, in any of the ways that men normally or formally serve it, to honor it. If most followers of the false god normally kiss the idol or put money before it, for instance, it is criminal idolatry to do so oneself;

C) nor to serve any idol in any of the four ways that God prescribes for His own Temple-service, whether the particular no-god is normally worshipped in that manner or not: neither by bowing, sacrificing, offering incense, nor, finally, pouring libations — liquid offerings — to it or before it.[66]

All these acts constitute the criminal practice of hard-core, first degree idolatry. They all exemplify error; they all harden people in error. In time, the whole world will treat such acts appropriately — as crimes, as betrayal, as evil.

Pending that time, these Universal prohibitions can't be fully, legally, enforced. His laws against idolatry are like His laws against sacrilege and blasphemy in that respect.

The world's nations as yet haven't learned enough about the Law, nor about the Lawgiver. They can't be expected to criminalize what they still haven't learned to recognize as crime — as misplaced loyalty, as treason. Meanwhile, every nation has its pioneering leaders. Individuals can still learn and keep the law as individuals. So they should, for their own good and for the world's. The rest of the human race will catch up. All humanity will be getting wiser.[67]

> To whom then will you liken God? Or what likeness will you compare unto Him? — *Isaiah 40:18*

God is One — a completely indivisible and perfect Unity.[68] That is, He is One in all respects: He alone is God, He is utterly unique, and also absolutely indivisible.[69] If this proposition is false then the Bible and the entire Hebrew Revolution is a fraud.[70]

He is spirit, not matter, which we know because all matter and everything corporeal can be divided, but God is no more divisible than a point in theoretical geometry — which is to say, He is totally indivisible. So He can't be represented physically: to do so would be to reduce Him, the Infinite, to finitude.

Even though His Essence fills the universe,[71] He is absolutely One, by virtue of a Unity beyond any other unity, and this, we see from Scripture, is an immutable element or feature of His never-changing Character. There are no other beings with Him, no other things or beings like Him,[72] and no one and nothing that deserves man's worship but Him.[73]

Despite all this, human beings persist in trying to put a face on God, as it were, to blasphemously delimit Him, by grounding Him in the corporeal.

Men try to divide the Indivisible, associating God with other beings: partners, family members, earthly intimates, and even challengers.[74]

Even though He is perfectly and purely One, people insist on treating "the Godhead"[75] — Divinity — as multiple, as something that He shares with others.

> I form the light, and create darkness; I make peace, and create evil; I am the Lord, I do all these things.— *Isaiah 45:7*[76]

Idolatry is the root of all evil.[77] To formulate effective policies against it, Israel has often debated the issue of which kinds of *associationism*[78] — of imagining God in a partnership,[79] or in an intimate Divine relationship with other godlike beings — are most idolatrous. This issue has never completely been resolved.

Some scholars regard associationism as less blameworthy than *substitution* — of trying to replace God with another thing or a substituting deity. Total pagans try to substitute different entities like Satan, Ba'al, the People, the Fatherland, or "the god within," for instance, for the One God. That is, they see in their gods *alternatives* to the God of Israel. (As opposed to merely linking some entity to Him as His associate — as His representative or stand-in. This is not totally pagan, because it at least aims at the Lord.) But many experts view associationism as worse than substitution — as more blameworthy, more devious, and more likely to keep people fixed in error.[80]

The starting point for all Israel is that every kind of associationism and every effort to place an intermediary between God and man is nonsense. Why should one need some third party between oneself and God, one's Father? Only if one has a primitive, misleading, and blasphemous conception of God — and nothing is more ultimately deranging than a false idea of the Ultimate.[81]

Does associationism and intermediation in worship, expressed by physical acts of worship,[82] violate the minimal requirements of the Noahide law? Most Jewish scholars believe that it does.[83]

Simple prayer, please note, is a private matter. One's thoughts and feelings are one's own. God gives no human court authority to punish anyone absent some wrongful action — unless one has committed some sort of unequivocal physical act.[84] So addressing a silent prayer to a no-god, without bowing and scraping before an image of it,[85] for instance, isn't necessarily a crime that must be addressed at law.[86] Even though sending off any such prayer is utterly idolatrous and foolish.

Israel also distinguishes between mere *veneration*, of the kind that one might direct to an unusually worthy person, for instance — believing that person to be especially close to or having some special influence with God — and *adoration*, or focused devotion.[87] Venerating the holy can lead to holiness, but no man improves himself by adoring a no-god. In this context adoration, which is truly worshipful, must always be exclusive: it must never be directed anywhere except to God alone. Veneration, which isn't really worship, doesn't necessarily try to give God any partners. It doesn't, unlike theological associationism, try to raise someone or something else to the level of true Deity — of interchangeability with the One Indivisible God.[88]

> Lest you corrupt yourselves, and make you a graven image, the similitude of any figure. — *Deuteronomy 4:16*

At its most clearly idolatrous and worst, veneration becomes adoration. It interposes a third party,[89] in a sense, between God — one's Father — and man — His cherished son. Even if one regards this party's intercession as being only helpful instead of utterly indispensable, the tendency here is to blasphemously delimit God. Does He not know one's heart?[90] Is He not Himself fair and straight and loving?

Relying on some intercessor can easily degenerate into substitution — into putting another being or no-god before Him.

No non-deity deserves to be honored like the Deity. Still, a man who merely venerates saints, or ancestors, or whatever,[91] isn't invariably substituting a no-god — an idol — for the One God.[92] Since one can approach God, to honor and petition Him, directly, one should, but that doesn't make all use of an intercessor in one's worship idolatry.[93]

> If Zeus is a god, licentiousness is no sin. If Aphrodite is a goddess, chastity cannot be a virtue. — *Heinrich Graetz*[94]

Men take their culture either from their gods or God, by learning from their fellow men.

The only culture that one can know or count on to be consistently, universally good and just and kind and holy comes solely from knowing Him. So whatever tends to take men away from true knowledge of God must be suspect.

The commission of crime leads men away from God but so, surely, does *every* kind and degree of idolatry, whether or not it is so gross or hardcore that the Noahide law necessarily calls it criminal. Which means that idolatry in Noahide jurisprudence is again, like blasphemy, something of a special case — it is *sui generis*, unique. And, in fact, the normal legal considerations, and procedures, don't always apply.[95]

Idolatry and Witchery

> There shall not be found among you any one that makes his son or his daughter to *pass through the fire,* or that uses divination, or an *observer of times* or an enchanter, or a sorcerer. Or a charmer, or a consulter with familiar spirits, or a wizard, or a necromancer. For all that do these things are an abomination to the Lord. — *Deuteronomy 18:10-12*

Israel speaks of such conduct as "the ways of the Amorite."[96] Each of these Torah crimes rests on an explicit Divine value: the listed practices are all *abominable*. They are inherently evil, disgusting and perverse, in the same sense as any act of oppressive cruelty or robbery or sexual depravity is perverse.

They all offend God, yet the Torah prescribes capital punishment for only some of them. So there's a question whether all of them violate the Noahide law.

Drawing a line between the minimal requisites of law — which the nations' courts must all enforce — and less urgent or compelling Torah precepts isn't necessarily supposed to be easy. As we've seen before, deciding where to place the line naturally gives rise to controversy.[97]

Some of these practices that Scripture condemns may not even constitute out-and-out idolatry. But all of them carry at least the germ — a kernel — of idolatry. Some — not all — authorities classify them all definitely as Noahide crimes. Beyond that, pending further answers, the nations must each define criminality for themselves. God calls Israel to holiness through the statutes here; other nations will profit from the Instruction. One must make further judgments about these sins for oneself:

- *Making one's child "pass through the fire,"*
  **this rite being connected to the worship of
  the idol known, thousands of years ago, as
  the Molech.**[98]

Scripture singles out Molech-worship as particularly loathsome, even compared to other kinds of idolatry.[99] In fact, if it weren't already Universally forbidden on other grounds — as idolatrous sacrifice, or as an otherwise forbidden act of customary service, honoring a no-god, this remains extremely hard-core idolatry — the Torah separately, emphatically, defines this sort of idolatrous service as a capitally punishable crime.[100]

Note, parenthetically, that capital punishment has absolutely nothing to do with human sacrifice, nor with any rite of legitimate worship. God abhors the sacrifice of human victims "with an infinite abhorrence."[101] Capital punishment serves the ends of punishment alone: retribution, restraint and deterrence, together with expiation — basically, the process of reforming the guilty person, morally and spiritually, by making him properly pay for his crime.[102]

The only true sacrifice to God is one's devoted submission to Him, through "a broken spirit: a broken and contrite heart."[103] This may involve a considerable degree of self-sacrifice or even actual martyrdom but never literal human sacrifice.

- *Witchcraft:* **practicing divination or acting as
  "*an observer of times*,"**[104] **an enchanter or a
  sorcerer.**[105]

Besides being false and deceptive — and also usually cruel and obscene — witchcraft violates the essential Revolutionary precept that one must "be whole-hearted with the Lord your God."[106] It invests other beings, forces or spirits with supernatural — godlike — powers, teaching that God has effectively "abandoned the Earth"[107] but that the followers of such lesser deities can, using occult methods,[108] achieve godlike results by harnessing the powers of these gods.

Who abstains from magic is closer to God than are angels.
— *Rabbenu ben Zeira* [109]

- *Divination* **denies the principle of God's Providence: the truth that even if some portent seems to point to a future event God may, in His wisdom, change it.** [110]

Man has a perfect right to try to guess at or estimate the future. One who does so by relying on occult powers to bolster his conjectures, stimulating his natural powers of intuition by "magical," irrational, and artificial methods, [111] is called a diviner. [112]

This practice — divining, not consulting with a diviner, "though the act of consulting him is blameworthy in the extreme" — is totally disallowed within and among the people of Israel. In the Hebrew Code, it constitutes a corporally punishable crime. [113]

Divining includes sinning by "observing times" — or literally, "cloud-gazing" — trying to foretell the future by means of occult omens, supernatural signs, mystic portents or astrology, the practice of the soothsayer.

A soothsayer may say that the shape of a cloud, for instance, portends some occurrence that isn't rationally related to clouds or weather, based on an arcane representation concerning the occult or mystic properties of cloud-shapes. The soothsayer deliberately leads his audience to believe that the world is governed by hidden forces and secret principles, all existing beyond the grasp of worldly logic, outside the scope of Torah, and beyond the ken of either history or science. He represents an irrational, fundamentally unreal way of looking at the world.

Naturally, if his way worked, soothsayers would rule the planet. Of course it doesn't and they don't. They never have; they never will. Those who follow him follow nonsense.

Scripture offers anyone who cares to read about it a much better way — the one true way of rationality and Torah —

immediately after God condemns the soothsayer's. Instead of following nonsense, God commands Israel to follow the logic of His Law, the way of the Hebrew prophets, sages and priests, and all who truly teach and exemplify Torah.[114] That is, He wants not just Israel but every man of every nation to follow truth, rather than lies, to be completely whole-hearted with Him, and to renounce the irrational and unholy for the rational and holy.[115]

> Who practices magic will be harassed by magic. — *Rabbenu Levi*[116]

Whatever denies the absolutely fundamental Torah Principles of God's Unity, God's Providence, and human free will also denies God.[117] To the extent that fortune-telling, astrology, etc., denies these truths — recognizing that some astrological and other acts of portent-watching may not[118] — the practitioner is subject, in the Hebrew Code, to corporal punishment.[119]

No one can know the future. Any teaching that man is a slave to the stars, or to other forces or objects apart from Providence, is blameworthy. It constitutes the teaching of idolatry. But mere descriptive astrology, for instance, which doesn't necessarily attempt to foretell the future (as by decreeing supposedly auspicious or inauspicious times) but only delves into individual character (as by trying to describe the personalities of people born at different times) isn't necessarily idolatrous, nor blameworthy.

Also, naturally, "whatever is recommended by reason is [always] permitted."[120] Faith in reason flows from Sinai. Science, or empirically connecting different phenomena and events with other phenomena and events, to predict a future event, represents the rational, truth-seeking best in man. Hunting up omens, or making predictive connections nonempirically, based only upon occult teachings or mystic and unscientific lore, isn't science. Representing the primitive and irrational worst in man, it is a perversion of human curiosity.

Some authorities include deceitful "magic" — sleight-of-hand or sensory illusion tricks — in the Torah prohibition here. That is, not tricks designed just to amuse or entertain an audience, but tricks meant to genuinely deceive, to permanently overturn the audience's view of the world as a well-ordered place, to make them actually believe in occult powers and in the more-than-human powers of the trickster.[121] At their worst, these same acts — this extremely wrongful practice — might also be seen as violating the more serious prohibition, against sorcery, below.

> You shall not suffer a witch to live. — *Exodus 22:17*[122]

- *Sorcery* is a capital crime in the Torah.[123]

Most sorcery concentrates on causing and curing disease.[124] If any real difference exists between the ordinary deceitful trickster and the sorcerer, or witch, the former knows that he is a trickster while the latter, the sorcerer, sincerely believes that he can manipulate spirits, demons, or other occult powers — no-gods.[125]

You should recognize that every such belief is nonsense. The great vice in it is that it can delude people into enslaving themselves to nonsense,[126] but people are too credulous when it comes to superstition and too susceptible to this evil to take it lightly.[127] It is enormously evil, and the Torah especially warns humanity's courts, or at least the courts of Israel, not to be lax concerning its destruction.[128]

- *Necromancy,* or acting as a counselor or a medium between the living and the dead, or with *"familiar spirits,"*[129] deserves separate condemnation as vile sorcery.[130]

Not only does the Torah forbid the practice of such sorcery, in most cases, as a capitally punishable crime,[131] most authorities regard it as inherently idolatrous.[132] Even the act of merely consulting with this kind of sorcerer is so very blameworthy that the Torah defines it as a corporally punishable crime.[133]

Necromancy involves seeking information from the dead. A desperate King Saul did so, infamously, the night before he died: he entreated a necromancer, the Witch of Endor, to disturb the prophet Samuel.[134] Most authorities regard the witch, and her whole production, as a fraud, from beginning to end.[135] Can the living raise the dead? In any case, fraudulent or not, it all ended, naturally, disastrously. Saul disgraced himself, pathetically, by turning away from the God who despises superstition.

While necromancy surely isn't being "whole-hearted with the Lord," God telling us clearly that He "abominates" sorcery and all such flirtation with "unclean spirits,"[136] certain varieties of the practice may not constitute out-and-out idolatry. For instance, some necromancers may just go to the place where the person they want to speak to lies buried, hoping that a spirit will come to them if they sleep there.[137]

That sort of conduct, taken alone, is not so terribly heinous. In such cases the Torah prescribes (for Israel) no more than a corporal penalty.[138] But if the necromancer performs distinct rites of worship, to propitiate the spirit, or if he pretends to communicate with it, to channel the spirit's supposed message to others, his crime if far greater. If a Hebrew, a Jew, conducts himself so, the Hebrew Code — the Torah — prescribes the death penalty.[139]

- ***Practicing spells, enchantments or charms,* is defined as a corporal offense in the Torah.**[140]

The charmer writes or recites certain "magic" formulas or phrases to gain power over things, events or beings that can't and don't understand his language. Scripture speaks of the *chover chaver,* the charmer of snakes or scorpions, who recites formulaic spells over them to supposedly render them harmless.[141]

Even if such spells contain words of Torah, and even if the spell-caster directs them at the Lord, this is a nonsensical and superstitious practice. It is an irrational, animalistic use of man's capacity for language; it leads men away from God.[142] Worse yet, most enchanters, being idolators, try through their spells to petition forces, deities or spirits other than God, and this is pure idolatry.

One should appreciate that spell-casting has nothing to do with true prayer. True prayer, known as "the service of the heart,"[143] doesn't test God by demanding that He create for one some instant miracles.[144] Neither does it ever put human life or limb in jeopardy.[145] Rather than trying to blackmail God into focusing *His* attention on the worshipper, the great benefit of prayer is that it works the other way, drawing the worshipper's attention *to* Him.[146]

False Prophesy

The seal of the Holy One is truth. — *Rabbenu Hanina bar Hama* [147]

"Keep yourself far from a false matter," God commands His followers.[148] Nothing is more of a lie than a lying prophecy. Right after setting out the witchcraft prohibitions above,[149] Scripture lists the two following crimes:

- ***Prophesying in the name of an idol.* That is, proclaiming either that God has commanded any man to worship any god but Him or that any such non-god commands man to worship it, promising reward if one obeys and threatening punishment if one does not.**

This constitutes a capital offense in the Torah, as Scripture immediately tells us.[150] It contravenes, among other basic principles, the Torah's explicit rule that one should never even recite or speak the name of any idol.[151]

- ***Prophesying falsely.* That is, speaking "presumptuously" in God's Name.**[152]

The crime here, a capital offense in the Torah, involves falsely claiming that God has prophetically given one some word or command when He hasn't, falsely claiming that God has prophetically commanded one to proclaim something to others when He didn't, or taking credit for a genuine message that the Master of the Universe issued through a real prophet — whether that prophet is living or dead, the false prophet claiming falsely that the Master of the Universe has spoken so to him.[153]

Scripture does not just condemn the false prophet but also those who follow him or who even, merely, fear him, or who believe that his false prophecies may conceivably be true. "You shall not hearken unto the words of that prophet."[154] "You shall not be afraid of him."[155] The obligation of Israel, at least, is to punish the false prophet who seeks to lead the people astray. His offense constituting a capital crime, the failure of any person to properly report or prosecute it constitutes another crime, for which the Torah prescribes corporal punishment.[156]

Advocating Idolatry

Like other blasphemies, one can commit idolatry by means of speech alone. Man need not actually worship a false god in order to serve it. One who announces to an idol, in its presence, "you are my god," or who publicly accepts a false god to himself, is liable. If he makes himself an advocate for that god, trying to incite his fellows to believe in it or worship it, Scripture calls him a misleader.[157] A Jew who commits this horrendous felony merits death at the hands of a Torah court, God tells us.[158] His sin constitutes one of those rare crimes that is fundamentally unforgivable.[159]

[T]o be cruel to those who lead people astray after foolishness is to be merciful to mankind. — *Yad, Hilchot Sanhedrin 11:5*

Revolutions don't succeed by coddling the counter-revolutionary. But neither is a Noahide, a Gentile, always held to the same standards as a Jew. The Noahide misleader doesn't necessarily directly threaten the integrity and survival of the core people of the Hebrew Revolution by attacking, from within, the core truth of the Revolution. Also, the Noahide misleader may not actually know any better, perhaps as a consequence of growing up surrounded by idolatry — while God expects every Jew to know better. So He explicitly commands Israel to punish, severely, the Hebrew who commits the crimes described below.

We list them here, recognizing that the same acts, if committed by a Noahide, are certainly wrongful, but that the larger stakes and the individual's legal culpability are, if anything, lesser.

- **Inciting others to idolatry. Even if he does not worship any false god personally, doing nothing but summoning or inciting even one other person to do so, the inciter commits a heinous sin: he is a misleader, pushing his fellow man away from the Father and into the arms of evil. For this advocate of evil the Torah prescribes capital punishment.**[160]

Make no mention of the name of other gods, neither let it [any such name] be heard out of your mouth. — *Exodus 23:13* [161]

- **Swearing by an idol. For making a vow or swearing an oath in the name of any no-god — as by saying, "By Jove/By Jupiter, I will do this-or-that," or "May the Devil strike me dead if . . . ." — which misguided souls in one's hearing may regard as some kind of true deity, the Torah prescribes corporal punishment.**[162]

This prohibition is so important that the people of Israel, at least, are legally forbidden to in any way encourage or incite even a non-Jew, an active idol-worshipper, to violate it. "You may not cause the idolator to swear by his deity."[163] But note, if only in this context, that Israel has held to the following belief — an authoritative legal opinion — for the last few centuries, from about 1570 CE:

> The nations of today swear by the name of the Lord, and believe
> in Divine Revelation and in the sanctity of the Torah. And
> although they associate with the name of Heaven other ruling
> powers, their intention is to swear by Him who created the heavens
> and the earth. — R. Moses Isserles [164]

In this matter of vows and swearing, a line exists between theological associationism and theological substitution. A Ben Noah who merely associates an idol or a no-god with God commits a terrible error. Yet his vow, or oath, in the name of his no-god is meant to invoke the Master of the Universe — the One God.

Without making more of the narrow legal ruling here than it actually represents,[165] such an oath is far less offensive than one that invokes an idol or a no-god as a substitute for God, that doesn't refer to Him in any sense, and that intends, in fact, to replace God with a different god or a "higher" good. Associationism aims, at least, at God. It heads in the right direction. But the vow or oath that tries to elevate any idol to the status of His substitute or replacement is purely pagan and utterly blasphemous and defiling.

- **Generally, concerning the misleader, the
  advocate for any idol, Scripture teaches: "You
  shall not consent [or "show affection"][166]
  unto him, nor hearken unto him; neither shall
  your eye pity him, neither shall you spare
  [him][167], neither shall you conceal him:[168]
  But you shall surely kill him[169] . . . Because
  he has sought to draw you away from the
  Lord your God."[170]**

Lesser or "Softer" Idolatry

Every type and species of idolatry for which the Torah prescribes capital punishment is a Noahide crime, as we've seen above.

Torah prescribes capital punishment for worshipping any non-god in a conventional manner — in the way that people usually worship that idol — and, even if it isn't a generally accepted way of honoring that idol, for bowing, sacrificing, offering incense, or pouring liquid offerings to it or before it.[171] But *any* act of worship that leads men away from the One God is idolatrous, and therefore also blasphemous. So even if the Torah doesn't prescribe the death penalty in such a case, that act must nonetheless be blameworthy.

> Take heed to yourselves, lest your heart be deceived, and you turn aside [from God's Law], and serve other gods, and worship them.
> — *Deuteronomy 11:16*

Most — not all — Torah authorities hold that the Universal Law forbids even those acts of idolatrous worship which a Torah court would *not* deem worthy of capital punishment.[172] That is, even though the Torah prescribes a corporal rather than a capital penalty, in cases where a Jew commits the sin, most authorities regard these sins — these idolatrous practices — as so damaging and defiling that they deserve to be banished not just from Israel but from the whole world.

Call it "soft" or second-degree idolatry, though it may lead to harder kinds. At the very least, these are all Torah-defying acts, and all morally suspect; these are all crimes if commited by a Jew. That they could ever be tolerated in the Holy Land, the land of Israel, when it is completely free and peaceful and Torah-true — i.e., in the Messianic Age — is hardly even conceivable.[173] Suggesting, perhaps, that the acts in question are so dangerously sinful that they shouldn't be tolerated anywhere. At any rate, at the very most, God expects the Noahide nations to ban such idolatry, to try to put a stop to it, to keep it from defiling any nation. But this doesn't necessarily mean that He requires the nations to prosecute it criminally.

A Jew, who is morally and legally blameworthy if he even "entertains the *thought* that there exists a deity except the Lord,"[174] is punishable by a worldly, Torah, court if he ever acts on that thought demonstrably — if he translates his idolatrous thought into an act of idolatrous devotion.[175] Every Jew should absolutely know better: the people of Israel are God's special "witnesses,"[176] pledged as a nation to His Truth. So God holds the Jews, as individuals, to the highest, truest, most stringent national standard here. He doesn't hold every Noahide to that standard.

In these cases of soft or second-degree idolatry, the minimal requisites of God's law do not require Noahide courts to criminalize every such act, or exact legal retribution — impose criminal penalties — against each individual sinner. *If* God calls on every nation to thoroughly cleanse itself of all idolatry, of every stripe and every degree, the Noahide nations need do no more than act to prevent, not criminalize, these lesser sorts of idolatry.[177] So, at most, it seems that the sinning individual Noahide need only be stopped, and warned, and prevented from proceeding with such evil.[178] Society has the right to eliminate idolatry in stages.

A Noahide is morally blameworthy if he strays from his Father, putting any thing or being before Him or beside Him.[179] By making his idolatry operative — by translating it into action — he becomes dangerous: to himself, because bad practices are hardening, or self-reinforcing; and to others, who may be infected or led astray by his terrible example. Society has the right, if not the obligation, to protect itself by stopping him.

Following Maimonides, the four kinds of conduct described below all fall under the proscription of this first Universal Commandment. But remember: every Divine law is an anti-idolatry law, the main point and purpose of all God's Commandments being the total destruction of all idolatry. So any effort to choose between His laws, saying that this one is more concerned with idolatry and that one is more concerned with something else, is obviously problematic. The Torah contains 613 Commandments. They all oppose idolatry.[180]

Jealously do I [God] exact punishment for idolatry, but in other matters I am merciful and gracious. — *Midrash*[181]

- **Any idolatry, or act of worship or devotion, for which the Torah prescribes corporal but not capital punishment.**[182]

This specifically includes: making any image of an object of worship, for the purpose of worship;[183] creating or turning any image into an object of worship by others;[184] honoring any no-god by any demonstrable action, such as kissing or embracing it, washing it, sweeping before it, hanging flowers around it, and so forth, these and all similar acts showing reverence and affection for an idol being, clearly, idolatrous.[185]

- **Wasting any time or attention on idolatry at all, and especially not with a view to pursuing it, or turning to any idol or a no-god by either word, thought or deed.**[186]

- **Following the irrational habits, customs or fashions of idolators.**

One should avoid their heathen ways and despise their heathen customs. "You are not to say: Since they [the pagans] go out dressed in purple, I will go out dressed in purple."[187] Rather, do not walk in their ways: don't follow their idolatrous customs; don't follow their idolatrous statutes, or the social customs that have become for them like statutes.[188] About all these, the superstitious "ways of the Amorite," the Scripture warns, "Take heed to yourself that you are not snared by following them."[189]

- **Establishing any physical facilities, monuments or images for promoting or assisting idolatry or any kind of idolatrous devotion.**[190]

This transgression includes setting up statuary, carved stones, sacred groves or the like, devoted to the service of some no-god.[191] But don't defile God's service by trying to convert or dedicate such defiled tools of idolatrous worship to Him.

God takes no pleasure in them.[192] In fact, constituting as they do — these strange monuments, sacred trees, idolatrous "holy" images or mystic carvings — such a terrible snare and enticement to idolatry, neither can they be dedicated to the service of mere art.

Connoisseurs may smile at mere antiques or curiosities dedicated to gods that now seem safely ridiculous, but "living" artifacts that retain any grain of potency, psychologically, are insidious, a snare for the unwary. Even if the artist says that he is making an idolatrous device only for the sake of beauty, one should treat him with suspicion. Normally such artifacts serve other purposes, and are not to be permitted.[193]

True Religion

Discovering what God condemns, virtue does the opposite. God is close at all times and He offers His love to men at all times. Turn to Him: He *will* turn to you.[194]

He from Whom we have our amazing free will Created us for exactly this: to recognize and call on Him, to love and follow Him; to develop ourselves, to even become more *like* Him! The God of this and every universe, perfect Goodness Himself, deigns to offer every human being nothing less than a profound and direct relationship with the One supernal Ultimate, with Him! God offers us, in a sense, His eternal loving Hand.[195] Idolatry spurns the offer.

Don't spurn God, the Lord your Judge. Remember that the end purpose of every Noahide law — and the goal of all the Torah — is to make man "know the Lord."[196]

> [W]hat does the Lord your God require of you, but to fear the
> Lord your God, to walk in all His ways, and to love Him, and to
> serve the Lord your God with all your heart and with all your soul?
> — *Deuteronomy 10:12* [197]

"Knowing" the Lord is the total, unconditional recognition that God exists; that He acts in history, guiding and directing it; and that He is the transcendental, all-powerful, all-knowing Being Who gives us life.

To know Him, as far as mere created beings can know the holy Infinite Creator, means to admit and live the fact that man didn't invent God, but He created man. "Knowing God" means to acknowledge that everything that Israel stands for, including the entirety of Hebrew history and the Bible, is *not* a fraud; that truth exists and that life is real — and that its One Eternal Owner is good. To "know" the Lord means to fully, unreservedly accept Him as one's Master.

> Do His will as if it were your will, that He may do your will as though it were His will.— *R. Gamaliel*[198]

What does your Master want from you? "To keep the Commandments of the Lord, and His Statutes, which I [God] command you this day for your own good."[199]

Knowing God, in other words, means submitting to His Rules. Whatever his Rules are for you: whether you belong to the "high priests" or *cohanim* of Israel, and He commands you to follow the laws that apply to the Jewish *cohanim*;[200] to the *Levi'im*, Levites, or the "priestly" tribe of Israel;[201] to the "nation of priests," B'nai Israel, the generality of the people of Israel;[202] or to B'nai Noah, the vast majority of the descendants of Noah, the human race in general.

Know and obey Him by knowing and keeping His laws for you. "Knowing God" means bending and subjugating your own will and ego to His, making God's Law yours — making His Will one's own. It means rising or beginning to rise to holiness in His service — for one's own good, for the good of the greater universe.[203]

> As soon as one departs from the words of the Torah, it is as though he attached himself to the worship of idols. — *Midrash*[204]

The root of the Hebrew word for commandment, *tzevet*, means "connection." Every act that man does in honest obedience to a Commandment *connects* him to his Commander.[205] Motivation matters. To obey the Commandments, not simply because one believes that they are wise, or useful, or because one's fellows expect it, but — beyond all that, regardless of it — because the Lord of the universe Himself *commands* them, is to effect this connection with one's Maker.

> May your fear of Heaven be as strong as your fear of man.
> — *Talmud*[206]

A pious person cultivates this active link — this God-blessed connection — with Ultimate Goodness. He tries, if only for his own good, to make his Master's Will his own. Man acquires a measure of the Law's eternity by doing so;[207] he discovers his own true place in things — his position in Creation — in the process. By fulfilling the Divine laws he both humbles and exalts himself — by bowing his head to the Almighty Lawgiver.

Pursue God by pursuing godliness. Pursue godliness by learning and keeping God's laws for you.

Learning comes before observance. Human beings don't pick up righteousness — Divine law — by instinct but by education. "An empty-headed person cannot be a sin-fearing person; the ignorant aren't genuinely saintly."[208] The fear of the Lord leads to the Lord, but only by means of learning. Because without learning you cannot serve Him as He would have you serve Him, as He commands you to serve Him.[209]

Learning True Religion

> Happy is he who comes to the Hereafter possessed of learning!
> — *Talmud*[210]

Learning must be sought.[211] "Get yourself a teacher and remove yourself from doubt."[212] Learn about God and goodness from all sources.[213] Learn from the Bible with its commentaries, books — this book among them — and your fellow students, and from God-fearing people generally.[214] Learn righteousness by doing righteousness — incorporate His Law into every aspect of your life — but don't be too proud, or shy, to study with those who can guide you on the way.

> Teaching [Torah to] an unworthy student is [a transgression] like
> worshipping idols. — *Mishnah Tosefta* [215]

Study for a proper purpose — to know the Lord, to increase
your love and fear of God, to carry out, so far as possible, His
Divine Instructions to you, to turn them into deeds. "Approach
the Torah with joy, and also with trembling." [216]

Remember that God didn't entrust Israel with the precious
detailed Guidance of the Torah for Israel to surrender it to others
for defilement.

> [L]et Your awe be manifest in all Your works, and a reverence for
> You fill all that You have created, so that all Your creatures may
> know You, and all mankind bow down to You to acknowledge You.
> — *Hebrew Prayer* [217]

A Ben Noah who studies Torah with no intent to carry out the
laws in it that apply to Him, or that point him to a Noahide law, is
an interloper, a thief, who deserves no help from Israel. [218] The
Torah itself forbids the Jews from sharing Torah with B'nai Noah
except for a proper purpose, [219] such as helping anyone honestly
seeking knowledge of God's laws in order to follow in His
Ways. [220]

> Make not of her [the Torah] a crown with which to aggrandize
> yourself, nor a spade wherewith to dig. — *Mishnah* [221]

Do not approach the Torah with a frivolous purpose,
arrogantly or pridefully; give your teachers the benefit of the
doubt. This is not to say, however, that you must accept everything
that your teachers tell you, or switch off your intellect, your
discriminating faculties, in the presence of those from whom you
hope to learn.

> Ask your teacher his reasons and his sources. — *Rashi* [222]

Learning God's laws, which necessarily involves *living* His laws,
requires one's full engagement. Further, since Torah, God and
Israel are so closely intertwined, the honest seeker will, sooner or
later, on some level, find himself personally engaged with Israel
— with Jews. But Jews are just people, with all the good, and bad,
that goes with being human. [223]

God alone is perfect. Human beings are never completely pure, or selfless, or correct.

Don't let the mere humanity of the Jews sour you on Israel or Torah.

This is a test for you. God can distinguish between those who love Him and those who hate Him by their attitude to Israel.[224] One who hates the Jews will hate humanity. To respect the Jews, despite their flaws, is to respect humanity. To respect humanity, despite its flaws, is to show respect and love to God.[225]

You should know this about your Torah teachers. When they teach you laws or principles that come to you endorsed by the whole people of Israel, you are learning holy laws and Principles; you are getting Truth about the Ultimate. If history tells you that practically every living Jew, including the greatest Jewish thinkers, has accepted any religious principle or Torah tenet over a span of many generations, consider: "If they [Jews] are not prophets, they are the descendants of prophets."[226]

Know that the collective wisdom of all Israel is true wisdom. "The sceptre [of Torah and Torah knowledge] shall not depart from Judah (*Yehuda*)."[227] The whole Jewish people cannot be wrong for long about either God or the Way of God.[228]

Obviously, this is not to say that every Jewish teacher or Jewish school of thought always has things right.

Beware of accepting the mistaken presumptions of your teachers. **If anything about the Torah ever strikes you as wrong, perverse or cruel, you are either misunderstanding it or it isn't genuine Torah.** If all Israel has historically endorsed it then it's genuine Torah and you're missing the point of it. If it lacks that collective endorsement, weigh it — in the light of everything that you can find that is reliable.

Israel has collectively endorsed every word of the Hebrew Bible, every page of the Talmud and Mishnah, every word of every prayer common to every Hebrew prayerbook, or *Siddur*,[229] and the amazing multi-volumed compilation of authoritative detailed law known as the *Shulchan Aruch*.[230] Not only that, the

Jewish people have validated other classic works — such as those of Maimonides, and of other geniuses like Rashi, Sa'adia Gaon, Nachmanides, and Ibn Ezra — which, though not universally accepted in every particular, have earned the reverence of all Israel.

> May the words of my mouth and the meditation of my heart be
> acceptable before You, O Lord, my Rock and my Redeemer.
> — *Psalm 19:15*

Remember that Infinite God — the God of Abraham, the God of David — hears your every prayer.[231] And that even very pious, careful teachers have been known to presume to ridiculously delimit Him.

Nobody can disparage God like one who claims to speak in His Name. In case of doubt, check your teachers' assertions against Israel's Thirteen Principles of Faith [See Appendix].

Rely on the reliable. Don't let the mistaken presumptions or misled agendas of self-styled experts prevent you from loving and celebrating the God of love. Pray to know how to celebrate Him, and where and how to direct your love and joy and grateful worship, but don't let anyone diminish your love for Him, the one Creator. Love Him and acknowledge Him in all things first.[232] Then work on improving your method.

Kabbalah, the Mystic Tradition

> The secret things belong unto the Lord our God, but that which
> has been Revealed belongs to us and our children forever, that we
> may do all the words of this Torah. — *Deuteronomy 29:29*

Beware the teachings that go under the name of *Kabbalah* — literally, "that which is received or handed down," "the received tradition," or simply "the Tradition."

Israel does have a mystic tradition and it represents something immensely deep and ancient, but it has little to do with anything being taught today in popular classes or books about kabbalah.

Nothing can harm people like a false idea about God. Popular kabbalah teaches false ideas about God. It claims to mystically bridge the gulf between the Lord, Who is ever-present but invisible and infinite, and the finite, visible world. It claims to take up where the Talmud and the Written Torah leave off. But mostly all it is is irrationality, idolatry, and nonsense.[233]

> The heavens were opened, and I saw visions of God.— *Ezekiel 1:1*

Some kabbalistic teachings go back at least as far as Moses,[234] and the Book of Ezekiel contains such elements.[235] Several of the Sages who are mentioned in the Talmud taught and practiced kabbalah.[236] In fact, even this book contains some kabbalah — see those color designations given to the Seven Rainbow Covenant Commandments — because a little mysticism can add "juiciness," depth and color to a presentation that might be too dry or demanding without it.

One must never try to make the vital, living Torah dry. But neither should one ever foster lawlessness, as by teaching anything that can be converted to idolatry or that leads to idolatrous habits of thought.

Kabbalah constitutes a vast body of mystic poetry — its details never validated by the full community of Israel — together with a non-rational way of looking at and dealing with the essentially unknowable. That is, kabbalah concerns itself with the "secret things that belong unto the Lord"[237] as opposed to practical Torah or anything at all concrete.

So no kabbalistic "truth" can be verified. Not in the real world, historically or scientifically; nor can it ever be checked against reliable sources. Naturally, there are no such sources, because the whole point of the kabbalah is that God never openly revealed it. This means that anyone can take any nonsense and call it kabbalah.

Eschew nonsense. Kabbalah can make you crazy.[238] Even the genuine article can be misleading,[239] let alone the godless drivel that commonly passes for the real thing.

Don't be so humble in your search for truth that you end up humbly accepting drivel in place of truth or common sense.

Finally, remember: the Way of God is not a way of magic; it is not occult nor hidden, nor the private property of a secret few initiates or mystics.[240] Don't let anyone tell you any differently.

> He [God] has shown you, O man, what is good, and what the Lord requires of you: Only to do justice and to love goodness, and to walk humbly with your God. — *Micah 6:8* [241]

NOTES

1. The Lord — *HaShem*, the Name, God's proper name, the Tetragrammaton (i.e., *Tetra*, four: *Y-H-V* and *H*). God, — *HaElo[k]im* or "the God."

2. Exodus 20:3 and Deuteronomy 5:7. Or "besides Me" or, literally, "no other gods [*Elo(k)im*] to My face." This is the second of Israel's Ten Commandments, following "I am the God. . . . ," the first Commandment identifying Him as *HaShem*, the King of freedom, who works through history, the Lord of the Exodus, the God of Abraham, Isaac, Israel and Moses. See commentaries.

3. *Moreh Nevuchim* 3:29. See, e.g., Exodus 19:6, Isaiah 43:10,12; *Yad, Yesodey HaTorah* 1:1, 1:6.

4. Rabbenu Bachya ibn Yosef, *Hovot HaLevavot* (c. 1161 CE) 9:2.

5. And, presumably, the only creature to live its life aware of its own mortality.

6. See, e.g., Genesis 1:26-27, Numbers 14:21, Deuteronomy 10:13, Isaiah 48:17, Proverbs 16:4.

7. The Koran, *Sura* 10:90, recalling Egypt's experience with the Exodus. See Exodus 12:32. Whether men call Him God or Allah, there is no god but the Eternal, the One.

8. The Christian Gospels. See Deuteronomy 6:4. These words, "Hear O Israel," etc., begin the first paragraph of the *Shema* ("Hear!"), Israel's basic statement of faith. See the *Siddur*/Prayerbook.

9. *Moreh Nevuchim* 3:29; *Yad, Hilchot Yesodey HaTorah* 1:6, 1:1.

10. See Midrash, *Mechilta* to Exodus 12:6.

11. *Yad, Hilchot Melachim* 9:1. Also see Talmud, *Sanhedrin* 56b, in the name of R. Yitzhak.

12. See Midrash, *Sifre* to Numbers 15:22.

13. Midrash, *Sifre*, ibid.

14. Bindman, *Seven Colors of the Rainbow*, supra, p. 103.

15. Bindman, supra, p. 124. See "The Third Commandment," above.

16. See Midrash, *Mechilta* to Exodus 20:2.

17. "And the Lord God commanded" — *Va-yitzav*, Commanded. *HaShem*, the Name. *Elo[k]im*, the Lord.

18. Talmud, *Sanhedrin* 56b.

19. Exodus 20:3 and Deuteronomy 5:7; Talmud, supra. See Exodus 32:8, describing how, before Israel received the Torah, the "mixed

multitude's" idolatry with the Golden Calf was itself a betrayal of the law that God had previously commanded them. See Novak, supra, p. 107; Midrash, *Genesis Rabbah* 16:16 (re: Hosea 5:11 and Genesis 2:16). Also see Mishnah, *Shevuot* 4:6, for the interesting proposition that man's true crime in the Garden (Eden) was nothing but the violation of this one Commandment, against idolatry.

20. See, e.g., Novak, supra, p. 90.

21. Mishnah, *Pirke Avot* 2:1. "Eye," "Ear," "Book" — metaphors describing the otherwise indescribable.

22. Talmud, *Sanhedrin* 102b. See Talmud, *Avoda Zorah*, generally; *Yad, Hilchot Avodat Kochavim.*

23. *Sifre* on Deuteronomy 43.

24. As the Nazis famously superimposed the swastika, a pagan cycle-of-life/rebirth symbol, over the white emblematic disk of the Sun god, and then ascribed extremely old-fashioned pagan meanings to the combination. See Nicholas Goodrick-Clarke, *The Occult Roots of Nazism* (New York University Press, NY, 1992) p. 20.

25. *Judaism and Modern Man* (Farrar, Straus & Cudahy, New York NY, 1951) p. 96.

26. R. Solomon ibn Gabirol, *Tikkun Middot HaNefesh* (c. 1055 CE). See Psalms 2:11, 19:10, 111:10. Also see Proverbs 1:7, 8:13, 9:10.

27. See *Horeb*, supra, Sec. 1, Chap. 3, paras. 8-12 (pp. 6-8).

28. Micah 4:5.

29. Psalm 96:5. See Jeremiah 10:11-15. "Idols" — no-gods, things without substance; in Hebrew, *elilim.*

30. See Deuteronomy 4:19 with commentaries.

31. Job 31:26-27 with commentaries; Zephaniah 3:9 with *Mishnah Tosefta* to *Berachot* 6:2 and Talmud, *Berachot* 57b; *Yad, Berachot* 10:9; *Shulchan Aruch, Orach Haim* 224. See Novak, supra, pp. 109-115. Also see, e.g., Jeremiah 10:11-15 and Habakkuk 2:18-20. Both Jews and Gentiles should know better than to follow non-gods, but Jewish idolatry, apparently, beyond being merely stupid, constitutes an especially grievous direct betrayal of God. See Novak, pp. 110-114.

32. Evidence including the peculiar role played by Israel in history and the accomplishments of the Jews among men since the invention of the alphabet, especially as checked against clear Bible prophecy; the sublimity and utter righteous consistency of the Torah (see Deuteronomy 4:5-8); and even the absence of character of Israel's many enemies, of every generation. Still, not everyone knows to look at the Bible through the eyes of the people who are its focus; history can be slanted, neglected or forgotten; supposed common sense and human logic can mislead. Scripture explains that the evidence of God's greatness will build, through history, until finally no man can deny it. See, e.g., Isaiah 2:2, 66; Psalm 105; Ezekiel 37:28.

33. Jeremiah 16:19; Talmud, *Hullin* 13b, *Shabbat* 116a, *Avoda Zorah* 27b.

34. See, e.g., Isaiah 66:23, Jeremiah 16:19; Habakuk 2:14, Zechariah 14.

35. *Sefer HaMitzvot* 2:1 (re: Exodus 20:3 and Deuteronomy 5:7).

36. *Yad, Hilchot Teshuva* 3:14. "It is tantamount to repudiating the whole Torah, the prophets and everything they were commanded, from Adam to the end of time." — *Yad, Hilchot Avodat Kochavim* 2:4.

37. Nahum 1:2. See Exodus 20:5; Deuteronomy 5:9. "Jealous," the

Hebrew root *kanna* being descriptive of the just indignation of one terribly and wrongly injured, in the sense of a lovingly devoted husband whose wife cruelly betrays him. See commentaries. "God"/*Elo[k]im;* "the Lord"/ *HaShem.* That is, the One God.

38. *Yad, Hilchot Teshuva* 3:15.

39. I.e., the foundation, the core, the everlasting center.

40. (Classic commentary, c. 1160 CE) on Exodus 20:2. An atheist follows his own man-made gods — perhaps a fellow creature or some idea of Creation, or abstract principles, animal impulses, money, or the self. Rid of orthodox belief, half-baked old orthodoxies and lawless invented beliefs accumulate in their stead. But no god restrains or humanizes his morality; he remains numb to the fear of God. See Genesis 20:11; Exodus 1:17, 18:21; Deuteronomy 25:18; Psalms 19:9 and 14:1.

41. All depends on one's deeds. See Mishnah, *Pirke Avot* 3.19, 1.15,17 and *Ta'anit* 2:1 (on Jonah 3:10, recalling that God relented as to the B'nai Noah due solely to their works); Talmud, *Kiddushin* 40a; Midrash, *Mechilta* to *Exodus* 12:6; *Kuzari* 2:46. This is not to say, though, that God never punishes individuals for mere bad intentions. But He doesn't grant that power to human courts.

42. "*Halakha* and Democracy" in *Tradition* 32:1 (Fall 1997), p. 16. Also see, e.g., Joshua 24:15.

43. Talmud, *Sanhedrin* 56b; *Yad, Hilchot Melachim* 9:2. See Job 31:26-27; Novak, supra, pp. 111-117. Still, God knows the heart — Psalm 44:21 — and He expects everyone (the Hebrew Code explicitly, repeatedly, and formally Commanding the Jews in this respect) to direct their hearts to Him alone. See, e.g., Deuteronomy 6:5; *Sefer HaMitzvot* 1:1-22.

44. Although crime may have consequences beyond man's knowing. Generally, see Deuteronomy 18:10 and commentaries; Talmud, *Sanhedrin* 56b.

45. Can any of His creatures hurt the Lord of the Universe? Not God but men, and the world of men, suffer from the evil that men do.

46. *Moreh Nevuchim* 1:36, citing, in the following order, Deuteronomy 11:16,17, 6:15, 31:29, 32:21, 6:15; Jeremiah 8:19; Deuteronomy 32:19, 22; Nachum 1:2; Deuteronomy 7:10; Numbers 32:21: Deuteronomy 16:22, 12:31.

47. Isaiah 11:9. Already, great parts of Torah — the so-called "Judeo-Christian ethic" — have instilled themselves in the Western world's civil life and conduct. Even people who aren't particularly pious live quite ethically, frequently, based on Torah norms that have been all but universally accepted.

48. Isaiah 66:23. See, e.g., Isaiah 13:11; Zephaniah 3:9 and Talmud, *Berachot* 57b.

49. See Micah 4:5; Talmud, *Yoma* 52a; Deuteronomy 4:19 and 2 Kings 5:18-19 with commentaries; Also see Exodus 18:11; Novak, supra, pp. 110-148. Idolatry is always at least somewhat blameworthy morally — see Jeremiah 10:11-15; Job 31:26-27; Proverbs 3:35 and commentaries; Talmud, *Megilla* 9b, *Avoda Zorah* 55a — but, in the case of Gentiles, not always or in every respect blameworthy legally.

50. Roland H. Bainton (Abingdon Press, Nashville TN, 1950), p. 21.

51. See, e.g., Exodus 20:5, 23:25; Deuteronomy 6:13, 10:20, 11:22, 13:5; Isaiah 66:23; Psalms 2,5,7, etc.

52. Genesis 17:5.

53. Genesis 18:19.

54. See, e.g., Exodus 19:6; Isaiah 43:10, 12.

55. See Isaiah 1:3; Jeremiah 2:13 with Rashi.

56. "Experience is a good school, but the fees are high." Attributed to Heinrich Heine (c. 1797-1856).

57. See e.g., Isaiah 11:9, 66:23, Jeremiah 3:17,16:19; Ezekiel 39:7; Habakuk 2:14, Zechariah 8:23, 14.

58. Not just historically, but — again on a national basis — through Israel's daily practice, constant exposure, and schooling in His Torah. See, e.g., Deuteronomy 6:7.

59. "Known" — *yada'ati*: select for more intimate relationship. See, e.g., Genesis 18:19 and commentaries.

60. Amos 3:2.

61. Exodus 4:22, "Israel is My son, My first-born."

62. See, e.g., Genesis 18:19; Exodus 19:5-6; Isaiah 2:3; Jeremiah 13:11, 33:7-9; Psalm 83.

63. See, e.g., Isaiah 34, 45:22; Jeremiah 16:19; Malachi 3:16-17.

64. And also to a false priesthood, idolatry permitting only certain adepts or familiars access to Divinity. The true God is directly accessible to all who humbly seek Him. See, e.g., Exodus 15:2; Zechariah 1:3; Psalms 3:4, 27:1, 31:24, 145:18; *Moreh Nevuchim* 2:39, 3:29; Novak, supra, pp. 147-148.

65. Talmud, *Sanhedrin* 56b; *Yad, Hilchot Melachim* 9:2; Aaron HaLevi, *Sefer HaHinnuch* (c. 1300 CE; Chavel ed., Mosad HaRav Kook, Jerusalem, 1952) p. 543. The Torah provides that only the clearest and most serious types and varieties of idolatry can be punished capitally, or by human courts at all.

66. *Yad, Hilchot Melachim* 9:2. See Exodus 20:5, 22:19; Leviticus 17:7, 20:3,5; Numbers 15:31, 25:3; Deuteronomy 12:30; *Sefer HaMitzvot* 2:5,6.

67. See, e.g., Numbers 24:17; Deuteronomy 28-30; Isaiah 2:2-4, 66; Jeremiah 16:19; Habakuk 2:14; Zechariah 14.

68. Deuteronomy 6:4. See commentaries. Also see *Moreh Nevuchim* 2:1.

69. See, e.g., *Moreh Nevuchim* 2:1.

70. See Israel's Thirteen Basic Principles of Faith, supra, Principle Two.

71. Deuteronomy 4:39. See Appendix, Principles Two and Three (Israel's Thirteen Principles of Faith), following.

72. Scripture "speaks in the language of men" — Talmud, *Berachot* 31b — figuratively and metaphorically referring to God as displaying bodily attributes, such as standing, sitting, speaking, wielding a sword, etc. See Deuteronomy 4:15 with commentaries; *Sefer HaMitzvot* 1:2; The Thirteen Principles, Appendix, Principle Three.

73. Exodus 20:3.

74. Challengers like Satan: in Hebrew, *Sotan*, "the Accuser," or prosecuting angel, God's loyal agent. See Talmud, *Bava Batra* 16a (R. Simon ben Lakish): "Satan, the Evil Inclination (the dark impulse or selfish dynamic in man), and the Angel of Death are one." Hebrew Scripture mentions this figure only in 1 Chronicles 21:1, Job 1:6-12 and 2:1-7, Psalm 109:6, and Zechariah 3:1-2. Note that "devil" comes from an East Indian word for "god" — *devi*. No well-translated copy of Israel's Bible includes the word, nor even the idea.

75. A theological term, beloved by the nations' theologians — students

of *theos*/divinity, from the Greek. Pagan concepts being very complicated, they require concentrated study. Israel, on the other hand, spends less time wrestling with questions of divinity (See Job 11:7) and much, much more on issues of religion (from the Latin *religare*, to tie back/to restrain). In other words, monotheists tend to emphasize observance, or what the Deity expects of man, not theology, or what man expects of Deity.

76. "Evil," denoting calamity, suffering and punishment for human sins. As opposed to moral evil, or the sins, crimes and wrongs that men commit. See Amos 3:6 and commentaries. "The Lord" — *HaShem*/the Name.

77. See *Sefer HaMitzvot* 2:10 with the Chavel commentary (in the Soncino edition of 1967, supra).

78. The Hebrew term is *shittuf* — associate. See Talmud, *Sanhedrin* 63b; Novak, supra, pp. 130-137.

79. The Hebrew term is *shuttfut* — partner. See Talmud, *Sanhedrin* 63a, *Sukkot* 45b; Novak, supra, ibid.

80. *Encyclopedia Talmudit*, 2:350. See Novak, supra, p. 131, with the other sources cited there.

81. See, e.g., Hosea 6:6 with commentaries; Mishnah, *Pirke Avot* 6:11; Talmud, *Sanhedrin* 98b.

82. That is, bowing, sacrificing, etc., before or to the thing being worshipped.

83. See Isaiah 44:6 and Deuteronomy 4:19 with Rashi; Mishnah, *Shevuot* 11:2; Talmud, *Sanhedrin* 63, *Sukkot* 45b, *Megillah* 9b with Rashi; *Yad, Hilchot Melachim* 9:2, *Shevuot* 11:2, *Hilchot Avoda Zorah* 1:1; *Sefer HaMitzvot* 1:7; Novak, supra, p. 130.

84. All depends on one's deeds. See, e.g., Mishnah, *Pirke Avot* 3:19, 1:15,17, *Eduyot* 5:7, *Ta'anit* 2:1 (on Jonah 3:10).

85. Or sacrificing, etc.

86. See *Yad, Hilchot Melachim* 9:2, *Hilchot Avodot Kochavim 3:4*.

87. See Rabbenu Tam, *Tosefot* to Talmud, *Avoda Zorah* 2a, *Sanhedrin* 63b; Novak, supra, pp. 131-134.

88. See Talmud, *Sanhedrin* 63a, *Sukkot* 45b; Maimonides, *Siraj,* Commentary on the Mishnah, *Avoda Zorah* 4:7.

89. See *Sefer HaMitzvot* 1:7.

90. See, e.g., Jeremiah 17:10 and commentaries; Psalms 7:10, 37:4, 147:3.

91. E.g., angels, or the Buddha, or Jesus/*Yeshua*, or a planet, natural force, leader or great teacher, imagined in the role of an intercessor with or a channeler between men and true Divinity, God.

92. See Mishnah, *Arachin* 4:13, *Sanhedrin* 8:7; Talmud, *Sanhedrin* 28a, *Yevamot* 101a.

93. See Exodus 32:4 with Midrash, *Exodus Rabbah* 42:3 and Talmud, *Sanhedrin* 63a. Even considering that the worshipper might go beyond merely reflecting on the intercessor mentally, by — for instance — honoring the venerated person's grave, or lighting a candle before the intercessor's image. But treating the intercessor like a god — bowing and scraping, say, before its image — is adoration beyond mere veneration, and intolerable. See above, with *Yad, Hilchot Melachim* 9:2.

94. Historian, c. 1817-1901 CE. Epigram attributed through *Jewish Quarterly Review of London*, 1889, Vol. 1, p. 9.

95. Talmud, *Sanhedrin* 63b. See Novak, supra, p. 131.

96. See Genesis 15:16; Exodus 34:11; Leviticus 20:23; Deuteronomy 12:30; Talmud, *Shabbat* 67a; *Sefer HaMitzvot* 2:30; *Moreh Nevuchim* 3:37. The Amorites were one of the (ancient) Canaanite nations.

97. For a scholarly treatment of some of the different considerations and points of view see Novak, supra, "Idolatry," pp. 107-148.

98. See Leviticus 18:21, 20:5; Deuteronomy 18:10; Leviticus 18:21 with Rashi; *Yad, Hilchot Avodat Kochavim* 6:4; *Sefer HaMitzvot* 2:7. Before Israel supplanted them, the ancient Canaanites used to serve their god Molech in this manner in the valley called Gehenna, or *Gei Hinnom,* just west of the Jerusalem city walls. See, e.g., Joshua 15:8 and Jeremiah 7:31-32. A defiled place, Gehenna later came to be associated with paganism's Hell — i.e., as an utterly unholy realm dominated by the Norse goddess Hel, queen of the underworld, daughter of Loki the Trickster. See Frazer, *The Golden Bough,* supra.

99. Deuteronomy 12:30-31. Whether Molech-worship actually involved the fatal burning of children or just passing them through a flame is disputed. See *Yad, Hilchot Avodat Kochavim* 6:3 and Nachmanides on Leviticus 18:21. The Canaanites certainly fatally sacrificed human beings to some idols. See, e.g., 2 Kings 17:31. Many commentators believe that the phenomenon of young Muslim suicide bombers, encouraged by their peers and loved one to immolate themselves — along with their targeted enemies — as fiery sacrifices to a "higher cause," such as the destruction of Jewish Israel or the humiliation of the West, represents a modern revival of this evil.

100. Mishnah, *Sanhedrin* 7; *Sefer HaMitzvot* 2:7.

101. On Israel's all-out war against human sacrifice see, e.g., Genesis 22, Deuteronomy 12:31, and Judges 11:30-40 with commentaries; Talmud, *Rosh HaShana* 16a; Hertz, supra, pp. 201 and 804.

102. See Exodus 21:24 and Leviticus 24:20; Talmud, Sanhedrin 37a; Yad, *Hilchot Melachim* 3:10; 9:14.

103. Psalm 51:19. See, e.g., Hosea 6:6.

104. A soothsayer: literally, a "cloud-gazer" — an omen gatherer, an observer of mystic "signs" or portents.

105. Deuteronomy 18:10. See Leviticus 20:23. Witchcraft and idolatry are not necessarily the same thing. Though witchcraft certainly carries an idolatrous germ, it doesn't necessarily or in every case constitute a total betrayal of God. See the discussion in the Talmud, *Sanhedrin* 56b-60a; *Yad, Hilchot Avodat Kochavim* 6:2; *Shulchan Aruch, Yoreh Deah* 179:22; Lichtenstein, supra, p. 66. But one could do worse than to heed every detail of Deuteronomy 18:10, especially in light of the Talmud's Rabbi Yossi's argument (*Sanhedrin* 56b) concerning the universal overwhelming pertinence of the Torah's eight anti-witchcraft ordinances.

106. Deuteronomy 18:13. See Leviticus 20:23; *Yad, Hilchot Avodat Kochavim* 11:16; Hertz, supra, p. 313.

107. *Sefer HaHinnuch*, Imperative 510.

108. "Occult" — concealed, hidden, never publicly revealed. The Torah teaches that God is close to all who humbly call on Him (See, e.g., Psalm 145:18), but idolatry generally, and witchcraft particularly, holds that effective communion with the Ultimate requires secret knowledge or supernatural powers.

109. Talmud, *Nedarim* 32a.

110. *Sefer HaHinnuch,* Imperative 510. God who gives man free will has free will Himself.

111. Such as throwing bones, or using cards or tea leaves. One such method, popular in ancient times, involved consulting a staff — a walkingstick or cane. See Hosea 4:12 and commentaries.

112. Deuteronomy 18:10 and commentaries. Many people are more or less amazingly intuitive and sensitive to very subtle clues about the people around them. Their natural, logical deductive power often seems uncanny to those less knowledgeable or gifted in those ways. Superstition is always ready, unfortunately, to declare the natural supernatural.

113. *Sefer HaMitzvot* 2:31.

114. Deuteronomy 18:14-22 and commentaries. See Deuteronomy 30:10-14. The central message of all the prophets can be summarized: "You! Remember the Torah of Moses My servant, which I commanded unto him in Horeb [Sinai] for all Israel, [including] decrees and laws." — Malachi 3:22. On the subject of prophecy generally, including grades of prophecy, criteria for recognizing a prophet, etc., see Kaplan, *Handbook of Jewish Thought,* supra, chapters 6-11. As for magic, see Rambam, Yad, *Avodat Kochavim* 11:16 and *Moreh Nevuchim* 3:37 for the classic proposition that magic is all nothing more than trickery — "foolishness." Also see, e.g., Isaiah 47:12 (on a closely related subject). But other commentaries posit a world or range of heavenly forces, under God, that adepts — like Pharaoh's court magicians, fighting against Aaron and Moses (see Exodus 7:22 with Rashi) — can sometimes influence to actual supernatural effect. See Ramban, *Derech HaShem* on Deuteronomy 18:9.

115. This being Israel's great mission, to lead the nations to God's truth. See Isaiah 42:6, 43:10, 59:21; Talmud, *Pesachim* 87b; *Yad, Hilchot Melachim* 8:10, 11:4.

116. Talmud, *Nedarim* 32a.

117. *Yad, Hilchot Teshuva* 5:5.

118. See Jeremiah 10:2 with Talmud, *Shabbat* 156a; *Yad, Hilchot Avodat Kochavim* 11:5,6,16.

119. Deuteronomy 18:10. See Exodus 22:17; Leviticus 19:26; *Sefer HaMitzvot* 2:31-34.

120. *Moreh Nevuchim* 3:37. People tend to think that just because some belief is old, there must be something to it. But if there were any truth to witchery, witches and warlocks would rule the earth and the Hebrew Revolution, including the laws here, would be a dead letter. Apparently, the false ideas of idolatry and witchery are bound to keep recurring until God's truth eventually universally supplants them.

121. Deuteronomy 18:10 and Midrash, *Sifre* to Deuteronomy 18:10. See *Sefer HaMitzvot* 2:32; *Yad, Hilchot Avodat Kochavim* 11:15.

122. Nor sorceress, nor a male witch, or sorcerer. Leviticus 20:27. See Hertz, supra, p. 313.

123. Exodus 22:17; Deuteronomy 18:10; Mishnah, *Sanhedrin* 6:4; *Sefer HaMitzvot* 2:34, 2:310.

124. God directs the sick among Israel to doctors — physicians, not doctors of divinity. See Exodus 21:19 and commentaries.

125. *Yad, Hilchot Avodat Kochavim* 11:15.

126. *Yad,* ibid, 11:16. Consider the influence of sorcery, or the fear of sorcery, in retarding the progress of almost the whole continent of Africa. See, e.g., Geoffery Parrinder, *Witchcraft* (Pelican, London, 1958); Jack Mendelsohn, *God, Allah and Ju Ju* (Beacon Press, Boston MA, 1962).

127. Some believe that women, speaking only very generally, tend to be more taken by the lure of the occult than are men. See Talmud, *Pesachim* 100b.

128. Mishnah, *Sanhedrin* 7; *Sefer HaHinnuch,* Imperative 62; *Sefer HaMitzvot* 2:34, 2:310. Also see Deuteronomy 22:24 and *Sefer HaMitzvot* 1:229 (sorcery as an offence punishable by stoning).

129. Leviticus 19:31. Literally, "attendant spirits," a spirit, ghost or demon hidden from other people.

130. Leviticus 19:31; Deuteronomy 18:10-11 and comentaries. See *Sefer HaMitzvot* 2:8-9, 2:36-38.

131. Leviticus 20:27.

132 See *Yad, Hilchot Avodat Kochavim* 6:2.

133. *Yad, Hilchot Avodat Kochavim* 11:11-12. See *Yad, Hilchot Yesodey HaTorah* 10:3.

134. 1 Samuel 28:7-20.

135. R. Shmuel ben Hofni Gaon, Maimonides, R. Ibn Ezra, R. Levi ben Gershom (Ralbag, or Gersonides). But, noting that the witch seemed to be more surprised than anyone by the success of her necromancy (1 Samuel 28:12), some — R. Saadya, R. Chai Gaon, Nachmanides — suppose that, in this one instance, God caused her to see an apparition of Samuel, to announce Saul's punishing fate.

136. Deuteronomy 18:11 with Rashi. "The dead"/*doresh el ha-metim.* Literally, "a spirit of uncleanness." God makes a clear distinction between the living and the dead; the living defile themselves when they try to blur it by seeking excessive contact with the dead. See, e.g., Genesis 3:19; 1 Samuel 28:7-20.

137. Talmud, *Sanhedrin* 65b.

138. *Sefer HaMitzvot* 2:38.

139. See Leviticus 19:31 with *Yad, Hilchot Avodat Kochavim* 6:1 and *Sefer HaMitzvot* 2:8-9 and 2:36-37, describing the sorcery of the *ob,* or "ghost," and the sorcery of the *yidde'oni,* or "familiar spirit."

140. Deuteronomy 18:10-11; *Sefer HaMitzvot* 2:35.

141. Deuteronomy 18:11; Midrash, *Sifre* to Deuteronomy 18:11; *Sefer HaMitzvot* 2:35.

142. See Mishnah, *Sanhedrin* 10:1; *Yad, Hilchot Avodat Kochavim* 11:12; *Moreh Nevuchim* 1:6.

143. Talmud, *Ta'anit* 2a.

144. "You shall not try the Lord your God." Deuteronomy 6:16. See *Sefer HaMitzvot* 2:64.

145. See *Yad, Hilchot Avodat Kochavim* 11:11-12. Naturally, the prohibition here doesn't apply to the use of special phrases solely to comfort or encourage someone, be he the speaker or the listener. Nor does it apply to blessings, or true prayer, meant to generally invoke God's favor. Neither does it apply to one who recites prayers or words of Scripture, "in order that he may be shielded by the merit of the recital and saved from trouble and hurt." *Yad,* ibid.

146. See 2 Samuel 22:7; Psalm 130:1; Mishnah, *Berachot* 5:1; Talmud, *Sanhedrin* 22a on Psalm 16:8.

147. Talmud, *Shabbat* 55a. See, e.g., Zechariah 8:16; Psalm 51:8; Proverbs 12:22; Daniel 4:34.

148. Exodus 23:7.

149. Deuteronomy 18:10-14 and 18:20-22.

150. Deuteronomy 18:20; *Sefer HaMitzvot* 2:26. See Talmud, *Sanhedrin* 89a (regarding the punishment).

151. Exodus 23:13. See *Sefer HaMitzvot* 2:26, 2:14; Leviticus 19:4; Talmud, *Sanhedrin* 63a with Rashi.

152. Deuteronomy 18:20.

153. Deuteronomy 18:20; *Sefer HaMitzvot* 2:27. The two prohibitions above, against prophesying in the name of an idol and against prophesying falsely, apply even if the false prophet tries, through his lies, to support the Torah or the validity of any one or all of its Commandments. Talmud, *Sanhedrin* 89a.

154. Deuteronomy 13:4; *Sefer HaMitzvot* 2:28.

155. Deuteronomy 18:22; *Sefer HaMitzvot* 2:29.

156. *Yad, Hilchot Avodat Kochavim* 5:7,9; Midrash, *Sifre* to Deuteronomy 18:22. See Maimonides, *Siraj*/Commentary on the Mishnah, Introduction to *Zera'im*.

157. Deuteronomy 13:7-14; Mishnah, *Sanhedrin,* 7:6; *Yad, Hilchot Avodat Kochavi*n 3:4. A *Meisit* — one who misleads an individual. A *Meidiach* — one who misleads a group or community. See Talmud, *Sanhedrin* 63b; *Sefer HaMitzvot* 2:15-16.

158. Deuteronomy 13:10.

159. *Yad, Hilchot Teshuva* 4:1. Unforgivable, even by a Heavenly Court, because one can fully atone only for one's own transgressions, not for those that one has misled or incited others to commit.

160. See Exodus 23:13; Deuteronomy 13:7-14; Talmud, *Sanhedrin* 63b, 67a; *Sefer HaMitzvot* 2:15-16.

161. "Make no mention." Even to the extent of one saying to his friend, "Wait for me at the place of such-and-such an idol." Talmud, *Sanhedrin* 63b.

162. Exodus 23:13; Leviticus 19:4; Talmud, *Sanhedrin* 63a-b; *Sefer HaMitzvot* 2:14.

163. Midrash, *Mechilta* to *Exodus* 23:13; *Sefer HaMitzvot* 2:14.

164. Rabbenu Moshe Isserles, Moshe ben Yisrael, also known as Ramo, Rama, or Rema, 1525-1572 CE), on *Shulchan Aruch, Orach Haim* 156:1.

165. See, e.g., Mishnah, *Sotah* 9:15; Talmud, *Sanhedrin* 97a, 98b and commentaries.

166. Midrash, *Sifre* to Deuteronomy 13:9.

167. That is, plead in his favor before a court. See *Sefer HaMitzvot* 2:20.

168. That is, suppress or withold any incriminating evidence against him. See *Sefer HaMitzvot* 2:21.

169. After trial and conviction before a properly constituted court. Deuteronomy 13:15. See Mishnah, *Sanhedrin* 5:1, *Sanhedrin* 7.

170. Deuteronomy 13:9-11. See *Sefer HaMitzvot* 2:17-21. Against the general, positive Imperative, "You shall love your neighbor as yourself." — Leviticus 19:18; *Sefer HaMitzvot* 1:206 — Scripture interposes the specific

legal prohibition, "You shall not consent [*tove*/"show affection"] to him [an idolator]." — Deuteronomy 13:9; *Sefer HaMitzvot* 2:17. Note, however, that Naomi incurred no guilt for advising her Gentile daughters-in-law to return to probably inevitable idolatry (Ruth 1:8-15, with commentaries). Naomi was no misleader; she was simply recognizing that people will do what they think they need to do. Also see 2 Kings 5:18-19 (the prophet Elisha and Na'aman, a Syrian).

171. *Yad, Hilchot Melachim* 9:2. See Exodus 20:5, 22:19; Leviticus 17:7, 20:3,5; Numbers 15:31, 25:3; Deuteronomy 12:30; *Sefer HaMitzvot* 2:5,6.

172. Following *Yad, Hilchot Melachim* 9:2. See the discussion of this issue in the Talmud, *Sanhedrin* 56b, 60b, and Lichtenstein, supra, pp. 59-67. Also see Clorfene and Rogalsky, supra, ch. 5, pp. 48-73, and the sources cited there.

173. See Habakuk 2:14; Isaiah 66; Zechariah 14; *Yad, Hilchot Melachim* 3:8, 8:10-11, 9:2.

174. *Yad, Hilchot Yesodey HaTorah* 1:6.

175. *Sefer HaMitzvot* 2:1 and 2:2-30; *Yad, Hilchot Teshuva* 3:14.

176. Isaiah 43:10.

177. Consider how Rachel stole away with her father Laban's idols (*teraphim*/idolatrous figurines), not to use them but to keep him from using them. See Genesis 31:19.

178. See *Yad, Hilchot Melachim* 9:2, and commentaries. But one who ignores official warnings or commands and continues to transgress a lawful prohibition, holding authority in contempt, may be punished, criminally, as a disorderly, rebellious person. See, e.g., *Yad, Hilchot Melachim* 3:8.

179. Exodus 20:3 and commentaries; *Sefer HaHinnuch,* Imperative 26.

180. See Midrash, *Mechilta* to *Exodus* 20:2; Talmud, *Shabbat* 87a, *Makkot* 23b-24a; *Sefer HaMitzvot* 1:1; Midrash, *Sifre* to Numbers 15:22; *Moreh Nevuchim* 3:29.

181. *Mechilta* to Exodus 20:5.

182. See *Yad, Hilchot Melachim* 9:2.

183. Exodus 20:4; Leviticus 19:4; Deuteronomy 4:15-19; *Sefer HaMitzvot* 2:2-3.

184. Exodus 20:20; Mishnah, *Avoda Zorah* 3; *Sefer HaMitzvot* 2:4.

185. *Yad, Hilchot Melachim* 9:2 and commentaries. See *Sefer HaMitzvot* 2:2-30.

186. Leviticus 19:4, Deuteronomy 11:16, 12:30, and commentaries; *Sefer HaMitzvot* 2:10.

187. *Sefer HaMitzvot* 2:30. See Zephaniah 1:8. Not just odd clothing but odd haircuts, jewelry, or mere attendance at such events as seances are objectionable, when they partake of witchery, idolatry, cruelty, lewdness, foreign religious mysteries, or the superstitious.

188. Leviticus 18:3, 20:23, and commentaries; *Sefer HaMitzvot* 2:30. See Talmud, *Shabbat* 67a.

189. Deuteronomy 12:30. See Talmud, *Shabbat* 67a, enumerating many or most of these practices.

190. Making or even directing someone else to make *any* image for anyone to worship constitutes, in Torah, a corporal offense. See Exodus 20:4, 20:20; Leviticus 19:4; Deuteronomy 4:15-19; *Yad, Hilchot Avodat Kochavim* 3:9; *Sefer HaMitzvot* 2:2-3.

191. *Yad, Hilchot Melachim* 9:2. See Leviticus 26:1; Deuteronomy 16:21-22; *Sefer HaMitzvot* 2:11-13.

192. Leviticus 26:1; Deuteronomy 16:22.

193. *Yad, Hilchot Melachim* 9:2. See *Yad, Hilchot Avodat Kochavim* 3:10-11 for the parameters of this restriction. Generally, representational art is perfectly permissible, but monumental three-dimensional images — sculptures or carvings — of human beings are not, if they go so far in depicting the details of the human face as to represent the pupils of the eyes. Such extremely realistic human reliefs or statuary may, eventually, turn into idols, or influence children badly. See Mishnah, *Avoda Zorah* 3; *Sefer HaMitzvot* 2:4.

194. Zechariah 1:3.

195. See, e.g., Exodus 15:2; Psalms 3:4, 27:1, 31:24, 145:18.

196. See Exodus 5:2 with commentaries.

197. "Fearing God" — the feeling that humanizes man's dealings with his fellow creatures, the voice of kindliness and conscience. See Genesis 20:11; Exodus 1:17; Deuteronomy 25:18; and commentaries.

198. Mishnah, *Pirke Avot* 2:4.

199. Deuteronomy 10:13. See Micah 6:8, and commentaries.

200. See Leviticus 21 and, e.g., *Sefer HaMitzvot* 2:68-71,84,158-162,165-168.

201. See Numbers 18; *Sefer HaMitzvot* 1:23,129. As for both the priest, or *cohen*, and the Levite, most but not all of their legal rights and obligations pertain only in the land of Israel, mostly relating to service in Israel's Temple — which is no more — in Jerusalem. See, e.g., *Shulchan Aruch, Yoreh Deah* 61:21.

202. Exodus 19:5. See, e.g., Isaiah 2:3.

203. Mishnah, *Pirke Avot* 1:2; Talmud, *Gittin* 59b. See, e.g., Psalms 19:8, 119:1,142,165.

204. *Sifre* on Numbers 43. "Words of Torah" — most certainly including the Noahide laws that are learned from Torah.

205. See *Yad, Hilchot Melachim* 8:11: Anyone who keeps the Seven Commandments is one of the Pious [the righteous] among the Nations and merits the World to Come [eternal life], but only if he accepts and fulfills them because God Himself commanded them. If he keeps them out of mere intellectual conviction [as to their social utility], without acknowledging them as Divine Commandments, he is neither Pious nor deserving of a share in the World to Come . . . ." Also see *Yad*, ibid, 9:1, and *Hullin* 7:6. Allegiance to the Lawgiver is a must if one hopes to completely fulfill or properly carry out His laws. Denying His power (including His ability to give men law) or existence, or the great and amazing truth that He loves us enough to give us this guiding Law, is itself impious.

206. R. Yochanan ben Zakkai, *Berachot* 28b. See Psalms 2:11, 19:10, 111:10; Proverbs 1:7, 8:13, 9:10.

207. *Mishnah Tosefta, Sanhedrin* 13:2; *Yad, Hilchot Teshuva* 3:5: "The pious of all nations have a share in the World to Come." See Midrash, *Sifre* to Leviticus 18:5; Talmud, *Avoda Zorah* 3a, *Sanhedrin* 105a.

208. Mishnah, *Pirke Avot* 2:6, in the name of Hillel.

209. See Talmud, *Kiddushin* 40b, in the name of Rabbi Akiva.

210. *Pesachim* 50a, in the name of R. Yosef ben Yehoshua. "[T]he

Hereafter" — the afterworld, Eternity. "Learning" — Torah knowledge, moral knowledge; learning in God's Law.

211. R. Shimon ben Lakish, Midrash to Proverbs 2:4.

212. Mishnah, *Pirke Avot* 1:16, in the name of R. Gamaliel.

213. "Who is wise? He who learns from every person." Mishnah, *Pirke Avot* 4:1. See Psalm 119:99.

214. See Talmud, *Ta'anit* 7a, in the name of R. Yehuda HaNasi: "I learned much from my teachers, more from my colleagues, and most from my students." Also see, e.g., Talmud, *Pesachim* 25b. "Get yourself a teacher and also [separately] a study partner." — *Pirke Avot* 1:6.

215. R. Shimon ben Eleazar, *Avoda Zorah* 6:18.

216. Talmud, *Yoma* 4b. "Study in joy and good cheer, in accordance with your intelligence and heart's dictates." — Rashi on *Shabbat* 63b. On qualifying as a good student, see, especially, Mishnah, *Pirke Avot* 6:6.

217. High Holiday (Rosh HaShana and Yom Kippur) Prayerbook/ *Machzor,* the *Amidah.*

218. See Deuteronomy 33:4; Talmud, *Sanhedrin* 59a; Bleich, *Contemporary Halachic Problems*, supra, Vol. 2, "Teaching Torah to Non-Jews," pp. 311-341. A Ben Noah who studies Torah with arrogant, frivolous or bad intent deserves punishment through God's courts, not from man's. See *Yad, Hilchot Melachim* 10:9 with commentaries.

219. Talmud, *Sanhedrin* 59a. See Bleich, "Teaching Torah to Non-Jews," supra.

220. See, e.g., Exodus 19:5; Deuteronomy 7:6; Isaiah 2:3, 42:6 with Rashi; *Yad, Hilchot Melachim* 8:10. A Jew should rush to help such a person: a Ben Noah who studies Torah to learn how to keep the path of the Noahide Law "is like a *cohen gadol/*a high priest of Israel." Talmud, *Sanhedrin* 59a. See Yosef ben Shlomo Hakohen, *The Universal Jew* (Feldheim, Nanuet NY, 1995) p. 105.

221. *Pirke Avot* 4:7, in the name of R. Tzadok. See Hillel, ibid. at 1:13, 4:7. Trying to turn the Divine gift of the Torah into a device for making money is a mortal sin. Although the teacher of Torah, no less than the laborer, or engineer, deserves a fair wage for his time and effort. See, e.g., Talmud, *Nedarim* 37a, *Bava Metzia* 85a (in the name of R. ben Eliezer), and *Sanhedrin* 19b.

222. Commentary on the Talmud, *Bava Metzia* 33b.

223. "The Jews are the intensive form of any nationality whose language and customs they adopt." *Epistle to the Hebrews*, (1882) in Morris Schappes, ed., *Emma Lazarus: Selections From Her Poetry and Prose* (Cooperative Book League, New York NY, 1944). "The Jews are just like other people, only more so." Proverb, quoted in Arthur Koestler, *Promise and Fulfillment* (Simon & Schuster, New York NY, 1949) p. 287.

224. See, e.g., Genesis 12:3, 27:29; Leviticus 20:26; Isaiah 42:6, 43:10, 54:17.

225. See, e.g., Genesis 1:27; Leviticus 19:18, 19:34; Talmud, *Shabbat* 31a; and commentaries.

226. Hillel, Talmud, *Pesachim* 66b.

227. Genesis 49:10 with Rashi; See, e.g., Deuteronomy 4:31, 30:11-12; Isaiah 59:21.

228. Some of the people can be wrong all of the time and all of the

people some of the time, but not all of the people all of the time. With credit to Abraham Lincoln.

229. This prayerbook, despite minor variations between the ones used over the centuries in Yemen, say, or Russia, Hungary or Babylonia/Iraq, etc., is always, everywhere, basically the same.

230. Literally, the Prepared Table, c. 1564 CE, together with the gloss by Rabbi Moshe Isserles (Ramo, or Rema, 1525?-1573?). In every part of the world, every Jewish community that succesfully maintained itself as Jewish has studied, accepted and lived the *Shulchan Aruch*, over many generations. The only significant exception is the Jewish community of Ethiopia — the Black Jews of Africa, who had the Bible but were cut off from their brethren and from every other Hebrew sourcebook. Recently, their situation has changed dramatically — largely, since 1980, with a massive airlift to Israel.

231. See, e.g., Psalms 55:17-18, 65:3, 94:9, 145:18; *Siddur*/Prayerbook, *Tachanun, Ana Melech* (end).

232. See Deuteronomy 6:5; Talmud, *Shabbat* 119b.

233. Along with kabbalah, a major, very vital school of Jewish thought, *hasidus (chasidus)*, the hasidic (chasidic), enjoys parables and stories "where the heart fools the mind." Each hasidic group, of which there are several, also strongly emphasizes the teachings of its own leaders — which teachings are *not* necessarily accepted by mainstream Orthodox Jewry.

234. See Exodus 24:10 or, e.g., Genesis 30:37-43, with commentaries.

235. See, e.g., Ezekiel 1:1,4.

236. Talmud, *Hagigah* 14b.

237. Deuteronomy 29:29. Where kabbalah frequently claims to represent the "soul" of the Torah, what passes for kabbalah frequently denies the central tenets of Torah, such as the Oneness of God and the "made in the [Divine] Image" quality of every human soul.

238. *Mishnah Tosefta, Hagigah* 2:1; Talmud, *Yoma* 69b, *Hagigah* 14b-15b.

239. One must be demonstrably mature and also possessed of independent Torah insight, being already fully versed in both the Written and Oral Torah, before being admitted to kabbalistic exercises or any such confusing mystic speculations. Mishnah, *Hagigah* 2:1; Midrash, *Exodus Rabbah* 3:15; *Yad, Hilchot Yesodey haTorah* 4:13; *Shulchan Aruch, Orach Haim* 664. How trustworthy can the teacher be who violates these extremely basic precepts?

240. See Deuteronomy 30:12.

241. To do "justice," or *mishpat*. Literally, lawfulness, rightness, the fair, square and decent thing. To love "goodness," or *hesed (chesed)*: loving-kindness, or the spirit of mercy translated into deeds. To walk "humbly," or *tzana* (see Proverbs 11:2): modesty, chastity, personal dignity and purity.

Revolutionary Doctrine

ISRAEL'S THIRTEEN PRINCIPLES OF FAITH

My soul thirsts for God, for the living God.
— Psalm 42:3
What is most essential to emphasize at this point is that the fundamental principles of our faith are embraced in thirteen basic principles. — Maimonides[1]

After finishing with idolatry, we need to attend to idolatry's opposite. If you try to break Revelation down into its fewest common elements, or consistent core ideas, you come out with just Thirteen Principles.* These are the underlying doctrines of the Hebrew Revolution.

They can be divided into three groups. The first five set out Israel's theology:

1) God exists.

2) He is one.

3) He is spirit, not matter.

4) He is eternal.

5) He alone may be worshipped.

The next four deal with the inspiration, or Revelation, of the Written and the Oral Torah:

6) God communicates with humanity through His prophets.

7) Moses is and was unique among all God's other prophets.

8) The Lord Revealed His Law — His Torah — through Moses.

9) His Law is eternal and immutable — the Law won't be replaced by another set of laws.

The last four go to man's responsibility, and reward and punishment:

10) The All-Knowing One knows every action and every thought.

11) He rewards those who obey His will and punishes those who reject Him.

12) Before the Earth ends, the Messiah will come.

13) Some of the dead will live again.

Israel has collectively accepted these Thirteen Principles, which are restated in every Hebrew *Siddur*, or prayerbook, and repeated in the daily Hebrew prayers.[2]

Naturally, every Ben Noah — every non-Jew — need not personally subscribe to each and every Principle. Even though Israel believes that one needs no inspiration but only logic to distill them from Revelation for oneself.

Correct knowledge of God has never been one of the minimal requisites of decent human conduct. But study, and logic, always lead back to these same Thirteen Principles.

Most of the commentary below follows the classic commentaries of Maimonides.[3]

I believe with perfect faith. . . . — *Siddur*[4]

ONE

Believe in the existence of the Creator, a perfect Being, the Supreme Cause of everything in existence. Nothing exists without Him. But He, Who is Self-contained, can exist without any other thing. All things and beings, in heaven, on earth, and everywhere in this and every universe, depend on Him for their existence.

> I believe in the sun, even when it is not shining; I believe in love, even when not feeling it; I believe in God, even when He is silent.
> — *Anonymous* [5]

TWO

Believe in the Unity of the Lord — that He Who is the Cause of all things is One; that He alone is God; that there are no gods nor other beings with Him nor besides Him; that He cannot be divided. He is One by virtue of a Unity which is unlike any other unity, that surpasses every other unity.

All is *not* one. God unifies Creation, and He alone faithfully sustains its every atom, but the Creator and Creation are not the same.

If all Creation were non-existent He alone would still exist.

The non-existence of His creatures would not involve His non-existence. All beings are dependent on Him but He is not dependent on them.

His real essence is separate from and unlike that of any of them. He Who is infinite is, by virtue of His essence, no more divisible than a geometric point.

It follows that, since there are no other gods than God, the One Creator, all human beings are equally His children — of Him, by Him, and (spiritually) even remarkably somewhat *like* Him. [6]

THREE

Believe that this One Being is incorporeal, without any physical shape or form whatsoever. [7]

Physical matter — even a single atom or electron — can always be divided. Everything corporeal is divisible; nothing corporeal can be a complete and perfect unity. Therefore, God in His total Oneness cannot be physically material. Neither is He reducible to a force or power within any physical body. Nor is He subject to any of the accidents that affect the material and physical, such as movement, growth or decomposition.

His essence is spiritual — spirit — rather than material.

Scripture repeatedly sets forth the truth that God cannot be a physical body. "The Lord is God in Heaven above and upon all the Earth beneath."[8] A physical body cannot be in two places at one time.

God has neither similitude nor peer.[9] "To whom then will you liken Me, or shall I equal?"[10] The answer is no one — none. If He were a corporeal, physical, material body, He would be like other bodies.

Every Scriptural expression that seems to impart animal or human attributes to God is rhetorical. Such attributes exist only in physical beings. God is infinitely blessed and exalted above the merely physical.

To all such expressions applies the saying, "Scripture speaks in the language of men."[11] The human mind can no more comprehend God's essential nature — His nature as He really is — than an ant can comprehend man's essential nature, or a dog grasp our highest thoughts. "Can you, by searching, find out God? Can you find out the Almighty to Perfection?"[12]

FOUR

Believe in God's eternity. The Universe and everything that has been, is, or ever will be exists only because of Him. He was first in time, He will be last in time. He is eternal and everlasting. He existed before the beginning and He will exist beyond the end of the Universe.[13]

FIVE

Believe that eternal God alone, the One Lord, the Creator, may rightly be worshipped and exalted. "The Eternal is the true God."[14] That is, He alone is divine; there are no other gods and there is no other god but God.

"There is no one else besides Him."[15] That is, there is nothing and no one like Him. So we are to worship nobody and nothing else than God Himself, and we are to act in such manner only toward Him.

Nothing else below Him deserves man's prayer or worship — neither His angels,[16] the stars, the elements or their compounds, nor forces, nor any of His other creations; nor any of man's creations.

SIX

Believe that God has communicated or "spoken" to human beings through His prophets.

We are to recognize that God chooses certain individuals who possess such excellent qualities and such pure and receptive souls that they can attain prophecy — the interaction of the prophet's powers of reason with the emanations from God's own divine Intellect.

Life has meaning. People are not just scuzz on the surface of a planet: we are each unique, and unique as a species; we exist in God's image! The Lord and Creator of the infinite cosmos can actually, as He wills it, communicate intelligibly with our species through our own kind — that is, through His prophets.

SEVEN

Believe that Moses is and was unique among all God's other prophets, and that his prophecy is not merely true, but of a quality unapproached by any other prophet before or since.[17]

Moses' prophecy differs from the prophecy of all others in four ways:

1) In the case of all other [genuine] prophets, the Creator communicates with them only indirectly, through intermediaries or angels. But with Moses He communicated directly, with no intermediary.[18]

2) In the case of all other prophets, prophecy comes to them only in the course of natural sleep,[19] or when overtaken by a deep and sudden sleep.[20] But prophecy came to Moses while he was conscious and awake.[21]

3) Even though coming by means of intermediaries, in visions cushioned by sleep, all other prophets are weakened, fatigued, pained or frightened by the experience of prophecy.[22] But "the Lord spoke unto Moses face to face, as a man speaks unto his friend."[23] Moses' reason was in such intense union with the Divine Intellect that Moses felt no fear — just as one feels no fear while conversing with a friend.

4) Other prophets prepare themselves, clear their minds, and wait for prophecy — sometimes for days, sometimes for years. Prophecy doesn't come to them by their own will but only by the Will of the Lord. But Moses, following a certain point in his career,[24] could confidently say: "Stay, that I may hear what the Lord will Command concerning you."[25]

Israel puts Moses as far above all other prophets as the great composer Beethoven, say, stands above the writers for Alvin and the Chipmunks. Still, putting Moses below another prophet can't be said to contravene the Law of the Rainbow Covenant.

People have every right to value wisdom, from whatever source it may derive, as they see fit. What is absolutely contrary to the Universal law, however, is to impute divinity to any human being — whether Moses, Jesus (Yeshua or *Yeshua ben Yosef* of Galilee), the Buddha (Siddhartha Gautama), or anyone else — or to try to channel prayer through any human (or other) idol.

Prophets are God's servants, not His peers. God can inspire or communicate with people much as people, through their prayer and service, can communicate with God. Naturally, many nations other than Israel have had their prophets.[26] But prophecy in the Biblical sense came to an end with Zechariah, Haggai and Malachi,[27] and won't return again until the Messianic Age.[28]

Once a great rabbi was arguing a point of law. A Talmudic legend recounts that he tried to strengthen his position by asking God to perform some supporting miracles. God obliged him! But his fellow rabbis still voted against him. They didn't accept his reasoning.

They based their decision upon their own (more rigorous) analysis — and also on the grounds that neither miracle nor prophecy ever supplants Torah. The rabbinic lesson being: God wants humanity to take responsibility for itself. He gave us His Torah complete, with all its pre-installed problem-solving processes and methods. So, obviously, just as He never contradicts Himself, nothing coming from Him — no miracle nor prophet nor mystic phenomenon whatever — will ever contradict, replace, or set aside this Torah.[29]

God's prophets have shown men the way. Now it's up to all of us to finish the work. When our race — the human race — has come closer to completing it, or at the beginning of the Messianic age, prophecy will come again.

Until then, and everywhere, if God wants us to be more responsible, He must restrict Himself from intervening in the legal process with Heavenly signs or miracles. The rabbis (in the case of Israel) must rule according to the Law.

EIGHT

Believe that the Five Books of Moses — *Humash* (*Chumash*), the Pentateuch, Law, or Torah, the first Five Books of the Bible, Genesis,

Exodus, Leviticus, Numbers, and Deuteronomy[30] — were all given to us, through Moses, from the Almighty.

Although the precise manner in which this was accomplished is unknown to us, having been known only to Moses, he was like a scribe who writes down what is dictated to him.[31]

Moses was absolutely trustworthy in this respect. "And Moses said: Hereby you shall know that the Lord sent me to do all these works, and that I have not done them of my own mind."[32]

Following Moses, other prophets, psalmists, and the authors of the Scripture's Writings also received varying degrees of Divine inspiration. As for the Written Torah's "other half," the so-called Oral Torah, the Mishnah and the Talmud, its wisdom is completely integral to the whole prophetic system.

The Oral Torah comes from consecutive revelations and a historically seamless process beginning from before Abraham, through Moses, and Sinai, carried on into the present through their heirs, the leaders and chief thinkers of the Hebrew Revolution.[33]

No generation of Israel ever completely dropped the baton. The Eternal Lord, by the hand of Moses, has entrusted Israel's Torah leaders, the Jews' judges, elders, priests and scholar-rabbis, with the continuing responsibility for interpreting and judiciously applying this Torah — and for precisely conveying it, according to revealed methods of exacting transmission, through successive generations.[34]

So this Oral Torah, including Israel's traditional interpretations of the Five Books, flows *very* reliably — Moses having done everything he could to ensure precisely that — from Sinai. The Written Torah itself guarantees it.[35] "You shall come unto the priests, the Levites, and unto the judges that shall be in those days, and inquire, and they shall tell you the sentence of judgment. And you shall do according to the sentence . . . according to the judgment which they shall teach you, you shall do."[36]

NINE

Believe that this Torah has been formulated by the Creator and by no one else. Its principles are eternal and immutable. Righteous conduct, as the Torah defines it, will always be righteousness. Evil, as the Torah defines it, will always be evil. Other, later Revelations may further elucidate God's commandments but will never reverse or contradict them.

We are to obey this eternal Torah now, immediately, as devotedly and precisely as we can. "Whatever I command you, observe to do it; you shall not add thereto, nor diminish from it."[37]

Knowing that the judgments and customary applications of the Law will always require an extension in some cases and curtailment in others, according to places, events and circumstances, God established the Hebrew Revolutionary system.

Israel may legislate certain temporary by-laws or fences around the Law, or agree to dispense with some religious act prescribed in the Law, if necessary, for the Law's own protection.[38] But none of God's laws can be changed or abrogated permanently. "By this method, the Law remains perpetually the same, and will yet admit at all times and under all circumstances such temporary modifications as are indispensable."[39]

TEN

Believe that God is conscious and aware of all the deeds and thoughts of humanity, and that His watchfulness over us is unceasing.[40]

This Principle is in total opposition to the opinion of those who maintain that the Lord has abandoned the Earth. Time and space impose no restrictions upon the Infinite Creator of time and space.

God is absolutely omniscient. He sees everything, from before the Beginning to beyond the end of this and every universe, and into the tiniest details of Creation. He even knows what people think. "The Lord sees not as men and women see . . . the Lord looks into the heart."[41]

ELEVEN

Believe that the Lord rewards those who fulfill His Law's commandments, and punishes those who transgress them.

Of all rewards, the greatest is that of inheriting a portion in the World to Come — i.e., after death. The greatest punishment is the soul's extinction.

God knows the transgressor and the sinner, and whom to reward and whom to punish. "Whoever has sinned against Me, him will I blot out of My book."[42]

Everything mortal must die;[43] their bodies will decompose. Our chemical particles are merely "dust."[44] But life is more than just gathered stardust. The soul, the animating spirit in all life, is not mortal. "Behold, all souls are Mine," God tells us.[45] "The dust returns to the earth as it was, and the soul returns to God who gave it."[46]

Every soul comes from God in an inherently pure condition: the way one leads his life affects the soul, for good or bad. "With the pure, God shows Himself pure."[47] The Eternal's love and mercy will envelope the beautiful soul with tender passion, forgiveness and redemption.[48] But for the coarsened souls of those who, rejecting His ways, have turned against Him, God's justice awaits. "The Lord is known for His justice."[49]

"[K]eep My statutes and My ordinances, which if a man do, he shall live in them" speaks not just of life but of life beyond life — of the World to Come.[50] It includes not just the Jews in its scope but every human being of every race and language.

"The righteous of all nations have a share in the World to Come."[51] As for the utterly evil person, "that soul shall be cut off."[52]

Much more than that we cannot know. God has not revealed it. "No living eye has seen the World to Come, O Lord, only you."[53]

Generally, Israel believes that a purgation or purging process may lie before most souls.[54] Based upon the Kabbalah, many Jews also believe that an incomplete soul may be reborn, or reincarnated.[55]

Remember that all Israel is called to believe that God is not merely just and not merely all-powerful but also loving, forgiving and kind. And that all the souls that receive even a tiny portion in the World to Come will receive incomparable goodness.[56] They will "delight in the radiance of the Divine Presence."[57]

TWELVE

Believe that the Era of the Messiah — in Hebrew, *HaMashiach*, or "The Anointed," God's appointed — will come. The human race, the people of Israel, and life on earth won't come to an end before all of them become drastically and obviously better.

> If you should happen to be holding a sapling in your hand when they tell you that the Messiah has arrived, first plant the sapling, then go and greet the Messiah.— *R. Yochanan ben Zakkai*[58]

Do not think that the new dispensation — the coming era's Redemption — will revoke the laws of nature. Don't expect any man or men, even including the Lord's Anointed, to perform miraculous signs or wonders, revive the dead, or do similar things. But do expect the Messiah to be a leader for Israel like Moses or King David. He will be a Jew of the tribe of Judah (rather than a Levite, *cohen* or "priest"), a descendant of David and his righteous ancestress Ruth (who was once a Noahide, then a convert).

Do expect the King Messiah to succeed.[59]

He will reign — he will rule Israel, not just as a moral leader but politically — for a long time. His influence will spread across the world while he lives; when he dies his own pious descendants will reign in his stead.[60]

We are to set no time for this Messiah's arrival,[61] nor try to use Scripture to calculate his coming. "Woe to them who make calculations of the End [i.e., the end of the current era]."[62]

Not only its time but the exact form the Redemption will take, and the processes that God might choose to use to effect it, must remain unknown until the time comes.[63] But the Messianic Age will take us to the last, highest stage of human evolution.

Knowledge, peace, world prosperity, unity, liberty and justice will be its hallmarks, right here on Earth: "it is not of Heaven."[64]

Eagerly, of their own accord, multitudes will pursue God and Torah.[65] Finally, the whole human race will come to recognize God's sovereignty, and accept His Universal laws.[66] Then "The earth shall be full of the knowledge of the Lord as the waters cover the sea."[67]

THIRTEEN

Believe in the resurrection of the dead. Some who are now dead, and some who live — or who will live — and die will live again.

God will deal with the souls of His creatures, after our bodies die, according to His Will, out of His infinite justice, love and compassion. But He is also all-powerful, and completely unrestricted in what He may do. So the details and mechanisms of resurrection are basically unknowable. Never revealed,[68] they are secret things; they are known and belong only to God.[69]

"This world [the world we live in] is like a vestibule before the World to Come. Prepare yourself in the vestibule so you can enter the banquet hall."[70]

Life on earth, in this world, deserves the concentrated attention of the living. "The way of life goes upward for the wise [person], that he may depart from the grave beneath."[71] Trust that the Lord, the God of judgment,[72] will do good unto the good.[73]

§§§§

NOTES

1. Commentary on the Mishnah (Cairo, 1168 CE), also known as the *Maor*, or Light, in Hebrew; first published in Arabic as the *Siraj*. Introduction to the Mishnah Torah, *Sanhedrin* 10.

2. In two frequently repeated prayers: *Yigdal* ("May He be Exalted") and *Ani Ma'amin* ("I Believe").

3. The *Maor*, or *Siraj*, supra, *Sanhedrin* 10; the *Mishneh Torah, Yad Hazaka*, or *Yad*; and *Moreh Nevuchim* ("Guide for the Perplexed").

4. *Ani Ma'amin* (recited after morning prayer), the *Shlosha Asar Ikkarim*, the Thirteen Principles of Faith.

5. On the wall of a cellar in the city of Cologne, where Jews had hidden from the enemy, this inscription was discovered after the Nazi Holocaust. Alfred J. Kolach, *Great Jewish Quotations* (Jonathan David, New York NY, 1996) p. 18.

6. Genesis 1:26, 27; Psalm 8:6; Job 31:15. "Man eats and drinks, performs natural functions and dies like an animal; he stands erect, thinks and has visions like an angel." — Midrash, *Genesis Rabbah* 14:3.

7. See, e.g., Deuteronomy 4:15; Isaiah 40:25.

8. Deuteronomy 4:39.

9. Deuteronomy 4:15.

10. Isaiah 40:25.

11. Midrash, *Genesis Rabbah* 31b.

12. Job 11:7.

13. See, e.g., Deuteronomy 33:27.

14. Jeremiah 10:10.

15. Deuteronomy 4:35.

16. "When God created the Universe, on the second Day He produced the angels, with their natural inclination to do good, and an absolute inability to commit sin." — Midrash, *Tanchuma* 76b. Some of Israel's great teachers consider the idea of angels to be largely or merely allegorical, while others maintain a literal belief in supernaturally potent angels. Angels, God's agents, are, at most, Divine instrumentalities — in Hebrew, *malachim*, or "messengers" — who are the totally faithful servants of their Creator. See, e.g., *Moreh Nevuchim* 2:6: "Everyone entrusted with a mission is an angel . . . all forces that reside within the body are angels." Generally, see Midrash, *Tehillim* (Psalms) 94; Talmud, *Sanhedrin* 103a and *Pesachim* 119a.

17. See Rav Nosson Scherman, *The Complete Artscroll Siddur* (Mesorah, New York NY, 1984) p. 179 (Commentary on the *Shlosha Asar Ikkarim/* Thirteen Principles of Faith, No. 7).

18. Numbers 12:8.

19. See, e.g., Genesis 20:3, 31:24; 1 Kings 3:5; Job 33:14-15.

20. See, e.g., Ezekiel 8:3.

21. Numbers 12:6-8. See Exodus 25:18-22.

22. See, e.g., Daniel 10:16.

23. Exodus 33:11.

24. That is, following the events described in Exodus 34:29-35, and Moses' transforming experience at Sinai.

25. Numbers 9:8.

26. See, e.g., Numbers 22:9-12.

27. Talmud, *Sotah* 48b. See Kaplan, *Handbook of Jewish Thought*, supra, Chapters 6 and 8.

28. See Joel 3:1-2 and commentaries.

29. Talmud, *Bava Metzia* 59b. Many Christians subscribe to the idea that God *does* contradict Himself — that one or more of the 48 latter prophets of the Bible after Aaron and Moses (See Talmud, *Megillah* 14a) have somehow nullified, invalidated or set aside all or most of the Law of Sinai, the Torah.

29. Talmud, *Bava Metzia* 59b.

30. *Chumash* — the Five. The books are called, in Hebrew, *Bereisheit* (Genesis), *Shemot* (Exodus), *Vayikra* (Leviticus), *Bemidbar* (Numbers), and *Devarim* (Deuteronomy).

31. See, e.g., Deuteronomy 33:21. Some believe that Joshua, not Moses, wrote the last eight verses of Deuteronomy. See the discussion in the Talmud, *Bava Batra* 14b-15a; Deuteronomy 34:5 with Rashi; Joshua 24:26 and commentaries.

32. Numbers 16:28. See Numbers 9:23; Deuteronomy 4:44.

33. See Exodus 3:15; Deuteronomy 17:8-9; Ezra 10; Nechemiah 9-10. Also see Talmud, *Nedarim* 32b: Abraham learned and emerged from the school of Shem (one of Noah's three sons; see Genesis 9:26), as did Jacob/Israel. Sinai validated Israel's Abrahamic heritage — his inspired true teachings, including many teachings from the school of Shem.

34. See, e.g., Deuteronomy 4:31, 12:21; 30:11-12-14; Isaiah 59:21. The great early Sages of the Mishnah and the Talmud learned directly from the schools of Israel's 48 latter Prophets. See, e.g., Talmud, *Megillah* 14b with Rashi. One can't overstate Israel's Sages' and Prophets' dedication to precision — to correctly and carefully transmitting the exact heritage of Sinai, letter-by-letter, and even in matters of pronunciation.

35. Genesis 49:10 with Rashi; Deuteronomy 4:29, 26:18. See, e.g., Psalm 94:14.

36. Deuteronomy 17:9-11. See *Sefer HaMitzvot* 1:174, 2:312-314.

37. Deuteronomy 13:1. Also see *Sefer HaMitzvot* 2:313-314.

38. See Leviticus 18:30; Numbers 15:16; Mishnah, *Pirke Avot* 1:1. Any modification can only be temporary and situation-specific; this is an emergency power. In Scripture, Elijah/Eliyahu invoked it (1 Kings 18:32), performing a sacrificial service on Mt. Carmel, even though such services should normally not be offered there. See Deuteronomy 12:13 and commentaries; Talmud, *Zevachim* 119b.

39. *Moreh Nevuchim* 3:41. Actually, the Law is, if anything, much more stable than this quote may imply.

40. See, e.g., Jeremiah 32:19.

41. 1 Samuel 16:7.

42. See Exodus 32:32-33. Note the allegorical expression, connoting "erase you from My memory" — *Moreh Nevuchim* 2:47 — or "blot you out of the book of life (kill you)." Talmud, *Rosh HaShana* 16b. Probably the clearest references in Torah, with its tremendous emphasis on life in this world, to an afterlife, or life after death, are to *kares* — the "cutting off" or extinction of one's immortal soul as a punishment for bad behavior. See, e.g., Leviticus 18:29 with Ramban (Nachmanides).

43. 2 Samuel 14:14; Ecclesiastes 2:14. Even though God has been

known to spare some souls the physical experience of death. See Genesis
6:24 (Enoch); 2 Kings 2:11 (Elijah).

44. Genesis 3:19.

45. Ezekiel 18:4.

46. Ecclesiastes 12:7, answering the question posed in Ecclesiastes 3:21.
Note that the Hebrew here for "soul" is *ruach* or "living spirit," or "animated
spirit." Man is also a "soul" or *nefesh* — a "speaking spirit," a personality
capable of thinking and making his thoughts known. See Genesis 2:7;
Ezekiel 18:4. Further, every human being has a "soul" or *neshama* — the
Heavenly spark or spirit of God in man that makes him a responsible moral
being. See, e.g., Talmud, *Berachot* 10a; *Moreh Nevuchim* 3:12.

47. 2 Samuel 22:27. See Deuteronomy 4:4, 10:12, 28:9 and
commentaries; Job 21:14.

48. See Psalm 130.

49. Psalm 9:17. Generally, see Talmud, *Nedarim* 32b, *Sanhedrin* 91a;
Nachmanides on Leviticus 4:2.

50. Leviticus 18:5 and commentaries. See, e.g., Deuteronomy 6:24,
11:21; Proverbs 15:24.

51. *Mishnah Tosefta, Sanhedrin* 13:2. See, e.g., Mishnah, *Sanhedrin* 10:1 with
commentaries. Also see Talmud, *Avoda Zorah* 18a, about a crude Roman
centurion who, through a single act of great humanity, acquired a seat
alongside one of Israel's foremost scholar-saints, at the same Heavenly table.

52. Numbers 15:31 (speaking of the punishment of *kares*). Also see,
e.g., Leviticus 7:22,27

53. Talmud, *Berachot* 34b, *Shabbat* 63a, *Sanhedrin* 99a.

54. For up to one full planetary year. Talmud, *Shabbat* 33b, *Rosh HaShana*
17a; *Sanhedrin* 104a.

55. See Talmud, *Niddah* 13b, *Hagigah* 12b; *Encyclopedia Judaica*, supra,
"*Gilgul*," and "Transmigration of Souls."

56. See Mishnah, *Pirke Avot* 4:22, in the name of R. Jacob: "Better is one
hour of bliss in the World to Come than the whole life of this world." Still,
"Better is one hour of repentance and good deeds in this world than the
whole life of the World to Come." In the next world one can only *receive*
good.

57. Mishnah, *Sanhedrin* 10:1; Talmud, *Berachot* 17a.

58. Midrash, *Avot d'Rabbi Nathan* 31 — meaning, among other things,
that trees and work will still be necessary to the world, even in the messianic
era.

59. See Isaiah 42:4. Besides the (Davidic) King Messiah, God may
actually or figuratively "anoint" (as the kings of ancient Israel were anointed,
see 1 Samuel 10:1) other people to serve as redeemers, to help him. Who can
say? See, e.g., Talmud, *Sanhedrin* 99a; Midrash, *Lamentations Rabbah* 2:2. So
there is not much point in putting a lot of effort into trying to identify any of
these anointees early. How could such a futile study make one a better
person, or affect one's love for God or fear of Him?

60. That is, if he dies. At some point following the beginning of his
reign, even death will come to an end. See, e.g., Isaiah 25:8.

61. Habakuk 2:3.

62. Talmud, *Sanhedrin* 97b. See, e.g., Daniel 11:35; *Mishnah Tosefta, Derech
Eretz* 6:13.

63. Talmud, *Sanhedrin* 97a.

64. Deuteronomy 30:12.

65. Talmud, *Avodah Zorah* 3b, in the name of R. Yose ben Halafta.

66. Midrash, *Mechilta to Exodus* 20:2. See, e.g., Isaiah 66:23; Zephaniah 3:9.

67. Isaiah 11:9.

68. "For since the beginning of the world men have not heard, nor seen, what God has prepared for him who serves You, O God." — Isaiah 65:3. At the same time, also see Isaiah 25:8 on the future of death.

69. See Deuteronomy 29:29.

70. Mishnah, *Pirke Avot* 4:21.

71. Proverbs 15:24. "[W]ise" — having insight, judgment. "[G]oes upward" — that is, up to [eternal] life, not down to [eternal] death. "[M]ay depart" — turn away from. "[T]he grave beneath" — *Sheol*, the pit, the grave. See commentaries. On life after death generally, see, e.g., Deuteronomy 30:4, 30:15-19, and Leviticus 18:5 with commentaries; Isaiah 26:19; 1 Samuel 28; Daniel 12:2; Mishnah, *Sanhedrin* 10:1. "The grave, like the womb, [both] receives and gives forth." — Talmud, *Berachot* 15b, in the name of R. Yosiah. "If a grain of wheat, buried naked, sprouts forth in many robes, how much more so the righteous!" — Talmud, *Sanhedrin* 90b, in the name of R. Meir. "The resurrection of the dead is only for the righteous." Midrash, *Genesis Rabbah* 13, and see Talmud, *Berachot* 18b.

72. Deuteronomy 32:4.

73. Psalm 125:4.

---

* Endnote: In his *Sefer ha-Ikkarim (Book of Fundamentals/ Book of Principles*, c. 1425 CE), R. Joseph Albo criticizes Maimonides' list as being too extensive. As an alternative, he sets forth just three root principles — belief in God, the Divine origin of the Torah, and ultimate reward and punishment — from which branching principles, or mere dogmas, such as belief in the coming Messiah, are derived (*Ikkarim* 1:3). He insists, very reasonably, that anyone who upholds and believes in the Law of Moses must be counted among the pious — even though that person may also hold certain erroneous theories (Ibid., 1:2).

For an assessment of R. Albo's often neglected contributions to Rainbow Covenant studies, see "Albo's Theory of Noahide Law" in Novak, *Image of the Non-Jew in Judaism*, supra, ch. 11.

Sources and Materials

Moses' authority to teach and explain the Hebrew Revolution's core text, the Five Books, Genesis through Deuteronomy, resides in the rabbis of Israel. That may sound sharp but it's a fact. The Pentateuch (in Hebrew, the *Chumash*, the Five Books), the Bible, and the unique moral universe of Torah as a whole can't be understood without the light provided by Israel.

Unless you're already a fluent Hebrew-reader, you need a good Bible translation. Get one, at least, that Israel considers acceptable. Without endorsing any company unconditionally, these publishers are generally well-regarded: Targum, Mesorah-ArtScroll, Soncino, Judaica Press, and Moznaim.

You should have at least one copy of the Written Torah that comes with a good rabbinic commentary, or at least with fairly reliable — i.e., rabbinic — explanatory notes. ArtScroll's Hebrew-English *Stone Chumash*, the *Cohen Chumash*, published by Soncino, and Rav Samson Raphael Hirsch's *Trumath Tzvi*, by Judaica Press, are all good, as is Aryeh Kaplan's *The Living Torah*, by Moznaim.

These works have largely overtaken Anglo-Israel's old Hebrew-English standby, the *Hertz Chumash* (*The Pentateuch and Haftorahs* — Hebrew text, English translation and commentary), by J.H. Hertz, the late Chief Rabbi of the British Empire. First issued in 1936 by Soncino, it has an interesting ecumenical spirit, in most of the notes and commentaries, and many are most worthwhile. Rabbi Hertz's detailed scholarly responses to the so-called Biblical-Historical school's attacks on the Bible's authenticity are especially deserving. These essays, though written long before post-war archaeology began discrediting the "Historical School's" main arguments, will still reward your attention.

Israel reads through the entire Pentateuch each year. Everywhere in the world, most Jewish communities follow the same cycle of readings. If you're going to study Torah, try reading the Torah this way, along with Israel.

What every student should know. All of Genesis and the first nineteen chapters of Exodus (plus Numbers 22:2 - 25:9) belong, in a sense, to everyone. The rest of the Bible, following the Book of Deuteronomy, is similar: even though its focus is on Israel, it speaks directly to all the world; its job, one might say, is to reveal God to the world. Starting with Exodus 20, though, God begins privately addressing Israel, setting out the (Hebrew) Law, the Guidance, or Way. From here to the end of Deuteronomy, Scripture is mostly given over to the transmission of this Law, the Torah.

Understand, please, that Torah study, narrowly defined — study of these Torah texts in Scripture, Talmud, and related complex legal esoterica — is not for everyone. Most people, indeed, outside the people Israel, should probably leave it alone, or anyway to other people; they should learn Torah morality from interpretive works (such as those mentioned below) and from other parts of Scripture, not by plunging impatiently into the details of Hebrew jurisprudence. But — this point can't be over-emphasized — nothing in those details is a secret.

Some people, not just Jewish people, simply won't be kept apart from Torah. They insist on studying the main sources. To them, and all Israel: may you make good use of the Torah references provided for you here.

Please always remember to treat a volume of Torah with respect. Even a translated copy contains holy names and holy concepts. God didn't entrust them to Israel for you to casually misuse them. Don't treat your copy, physically, sacrilegiously.

Israel's Oral Law, in the Mishnah and Talmud, has been published and republished in several English translations. Still, a student of the Universal Law is best advised to end his studies with the Talmud's intricacies rather than begin them there. The great exception to this is *Pirke Avot*, or *Sayings* [or *Ethics*] *of the Fathers*, an ethical-philosophical tractate of the Mishnah, and a great classic of world literature. Read its six short chapters of wise moral sayings and edifying wisdom to learn what the Hebrew Revolution is all about. *Avot* is a part of every *Siddur*, or Jewish prayerbook, but even general libraries and bookstores often have it in English translation.

For an overview of the Oral Law, and the Talmudic method, Rabbi Adin Steinsaltz's *The Essential Talmud* (Basic Books, New York, 1976) is very good. So is *Everyman's Talmud,* by A. Cohen (Schocken). A work intended for those seeking more basic spiritual knowledge, the distinguished novelist Herman Wouk's readable, popular and remarkably information-rich *This Is My God* (Little, Brown, 1959), now available in many reprints and later editions, is also good.

To briefly taste the flavor of all the principal Hebrew source-books, including the Bible, the *Siddur*, the Oral Law, the *Midrash*, or ancient Biblical commentaries, and other great works of law and commentary, try *Back to the Sources: Reading the Classic Jewish Texts* (Barry W. Holtz, general editor, Summit Books, 1984).

A word of warning about the last work, and all the many books that are somewhat like it. Speaking very frankly: please don't take the conventional — that is, the largely irreligious — commentary of religiously non-observant editors without a grain, at least, of salt. Not to single out *Back to the Sources* unfairly. This sort of thing just comes with the times: it's part of the superior posture of the modern academy, a bad habit of an unredeemed age. Most secular scholars of religion speak in similar tones. Some of them disbelieve in the God of Israel while others simply don't trust their fellow men to accurately communicate anything concerning Him.

(Unfortunately, it is those doctrines that tend to make their way into ordinary libraries and bookstores. Excuse the interjection, please; one has to address this somehow. Man-made religion has helped generate such tremendous antagonism to all religion that the most pompous assumptions of a hectoring, debunking, anti-religious pseudoscience frequently pass as science. So long as modern science hasn't yet discovered archaeological clear proof of Moses' complete historicity, for instance, real scientists, instead of smugly proclaiming therefore that Moses never existed, should instead be pressing the virulently anti-Israel modern Arab countries where such proof would most likely be found to stop obstructing every effort to find it!)

You can try to read around the stranger assertions in works of that current, conventional persuasion — and find yourself very well-rewarded for the effort, too. Diamonds can often be found in the mud. You can also search out less conventional but better book outlets. Genuine works of Torah are still only rarely found in general-purpose libraries or bookstores. Try following observant Israel to its sources. If you want Torah, go to the booksellers and libraries that concentrate on Torah.

Catalogs. You can get a lot of information from publishers themselves. They all have catalogs: try the catalogs from the different Judaica providers recommended earlier. These two companies also have extensive backlists: Feldheim Publishers, of Nanuet, New York (www.feldheim.com), and Jason Aronson, Inc, of Northvale, New Jersey (www.aronson.com). Generally, however, one should try to support one's own local providers, if one is lucky enough to have them: a Jewish bookstore in any community is a good place to go for all kinds of things, including music, art, magazines and newspapers, and to help connect you to local cultural events and classes. The best thing about publishers' catalogs, perhaps, is just the leg up they offer when you're working with the local library or bookseller.

One superlative desk reference. To know or explore the Noahide Code you must explore the Hebrew Code. We are blessed in having Maimonides' *Sefer HaMitzvot* — *"Book of the* [Written Torah's 613] *Commandments"* — available to study. We are doubly blessed in having Rabbi Dr. Charles B. Chavel's superb annotated translation: *The Commandments*, published by Soncino. The first section enumerates the Torah's 248 Positive Commandments, the second section covers the 365 Negative Commandments, or Prohibitions. This book is an education in itself. You can look at the other English-language compilations of the 613 Commandments. I like this one. I'd call it a must-read, well worth buying, if only for its information-packed appendices.

Torah Digests: Rabbi Aryeh Kaplan gives us *The Handbook of Jewish Thought* (1979). A concise English-language guide to the ideas and principles represented by the Torah, it's very well-written, like most of R. Kaplan's works, and supported by useful source notes. Moznaim, the publisher, compiled several successor volumes after the author's death; those, unfortunately, I can't vouch for. But the first volume stands complete on its own. The sections on prophecy and inspiration, and the detailed breakdown of the levels and varieties of same, are really noteworthy.

For more challenging reading, going beyond the basics to get at the "why" of the different Sinaitic observances, let me recommend one of my all-time favorites: *Horeb*, by Rabbi S. R. Hirsch. *Horeb* is another name for Mt. Sinai (see, e.g., Exodus 3:1; Deuteronomy 1:6) and Rav Hirsch, who was a great teacher, reveals many of the underlying ideas and philosophy of Sinai. In fact, the main thrust of *Horeb* is much more metaphysical and spiritual than legal. This weighty tome, first published in 1837 most worthwhile. Translated from the original German and introduced by the late Rabbi Dr. Isidor Grunfeld, *Horeb* is published by Soncino.

Rav Hirsch's *The Nineteen Letters*, or *Nineteen Letters about Judaism* (also known as *The Nineteen Letters of Ben Uzziel*), which first came out in 1836, covers some of the same material but it is far smaller and far more accessible than *Horeb*. Several publishers have brought this classic work of Torah philosophy into the world in English. Whether you plan to read *Horeb* or not, you ought to read *Nineteen Letters*.

Other important resources. Some critics call it apologetic literature, in the sense that it offers a defense or "apology" of the religion of Sinai, but *The Kuzari,* from 1140 CE, a work usually attributed to the great Spanish religious poet, Rabbi Yehuda HaLevi, sets out the principles and philosophy of Torah in such a simple, clear-headed way that people often mistake the wisdom in it for mere artistry. Written in the form of a dialogue between a rabbi and a genuine historical figure, the King of Khazaria (who eventually converted to Judaism), depicted here as a highly sophisticated Gentile interlocutor, this lovely little book is, in many ways, as many a rabbi has called it, "holy of holies."

Maimonides' *Moreh Nevuchim,* or *The Guide for* (or *of,* or *to*) *the Perplexed,* represents the gold standard in Torah philosophy. Maimonides — Rabbi Moses (Moshe) ben Maimon, known as Rambam (RaMBaM) from his initials — wrote it for those who follow both Torah and secular philosophy, who are "perplexed" by the seeming contradictions between the two. So it tends to strike most readers as a very modern book. In fact, the *Guide* first came out in the early Middle Ages, in the twelfth century CE. And it's definitely not for everyone: it's long and closely argued and the secular philosophy can be mind-numbing. Still, after all this time, it remains very controversial. As a well-recognized classic of world literature, you can find it, in several English-only versions, in better general-purpose libraries and bookstores.

Maimonides' brilliant *Commentary on the Mishnah* — known as the *Siraj,* or *Maor ("Light")* — and his greatest work, the fourteen volumes of his *Mishneh Torah* — the "*Repetition of the Torah,*" also known as the *Yad,* or *Yad Hazakah* ("*Strong Hand,*" or "*Mighty Hand,*" reflecting the use of that term in, e.g., Exodus 3:19, Deuteronomy 4:34 and 17:18, and Joshua 8:32; a *yad,* or hand, also connotes a ritual object, a hand-shaped silver pointer, used in religious services to help point the way to the person reading from a Torah scroll; the letters in *yad,* each letter in the Hebrew alphabet having a numerical value, add up to fourteen) — are seminal texts that have all been translated into English. Many careful, cautious students of the Torah consider their author to have been divinely inspired. These books are, at a minimum, the works of a faithful, totally dedicated Torah genius. They are legal works, however, classics of Hebrew jurisprudence, and somewhat difficult at that;

as such, they definitely aren't for everyone.

One of the volumes of the *Yad,* the last, *Hilchot Melachim,* or "*Laws of Kings,*" broadly pertaining to the legal duties of Israel's coming Davidic (Messianic) kings, is particularly important in Noahide studies. Much of what we know about the Seven Laws we know because Maimonides has recalled and condensed it here.

Histories: God, the God of Israel, is a historical God, Who acts in history, Who manifests Himself to the world through history — particularly through the history of Israel. Of course the story of the Jews doesn't end, with the Bible, in the land of Israel, in or about 450 BCE. Instead, it goes global, as the rest of the world becomes gradually educated to the knowledge of God. So this history, too, including, e.g., the Maccabean wars (associated with *Hanuka*), is sacred history. It serves, in fact, almost like an extension of the Bible. By example and by warning, it teaches or can teach us about God and His Ways, very like the Bible's histories. And, like them, it validates, illustrates, and elucidates His Torah.

Solomon Grayzel's *A History of the Jews* (Jewish Publication Society, Philadelphia PA, 1970), Cecil Roth's book by the same name (Schocken Books, New York NY, 1970), as well as his classic *The Jewish Contribution to Civilization* (Harper and Brothers, New York NY, 1940), are all quite good. You might also try the late Max I. Dimont's dramatic, excitingly written popular histories: *Jews, God and History, The Amazing Adventures of the Jewish People,* and *The Indestructible Jews,* by various publishers and in several different editions and later reprints.

Rabbi Joseph Telushkin's *Jewish Literacy: the Most Important Things to Know About the Jewish Religion, Its People, and Its History* (William Morrow & Co., New York NY, 1991), has 688 pages, nice big type, and pretty much lives up to its name.

Turning to the matter of the Arab world's seemingly never-ending war against Israel, history's Third Jewish Commonwealth, let me recommend: *Battleground: Fact and Fantasy in Palestine,* by Samuel Katz (Bantam, New York NY, 1973/Steimatzky, NewYork and Jerusalem, 1985); *From Time*

Immemorial: the Origins of the Arab-Jewish Conflict Over Palestine, by Joan Peters (Harper & Row, New York NY, 1984); and *The Zionist Revolution*, by Harold Fisch (St. Martin's Press, New York NY, 1978). I can't say enough good about these three superb — but terribly neglected books. Get hold of them if you can, even if you have to borrow them or buy them used; the news reports and headlines from the Mideast will never look the same to you again.

Aviezer Ravitsky's *Messianism, Zionism, and Jewish Religious Radicalism* (University of Chicago Press, Chicago IL, 1996) explores the fascinating world of Jewish radical ultra-Orthodoxy and its anti-Zionist philosophy — a peculiarly anti-historical approach to Torah that holds that God's promises to redeem the world can't be realized within nature but only by means of supernatural processes and obvious outright miracles. This philosophy has influenced a good deal of recent Jewish history; as Professor Ravitsky proves, it still is influential. 303 pages, including sixty pages of notes, this book is not for most people but those who do read it won't forget it.

Concentrating directly on the Rainbow Covenant Code itself: taking advantage of modern scholarship, a number of fairly recent books and articles should help you develop your understanding of the Law. These five books all go straight to our subject. While I also have some problems with them — concerning philosophy, perspective or even facts; but then I wouldn't have written this book if I'd been perfectly satisfied with the others — they all make a notable contribution.

Rabbi Professor Aaron Lichtenstein's *The Seven Laws of Noah* (first edition, 1981; 2nd ed., 1986. Rabbi Jacob Joseph School Press/Z. Berman Books, New York NY). Only 120 pages long, this little giant of a book helped trigger the explosion in modern Noahide studies. It is a must-read for anyone exploring the full scope and nature of the Universal Law.

Professor David Novak's *The Image of the Non-Jew in Judaism: an Historical and Constructive Study of the Noahide Laws* (Edwin Mellen Press, Lewiston NY, 1983), uses the Universal Law to interpret or explain different aspects of Torah scholarship. This is a religiously non-Orthodox study. It is also very expensive, and not an easy book to find in libraries. 480 pages, including extensive source citations and a superb bibliography.

Chaim Clorfene and Yakov Rogalsky's The Path of the Righteous Gentile: an Introduction to the Seven Laws of the Children of Noah (Targum Press, Southfield MI, distributed by Feldheim Publishers, 1987). A book about Noahide Law that actually addresses Noahides, this work tries to turn mere legal theory into the sort of practical guidance that normal people need. 142 pages long, with endnotes listing sources.

Rav Yoel Schwartz's A Light Unto the Nations (Translated from the Hebrew, Or-La'amim, by Mordechai ben-Aharon and edited by Yirmeyahu Bindman, published by The Jerusalem Academy of Jewish Studies/Yeshivat D'var Yerushalayim, Jerusalem, 1988). 95 pages. Less a practical guide to the laws than a call to righteously observe them, this readable little book can now be found in many Jewish bookstores.

Yirmeyahu Bindman's The Seven Colors of the Rainbow (Schueller House, Colorado Springs CO, 1995). 138 long, softcover, with a subject index and an index of Torah sources. This treatise on the Noahide Law, written from a mystic's perspective, may strike you — it did me — as eccentric. Even so, the author sets out quite a lot of information in a relatively small space. Best of all, I think, he tries to direct usable advice to the proper audience, to the people who need to be most concerned about Noahide Law: that is, to Noahides themselves.

One more book, an important study, came out just a few years ago — unfortunately, too late for me to incorporate more of it in The Rainbow Covenant. You may already be familiar with the name of Professor Nahum Rakover, if only from citations to his seminal English-language articles. Now Rabbi Rakover, former Deputy Attorney General of the State of Israel, gives us Law and the Noahides: Law as a Universal Value (The Library of Jewish Law, Israel Ministry of Justice, Jerusalem, 1998). 148 pages, with a detailed subject index, source index, and appendices, this work explores just one Commandment: the Noahide obligation of dinim, the Universal law against lawlessness.

Professor Rakover indicates that The Library of Jewish Law is planning a whole series of similar books on the Rainbow Covenant Code. One eagerly awaits them.

My friend Rabbi David Sears gives us *Compassion for Humanity in the Jewish Tradition* (Jason Aronson, Northvale NJ, 1998), a sourcebook of classic universalistic rabbinic and hasidic texts.

You can go through the footnotes in *The Rainbow Covenant* to find other sources and materials. See, especially, Rabbi J. David Bleich's *Contemporary Halachic Problems*, Volumes 1-3 (Yeshiva University Press/Ktav, New York NY, starting with the first volume, 1977). Professor Bleich's writings, which are wonderfully erudite and source-rich, go right to the heart of some of the most controversial Noahide issues. They are scholarly articles, however, providing more in the way of theory than of practical or day-to-day advice.

For B'nai Noah, by B'nai Noah. All over the world, Gentiles — Noahides, or Noahites — are turning to Torah, and more and more are writing about it, speaking about it, making art and music, books and videos and pamphlets about it, building up websites and talking about Torah on the Internet.

Some of this stuff is really excellent. You can get a lot of practical information from these sources, and a whole world of art and inquiry and profoundly sophisticated learning too. But don't be surprised if you also encounter a lot of muddled thought and poor work. You may also find, unfortunately, that some of the new product goes beyond being merely bad; it can be awful, disgusting and malignant. Fortunately, it's usually fairly easy to spot trash of that sort: if you find anything questionable at all, test it against Israel's Thirteen Principles.

Quite a few Noahide groups have a presence on the Internet. Find them by doing a search using the key terms Noahide, B'nei Noah, Rainbow Covenant, or Noahide Law.

Without recommending any particular site, and passing over several others that might be at least as worthy, these sites, which have all been in business at these addresses for some time, specialize in matters pertaining to B'nai Noah and offer hyperlinks to other sites and resources: www.asknoah.org, www.vendyljones.org.il, www.geocities.com/Athens/Oracle/2120/, and www.rb.org.il.

Many of the better websites, you should know, are weighted in favor of the hasidic, mystical teachings of Chabad Lubavitch. This is a growing, activist Jewish group or movement that shares much, but not everything, in common with mainstream observant Jewry. Under the leadership of the late great R. Menachem Schneersohn, "The *Rebbe*," Chabad has dedicated itself to making Torah more readily available to all — not just to secular or unaffiliated Jews

---

Chaim Clorfene and Yakov Rogalsky's book, *The Path of the Righteous Gentile*, is Chabad-influenced, and it seems that Rabbi Bindman's book, *The Seven Colors of the Rainbow*, is too. Some of their comments there, discussing the relative status or the inherent refinement — or lack of refinement — of different human souls, are very puzzling and disturbing. This stuff, which comes from mysticism, smacks, in fact, of Jewish ethnocentrism. Indeed, it seems much more Eastern than Hebrew in its tone and content. So please accept this warning. Once people begin occupying themselves with mysticism, anything is possible; the first things to go can be intellect, reason, and observation. Israel's Law teaches very clearly that the measure of every human soul depends not on any accident of birth but on one's **own** efforts and accomplishments in life. (See Maimonides, *Moreh Nevuchim* 4:44.)

---

but, through the organization's focus on the Seven Laws, to Noahides as well. It has, indeed, done remarkably well at it; the Lubavitchers have done great things to better promulgate the Law. No one can detract from that record. Still, like many other Hebrew sects, Chabad speaks mainly for itself. It emphasizes, very strongly, the mystic and other teachings of its own leaders. Please recognize, at least, that you can also learn from *other* teachers.

Many people of widely varying backgrounds have come to follow the path of the righteous Gentile. Only a few have written books about the experience. One of the classics of this personal-passage genre is Aimé Pallière's *The Unknown Sanctuary: a Pilgrimage from Rome to Israel.* First published in France in 1926, and then in Germany one year later, it's now available in English — translated by Louise Waterman Wise — with an informative preface by David Novak (Bloch Publishing, New York NY, 1993). I should also like to endorse two similar books — Kimberly E. Hanke's *Turning to Torah* (Jason Aronson, 1993), and J. David Davis's *Finding the God of Noah: the Spiritual Journey of a Baptist Minister from Christianity to the Laws of Noah* (Ktav, 1996). But, I should admit, I'm probably too friendly with these two authors to be the most objective judge here.

Aimé Pallière learned about the Universal laws from Rabbi Eliyahu Benamozegh, one of the leaders of the Jewish community of nineteenth-century Livorno (Leghorn), Italy. The rabbi's own work, *Israel and Humanity,* an eccentric, deeply mystical treatise on Rainbow Covenant ideology, has been republished in condensed form as *Elijah Benamozegh: Israel and Humanity* (Maxwell Luria, editor and translator. Paulist Press, Mahwah NJ, 1995). 436 pages.

The Root and Branch Association in Jerusalem is devoted to advancing the cause of Universal Covenant. Visit their website at www.rb.org.il. They published *The Root and Branch Noahide Guide* 1991-5752, edited by Aryeh Gallin, a directory of some of the leading Noahide groups, events and learning resources. For their other materials, or for regularly updated schedules of the lectures they sponsor, contact them at P.O. Box 8672, German Colony, 91086 Jerusalem, Israel; or by e-mail at rb@rb.org.il.

In coming years one expects an outpouring of new books and materials about the Noahide Law. They should substantially increase mankind's understanding.

Deeper understanding begins, as this book argues, with the fact that Noahides must determine the details of their own laws for themselves. The general guiding drift of Revelation provides the Law in outline, but every nation's special needs and history and existing laws and customs all figure in the details.

It doesn't take a genius to figure out the general guiding drift of Revelation. The Written Torah has been translated. Many commentaries, drawing from the Oral Torah, shed light on it. Other books, like this one, have set out the Noahide Law's basic framework. That's a lot of information, and the nations have more than enough already to shape a better, more righteous future for themselves. Still, whenever people aspire to go beyond the general drift of Torah to the Torah's deeply layered details, they reject the Torah's essence if they think they can do it all alone. At that point, one needs to follow Revolutionary Israel and inquire of the rabbis.

If you want to know what God expects of man, beyond civilization's minimal requisites of prohibitive law, in the way of positive absolute morality and affirmative compliance with the holy statutes and ordinances of Torah, you need to check with Israel. The Torah particularly belongs to the people Israel, the Jews; the crown of Torah, as poets say, will never leave them.

People turn to Torah, usually, because they want to know the Jewish people's God. You should consider that getting to know Him better normally ought to involve getting to know them better, too — individually and as a people. Certainly, in my own encounters over the years with different groups of Torah-seeking Gentiles, I have found that those groups that had the least to do with Jews and the coolest relations with them had, by far, the least success in terms of adopting a Torah lifestyle — that is to say, a holy lifestyle, dynamic, passionate, morally alert, and God-centered. I have also found that those groups having the warmest relations with Jews (like-minded, Torah-loving Jews particularly, of course, and not just rabbis), whether as friends or teachers or both, have, by far, beyond any doubt, the most success.

Of course nothing can stop people from trying to interpret Torah on their own. Israel's proprietary national relationship with Torah does not mean that Noahides can't, working independently, discover things about it to help *all* men understand it better. The Torah's depths are infinite and anyone of any nation may both draw from it and teach it. But the Torah itself also establishes the Hebrew Revolutionary system. The rabbis of Israel are the Torah's chief guardians.

Give the system its due. People have a genius for getting things — especially ultimate things — wrong. Fortunately, Israel has this core of expert representatives, these rabbis, who are finally responsibile for judging and validating every proposition of or relating to Torah. Please remember that, as you weigh every clever new approach or supposed fresh insight into Hebrew Revelation. Chafe at the rabbis' authority as you will but ignore them at your peril. They speak for Israel. However much you think you know about it or however much your teacher claims to know, it is not Torah unless Israel says it's Torah. So feel free to inquire, and to consult with the Jews. And may you study in good health.

§§§§

Index

About the Author

*Michael Dallen, an attorney and writer, is a co-founder of the
Rainbow Covenant Foundation and serves on its Board of Trustees.
He lives in Detroit.*

Publishers for the Torah Revolution

You can order *The Rainbow Covenant*
and other books and videos:

Phone (479) 306-4459 to place your order, or for information.
VISA and Mastercard accepted.

Visit our website at www.lightcatcherprod.com
Secure online orders using Mastercard or Visa.

Or by mail. Send your ordering information with a personal check
or money order (please, no cash) to:
Lightcatcher
842 Kissinger Ave.
Springdale AR 72762-9738

§ § § §

Many people associate the rainbow with groups and causes that have nothing
to do with Bible values or regard for the Creator's covenant with every living
creature. Yet, as the Bible teaches, God Himself has set apart the rainbow, to
serve Him and all humanity as the eternal symbol of that covenant. It belongs
at least as much, surely, to those of us who think of it in connection with God
and holiness, as it does to any group of people to use for other purposes.

The Rainbow Covenant Foundation was founded and exists to help increase
knowledge and advance public awareness of the Universal Covenant.

If you have an interest in this too, you may want to join us as a Fellow.

For more information about the foundation, its mission, and its current projects,
or to receive a free newsletter, go to our website, www.RainbowCovenant.org, or
write: The Rainbow Covenant Foundation, 61 4th Avenue, Suite 111, New York
NY 10003.

Notes

Notes

Notes

Notes